Conservation on the High Seas

NEW HORIZONS IN ENVIRONMENTAL AND ENERGY LAW

Series Editors: Kurt Deketelaere, *Professor of Law, University of Leuven, Belgium and University of Dundee, Scotland and* Zen Makuch, *Reader in Law, Barrister, Imperial College, London, UK*

Environmental law – including the pressing considerations of energy law and climate change – is an increasingly important area of legal research and practice. Given the growing interdependence of global society and the significant steps being made towards environmental protection and energy efficiency, there are few people untouched by environmental and energy lawmaking processes.

At the same time, environmental and energy law is at a crossroads. The command and control methodology that evolved in the 1960s and 1970s for air, land and water protection may have reached the limit of its environmental protection achievements. New life needs to be injected into our environmental protection regimes – perhaps through the concept of sustainability in its environmental, economic and social forms. The same goes for energy policy and law, where liberalisation, environmental protection and security of supply are at the centre of attention. This important series seeks to press forward the boundaries of environmental and energy law through innovative research into environmental and energy law, doctrine and case law. Adopting a wide interpretation of environmental and energy law, it includes contributions from both leading and emerging international scholars.

Titles in the series include:

Climate Law and Developing Countries
Legal and Policy Challenges for the World Economy
Benjamin Richardson, Yves Le Bouthillier, Heather McLeod-Kilmurray and Stepan Wood

The Law and Governance of Water Resources
The Challenge of Sustainability
Douglas Fisher

Climate Change Liability
Edited by Michael Faure and Marjan Peeters

Natural Resource Investment and Africa's Development
Edited by Francis N. Botchway

Myths and Realities of Business Environmentalism
Good Works, Good Business or Greenwash?
Kurt A. Strasser

European Emissions Trading in Practice
An Economic Analysis
Stefano Clò

Conservation, Biodiversity and International Law
Alexander Gillespie

Comparative Ocean Governance
Place-Based Protections in an Era of Climate Change
Robin Kundis Craig

Environmental Governance of the Great Seas
Law and Effect
Joseph F.C. DiMento and Alexis Jaclyn Hickman

Conservation on the High Seas
Harmonizing International Regimes for the Sustainable Use of Living Resources
Simone Borg

Conservation on the High Seas

Harmonizing International Regimes for the Sustainable Use of Living Resources

Simone Borg

Resident Academic and Head, Department of Environmental Law and Resources Law, University of Malta, Visiting Lecturer at the Katholieke Universiteit Leuven, Belgium and at the IMO International Maritime Law Institute, Malta

NEW HORIZONS IN ENVIRONMENTAL AND ENERGY LAW

Edward Elgar

Cheltenham, UK • Northampton, MA, USA

Published by
Edward Elgar Publishing Limited
The Lypiatts
15 Lansdown Road
Cheltenham
Glos GL50 2JA
UK

Edward Elgar Publishing, Inc.
William Pratt House
9 Dewey Court
Northampton
Massachusetts 01060
USA

A catalogue record for this book
is available from the British Library

Library of Congress Control Number: 2012935299

MIX
Paper from responsible sources
FSC® C018575

ISBN 978 0 85793 563 2

Printed and bound by MPG Books Group, UK
Typeset by Servis Filmsetting Ltd, Stockport, Cheshire

Contents

Foreword

It is over three decades since the adoption by the Third United Nations Conference on the Law of the Sea of the treaty with that name containing general provisions on the living resources of the sea and it is more than a half century since the initial consideration of this subject by the International Law Commission. Observably, the effort devoted to fisheries conservation and management at national and international levels has increased enormously since the 1950s and very substantially in the past three decades. During the earlier years, the conservation of marine living resources on the high seas was regulated by a specialized branch of international law commonly referred to as fisheries law. In addition, during this interval, the scope of international concern grew noticeably to include the overall general condition of the marine environment, its characteristics and contents. This development occurred under the aegis of another specialized branch of international law, namely environmental law, which addresses *inter alia* the conservation of wildlife in general.

These regimes adopt different methodologies but share the same objective, namely conservation of high seas living resources through sustainable use. The 1982 Convention on the Law of the Sea sought to achieve a balance between the different perspectives underlying the regulation of the conservation and sustainable use of high seas living resources and the right of freedom of fishing. Nevertheless the general provisions of the United Nations Convention on the Law of the Sea (UNCLOS) did not help to resolve fragmentation resulting from the different strategies, standards and rules that different applicable regimes have adopted. Subsequent state practice may also not be in conformity with the applicable UNCLOS provisions themselves but the Convention's provisions serve as a basis for objection. These circumstances have led to fragmentation providing conflicting legal interpretation as to what constitutes conservation and sound management of marine living resources on the high seas.

The changes and interactions of the decision processes involving the law of the sea, fisheries law and environmental law from an international perspective, are the main focus of Simone Borg's comprehensive work, moving beyond a study of UNCLOS alone. The major theme of the book is the evolution of agreements, both on fisheries and on more general environmental matters that have been negotiated following the creation of UNCLOS. The discussion is organized about the competence of states to proscribe for the issues involved, about the prescriptions that result from the exercise of this competence and their enforcement. The title of the book itself captures the essence of the analysis, namely the need to harmonize international regimes that seek to achieve sustainable use of living resources beyond national jurisdiction. The introductory chapter spells out the methodology of the project, calling attention to the developing fragmentation as agreements are required for specific fisheries over time and to the resulting need for their harmonization. The following chapters are organized thus; jurisdiction to regulate high seas living resources (Chapter 2); the specific content of the general obligation to conserve high seas resources (Chapter 3); specialized conservation measures for particular categories of species (Chapter 4); specific elements of the general conservation regime for high seas living resources, including promotion of compatibility between measures adopted unilaterally by high seas fishing states and consideration of the precautionary and ecosystem approaches (Chapter 5); the general regime for seeking compliance and enforcement on the high seas involving flag state jurisdiction (Chapter 6); the specific elements involved in compliance and enforcement actions, including registration of fishing vessels, control, monitoring and surveillance, reporting, observers, port state controls, and dispute settlement (Chapter 7); and the conclusion summarizing the major causes for fragmentation of regimes and recommendations for harmonizing regimes (Chapter 8).

In order to identify major conflicts, the author has traced the history behind the applicable UNCLOS provisions and then carried out a comparative analysis between later developments and the same provisions. She highlights the four main types of normative conflicts that may arise between different regimes: those arising as a result of prior and subsequent norms addressing the same circumstances, conflicts between special and general rules, laws emerging from different sources and the diverse application of the same rules in different contexts. The author then skilfully identifies potential and apparent conflicts according to the basic elements constituting any regime aiming at the conservation of living resources on the high seas, namely jurisdiction, regulation of conservation, enforcement, the link with scientific research and institutional capacity as a basis for cooperation amongst stakeholders. Simone Borg's discussion, as a whole, is a formidable piece of work that highlights the great range and variety of prescriptive and enforcement measures that are necessary to cope with widespread fishing activity over the vast part of the world ocean beyond national jurisdiction. The resulting analysis particularly emphasizes the important and continuing need for cooperative action to realize the enormous benefits available from high seas living resources.

William T. Burke
Professor of Law Emeritus
University of Washington School of Law

Preface

Having practised as an environmental lawyer in the public sector for 15 years, I have always been intrigued by the invasive nature of environmental law and its influence on other legal fields that had evolved before it. Securing the sustainability of stocks was already a fundamental aspect of international fisheries law when the 1992 Earth Summit highlighted the need for regulating the utilization of natural resources on the basis of sustainable development. Nevertheless UNCED has been highly influential upon the development of fisheries law in these last two decades. It stressed, amongst other things, the need for a more holistic perspective and sought the integration of socio economic issues into environmental concerns and vice versa. Since 1992, the International community has struggled to come to terms with translating this common objective into substantive norms so as to ascertain the sustainable use of high seas living resources. Above all, it sought to elicit the legal obligations and the required methodology to reach this goal. This process, however, also exposed the fragmentation of applicable international regimes addressing the conservation of high seas living resources. This is mainly due to its different sources and the diverse interpretation of the same legal terms as perceived by various international fora. I believe it was the perplexed feelings of my non-legal colleagues, who expect the law to be both certain and specific, which instilled in me the desire to write on this subject.

Carrying out research to assess to what extent harmonization may be achieved amongst the applicable regimes regulating the sustainable use of high seas living resources has proved to be a more fascinating subject than I ever imagined. The conservation of high seas living resources is a perfect example of how international law, in its infinite variety, has become super specialized as it adapts to contemporary needs and expectations, despite its dependency upon a primitive law-making system. Marine living resources have immensely diverse characteristics and life cycles. They roam freely, ignoring jurisdiction claims pertaining to human-made boundaries. They remain an essential source of sustenance not only for humans and states' economies but also for biodiversity in its entirety. In sum, effectively regulating the sustainable use of such resources is, euphemistically speaking, a tall order. Furthermore a harmonized regime is a *sine qua non* for ensuring the conservation of stocks that constitute a vested interest for many stakeholders.

This research project has also been in itself an unforgettable experience due to my mentor, Professor W.T. Burke, whose standing as a professor of maritime law, and of fisheries law in particular, is legendary. I am very grateful for his support, guidance and patience, especially for his frank remarks and constant encouragement. It has been an honour to work under his tutorship. I would also wish to express my deep gratitude towards Professor David Attard, Judge International Tribunal for the Law of the Sea and Director of IMLI, who has always encouraged me to pursue my studies and to whom I am especially grateful for introducing me to the subject of international environmental law at the beginning of my career. I am indebted to Dr Evelyn Meltzer for generously sharing with me her matrices on RFMOs, whilst she was still doing her research work. I am also very grateful to Dr Matthew Camilleri at FAO, who has made it possible for me to visit the FAO library and access FAO documents. Thanks also go to the staff at the IMO International Maritime Law Institute for their cheerful disposition when visiting the library. I wish to thank all the people at Edward Elgar Publishing involved in the making of this book, especially the editors of this series, Zen Makuch and Kurt Deketelaere who are both good friends and colleagues, Ben Booth, Laura Seward, Gillian Wright and Madhubanti Bhattacharyya, for making this dream a reality. I also wish to express my gratitude towards my many friends for their unity and prayers; when times were tough they kept me going. Above all I thank my family: my father for instilling within me love for learning and my mother for teaching me how to bear it all when pursuing it. I thank my daughters heartily for bearing with me these last three years. They will be relieved to hear that finally, 'mum has finished writing her book about sea creatures'. To my husband Paul, I am especially grateful for believing in me, for making it possible, for being there to listen. This work is yours just as much as it is mine.

Abbreviations

ACCOBAMS	Agreement on the Conservation of Cetaceans of the Black Sea, Mediterranean Sea and Contiguous Atlantic Area
Am. J. Int. L.	American Journal of International Law
BYBIL	British Year Book of International Law
CBD	United Nations Convention on Biological Diversity
CCAMLR	Convention on the Conservation of Antarctic Marine Living Resources
CCSBT	Commission for the Conservation of Southern Bluefin Tuna
CITES	Convention on International Trade in Endangered Species of Wild Flora and Fauna
CMS	Convention on Migratory Species of Wild Animals
COP	Conference of the Parties
EEZ	Exclusive Economic Zone
EU	European Union
FAO	Food and Agriculture Organization
FSA	Agreement for the Implementation of the Provisions of the United Nations Convention on the Law of the Sea of 10 December 1982 Relating to the Conservation and Management of Straddling Fish Stocks and Highly Migratory Fish Stocks
GFCM	General Fisheries Commission for the Mediterranean
HMS	Highly Migratory Species
IATTC	Inter-American Tropical Tuna Commission
ICCAT	International Convention for the Conservation of Atlantic Tuna
ICCAT PWG	ICCAT Permanent Working Group for the Improvement of ICCAT Statistics and Conservation Measures
ICJ	International Court of Justice
ICRW	International Convention for the Regulation of Whaling
IJMC	International Journal of Marine and Coastal Law
ILC	International Law Commission
IMO	International Maritime Organization

IOTC	Indian Ocean Tuna Commission
IPOU	International Plan of Action
ISBA	International Sea Bed Authority
IUCN	International Union for the Conservation of Nature
IUU	Illegal, unreported and unregulated fishing
IWC	International Whaling Commission
MEA	Multilateral Environmental Agreement
MSY	Maximum sustainable yield
NAFO	North Atlantic Fisheries Organization
NASCO	North Atlantic Salmon Organization
NEAFC	North East Atlantic Fisheries Commission
NGO	Non-Governmental Organization
ODIL	Ocean Development and International Law Journal
OSPAR	Convention for the Protection of the Marine Environment of the North East Atlantic
RFMO	Regional Fisheries Management Organization
SBSTTA	Subsidiary Body on Scientific, Technical and Technological Advice
SFS	Straddling Fish Stocks
SPAMI	Specially Protected Areas of Mediterranean Importance
TAC	Total Allowable Catch
UN	United Nations
UNCED	United Nations Conference on Environment and Development
UNCLOS	United Nations Convention on the Law of the Sea
UNEP	United Nations Environment Programme
UNGA	United Nations General Assembly
UNTS	United Nations Treaty Series
VCLT	Vienna Convention on the Law of Treaties
VMS	Vessel Monitoring System
WCED	World Commission on Environment and Development
WCPFC	Western and Central Pacific Fisheries Commission
WSSD	World Summit on Sustainable Development
WTO	World Trade Organization
Yb IEL	Yearbook of International Environmental Law

Table of cases

Table of treaties

*This work is dedicated to my daughters,
Raquel Ann and Michaela Ruth.*

1 Introduction

1.1 THE OBJECTIVES, METHODOLOGY AND SCOPE OF THIS BOOK

The 1982 United Nations Convention on the Law of the Sea (UNCLOS) requires States to maintain the sustainability of fish stocks[1] and to cooperate in the taking of conservation measures on the high seas. In order to fulfill these two obligations, states have concluded various agreements between themselves concerning fishing for identical species or in the same areas[2] on the high seas. Ten years after the conclusion of UNCLOS, the 1992 United Nations Conference on Environment and Development (UNCED)[3] served to emphasize, amongst other things, the need for states to adopt a holistic perspective towards conservation that aims to integrate environmental concerns into socio-economic needs. In the years that have followed, the international community has striven to come to terms with translating this holistic approach into substantive norms via the conclusion of new conservation treaties and by reviewing existing ones. In this manner, both UNCLOS and UNCED have strongly contributed to the specialization and fine-tuning of international law with respect to the sustainable use of living resources on the high seas. They have been less successful, however, in curbing its fragmentation, since coordination between the diverse fora which generated this accumulation of norms has often been lacking. The purpose of this book is to assess how these various applicable norms interrelate with each other. It aims to identify which legal techniques can be used when interpreting and applying these norms to harmonize their goals, methodologies and scope of applicability. Additionally, this book will demonstrate that in some cases, addressing gaps and conflicts in the existing legal framework may require the formulation of new instruments so as to provide a more coherent set of applicable norms. In both instances, harmonization cannot be achieved by riding roughshod over the diverse concerns of the parties concerned.[4] On the contrary, all stakeholders need to be involved so as to facilitate compliance with a revised set of consistent legal benchmarks that will ensure a level playing field for all parties.

To address these objectives, the discussion in this book focuses upon three basic legal aspects that are inherent to all international regimes aiming at the conservation of living resources on the high seas. These are:

- jurisdictional issues;
- the legal implications of the content of conservation obligations; and
- compliance and enforcement.

This chapter explains how international law, because of its dynamic character, develops to adapt to a variety of issues relating to these three main aspects. Its unity, however, may be challenged as it becomes more and more complex and specialized.[5] This happens because the norms which evolve have different functions: some serve as a fallback, establishing basic rights and obligations; others specify more detail, adding on to and fine-tuning earlier and more general norms. As norms accumulate and interact, they may not always complement and supplement each other and may even appear to express different or conflicting rights and obligations. Chapter 2 assesses how jurisdiction over marine living resources has evolved in a manner that is intrinsically linked to the zone where they occur and the type of species they are. It discusses whether international regimes are coherent in determining who has jurisdiction over living resources on the high seas and how this affects the legal status of such species. Chapter 3 provides a comparative analysis on how the term '*conservation*' is interpreted and translated into substantive norms under the various applicable regimes. The interface between legal obligations relating to conservation from a species-based approach is considered in Chapter 4. Chapter 5 examines how to achieve the systematic integration of conservation obligations as they emerge from a plurality of norms so as to ensure a level playing field for implementation purposes. Chapter 6 analyses the various compliance and enforcement measures adopted by these legal regimes to implement the regulatory framework. Chapter 7 proposes elements for a harmonized approach between the same. Other cross-cutting legal issues are also considered throughout the different chapters, including the link between scientific research and decision-making and the requirements for adequate institutional capacity.

The UNCLOS provisions[6] relating to the conservation of marine living resources were negotiated and agreed to as part of a package, together with all the other provisions regulating State maritime activities. As the provisions on living resources on the high seas could not be voted upon separately, the use of generic legal language[7] reflects the political compromise achieved during the UNCLOS negotiations. The 1982 Convention postpones the specific regulation of controversial issues, such as the allocation of fish catches on the high seas and the determination of the maximum sustainable yield.[8] UNCLOS leaves these legal issues to be determined either by subsequent international agreements or according to the discretion of individual states. As a result, conflicting claims intensified and became more widespread after the conclusion of the 1982 Convention. The methodology adopted in this book is based on the premise that the provisions of the 1982 UNCLOS serve as a basis for objection vis-à-vis subsequent international regimes and state practice regulating the conservation of marine living resources. This is the underlying reason why the various chapters first examine the UNCLOS provisions and then carry out a comparative analysis between these same provisions and later developments in international law. This methodology serves to identify whether the current state of play manifests compatibility or perhaps even gaps and conflicts between the different norms since, unlike UNCLOS, subsequent treaties have sought to limit the discretionary nature of state parties on the kind of conservation measures they may adopt on the high seas to ensure the sustainability of stocks.[9] This book focuses mainly on the applicable norms emanating from treaties. It also refers to those rules of customary international law recognized by international case law. At times the chapters also refer to the *possibility* that new customary rules may have evolved from state practice in more recent years but it needs to be stressed that in such circumstances this is merely hypothetical as their legally-binding nature has not yet been put to test.

The scope of this book is restricted to an assessment of international norms regulating the *direct* use of high seas living resources during anthropogenic operations that lead to their direct exploitation or incidental capture. This does not only include the harvesting of fish stocks but also any form of human activity that leads directly to the exploitation of *all* living resources occurring in maritime areas beyond national jurisdiction. It will not address anthropogenic activities that have an indirect, negative effect on the sustainability status of such resources, such as climate change or pollution from dumping, shipping or land-based sources. Similarly conservation regimes applicable in other maritime jurisdictional zones apart from the high seas do not fall within the direct scope of this work. These two aspects will be marginally referred to, so as to demonstrate that an effective conservation regime for the high seas does not only depend upon adopting legal measures to curb the unsustainable exploitation of living resources occurring therein, but also requires the efficient regulation of anthropogenic activities across all maritime zones.

There are various key terms used in this book that have a particular meaning for the purpose of this work.

- '*Harmonization*' of norms is given the same meaning as that intended in the ILC Report of the Study Group of the International Law Commission entitled *Diversification and Expansion of International Law. Fragmentation of International Law: Difficulties Arising from Diversification and Expansion of International Law*.[10] Harmonization does not mean uniformity; it is not intended as an exercise where the views of one legal stream prevail over those on the other side but rather as a means of systematic integration of the various sources of international law that may be applied in the circumstances. This implies that the relevant norms would all contribute towards achieving the same objectives by using compatible standards, rights and obligations. In the absence of a hierarchy of norms in international law, harmonization can be achieved even via certain techniques in legal interpretation. At other times, especially if there are gaps in the applicable laws or even normative conflicts, new legally binding instruments need to be formulated. States may also adopt non-binding instruments such as guidelines or codes of practice to achieve harmonization amongst applicable regimes. Harmonization in this sense reflects also what the provisions of the Vienna Convention on the Law of Treaties (VCLT) recommends, namely that users are to apply international law as an integrated whole.[11]
- '*Fishing*', '*harvesting*' and '*taking*' have been used interchangeably in this book to refer to the various forms of exploitation of living resources on the high seas.
- '*Freedom of fishing*' entails the right of all states to have access to living marine resources on the high seas, which includes access for the purpose of exploitation.
- '*Living marine resources*' does not only refer to fish or harvestable species but to all animal species that occur in the marine environment.
- '*Harvestable species*' is used to refer to those marine species that are exploited for commercial reasons.
- '*High seas*' has the same meaning as that provided by the 1982 UNCLOS.[12]
- '*Marine areas beyond national jurisdiction*' is used interchangeably with the term high seas, although in the case of living marine resources, the latter term also covers species that occur on the deep sea bed. It is to be noted that the 1982 UNCLOS does not actually regulate the latter. It refers to the deep sea bed as the '*Area*'[13] but it is only the mineral resources of the Area that are subject to the common heritage regime.[14]

- *'Flag state'*, *'distant water fishing state'* and *'high seas fishing state'* have been used interchangeably to refer to states which have vessels registered under their flag that exploit living resources on the high seas.
- *'Applicable international regimes'* refers to the body of treaty rules that regulate living marine resources. The book does not aim to provide an exhaustive list of these treaties but the individual chapters focus upon the salient provisions of the most influential amongst these legal instruments, examining how they relate to the different aspects discussed therein.

1.2 DIVERSIFICATION AND FRAGMENTATION UNDER INTERNATIONAL LAW

International law is constantly evolving to regulate a wide variety of state operations that elicit international concern. Its dynamic and flexible nature allows it to diversify into an ever increasing myriad of norms so as to meet with the needs of its subjects. There is always the risk of fragmentation, however, when a more specialized body of norms deviates from the general perspective of international law and fails to integrate with or supplement other applicable rules. Apart from generating confusion and ambiguity in the law, fragmentation also increases the chance of conflict between the various legal sources[15] and institutional practices.[16] National law also deals with similar causes of fragmentation but, unlike international law, it is endowed with an established legal hierarchy as well as a centralized law-making and a law-enforcement body. These tools facilitate the national authorities' task in overcoming substantive and institutional conflicts resulting from the accretion of legal instruments. Users of national law have a simpler life when it comes to discerning the applicable legal norm that regulates a particular activity under national legislation. One may refer to written legal instruments such as statutes, Acts of Parliament or subsidiary legislation and examine how these are interpreted by the courts. At most, one may further delve into the records of the debates that led to the negotiation and the formulation of the said legal instruments to comprehend better the goals and motives that led to their conclusion. In the case of common law systems court decisions may also be a source of law in themselves in the absence of a written legal instrument. National law endows the competent domestic authorities with the power to implement and monitor compliance with the legal obligations imposed therein. Any infringements are subject to arraignments by the police before the law courts that have compulsory jurisdiction. Apart from awarding punishments and claims for damages, national law courts also have the executive power to ensure that offenders comply with the legal obligations imposed upon them. Under international law, there is no single legal body able to create laws binding on all states without their consent.[17] There is no centralized executive authority entrusted with implementation and international courts and tribunals have no compulsory or comprehensive jurisdiction. It is sometimes difficult to trace the origins of a particular norm under international law and to ascertain when it took effect. In those cases where a plurality of norms may apply the subjects of international law cannot rely on an institutional set up or a hierarchy of laws like their counterparts within the national sphere. They must depend on other techniques to avoid and overcome fragmentation resulting from the specialization of international law into different legal fields.[18]

1.3 A BRIEF OVERVIEW OF THE SOURCES OF INTERNATIONAL LAW

Users of international law require a different approach when it comes to identifying sources where the applicable norms are to be found. Apart from the absence of a centralized law making authority, most publicists insist that there is no *a priori* hierarchy of sources under international law.[19] The only exception is *jus cogens* – peremptory norms of international law, which can only be superseded by another rule of the same status.[20] Article 38(1) of the Statute of the International Court of Justice (ICJ) refers to treaties, customary international law and general principles of law as the formal sources that establish the position of the law *per se*, whilst judicial decisions (binding on the contesting states that voluntarily submit their dispute for adjudication) and the writings of publicists constitute evidence of applicable international norms.[21]

The chronology in the list of sources provided by article 38(1) has only an operational[22] value. Although treaties 'to which the contesting States are Parties' top this list, it is because they usually provide clearer and more specific legal rights and obligations upon states than customary international law or general principles of law.[23] Treaties are an explicit expression of the states' consent; the day when a treaty norm comes into force is clearly identifiable and generally speaking they are more specialized in nature than other sources of international law. This may not always be the case, however, and one cannot ignore the possibility that a new customary rule may alter the content of an earlier treaty.[24] One may also argue that prominence should be given to treaties because, apart from the clarity a written text provides, it is adopted via a more transparent and democratic process.

On the other hand, some states may favour the application of international custom, which article 38(1)(b) defines 'as evidence of general practice accepted as law'. Custom may be perceived as being more flexible than negotiating a multilateral treaty and therefore more likely to safeguard both national and international interests. This is what happens for instance, when one state acts unilaterally, contrary to the established position of international law at the time, and other States follow suit. If this new form of state practice acquires the requisite *opinio juris sive necessitatis* (that is, acceptance that such behaviour is legally binding),[25] it crystallizes into custom. The problem with international custom is that unless its legal nature is tested and confirmed, its status as a norm of international law remains vague. Consequently, whenever this work discusses a customary rule of international law as an applicable source, it does so by referring to international case law, which has declared that there is evidence of its existence. In all other cases, one can only highlight that current state practice seems to *indicate* the possibility of the crystallization of a customary norm. It is certainly not within the competence of any author to assert the existence of a customary rule if its legal status has never been discussed and confirmed before an international adjudicating body.

The role of general principles of law is similar to that of international custom although principles establish overarching objectives of substantive or procedural law rather than specific rights and obligations.[26] Thus, for example, one refers to sustainable development and the precautionary approach as emergent legal principles.[27] Some publicists refer to the high seas freedoms as general principles of law.[28] Principles are normally qualified and supplemented by more specific norms arising from treaties and custom. International case law has occasionally referred to and even based its decisions on the strength of such principles adhered to by the international community.[29]

The role of international case law, although not a formal source in itself, cannot be underestimated. The decisions of international adjudicating bodies are binding only upon the parties to the dispute. They also provide evidence of the applicable international norms under particular circumstances. This book will often refer to a number of international disputes that have been settled before the ICJ and other international tribunals, since some led to landmark judgments that have influenced the course of behaviour of states in regulating the conservation of living resources in marine areas beyond national jurisdiction.[30] States and international organizations have at times reacted to some of these decisions by conducting bilateral, regional and multilateral agreements to further develop the law when international case law has exposed lacunae or the inadequacies of international law in promoting conservation.[31] Like all the other sources, however, international case law must be evaluated in the light of later developments, especially if subsequent treaties were concluded to address the same topics or a new rule of customary international law has been acquiesced to by states.

The writings of publicists may also constitute evidence of international law and their contribution is particularly valuable when they address topics that are contentious or subject to conflicting interpretation. The Report of the Study Group of the International Law Commission entitled *Diversification and Expansion of International Law. Fragmentation of International Law: Difficulties Arising from Diversification and Expansion of International Law*,[32] for example, discusses the problem of ambiguity and conflict in international law when a plurality of norms may apply and suggests legal techniques which can be used to overcome the problem.

More recently the term '*soft law*' has raised various discussions as to whether it can be regarded as another source of international law.[33] Soft law is used to refer to declarations, recommendations and resolutions that states adopt either at *ad hoc* meetings or at the various conferences organized by international organizations. United Nations General Assembly resolutions are considered to be an example of soft law. They are not, generally speaking, binding on member states[34] but as this organ of the UN is the widest forum where states are represented, such resolutions constitute valuable evidence of the opinions of their governments.[35] Similarly guidelines published by international organizations[36] and declarations at ministerial meetings or summits[37]which are adopted unanimously are also considered to be examples of soft law. States usually conclude such instruments with the intention of ensuring consistency in state practice and agreeing on certain standards in the implementation of international law.[38] What distinguishes soft law from hard law is that states adopt the former type of instruments with the full knowledge that they are *not* legally binding. Hence the term 'soft law' is both misleading and a misnomer because what is not legally binding is not law. It must be stressed, however, that some instruments of soft law have generated concepts and principles that have eventually been incorporated in treaties or acquired the requisite *opinio juris* as customary rules of international law.[39] The importance of soft law lies in mobilizing states to initiate discussions when issues of international concern arise, thereby facilitating the possible development international norms where a lacuna exists or applicable treaties are too open-textured.[40] In this context, the role of soft law in facilitating the harmonization of the applicable international regimes for the conservation of high living resources is crucial.[41] As we shall see in the coming chapters, many non-binding instruments published by the FAO provide guidance on the interpretation of terms and principles that are found in hard law instruments[42] which address the conservation of living resources on the high seas. Furthermore some Resolutions or Decisions approved by conferences between the parties to treaties and international organizations may be binding upon the parties, whenever the constituent treaty provides for this methodology.[43] If non-parties accept them they may even crystallize into custom.

This short discussion on the complexities surrounding the sources of international law sheds some light on the challenges that users face when identifying the applicable international norms. Fragmentation has further exacerbated this dilemma, particularly for judges sitting on international adjudicating bodies who must discern the position of international law in the circumstances[44] and apply the law in its entirety. In fact the ICJ has reiterated the need to interpret and apply treaties in the context of and together with other relevant sources of the law. The plurality of norms that have developed since the conclusion of the UNCLOS negotiations that are found in a variety of international law sources have to be taken into consideration. According to the ICJ in the *Gabčikovo–Nagymaros Dam Case*, new standards are to be given proper weight not only when states contemplate new activities but also when continuing with activities agreed upon beforehand.[45] The ICJ has not hesitated in accepting that a new customary rule may have evolved, which should prevail over an earlier treaty concluded between the parties.[46]

There are various political and historical reasons behind the unprecedented accretion of norms which have occurred in these last few decades that also explain why there is an increased risk of conflict amongst the sources of international law. The post Cold War era has brought added value in the perceived role of international law from what was previously a legal framework that guarantees peaceful coexistence to one that also promotes mutual cooperation.[47] Inter-state relationships have intensified during this period, leading to an exponential rise in the number of multilateral and regional treaties and a proliferation of international organizations. As discussed above, these developments have spawned an accumulation of new norms and facilitated subspecialization.[48] The cohort of international norms that currently regulates the conservation of high seas living resources is tangible proof of this trend as international law adapts to contemporary needs and expectations so as to regulate conflicting interests over the same. Inevitably, as discussed in the first part of this chapter, this diversification also has its negative effects.

More recently, globalization has promoted liberalization of international trade and states have tried to mould international law to address both the socio-economic benefits as well as the negative environmental impacts of this phenomenon, thereby increasing the potential for conflict between international environmental law and other international legal substreams. Various disputes before the Appellate Body of the World Trade Organization have been trade disputes on harvesting methods for imported fish products imposed by coastal states, claiming that such measures were adopted for conservation purposes. However, the distant water fishing states rebutted them, alleging that they constituted a breach of WTO rules since they were a barrier to trade.[49]

On a more positive note, the international community has witnessed an emerging hierarchy of values that have also influenced the evolution of international law. The ILC *Draft Articles on the Responsibility of States for International Wrongful Acts* reflect this trend and establish that particular importance should be attached to those obligations under the various sources of international law[50] which express collective interests or obligations that are owed to the community as a whole.[51] This approach has also increased the chances of conflict, because norms expressing a collective interest may not sit comfortably with established general principles of law. For instance, robust conservation standards that may impose closed fishing seasons on the high seas for endangered species challenge the general principle that states have right of access over living marine resources occurring in areas beyond their national jurisdiction.

1.4 THE CONSERVATION OF LIVING RESOURCES ON THE HIGH SEAS: A FRAGMENTED INTERNATIONAL LEGAL FRAMEWORK

The Report of the Study Group of the International Law Commission entitled *Diversification and Expansion of International Law. Fragmentation of International Law: Difficulties Arising from Diversification and Expansion of International Law*[52] considers the applicable regimes addressing the conservation of living resources on the high seas to be one of the primary examples of fragmentation under international law. This is mainly due to the fact that the body of rules for the conservation of marine living resources on the high seas has developed on an *ad hoc* basis, as a reaction to the historical and political developments that have occurred throughout the centuries as referred to in the 1.3 above. It is only recently that there has been some effort to achieve coordination and integration between the applicable legal norms.[53] The exploitation of marine living resources was originally subject to the closed sea doctrine and from the eighteenth century to the high seas freedoms.[54] Throughout the twentieth century, various conventions on the law of the sea[55] addressed, amongst other issues, the conservation of marine living resources, albeit in general terms. The most recent of these conventions, the 1982 UNCLOS, is regarded as the primary, although not the only, source of international law regulating the conservation of marine living resources in various maritime jurisdictional zones. UNCLOS, popularly referred to as the constitution for the oceans, regulates a plethora of uses and resources of the sea, including the legal relationship between coastal states and distant water fishing states when it comes to the exploitation of living resources on the high seas. Many of its provisions are considered to have codified the customary international law that existed at the time when it was negotiated,[56] whilst it is also considered to be a norm-creating treaty as some of its provisions served to generate new customary international rules.[57] Nevertheless UNCLOS constitutes an international legal framework and does not establish specific, substantive legal measures as to how such conservation of living resources beyond national jurisdiction may be achieved. The negotiators expected it to be supplemented by more detailed international and regional legal instruments which either already existed at the time or which could be concluded at a later stage. This is evident from some of its provisions which refer to 'generally accepted international rules and standards'[58] and the various obligations upon flag states and coastal states to cooperate in relation to specific fish stocks[59] and marine mammals.[60] Furthermore, article 237 establishes that the provisions of Part XII on the Protection and the Preservation of the Marine Environment are 'without prejudice to special conventions and agreements concluded previously and to agreements which may be concluded in furtherance of the general principles set forth in this Convention'.[61]

Alongside the evolution of norms on the law of the sea, a specialized international regime on the exploitation of fisheries had originated by the end of the nineteenth century with the conclusion of the first treaties specifically regulating fisheries[62] and the fur seal trade.[63] This process, which further developed and intensified throughout the twentieth century led to the formulation of various regional Regional Fisheries Management Agreements (RFMAs) and Regional Fisheries Management Organizations (RFMOs). RFMAs establish fisheries management mechanisms without establishing a formal institution established under the agreement. This task is usually assigned to the Food and Agriculture Organization (FAO) or another RFMO or shared between the parties to the RFMA. The reason for adopting such an approach is that it may be too cumbersome for the parties to set up an institution for this purpose, when they can make use of existing mechanisms, allowing for more flexibility and better cost-effectiveness.[64] On the other hand, RFMOs establish, via their constitutive treaty, a permanent institution that takes over both management and possibly enforcement responsibilities. Examples include the Convention on Future Multilateral Cooperation in Northwest Atlantic Fisheries (NAFO) and the Convention for the Conservation of the Southern Bluefin Tuna (CCSBT). The FAO can establish both RFMOs and RFMAs by virtue of articles VI[65] and XIV[66] of its Constitution. For the purposes of this work, any further use of the term RFMOs should be taken to also include RFMAs.

The major sources of international fisheries law consist of customary law as well as multilateral treaties and regional fisheries agreements that have evolved over time. The major treaties include:

- the 1946 International Convention for the Regulation of Whaling (ICRW);
- the 1950 Inter-American Tropical Tuna Commission (IATTC);[67]
- the 1969 International Commission for the Conservation of Atlantic Tunas (ICCAT);
- the 1979 NAFO;
- the 1982 Commission for the Conservation of Antartic Marine Living Resources (CCAMLR);
- the 1993 FAO Compliance Agreement;
- the 1994 CCSBT;
- the 1995 Convention for the Conservation and Management of Pollock Resources in the Central Bering Sea (Donut Hole Convention);
- the 1996 Indian Ocean Tuna Commission (IOTC);
- the 1995 United Nations Agreement for the Implementation of the Provisions of the United Nations Convention on the Law of the Sea of 10 December 1982 relating to the Conservation and Management of Straddling Fish Stocks and Highly Migratory Fish Stocks[68](FSA);
- the 1997 General Fisheries Commission for the Mediterranean (GFCM);[69]
- the 2003 Convention on the Conservation and Management of Fishery Resources in the South East Atlantic Ocean (SEAFO); and
- the 2004 Western and Central Pacific Fisheries Commission (WCPFC).

Whilst UNCLOS was under negotiation, the international community witnessed the rapid development of international environmental law, an emerging regime based mainly on treaties, which also addresses the conservation of living marine resources. Following the 1972 United Nations

Conference on the Human Environment (UNCHE), there was a proliferation of multilateral environmental agreements (MEAs). Some of these treaties also addressed the conservation of living resources on the high seas. The earliest examples include the 1973 Convention on International Trade in Endangered Species of Wild Flora and Fauna (CITES) and the 1979 Bonn Convention on the Conservation of Migratory Species of Wild Animals. More recent MEAs include the 1992 Convention on Biological Diversity, the 1995 Agreement on the International Dolphin Conservation Programme (IDCP)[70] and the 2001 Agreement on the Conservation of Albatrosses and Petrels (ACAP). Apart from these MEAs, one can also mention the various protocols on the conservation of marine biodiversity falling under the Regional Seas Programmes.[71] The legal component of these Programmes consists of framework treaties that were originally promoted by the United Nations Environment Programme (UNEP) to protect the marine environment from a regional perspective.

Some treaties like CCAMLR and FSA are also considered to fall under the category of MEAs. The FSA was the first serious attempt to approximate the ultimate goals and objectives of the international fisheries regimes with those of MEAs and other sources of international environmental law. The FSA and the CBD also influenced other RFMOs and regional seas programmes to revise their constituent treaties and incorporate more holistic conservation goals.[72] These developments have served to take into consideration not only the interests of coastal states and high seas fishing states but also environmental issues that concern all states.[73]

One cannot ignore the influence of soft law instruments such as:

- UNCED's Agenda 21 (particularly its Chapter 17);
- UNGA resolutions 46/215 Drift Net Moratorium, 49/118 on Bycatch and Discards, 54/32 on Illegal, Unreported and Unregulated (IUU) Fishing and 60/31 on Sustainable Fisheries;
- the 1995 Rome Consensus on World Fisheries;
- the 1995 Jakarta Mandate;
- the 1995 FAO Code of Conduct for Responsible Fisheries;
- the 2001 Reykjavik Declaration on Responsible Fisheries in the Marine Ecosystem;
- the 2002 Johannesburg Declaration on Sustainable Development;
- the 2002 WSSD Plan of Implementation;
- the 2005 Rome Declaration on Illegal Unreported and Unregulated Fishing;
- the Ministerial Declaration of the St John's (Newfoundland) Conference on the Governance of High Seas Fisheries;
- the UN Fisheries Agreement; and

- the 2005 APEC Joint Ministerial Declaration for the Bali Plan of Action Towards Healthy Oceans and Coasts.

The FAO has issued various other soft law instruments under the aegis of its Code of Conduct for Responsible Fisheries. These include Technical Guidelines,[74] International Plans of Action (IPOAs)[75] and the Strategy for Improving Information on Status and Trends in Capture Fisheries. As is evident from these developments, the distinction between international fisheries and international environmental soft law has become rather blurred and these instruments can easily be considered to fall under either stream.

This brief historical account of the regulation of living marine resources beyond national jurisdiction demonstrates its cross-sectoral nature and explains why it falls within the scope of various international regimes. Ultimately, issues relating to the application of laws in a particular context may also arise, as the conservation of harvestable species remains predominately under fisheries law, whilst the conservation of marine living resources in general is normally addressed by environmental law. As the judges of the International Tribunal on the Law of the Sea in the *MOX Plant* case held, the application of the same rules by different fora and institutions may vary due to 'differences in respective context, object and purpose as well as the subsequent practice of parties and travaux preparatoires'.[76]

Both international fisheries agreements and MEAs addressing the conservation of living resources on the high seas share a common objective but, as demonstrated above, they have developed in parallel. In the next chapters, we shall see how these two streams of international law have adopted different strategies, standards and rules to regulate these same goals. Furthermore, the diverse fora from where they originate tend to interpret differently the applicable norms that are common to both sectors, such as section 2 of Part VII of 1982 UNCLOS, which deals with the conservation of marine living resources on the high seas. The provisions of UNCLOS do refer to dependent and incidental species and many RFMOs regulate to limit bycatch and fishing effort. International fisheries regimes *aim* at the conservation of fish stocks but the rationale behind their objective is to ensure the harvesting of these species. Environmental law seeks, as its ultimate goal, the conservation of the marine living resources *per se* and regulates living resources whether they are harvestable or not. It tends to impose the same conservation measures for states in whichever capacity they act, whether they play the role of coastal states or flag states. Environmental law in its purest form considers the oceans as one habitat and envisages conservation of the species and the habitat as one ecosystem. As already highlighted before this perspective is popularly referred to as the '*ecosystem approach*'.[77] In recent years, the objective of conservation under environmental law has been assimilated with sustainable use due to the influence of the concept of sustainable development. Nevertheless, certain environmental groups, including legal experts, may distance themselves from this stance and sometimes interpret the obligation to take adequate conservation measures as implying *non use* rather than *sustainable use*.[78] Since the 1992 United Nations Conference on Environment and Development (UNCED), however, states have not, generally speaking, pursued this preservationist approach when negotiating and applying MEAs. The efforts to approximate applicable legal regimes were taken more seriously after UNCED and the main soft law document of this Conference, Agenda 21,[79] dedicated the whole of chapter 17 to the marine environment, which spurred both MEAs and fisheries agreements to ensure better coherence in their efforts towards regulating conservation in a sustainable manner. Together with the 1995 FSA, the 1992 CBD was a fundamental step ahead in this direction. The CBD,[80] at its second conference of the parties, adopted the Jakarta Mandate for Marine and Coastal Biodiversity.[81] This mandate articulates a programme of action for implementing the Convention's provisions with respect to marine and coastal biodiversity and singles out for special attention amongst other issues sustainable use of marine and coastal living resources.

In turn, both international fisheries law and international environmental law operate within the wider realm of international law and its other ramifications such as maritime law, the law of the sea and the law of natural resources. The law of the sea establishes the generic obligation to take the necessary conservation measures when exercising the freedom of fishing but although important it relies on other legal streams to regulate the use of living resources on the high seas.[82] Maritime law allows flag states the discretion to take unilateral conservation measures for their nationals fishing on the high seas and bestows upon them exclusive jurisdiction to ensure compliance and enforcement. It also requires flag states to cooperate with both coastal states and other flag states in taking conservation measures on the high seas, especially with respect to particular species. International law regulating the use of natural resources stresses that all states have a right to access those resources that occur in areas outside national jurisdiction. In conformity with the high seas freedoms, the appropriation of marine living resources on the high seas by any single state or group of states is prohibited. UNCLOS, in section II of Part VII,[83] requires states to take conservation measures that 'maintain or restore populations of harvested species at levels which can produce the maximum sustainable yield as qualified by relevant and economic factors'. The evolution of environmental treaties has continued to lay further emphasis on the sustainable use of such resources in order to ensure their conservation. As Orrego Vicuna observes, although originally international law regulated the availability of the resource to ensure the economic performance of the fishing industry, it has more recently started to address conservation issues required by environmental standards. The socio-economic issues addressed by the older sources of international law relating to high seas living resources acquired a different perspective and also had to accommodate environmental concerns. This process has given rise to new legal concepts and to the reinterpretation and reformulation of traditional principles of international law.[84]

1.5 HARMONIZATION: SYSTEMATIC INTEGRATION TO OVERCOME FRAGMENTATION

The fragmented nature of international law is not a recent phenomenon, so much so that the 1969 Vienna Convention on the Law of Treaties (VCLT) addresses the situation when the same set of facts is regulated by more than one legal source leading to incompatible results. Conflicts may be either apparent or genuine and inherent. Apparent conflicts may be 'interpreted away'. In such cases the integrated approach serves to clarify any ambiguities found in the treaty provision when users refer to other treaties or other sources of international law. For instance, in the *US–Mexico Shrimp Case*,[85] the WTO Appellate Body interpreted the WTO term 'exhaustible natural resources' in GATT article XX(g) with reference to 1982 UNCLOS, the CBD and CITES amongst other sources. It is not always possible to rely on interpretation as a legal technique to achieve harmonization amongst different applicable rules. This is what happens when there is a genuine and inherent conflict, which arises when the application of one norm is in direct breach of another. It could be a conflict between two commands, or between a command and a prohibition, or between a command and a right, or even between a prohibition and a right.[86] In the first two cases the chance of conflict is inherent because the application of one norm leads to a breach of obligation under the other and therefore cannot be resolved by conflict-resolving techniques. In the other two cases there is a potential conflict, which will occur if the exercise of a specific right under one norm breaches another under the conflicting rule. Conflicts may happen not only when successive treaties address the same subject and have the same title, such as for example the various conventions on the law of the sea[87] but also when more than one treaty may be applied to regulate a particular situation. The *MOX Plant Request for Provisional Measures Order Case*[88] referred to earlier, related to a nuclear facility namely, the MOX Plant at Sellafield in the United Kingdom, which Ireland claimed was causing negative effects on the environment as a result of its operations. The dispute was subject to the multilateral and general rules of UNCLOS, the regional rules of the OSPAR Convention[89] (since the dispute related to pollution in the North Sea) and the application of EU *acquis communautaire* as embodied in the EURATOM treaty (because both parties are members of the EU). As a result, the dispute was raised at three different institutional procedures: under the international Tribunal for the Law of the Sea (ITLOS), under the compulsory dispute settlement procedure set up under the OSPAR Convention and before the European Court of Justice because of the EC/EURATOM treaty. Conflicts may also arise when two or more treaties regulate the same issues but have divergent objectives. For instance, the 1958 High Seas Fisheries Convention perceives conservation as a measure to ensure food security whilst more recent treaties such as the 1992 CBD and the 1995 FSA[90] aim at conservation of the species *per se*. Additionally, conflicts may also occur when emerging norms are inconsistently applied to regulate similar circumstances, or when parties or different fora interpret the same treaty in a different manner.

Sometimes norms from different sources of international law may be eligible to regulate the same situation. If there is an apparent or an actual conflict between treaty and custom, the general trend is that the treaty provisions will prevail, whenever both states involved in the dispute are parties to the same treaty.[91] Nevertheless a more recent customary rule of international law may have modified and superseded the treaty provisions.[92] The onus of proof falls upon the contestant alleging the change in the law brought about by custom.[93] The same can happen when a treaty refers to general principles of international law[94] and any subsequent developments that seek to fine-tune it are interpreted as an infringement of the same general principles. One of the biggest bones of contention between states relates to the adoption of unilateral conservation measures by flag states on the high seas. Coastal or high seas fishing states consider that flag states cannot adopt measures that are inferior to those adopted via cooperation by other flag states harvesting identical species and/or fishing in the same marine areas beyond national jurisdiction. Their argument is based on the UNCLOS provision that requires all states harvesting species in this manner to cooperate.[95] Flag states taking this approach, however, contend that any constraints on their right to take unilateral conservation measures[96] hinder the general principle of freedom of access to these same resources codified under the 1982 UNCLOS. This conflict in the interpretation and application of the UNCLOS provisions as further developed by subsequent treaties is dealt with in detail in Chapter 3.[97]

The VCLT provides that states are to ensure that a treaty is interpreted in good faith in accordance with the ordinary meaning to be given to the terms of the treaty in their context and in the light of its object and purpose. Apart from its context and other agreements that were concluded to this effect,[98] state parties shall take into account 'any relevant rules of international law applicable in the relations between the parties'.[99] This implies that there is a presumption *against* conflict and that users must aim for the harmonization of applicable norms when they interpret treaties accordingly. Harmonization entails the identification of the most adequate legal techniques to avoid, minimize or mitigate conflict amongst the various sources of international law that may apply to a particular situation. Ideally, harmonization should be exercised at the negotiations stage, rather than as an afterthought, because in most cases it is the language of these same norms that gives rise to ambiguity and conflict every time the effects of political compromise lead to general provisions that leave too much discretion in the hands of the state parties. Apart from conflict prevention at the negotiations stage, the process of interpretation when a treaty is applied should be used to avoid conflict. Article 30 of the VCLT suggests the required legal techniques to achieve harmonization of conflicting treaty norms and regulates how a subsequent treaty may qualify an earlier treaty on the same subject.[100] Amongst the compendium of international norms that regulate the conservation of living resources on the high seas, one finds examples of *lex priori* and *lex posteriori*. UNCLOS itself and the CBD take this situation into consideration.[101] Article 30 of the VCLT applies when, 'successive treaties relate to the same subject-matter', and establishes that if a subsequent treaty specifies that it is subject to an earlier treaty or not in conflict with it, this should be interpreted to mean that the provisions of the earlier treaty 'shall prevail'. If a treaty is not suspended although it has been replaced by another, it remains applicable vis-à-vis those states that are parties to it and which are also parties to the new treaty, insofar as it does not conflict with the provisions of the latter. The provisions of the earlier treaty would, however, still prevail if in the case of a dispute where it is applied, one of the states is a party to it but not to the new treaty. The use of certain terminology in treaties such as 'without prejudice to' and 'further to' are often utilized to overcome the potentially conflicting interpretation of subsequent treaties vis-à-vis the previous one.

The VCLT also refers to other procedural legal measures to ensure harmonization between applicable treaties, such as determining the hierarchy of laws according to the relationship between the *lex specialis* and the *lex generalis*. One can notice that the international legal sources which regulate conservation of living resources on the high seas, range from norm-creating treaties like UNCLOS to subregional and bilateral agreements. Additionally, some norms relate to particular species like straddling stocks, marine mammals and anadromous species that raise issues of priority and specialization as the *lex specialis* that supplements and fine-tunes the *lex generalis*. A multilateral treaty may, because of its general nature, appear to be in conflict with more specialized norms emerging from subsequent treaties or possibly even customary international law that have developed at a later stage. The relationship between treaty law and customary international law may lead to the same situation of conflict between prior and subsequent legal sources addressing the same circumstances. A treaty in fact may predate the crystallization of a more recent customary rule of law.[102]

1.6 CONCLUSION

Living marine resources have diverse characteristics and life cycles. They roam freely ignoring human-made boundaries and jurisdictional claims arising therefrom. They also remain an essential source of sustenance not only for humans and states' economies but also for biodiversity in its entirety. The conservation of such resources on the high seas constitutes a vested interest for the international community as a whole and any attempts to harmonize the interpretation and application of the various international regimes is not only in keeping with the VCLT provisions, but also a *sine qua non* for the effective conservation of high seas living resources. Confusion, ambiguity and conflicts amongst applicable norms would inevitably hamper and weaken any legal framework on conservation. As we shall see in the coming chapters, despite the innumerable legal and non-legal challenges that render the regulation of sustainable use of living resources on the high seas a near-to-impossible task, there have been some success stories amongst many failures. Harmonization is possible and happening to some extent. There have been various attempts and some good examples of convergence between fisheries law and environmental law but these two legal streams have interacted less successfully with maritime law and the law of the sea, which are the sources regulating jurisdiction, enforcement and the nationality of fishing vessels. Despite the importance and the requirement to seek harmonization techniques, this approach has its limitations and cannot fill in legal lacunae or disregard the obligations of specific norms that are still in force. It must be stressed that whilst there is a presumption against conflict of norms under international law,[103] there is no similar presumption against change and legal stability cannot hamper the dynamism of the law.[104] Sometimes a temporary solution may be found as a political caveat but the stakeholders would at some point be constrained to negotiate new norms to resolve the conflict. A case in point is the imminent need to regulate bioprospecting for sedentary species on the deep sea-bed, outside the national jurisdiction of any state. This is discussed in Chapter 4. It is this requirement to replace ambiguity or overcome conflicting interpretation that often spurs states to call for the negotiation of new treaties. The FSA, for instance, sought to clarify UNCLOS' general rules, which had left open to interpretation the rights and duties of the coastal states and how these impinge on the freedom of fishing of straddling stocks and highly migratory fish stocks on the high seas. Sometimes the legal status of successive treaties in relation to the previous ones they ought to have fine-tuned, remains nebulous. States are bound by treaties they are parties to and if the new treaty is not adhered to by those states that were parties to the previous treaty, then its purpose to generate clearer legal obligations remains in abeyance. Harmonization may therefore occur via the adoption of techniques in legal interpretation permitted under international law or the formulation of a new legally binding instrument. It will only serve its purpose if it takes into account the different interests of states involved. The underlying reason why international law diversifies itself into different legal streams is to ensure the required degree of flexibility to meet with these different interests. Indeed, progress is registered whenever, 'the rules of maritime law have been the product of mutual accommodation, reasonableness and co-operation'. The words of the ICJ in the *Fisheries Jurisdiction Case*[105] sound as valid today, as on the day they were delivered.

NOTES

1. See UNCLOS article 119(1)(a) which says, 'In determining the allowable catch and establishing other conservation measures for living resources on the high seas States shall: take measures which are designed, on the best scientific evidence available to the States concerned to maintain or restore populations of harvested species at levels which can produce the maximum sustainable yield, as qualified by relevant environment and economic factors . . .'
2. See ibid, article 118.
3. The 1992 UNCED is also referred to as the Earth Summit. States at the Summit unanimously endorsed Agenda 21, an action plan which laid out how sustainable development and the sustainable use of natural resources may be achieved. See below at p 15.
4. See explanation of the term 'harmonization' for the purpose of this book, below p 4.
5. See speech by His Excellency Judge Gilbert Guillaume, President of the ICJ to the Sixth Committee of the United Nations General Assembly (UNGA), delivered on 27 October 2000, 'The Proliferation of International Judicial Bodiues: The Outlook for

the International Legal Order', p 4. www.icj-cij.org/icjwww/ipresscom/SPEECHES/iSpeechPresident_Guillaume_SixthCommittee.20001027.htm.

6. Section 2 of Part VII of UNCLOS, articles 116–20 and the cross reference made in article 116(b) to articles 63(2), 64–7.
7. See discussion in Chapter 3, pp 101–4.
8. Ibid, at note 53.
9. Some fisheries agreements such as the North Atlantic Fisheries Organization (NAFO) impose conservation measures in the high seas areas within the jurisdictional scope of the agreement (NAFO Regulatory Area) that if not abided by, lead to the classification of the fish caught in the same area as illegal, unregulated and unreported fishing (IUU). IUU fish landings are prohibited by port States, Parties to the NAFO. See Chapter 6 for a discussion on the subject at pp 247–9. See also Ball, W.S. (1996), 'The old grey mare, national enclosure of the oceans' ODIL, 27(1–2), 97–124; Birnie, P. (1997), 'Are twentieth-century marine conservation conventions adaptable to twenty-first century goals and principles?' Part II, IJMC 12(4), 488–532.
10. Document A/CN.4/L.682, 13 April 2006, 58th Session of the ILC, Geneva.
11. See VCLT, article 31.
12. See UNCLOS, article 86 which says that the provisions of Part VII on the high seas apply to all parts of the sea that are not included in the exclusive economic zone (EEZ), in the territorial sea and in the internal waters of a state or in the archipelagic waters of an archipelagic state. Also subject to freedom of fishing in accordance with section 2 of Part VII of UNCLOS are those living resources occurring in the superjacent water column of the continental shelf (beyond the territorial sea) where the coastal state has not declared an EEZ or an EFZ.
13. See UNCLOS, Part I, article 1(1) and Part XI, article 134.
14. Ibid, Part XI, article 133(a)(b).
15. Article 38 of the Statute of the International Court of Justice (ICJ), refers to a list of sources of international law, which the Court is to apply when settling disputes, namely: '(a) International Conventions, whether general or particular, establishing rules expressly recognized by contesting States; (b) international custom, as evidence of general practice accepted as law; (c) the general principles of law recognized by civilized nations; (d) subject to the provisions of article 59 judicial decisions and the teachings of the most highly qualified publicists of the various nations, as subsidiary means of rules of law.' Article 59 of the Statute of the ICJ establishes that judicial decisions of the International Court have no binding force except between the parties and in respect of that particular case. See Brownlie, I. (2003), *Principles of Public International Law*, 6th edn, Oxford: Oxford University Press, p 5.
16. See discussion on the *MOX Plant Case*, pp 14 and 17.
17. See Brownlie (2003), p 3.
18. See Report of the Study Group of the International Law Commission entitled *Diversification and Expansion of International Law. Fragmentation of International Law: Difficulties Arising from Diversification and Expansion of International Law*, document A/CN.4/L.682, 13 April 2006, 58th Session of the ILC, Geneva, paras 1–4.
19. See Brownlie (2003), p 5; see also Pauwelyn, J. (2003) *Conflict of Norms in Public International: How WTO Relates to Other Rules of International Law,* Cambridge Studies in International and Comparative Law, Cambridge: Cambridge University Press, p 94 et seq.
20. See VCLT articles 53 and 64. See also Shaw, M.N. (2003), *International Law,* 5th edn, Cambridge: Cambridge University Press, p 115.
21. See Brownlie (2003), p 5. See also Shaw (2003), p 103 and Pauwelyn (2003), p 90.
22. See Pauwelyn (2003), p 94.
23. See Shaw (2003), p 88.
24. See *Air Transport Services Agreement Arbitration* (1963) ILR 38, 182.
25. See Pauwelyn (2003), pp 143–5.
26. See ibid, p 148 et seq. See also Brownlie (2003) pp 15–19.

27. See Brownlie (2003), pp 274–7.
28. Ibid, p 18. See Orrego Vicuna, F. (1999), *The Changing International Law of High Seas Fisheries* Cambridge Studies in International and Comparative Law series, Cambridge: Cambridge University Press, p 1, who considers the freedom of fishing as, 'one of the fundamental principles underlying the regime of the oceans beyond the limits of national jurisdiction, a principle embodied both in customary international law and in the major codification conventions on the law of the sea'.
29. Examples of such cases include the *Corfu Channel Case,* ICJ Reports (1949), 18; *Right of Passage over Indian Territory* (Preliminary Objection) ICJ Reports (1957) 141–2.
30. Examples include the *Behring Sea Fur Seals Arbitration* (1898), 1 Moore's International Arbitration Awards 755, represented in 1 International Environmental Law Reports (1999) 43. See discussion in Chapter 3, pp 96–7 and 100–101.
31. The FSA is an example. It was negotiated to supplement the UNCLOS provisions that require coastal states and flag states to cooperate when exploiting straddling and highly migratory fishstocks under articles 63(2), 64 and article 116(b) of UNCLOS.
32. See above, note 10.
33. For a detailed discussion on the role of soft law vide Birnie, P., Boyle, A. and Redgwell C. (2009), *International Law and the Environment,* 3rd edn, Oxford: Oxford University Press. See also Dupuy (1991) 12 Michigan Journal of International law 420; Shelton, D. (ed.) (2000) *Commitment and Compliance: The Role of Non Binding Norms in the International Legal System*, Oxford: Oxford University Press.
34. See the separate opinion of Judge Lauterpacht in the *South West Africa* case (Voting Procedure), ICJ Reports (1955), 67 at 118–19.
35. See Brownlie (2003) pp 14–15. See also *Nicaragua v United States* (Merits), ICJ Reports (1986), 98–104, paras 187–95, pp 107–8, paras 203–5.
36. Examples include the FAO Code of Conduct for Responsible Fisheries, the United Nations Environment Programme (UNEP) 1987 Guidelines on Environment Impact Assessment. See Birnie, Boyle and Redgwell (2009), p 35.
37. Both the 1972 Stockholm Declaration of the United Nations Conference on the Human Environment (UNCHE) and the 1992 Rio Declaration of UNCED are considered to be examples of soft law.
38. See Brownlie (2003), p 15 and Birnie, Boyle and Redgwell (2009), p 35.
39. Principles referred to in both UNCHE and UNCED. Declarations such as the precautionary principle have eventually been incorporated in treaties like the FSA and may be considered by states to have crystallized as norms of customary International law. See *EC-Hormones: European Communities – Measures Affecting Livestock and Meat (Hormones),* complaints by Canada (WT/DS48) and the United States (WT/DS26), panel and Appellate Body reports adopted on 13 February 1998. In this case the European communities claimed that their ban on hormone-treated beef, which the applicant states claimed were allegedly inconsistent with WTO rules for not being based on sound science, was justified with reference to the precautionary principle – a principle which in the EC's view was part of customary international law.
40. This has been the role for example of the various Guidelines published by UNEP and Plans of Action promoted by the FAO.
41. For a detailed discussion on the role of soft law in this sense, see Birnie, Boyle and Redgwell (2009), pp 34–7.
42. The FAO has provided various Technical Guidelines on the Precautionary Approach, Fishing Operations, Fisheries Management, Sustainable Development Indicators, Illegal, Unregulated and Unreported Fishing (IUU) and the Ecosystem Approach. It also has formulated four International Plans of Action on seabirds, sharks, capacity and IUU. It has also provided a Fishery Resources Monitoring System. See Meltzer, E. (2009), *The Quest for Sustainable Fisheries*, Ottawa: NRC Research Press, p 12, Figure 2.1.
43. Some fisheries organisations for example use qualified majority voting, not unanimity, such that decisions would become binding on all parties if the constituent instrument

so permits. See Meltzer (2009), pp 270–91. For example the North East Atlantic Fisheries Commission (NEAFC) which requires both simple and at times qualified majority voting from a quorum of two-thirds of the contracting parties. Any contracting party may object to a recommendation for management measures only. Since the amendment of the constituent treaty in 2004, parties are to provide in writing, reasons for objection and declare alternative conservation measures they will be taking.

44. See Jennings, R. (1981), 'What is International Law and How Do We Tell It When We See It?', 37 ASDI 59.
45. See *Gabčikovo–Nagymaros Case* (Hungary-Slovakia), ICJ Reports 1997, para 140.
46. See *La Bretagne Arbitration Decision*, (1986) 90, *Revue General de Droit International Publique* (RGDIP), 716, para 58.
47. See Pauwelyn, (2003), p 17 and footnote 31.
48. See ibid, p 19, where the author argues that the transformation of international law into a law of both co-existence and cooperation has led to the significant potential increase in conflict between applicable norms and has generated apparent and genuine conflicts between general international law and the different substreams of specialized norms as well as amongst the substreams themselves.
49. US-Shrimp: *United States-Import Prohibition of Certain Shrimp and Shrimp Products*, complaints by India, Malaysia, Pakistan and Thailand (WT/DS58), panel and Appellate Body reports adopted on 6 November 1998.
50. See article 48 of the *Draft Articles of the ILC on State Responsibility for International Wrongful Acts*.
51. See also *Barcelona Traction Case* ICJ Reports (1970) 3. See also Birnie, Boyle and Redgwell (2003), pp 232–6.
52. See above, note 10, paras 1–4.
53. After the United Nations Conference on Environment and Development (UNCED) and the Cancun International Conference on Responsible Fishing in the year 1992, many fisheries agreements were reviewed to adopt an ecosystem approach. See Chapter 5 for a discussion on these developments at pp 182–7.
54. For a historical account on the early developments on the law of the sea vide McDougal, M.S. and W.T. Burke (1962), *The Public Order of the Oceans*, 2nd edn, New Haven, Conn.: New Haven Press, 1987; Churchill, R.R. and A.V. Lowe (1999), *The Law of the Sea*, 3rd edn, Manchester: Manchester University Press, pp 203–432; Brownlie, I. (2003) pp 223–7. For a more recent history see also Burke W.T. (1994), *The International Law of Fisheries: The 1982 UNCLOS and Beyond*, Oxford: Clarendon Press, pp 1–25.
55. There were four 1958 United Nations Conferences on the Law of the Sea: the Convention on Fishing and Conservation of Living Resources of the High Seas, which defined conservation and came into force on 20 March 1966, the Convention on the High Seas, which codified fishing as one of the high seas freedoms and came into force on 30 September 1962, the Convention on the Continental Shelf in force on 10 June 1964 and the Convention on the Territorial Sea and Contiguous Zone in force on the 10 September 1964. All were done in Geneva. The 1982 UNCLOS addressed all the issues in these four treaties. It qualifies the freedom of fishing making it subject to the obligation to conserve living resources and regulates exploitation both on the high seas and in the areas subject to national jurisdiction. See Burke, W.T. (1996), 'Introduction: The Importance of the 1982 UN Convention on the Law of the Sea and Its Future Development', ODIL, **27** (1–2).
56. See Shaw (2003), p 492 Birnie, Boyle and Redgwell (2009) pp 382–4.
57. See Brownlie (2003), p 200 and footnote 145.
58. See UNCLOS, articles 119 and 197.
59. See UNCLOS, articles 63, 64, 66 (3)(c), 67(3).
60. Ibid, article 65.
61. Article 237(2) also stipulates that specific obligations assumed by states under special conventions with respect to the protection and the preservation of the marine

environment should be carried out in a manner consistent with the general principles and objectives of the 1982 Convention.

62. The 1882 North Sea Over-Fishing Convention.
63. 1911 Treaty for the Preservation and Protection of Fur Seals (Washington) superseded by the 1957 Interim Convention on the Conservation of North Pacific Fur Seals Convention (discontinued).
64. Examples of such agreements include the South Tasman Rise Agreement and the Central Behring Sea Donut Hole; see Meltzer (2009), p xxxiii.
65. RFMOs and RFMAs established under this article have only advisory powers and may at best only make recommendations; they are funded by the FAO. They are not considered as RFMOS and RFMAs according the 1995 UN Fish Stocks Agreement definition of the same. The Fisheries Council for the Eastern Central Atlantic is an example.
66. These have a budget of their own from contributions made by the parties. The constituent treaty establishes the range of decision-making powers. The General Fisheries Commission for the Mediterranean is an example of such an RFMO.
67. This agreement is not in force.
68. The FSA came into force on 11 December, 2001.
69. The 1997 GFCM replaced the 1952 Agreement for the Establishment of a General Fisheries Council for the Mediterranean.
70. As amended in 2005.
71. Each of these programmes has a legal component that includes a Convention and various Protocols issued thereunder such as, for example, the 1976 Barcelona Convention on the Protection of the Mediterranean Sea Against Pollution as amended in 1995, namely The Barcelona Convention for the Protection of the Marine Environment and the Coastal Region of the Mediterranean and its 1995 Protocol Concerning Specially Protected Areas and Biological Diversity in the Mediterranean. See also Chapter 2, p 29, footnote 35.
72. See above at note 53.
73. See Orrego Vicuna (1999), p 2.
74. Examples include Precautionary Approach No. 2, 1996, Sustainable Development Indicators, No. 8, 1999, IUU No. 9, 2002 and the Ecosystem Approach, No. 4 Supplement 2, 2003.
75. See above at note 41.
76. *MOX Plant, Request for Provisional Measures Order Case* (*Ireland v United Kingdom*), (3 December 2001), (ITLOS), ILR vol. 126 (2005) p 273, para 51.
77. See above at note 53. See Birnie, Boyle and Redgwell (2009), pp 385, 386. See also discussion in Chapter 5, pp 182–7.
78. See Birnie, Boyle and Redgwell (2009), pp 11–12
79. See above at note 3. Agenda 21 is a soft law instrument which nonetheless has greatly influenced the trends adopted by treaties that address environmental issues and resource management since 1992.
80. The CBD came into force on 29 December 1993.
81. See CBD COP Decision II/10. See also CBD Subsidiary Body on Scientific, Technical and Technological Advice (SBSTTA) Recommendation III/2 as amended by COP III.
82. See Orrego Vicuna (1999), p 1.
83. Article 119(1)(a).
84. See Orrego Vicuna (1999) p 3.
85. See above at note 49 *US-Shrimp* WTO dispute paras 128–32.
86. See Pauwelyn (2003), pp 178–9.
87. Vierdag, E.W. (1988), 'The Time of the "Conclusion" of a Multilateral Treaty: Article 30 of the Vienna Convention on the Law of Treaties and Related Provisions', BYBIL vol. 59, p 100.
88. *MOX Plant Request for Provisional Measures Order Case* (*Ireland v United Kingdom*),

3 December 2001, International Tribunal for the Law of the Sea (ITLOS), ILR vol. 126 (2005) p 273, para 50.

89. The 1992 Convention for the Protection of the Marine Environment of the North East Atlantic (OSPAR) combines the 1972 Oslo Convention on the Dumping of Waste at Sea and the 1974 Paris Convention on Land Based Sources of Marine Pollution. It has 15 state parties apart from the EU.
90. The FSA came into force on 11 December 2001.
91. See 1995 Resolution of the Institute of International law 1995-I 66, *Yearbook of the Institute of International Law* 245 at 248. See also Pauwelyn (2003), p 133.
92. See Schacter, O. (1998), 'Entangled Treaty and Custom' in Yoram Dinstein and Mala Tabory (eds) *International Law in a Time of Perplexity – Essays in Honour of Shabtai Rosenne*, Dordrecht: Martinus Nijhoff, p 720.
93. See Pauwelyn, (2003), p 139.
94. See Brownlie (2003), pp 5, 18–19, where he explains that, 'They are primarily abstractions from a mass of rules and have been so long and so generally accepted as to be no longer directly connected with state practice.' He quotes as examples the freedom of the seas, principles of consent, reciprocity and equality of States. Furthermore he argues that, 'certain fundamental principles have recently been set apart as over-riding principles of jus cogens which may qualify the effect of more ordinary rules'.
95. See UNCLOS, article 118.
96. Ibid, article 117.
97. See below pp 116–28.
98. See VCLT, article 31(2)
99. Ibid, article 30(2), which establishes that, 'When a treaty specifies that it is subject to, or that it is not to be considered as incompatible with, an earlier or later treaty, the provisions of that other treaty prevail.' Article 30(3) provides, 'When all the parties to the earlier treaty are parties also to the later treaty but the earlier treaty is not terminated or suspended in operation under article 59, the earlier treaty applies only to the extent that its provisions are compatible with those of the later treaty.'
100. Ibid.
101. See 1982 UNCLOS articles 237 and 311 and CBD article 22(1)–(2).
102. A treaty may be amended by a subsequent norm of customary law where acquiescence to the latter is recognized by state practice of the same parties to the treaty concerned; vide for example *Air Transport Services Agreement Arbitration*, 1963, ILR 38, 182.
103. See *Right of Passage over Indian Territory* (Preliminary Objections) ICJ Reports 1957, 142 where the judges of the ICJ held that a rule of interpretation must be such as to intend to produce effects in accordance with existing law not against.
104. See Pauwelyn (2003), footnote 14, p 242.
105. *Icelandic Fisheries Cases (United Kingdom and Germany v Iceland) (Merits)*, ICJ Reports, (1974) (para 53).

2 Regulatory jurisdiction over living resources on the high seas

2.1 INTRODUCTION

State jurisdiction has two distinct but complementary aspects. Regulatory jurisdiction refers to the legal competence of a state to make decisions and prescribe rules, whilst enforcement jurisdiction refers to its power to implement and enforce them. Municipal law determines the application of jurisdictional powers by the legislative, executive and judicial organs of the State,[1] whereas the extra-territorial application of state jurisdiction is regulated by international law.[2] The regulatory jurisdiction of states over living resources on the high seas is governed by various norms that emerge from customary international law, treaties and general principles of law. These norms evolved over the centuries to meet the emerging needs, priorities and interests of the international community. This chapter will focus upon the right of access over these resources and how this right is qualified vis-à-vis third parties. Another aspect of the regulatory jurisdiction of states whose nationals exploit living resources on the high seas includes their obligation to take conservation measures; this will be discussed in the next three chapters. Enforcement jurisdiction will be dealt with in Chapters VI and VII.

UNCLOS establishes[3] that all states, whether coastal or landlocked, have access to the high seas, and that no state can appropriate these areas by exercising sovereignty or sovereign rights over all or any part thereof.[4] Article 87 codifies the so-called high seas freedoms, founded upon Grotius' legendary work *Mare Liberum,* which promotes the free seas common property approach as an inclusive interest vested in the international community as a whole.[5] In his work[6] Grotius refers to two main legal principles relating to the use of the high seas and their resources: non-appropriation by private individuals or by any state or group of states, and the principle that use by one state would not prejudice access to same resources by other states. Grotius based his arguments on the perception, prevalent in his time, that it is impossible to occupy these marine areas or to exhaust the resources located therein. One can understand that such an assumption on the infinite nature of the oceans and their resources[7] proved to be fallacious with the passage of time.[8]

For many years the high seas freedoms comprised only negative elements and consisted basically of prohibitions[9] whereby users of the sea were obligated, save in the case of a few exceptions, to observe an attitude of abstention towards one another.[10] The high seas freedoms are still directed against the individual or collective exclusiveness of use[11] by states. The absence of territorial sovereignty, as the basic principle of the freedoms, is supported by state practice[12] and jurists[13] alike. It is also evident, however, that states do not interpret freedom from territorial sovereignty to mean that the sea is free from all juridical sovereignty[14] or that the high seas fall outside the rule of law.[15] In the absence of an international authority having jurisdiction to regulate and police the high seas, the maintenance of international law and order depends upon flag state jurisdiction. Each vessel is subject to the national legal system of a state that registers it under its flag. Consequently, any obligations resulting from registration devolve on the flag state, which must assume jurisdiction and control over the vessel.[16] Flag state jurisdiction on the high seas is exclusive,[17] and this norm applies to all ships including fishing vessels or any other seacraft which conduct operations that exploit living resources beyond national jurisdiction.

This historical background to the high seas regime explains why the term 'freedom of fishing'[18] implies that access to living marine resources beyond national jurisdiction is *prima facie* a predominant right vested in all states. Over the years, various international norms have evolved which qualify this general position whilst presently, coastal states may claim sovereign rights over living marine resources up to 200 nautical miles from their baselines, when they declare an exclusive economic zone (EEZ).[19] Consequently, jurisdictional claims over marine living resources have evolved in tandem with developments in the delimitation of maritime boundaries[20] by coastal states. The extension of coastal state jurisdiction over the years, particularly the establishment of EEZ and Exclusive Fishing Zone (EFZ) in the second half of the twentieth century, has caused the span of maritime areas falling under the high seas regime to shrink considerably in size when compared to Grotius' time. The extension of coastal State jurisdiction from 3 to 12 nautical miles for fishing purposes was initially accepted as a norm of customary international law by the ICJ in the *Icelandic Fisheries*[21] cases. The extension to 200 nautical miles as a matter of state practice came about later,[22] and largely because of the UNCLOS negotiations which made it clear that this limit would be adopted in the new treaty when it was concluded. The insistence of coastal states on the establishment of the EEZ[23] exerted unprecedented pressure during the negotiations leading to the 1982 Convention because of the severe impact which the extension of coastal state jurisdiction had upon high seas fishing.[24] Overwhelming support for the establishment of the EEZ was based on the pretext that subjecting living resources to coastal state jurisdiction would curtail the over-exploitation that threatened the sustainability of living resources on the high seas, particularly with respect to those species which had a significant economic value. One of the reasons that spurred the extension of coastal state jurisdiction was the international community's failure to agree upon a basic list of conservation principles for high seas fisheries. Although a good number of regional and subregional fisheries agreements, supported by a permanent institutional structure,[25] were concluded, state parties did not always bestow upon them the necessary powers to monitor and enforce the implementation of the same conservation obligations enshrined in the constituent treaty. Furthermore, these treaties cannot bind third parties without their consent[26] and enticing them to adhere to conservation standards established by fisheries agreements has proved to be largely unsuccessful.[27] These severe shortcomings, fuelled by the lucrative prospect of exclusively exploiting fish stocks adjacent to their coasts, led many coastal states to extend national jurisdiction over marine living resources by declaring an EEZ or an EFZ,[28] thus acquiring sovereign rights over marine living resources located therein.[29] The impetus to appropriate these resources for economic benefit to the exclusion of other competitor states was a strong motive behind the urge to extend coastal state jurisdiction. The EEZ was proposed as the appropriate legal solution to give coastal states responsibility for the conservation of the marine living resources occurring in areas that were previously part of the high seas. This legal and factual development had two major consequences on the jurisdictional aspects of a conservation regime for living marine resources in general. In the majority of cases and insofar as the aggregate of fisheries is concerned, jurisdiction shifted from the flag state to the coastal state which now had sovereign rights for exploitation and legal responsibility for the conservation of resources living in its EEZ. UNCLOS established some parameters for conservation and allocation of stocks in the EEZ under its articles 61 and 62, but the view as to whether conservation is attempted or indeed achieved is left to the discretion of the coastal state. The extension of coastal state jurisdiction therefore eliminated freedom of fishing over the vast majority of previously available fish. Secondly, states intensified distant water fishing in the remaining marine areas of the high seas. To address the problem of regulating open access fishing claims, UNCLOS still had to come to terms with striking a balance between the demands of flag states, whose exercise of freedom of fishing had been severely curtailed and the establishment of an effective regime for the conservation of marine living resources on the high seas[30] to safeguard the rights and interests of all the stakeholders over the same resources.

UNCLOS, which embodies developments in international law resulting from centuries of state practice, strives to achieve this balance of interests via a number of provisions that qualify the right of freedom of fishing. These qualifications may be general and therefore applicable to all the freedoms. For instance, article 87 provides that all the freedoms must be exercised under the conditions laid down in the Convention and other rules of international law[31] as well as with 'due regard for the interests of other States' in their exercise of the high seas freedoms and with respect to activities in the Area.[32] They can also be specific to particular freedoms. Article 87(1)(e) then establishes that the freedom of fishing itself is subject to the conditions of section two of Part VII of the 1982 Convention which deals with the conservation and management of living resources on the high seas. Under section 2, flag states have various qualifications particular to the freedom of fishing, including the duty to cooperate with coastal states whose maritime zones are adjacent to the high seas and other flag state participants in the fishery. In line with their duty to cooperate, states have concluded various treaties both before and particularly after the 1982 UNCLOS that regulate the operations of distant water fishing vessels.[33] Some of these treaties concern the exploitation of living marine resources in specific regions on the high seas. Examples include the various regional and subregional fisheries agreements[34] as well as the UNEP Regional Seas Programmes.[35] The 1992 CBD marks an important turning point in the development of international conservation law as it addresses biodiversity in its entirety, whereas other treaties mainly focus on certain species, such as highly migratory fish stocks[36] or endangered species[37] or marine mammals.[38] Some of these Agreements, like the CBD, CITES and the Bonn Convention, were negotiated as multilateral environmental agreements (MEAs), but all these treaties have a common goal, namely that state parties comply with a list of conservation measures aiming at the sustainability of stocks.[39] The parties retain, as flag states, their exclusive jurisdiction on the high seas, but the treaties limit their discretion on the kind of conservation measures they are to adopt. Furthermore, multilateral environmental agreements (MEAs) have introduced various legal principles and methodologies, such as the ecosystem approach, the precautionary approach and the need for adopting tailor-made conservation measures specifically designed for certain categories of marine species, including non-harvestable species.[40] The influence of these principles from a conservation perspective is discussed in the next three chapters. Their incorporation in treaties, and possibly their crystallization as rules of customary international law, has also influenced the manner in which states may have come to perceive the exclusive nature of the regulatory jurisdiction of flag states. The 'original' interpretation of the states' freedom of fishing is based on arguments that date back to the time when the sustainability of stocks was not an issue of international concern. The more recent conservation principles challenge the rationale of this 'original' interpretation. As highlighted above, however, states cannot be coerced to adopt treaties[41] and they may persistently object to acquiescing to a norm of customary international law.[42] Consequently, any agreements which qualify the freedom of fishing may be rejected by some states and endorsed by others. As a result, the position of international law under applicable sources is riddled with various legal uncertainties due to the plurality of sources that affect jurisdictional issues. For instance, to what extent is the flag state's exclusive jurisdiction subject to the rights, duties and interests of the coastal states of other flag state participants in the fisheries' and the international community at large? What is the legal status of high seas' living resources? Does international law safeguard them as a common resource, vested in the international community at large? Despite the unsettled nature of international law in this context, there is strong evidence that states consider both their right of access over living resources occurring on the high seas as well as the non-appropriation of such resources by any state as being general principles of international law.[43] Similarly, the obligation that states have to take necessary conservation measures on the high seas[44] and the premise that their rights of access over the resources occurring therein are relative to those of other states[45] have been reaffirmed various times in international case law[46] and by jurists.[47]

It must be clarified that whenever states have made claims supporting the taking of unilateral conservation measures by imposing abstention upon other states to access living resources on the high seas, these have been turned down.[48] However, international tribunals, various treaties as well as international conferences and organizations have recognized the obligation on the part of any state whose nationals fish on the high seas to take conservation measures. This obligation, found in UNCLOS article 117, is said to codify customary international law and arises from the exercise of the high seas' freedoms in a manner that ensures orderly access to such resources by others. In other words, the freedom of fishing as a norm of international law cannot be considered in isolation but should be applied in accordance with other sources of customary international law, namely the obligation to act with reasonable regard and to refrain from abuse of rights towards others who share the same rights. This kind of reasoning is evident in the *Behring Fur Seals Arbitration* which reaffirmed the high seas' freedom of fishing but also recognized the need for restraint and called for conservation to prevent over-exploitation. The same can be said for the decision of the ICJ in the 1994 Icelandic fisheries cases, which upheld rights of fishing on the high seas but emphasized the obligation of reasonable use, the need of conservation, equitable allocation and good faith. To paraphrase the words of Orrego Vicuna, these developments in international law manifest that the principle of freedom of fishing is not derogated from, but it is no longer tantamount to uncontrolled or depredatory fishing activities.[49] It is the manner in which these qualifications should be implemented that remains controversial.

The next part of this chapter discusses the impact which the qualifications to the freedoms, as they occur under the UNCLOS provisions, may have upon the exclusive nature of the flag state's regulatory jurisdiction and to what extent treaties and state practice since the 1982 Convention may have further fine-tuned the Convention's provisions. Another jurisdictional issue that is cause of considerable debate in legal spheres, namely the legal status of living marine resources under UNCLOS and other sources of international law, will also be examined. The discussion will then assess whether contemporary international law can provide a harmonized set of norms that regulate the exclusive jurisdiction of states exercising freedom of fishing in a manner that is conducive to the conservation of living resources on the high seas. As we shall see, there are various complex and interrelated legal arguments which may have influenced the development of international law in this regard.

2.2 THE QUALIFICATIONS TO THE RIGHT OF FREEDOM OF FISHING AND THEIR EFFECT UPON REGULATORY JURISDICTION

Article 92 of UNCLOS codifies international law regarding the flag State's exclusive jurisdiction on the high seas affirming that:

> Ships shall sail under the flag of one State only and, save in exceptional cases expressly provided for in International treaties or in this Convention, shall be subject to its exclusive jurisdiction on the high seas.[50]

There is a symbiotic relationship between the relative nature of the flag state's exclusive jurisdiction and the qualifications to the freedom of fishing.[51] The qualifications require the flag state to assume certain obligations that impinge upon its discretion as to how it may exploit living resources[52] on the high seas. It is through these qualifications that international law aims to achieve this balance of interests between states, referred to above. Some qualifications are general in scope and are applicable to all the freedoms. Article 94 of UNCLOS, for instance, lists the duties of the flag state vis-à-vis ships flying its flag and provides a list of measures[53] which masters and crew must know about and comply with, such as generally accepted regulations, procedures and practices. The observation of these measures is mandatory[54] upon the flag state. Article 87 gives an inclusive[55] list of the freedoms and in subparagraph 1 declares that the freedoms shall be exercised 'under the conditions laid down by this Convention and by other rules of international law'. This provision is stating the obvious; international law should always be applied in its entirety, and the law of the sea is no exception. So one may argue that article 87(1) of Part VII is accentuating the relative nature of the freedoms so that states apply them within the wider context of the Convention itself and international law in general. The fulfilment of this obligation, however, is grossly hampered by the fragmentation of applicable international rules. Different legal sources emanating from various fora tend to adopt diverse legally binding standards and methodologies even if they have a common objective. Amid this plurality of norms it becomes a gruelling task for the flag state to decipher the relative nature of its regulatory jurisdiction in substantive terms. The efforts by states to harmonize fragmented regimes via the revision of treaties is discussed below; it is an exercise that facilitates the adoption of an integrated approach as advocated by article 87(1). However, the qualification under article 87(1) does not only relate to treaties but to all sources of international law.[56] Customary international law presents a bigger challenge for harmonization purposes, due to the uncertainty that may surround the legally binding nature of certain trends in state practice. Treaties may seek to codify custom but one should always exercise caution as to whether a treaty provides an exhaustive set of applicable norms, because in the meantime new customary rules may have emerged.[57] The next sections of this chapter will assess the various qualifications to the freedom of fishing and their legal implications upon the exclusive jurisdiction of the flag state.

2.2.1 The Vested Interest of all States over Living Resources on the High Seas

UNCLOS article 87(2) provides a general qualification, namely that the freedoms shall be exercised by 'all States with due regard for the interests of other States in their exercise of the high seas freedoms. . .'.[58] This provision addresses a wider category of states when compared to article 116(b), which refers to coastal states whose jurisdiction extends over maritime areas adjacent to the high seas and article 118 that affects other flag states, participants in the same high seas fishery. These two categories of states, as we shall see below, benefit from additional qualifications to the freedom of fishing,[59] but it is only article 87(2) that refers to the interests of 'other' states but only with respect to their exercise of the high seas freedoms. UNCLOS does not elaborate on how compliance with article 87(2) affects the flag state's exclusive jurisdiction on the high seas, leaving the legal issue open to interpretation. Notwithstanding various treaties on the subject, including the four conferences on the law of the sea,[60] disputes relating to the balance of rights and interests between states in their exploitation of high seas living resources have been amongst the most dominant subjects of international case law. Most fisheries' cases discuss the juridical relationship between coastal states and high seas fishing states, but some do refer to freedom of fishing as being subject to a general interest vested in all states. The *Behring (Fur Seals) Arbitration*[61] is one of the earliest disputes, where the decision of an international tribunal supported the need for restraint in exploitation and affirmed that the freedom to fish was not absolute but had to take 'reasonable account of the interests of other States'.[62] It considered that conservation measures were necessary to ensure that other participants' rights of access to these resources on the high seas were not prejudiced. The 1958 Convention on the High Seas established that states shall exercise the freedoms[63] with 'reasonable regard to the interests of States in their exercise of the freedoms of the high seas'. The other 1958 Convention on Fish Conservation and Management in the High Seas did not refer to these interests but reiterated the right of freedom of fishing subject to coastal states' rights.[64] In the *North Sea Continental Shelf Cases*[65] the parties were held to be under an obligation to negotiate and cooperate in good faith so as to accommodate their respective rights and interests under article 2 of the High Seas Convention. They had to balance equitably and regulate catch limitation, and take full account of fishery conservation needs in discharge of their duty to exercise 'due diligence'. In the *Icelandic Fisheries Case* the International Court of Justice (ICJ) was asked to decide upon the legality of Iceland's extension of its fisheries jurisdiction and the rights of the UK and the Federal Republic of Germany as flag states whose nationals fish in the area.[66] The relevance of the *Icelandic Fisheries Cases* in this chronological account revolves around a discussion on the relative nature of the rights of the states involved. The ICJ upheld as customary international law Germany's and the UK's right to exercise freedom of fishing. It declared that the parties' respective rights, both as the high seas fishing states and the coastal state, were not absolute but:

> had to take full account of each other's rights and of any fishery conservation measures . . . It is one of the advances of maritime international law, resulting from the intensification of fishing, that the former laissez-faire treatment of living resources of the high seas has been replaced by a recognition of a duty to have due regard to the rights of other States and the needs of conservation for the benefit of all.[67]

This decision of the ICJ in the *Icelandic Fisheries Cases* recognized that international law had evolved to consider that the flag state's duty to take conservation measures on the high seas was also intended for the benefit of *all* states and not only to safeguard the preferential rights of coastal states adjacent to the high seas and other flag states participants to a fishery.[68] It is significant to note that the ICJ reached this decision after it assessed the existing fisheries conventions and state practice at the time, before the UNCLOS negotiations were concluded.

The treaties and international case law quoted above served as precursors to UNCLOS Part VII. The negotiators of the 1982 Convention opted for the term 'due regard' instead of 'due diligence', referred to in the *North Sea Continental Shelf Cases*[69] or 'reasonable regard', found in the 1958 Convention on the High Seas. Due diligence is normally used as a qualification to the individual right of states to exploit natural resources[70] in areas beyond national jurisdiction. It expresses the need of good management when states are exercising their rights under international law and calls for the setting of minimum standards to safeguard the sustainable use of a common resource.[71] Some authors contend that due diligence guarantees exploitation as being subject to the conservation and management of the resource for the benefit of all interested states.[72] Paying 'due regard' to the interests of other states is regularly referred to in international law, as a manifestation of the obligation of good neighbourliness and reasonable use of common resources. The criterion of reasonable use has been interpreted by various jurists as ensuring unrestrained access by all states.[73] This implies that the enjoyment of high seas living resources is permissible so long as there is no abuse of rights. There seems to be consensus on this line of interpretation[74] but it is still considered difficult to put into practice what constitutes 'reasonable use', 'non abuse of rights' and 'equitable utilization of resources'.[75] The threshold beyond which, the exercise of the freedom of fishing is deemed 'unreasonable' remains at the discretion of the high seas fishing states.[76] Although the terms due diligence and due regard are applied and used in similar circumstances, there may be a subtle but significant difference in their legal interpretation. Whilst the application of due diligence is seen to focus on the exercise of one's rights without causing any harm or nuisance to others, paying due regard to the interests of other states appears to go beyond the exercise of diligence and acknowledges that the exercise of one's rights should not prejudice the interests, which other subjects may have over the common resource.

The competing uses of the high seas may lead to conflicting claims. For instance, the establishment of marine conservation areas may be considered as an encroachment upon the freedom of navigation; deep sea trawling can in turn hinder the laying of submarine cables and pipelines, whilst the regulation of bioprospecting on the deep seabed may be considered as obstructing the freedom to carry out scientific research. It is probably for this reason that under article 87(2) of UNCLOS the obligation to exercise due regard is tied to the other states interests in their exercise of the high seas freedoms. This link serves as a guarantee, which allows other states to enjoy the freedoms[77] in an equal manner. It may be argued that article 87(2) is more restrictive than what the ICJ declared in the *Icelandic Fisheries* cases because, under UNCLOS, flag states have a duty to pay due regard only insofar as this may affect the interests of other states in their exercise of the freedoms and the exercise of rights under the 1982 Convention in the Area.[78] This appears to exclude other interests third states may have over high seas living resources such as the conservation of the marine habitat and marine biodiversity for its own intrinsic value and not in relation to exploitation. The chapeau of the same article 87, however, clearly indicates that the freedoms cannot be interpreted in isolation.[79] The general qualification for states to exercise the freedom of fishing with 'due regard' under article 87(2) is supplementing the obligation for all flag states to comply with section 2 of its Part VII entitled 'Conservation and Management of High Seas Living Resources',[80] as well as any other relevant UNCLOS provisions and any other applicable international norms. The chapeau clearly indicates that the freedom of fishing has to be interpreted in the light of other international norms that widen the scope of the qualifications to freedom of fishing already imposed by section 87(2) and section 2 of Part VII although even these latter provisions may serve to express the international community's interest in living resources on the high seas. For instance the 1982 UNCLOS does not define 'conservation'. Its negotiators refrained from adopting the 1958 Convention's restrictive interpretation of the same term as 'the aggregate of the measures rendering possible the optimum sustainable yield from those resources so as to secure a maximum supply of food and other marine products'.[81] Instead, UNCLOS in article 119 establishes that conservation measures are to be 'designed to maintain and restore populations of harvested species', to produce the maximum sustainable yield qualified by environment, and economic factors, taking into account fishing patterns, the interdependence of stocks and generally recommended minimum standards. The 1982 Convention requires states to take into consideration the effects on associated and dependent species 'with a view to' maintain or restore their populations above levels at which their reproduction may become seriously threatened.[82] The wide scope of the objectives prescribed by article 119 suggest that the obligation to take conservation measures goes beyond ensuring sustainability of stocks on the high seas solely for exploitation purposes as specified under the 1958 Convention[83] and promotes conservation via an ecosystem approach. As will be discussed below, substantive obligations in post UNCLOS treaties build upon this perception.[84] This wider approach towards conservation was mainly developed around UNCED in 1992, which was crucial in promoting the ecosystem approach as a basis for the conservation of the marine environment and its biodiversity because of their intrinsic value for the benefit of all states. If one considers the UNCLOS provisions in the light of these more recent developments, these appear to include also the conservation of non-harvestable species as well as the marine habitat itself because the sustainability of living resources on the high seas depends on the adoption of a holistic set of conservation measures. UNCED and its Agenda 21, prompted by strong scientific evidence to this effect, have led parties to the various fisheries' Agreements to review the constituent treaties and include a more comprehensive set of conservation measures.[85] Some of these treaties were concluded by coastal and high seas fishing states in fulfilment of their obligation to cooperate under UNCLOS section 2 of Part VII. This gives more weight to their normative role and may therefore be considered as having crystallized into customary international law. Even if their legally binding nature may be contested, they constitute at the very least examples of best practice, when it comes to determining what are the necessary conservation measures flag states should adopt for their nationals who exploit living resources on the high seas. Apart from the generation of norms that further elaborate upon what the taking of conservation measures entails, the vested interest of all states over living marine resources has been developed by virtue of other articles in section 2 of Part VII that further supplement this obligation such that it has different permutations depending upon where the high seas fishery takes place[86] and which are the species involved.[87]

Despite these developments, uncertainty prevails as to whether any state under international law would have a legal standing to challenge abuse of rights by flag states on the high seas solely on the basis that this is detrimental to it either as a potential user of the freedoms or because it has a vested interest in the conservation of living marine resources *per se*. In other words, the capacity of a state to bring forward such a generic international claim is much weaker than that of coastal states with an EEZ adjacent to the high seas where the flag state is operating, or of states participating in the same fishery in an area beyond national jurisdiction. The latter two categories of states have the comfort of relying on other UNCLOS articles.[88] A causal link must be established between the manner in which the flag state is exploiting high seas living resources and the way this jeopardizes the interests of other states. The best way to substantiate the legal standing of any state to make such a claim against another flag state would be within the whole context of section 2 of Part VII. On the strength of the provisions of this section, the flag State, whether in cooperation with others or acting unilaterally, has to take the 'necessary' conservation measures in accordance with article 117.[89] States acquiesce to the obligation that their nationals take conservation measures on the high seas,[90] but as unilateral measures are also permitted[91] there is disagreement on whether the taking of less onerous measures than those agreed to by other participants via cooperation constitutes a breach of international law.[92] The FSA and the FAO Compliance Agreement tried to overcome this impasse. They do not impede flag states from taking unilateral measures but consider conservation measures adopted via cooperation as constituting the minimum necessary requirements to guarantee the conservation of species affected by high seas' fishery in the regions within the scope of the latter Agreements.[93] An international adjudicating body will not interpret UNCLOS article 118 as subjecting flag state jurisdiction to forced cooperation, because international law does not support this view,[94] but it may accept the argument that the obligation to cooperate under article 118 implies that measures are more effective when taken collectively.[95] Furthermore, article 119 of UNCLOS refers to 'the taking into account of recommended international minimum standards, whether subregional, regional and global'. The FSA and the Compliance Agreement build upon these provisions and consider that, where fisheries agreements exist, the 'necessary' conservation measures are more likely to be embodied in these rules or standards, which may be deemed to constitute best practice, especially if they are based upon independent and updated scientific advice. To affirm a claim against a flag state for failing to safeguard its interests, the applicant state must prove that these are not hypothetical but identifiable juridical claims arising from the flag state's concomitant duty to take the 'necessary' conservation measures under UNCLOS and as they may be further fine-tuned by other sources of international law. The applicability of various sources regulating the same issues but which interpret differently the relative nature of flag state jurisdiction may be harmonized by adopting such an approach.

Another relatively recent development may also support the right of any state to make a claim against flag states for failing to take adequate conservation measures on the high seas. The 1992 CBD in its preamble has classified biological diversity as a common concern of humankind and this would include marine living resources, which do not fall within the jurisdiction of states.[96] The term 'common concern of humankind' refers specifically to a common resource whose vulnerability requires a concerted effort from all states.[97] So far it is included only in United Nations Resolutions and preambular paragraphs in treaties,[98] but it may serve to strengthen the legal standing of a state to make a claim without having to prove a direct interest against another state for failing to adopt conservation measures to safeguard a common resource. It is useful to examine any legal implications the notion of common concern may have, bearing in mind that at this point in time it is in its embryonic phase. It was presented in the light of prevailing circumstances, which highlighted the precarious state of natural resources such as climate and biological diversity.[99] By declaring in the preamble of the CBD that biodiversity is a common concern of humankind, the parties acknowledge the limitations of regulating such resources only on the basis of jurisdictional zones. The CBD is not subjecting living resources on the high seas to global management as UNCLOS does with the mineral resources of the deep-sea bed under Part XI. Instead, it implies that because of their particular nature and importance, living resources as components of biodiversity (including those occurring on the high seas) are of vital interest to humankind and constitute a global unity. Any threats to their conservation status may affect the whole community of states or humanity as a whole. The first element of the common concern notion implies that, whilst the resource cannot be appropriated, global responsibilities towards it become *erga omnes* in character, owed to the international community as a whole. The second aspect emerged and developed mainly around the 1982 UNCED: global responsibilities towards the conservation of biological diversity are common but differentiated, in the sense that some states have a major say when it comes to equitable balancing in the access to these resources and may also be allowed preferential treatment. The provisions of UNCLOS do in fact make a similar provision by referring to the 'special requirements of developing States' when determining the allowable catch of marine living resources occurring on the high seas.[100]

These arguments also serve to highlight a link between the resources vested in humanity as a whole and *erga omnes* obligations under international law. *Erga omnes* obligations were widely discussed in the *Barcelona Traction Case*[101] where the ICJ distinguished between two different types of obligations which states may have, namely contractual obligations that arise vis-à-vis only those states with whom they may have concluded an Agreement and *erga omnes* obligations whose binding effect is collective and owed to the international community as a whole. The issue of *erga omnes* obligations in an environmental context was raised in the 1974 Nuclear Test Cases when Australia and New Zealand complained that nuclear experiments by France in marine areas beyond national jurisdiction constituted an interference with the high seas' freedoms of all states.[102] The ICJ did not accept that Australia and New Zealand had the required legal standing to bring forward such a claim against France, and so dismissed the applicability of the *erga omnes* concept in this context. The developments brought about by the evolution of international environmental law in the meantime may lead to an international adjudicating body to adopt, today, a different stand. In fact, the possibility that conservation of high seas living resources may be considered by states as an *erga omnes* obligation may be inferred from the *Gabčikovo–Nagymaros* case when Judge Weeramantry, in his dissenting opinion, referred to sustainable development as an *erga omnes* obligation.[103] This affirmation equates inter-generational and intra-generational rights and obligations, an intrinsic component of sustainable development, with *erga omnes* obligations. What is particularly relevant in our case regarding the status of marine living resources on the high seas is the fact that, if international law considers states to have an *erga omnes* obligation to conserve biological diversity, this would imply that each component of biological diversity, whilst retaining its original status wherever it occurs, becomes subject first to the international community's legitimate interest to safeguard resources of global significance and second to its common responsibility to achieve sustainable development. Any state would have the legal standing to make an international claim against any other state for lack of compliance with these obligations under international law. To date, however, the ICJ has not applied the concept of *erga omnes* obligations outside human rights or humanitarian law, and therefore the applicability of *erga omnes* obligations' concept to living marine resources beyond national jurisdiction remains untested.[104]

Even if international law does not yet consider the conservation of living marine resources as being the subject of *erga omnes* obligations, the classification of biodiversity as a common concern of humankind may serve to demonstrate that states are legally bound to adopt conservation measures that comply with minimum standards agreed upon by other stakeholder states; otherwise they would be interfering with the other states' right to enjoy the freedoms of fishing. In theory, these arguments seem solid enough but the concept of conservation, at least from a fisheries law perspective, remains closely linked to satisfying human needs albeit on a sustainable basis. The UNCLOS provisions are too vague when referring to reasonable use and equitable utilization. Post UNCLOS developments supplement the provisions of the 1982 Convention in stressing this concept of common responsibility towards the conservation of marine living resources occurring on the high seas. Throughout the negotiations leading to the 1982 Convention, there had been some unsuccessful proposals to subject fisheries on the high seas to international management.[105] Lebanon, in its statement in the Seabed Committee, had called for the collective organization of high seas fisheries[106] and Mexico had suggested the establishment of an international authority for high seas fisheries.[107] The post UNCLOS legal developments have not taken this route: the regulation of the freedom of fishing has not evolved within the context of collective undertakings and global management, but as a means to incorporate environmental concerns. Public opinion has mobilized the international community to take a series of measures that focus on the ecological impacts of high seas fisheries. The exclusive jurisdiction of flag states over living marine resources has thus assumed different meanings over the centuries: from an absolute freedom to one that largely sought to maintain a balance of interests between coastal states and distant water fishing states, dominated by economic interests, and more recently, to incorporate conservation obligations that ensure the sustainability of stocks over which both the participants in the fishery and the entire international community has an interest.

2.2.2 The Specific Qualifications to the Freedom of Fishing

(i) The provisions of section 2 Part VII

Article 87(1) provides an inclusive list of the high seas freedoms and its sub-article (e) refers to the freedom of fishing subject to the conditions laid down in section 2 of Part VII, entitled 'Conservation and Management of the Living Resources of the High Seas'. This qualification is specific to the freedom of fishing and supplements the qualifications discussed above.[108] Article 116 of the same section reiterates this qualification to the right, which all states have for 'their nationals to engage in fishing on the high seas'. It also subjects it to any treaty obligations states may have,[109] as well as the rights, duties and interests of coastal states.[110] Under article 117, flag states have the duty to take, 'such measures for their respective nationals, as maybe necessary,' when exploiting living resources on the high seas, either unilaterally or via cooperation. Furthermore UNCLOS establishes a general obligation for states to cooperate in the 'conservation and management' of living resources on the high seas. States are required to 'enter into negotiations with a view to taking the measures necessary for the conservation of living resources'[111] when their nationals either fish for identical species or for different species in the same area of the high seas.[112] The rest of the provisions refer to the obligation of high seas fishing states to take certain factors into consideration when adopting conservation measures and to cooperate in the conservation and management of marine mammals.[113] All of these qualifications, together with ones mentioned in the previous section, impinge upon the kind of conservation measures the flag state needs to adopt when its nationals fish on the high seas. Although it has the right to act unilaterally, the flag state's measures cannot disregard any of the obligations it has under the articles of section two of Part VII, the other provisions of the Convention and the rules of international law.

The subjection of freedom of fishing to the conditions of section 2 of Part VII has other legal implications. First, access to living marine resources beyond national jurisdiction is primarily governed by the norms laid down in articles 116 to 120 of the 1982 Convention. Sedentary species occurring on the continental shelf of the coastal state are an exception and are regulated by the continental shelf regime under Part VI, even when the superjacent water column forms part of the high seas.

The articles of section 2 of Part VII may be considered as the primary source regulating the exploitation of living resources on the high seas, according to which flag states, coastal states and the international community should operate. Later developments even required by UNCLOS are considered to fine tune these provisions.[114] If they are considered to codify customary international law, they acquire even more significance when considering the position of states which are not parties to post UNCLOS fisheries agreements or MEAs.[115] Although, as mentioned above, UNCLOS requires states to adopt an integrated approach and apply the norms of section 2 Part VII within the entire context of its other provisions and international law, non parties to other applicable treaties are likely to give these UNCLOS articles more weight in case of conflicting interpretation. Their norm-creating character is accepted by most states whilst the provisions of subsequent and more specialized applicable treaties like the FSA may have not been tested as to whether they have mustered the same degree of universal acquiescence. Nevertheless on the strength of these UNCLOS provisions, post UNCLOS treaties regulating the conservation of living marine resources may still have an indirect effect upon flag states, which are non parties. Flag states may find themselves applying the same or at least compatible conservation measures emanating from post UNCLOS treaties, in order to fulfill the UNCLOS obligations under article 116(b) for instance, where the freedom of fishing is subject to the rights, duties and interests of the coastal states[116] and/or articles 118 and 119 where states are obligated to cooperate with other participants in a high seas fishery[117] and to adopt conservation measures that take into account existing international and regional standards.

The subjection of freedom of fishing to the provisions of section 2 of Part VII also signifies that it is the flag state's responsibility to regulate the conservation of species on the high seas every time its nationals fish therein. UNCLOS article 117 obligates states 'to take or co-operate in taking such measures for their respective nationals as may be necessary for the conservation of living resources of the high seas'. Article 119 delineates the parameters of the conservation measures flag states are to adopt; their general nature is in stark contrast with the detailed ones that coastal states may impose upon foreign vessels allowed to fish in their EEZ.[118] This bestows upon flag states a wide margin of discretion and may result in subjecting high seas living resources to disparate standards of conservation compared to those in the EEZ. This has prompted post UNCLOS treaties to insist on the obligation for compatible conservation measures which UNCLOS only implies. Article 118 declares that, 'States shall co-operate with each other in the conservation and management of living resources on the high seas', through appropriate global and regional organizations in the formation and elaboration of international measures, particularly when their nationals fish for identical species or in the same areas of the high seas.[119] Despite the mandatory language, UNCLOS provides no indication as to what should happen when cooperation fails. The problem of inconsistency is a direct effect of the subjection of high seas fisheries to exclusive flag state regulatory jurisdiction, despite its various qualifications. One of the major challenges is the difficulty in proving that amid the various applicable norms that supplement the UNCLOS provisions of section 2 of Part VII,[120] international law has generated a minimum set of conservation standards that enjoy universal acquiescence. The regional fisheries agreements are supported by the FSA and the FAO Compliance Agreement in promoting their conservation measures as constituting the required minimum within the high seas area that falls under the scope of their jurisdiction. Some distant water fishing states however may refuse to abide by certain conservation measures widely applied by other participants in the same fishery on the high seas because they argue that UNCLOS article 117 allows for unilateral measures and therefore no minimum set of conservation measures can be imposed upon any state unless it specifically agrees to them. However this conflict may be only apparent because although article 117 allows for unilateral conservation measures it still refers to *necessary* conservation measures, not *any* conservation measures. To achieve harmonization between UNCLOS article 117 and these regional and later developments, one can argue that the conservation obligations achieved via cooperation reflect *prima facie* these necessary measures. Unilateral measures also need to satisfy this requirement, so the more similar the unilateral measures are to those agreed via cooperation, the more they can be interpreted as achieving this goal. Therefore it is up to the flag state taking unilateral measures to prove that the goals adopted satisfy the 'necessary' criterion, especially if the unilateral measures it adopted differ from those required via cooperation agreements.[121]

This line of argument avoids the controversial argument that a group of states may for conservation purposes preclude access to other states from fishing in a region of the high seas to support their conservation programme from being prejudiced by non parties. The exploitation of living resources occurring in the superjacent water column over the deep seabed,[122] as well as those located on the deep seabed and its subsoil, were categorically excluded from international management under the common heritage regime.[123] Although the concept of general interest of the international community to conserve resources beyond national jurisdiction also pertains to the common heritage regime, the similarity stops there; the subjection of freedom of fishing to section 2 of Part VII excludes the conservation of living resources on the high seas from global management as is the case with the common heritage regime in Part XI or appropriation and management by a group of states.[124] In his dissenting opinion in the *Estai Case*,[125] Judge Shigeru Oda insisted on this point, by remarking that the NAFO Convention neither provides for the unilateral adoption by coastal states of fishery regulations intended to apply in the Regulatory Area, nor entrusts coastal states with the enforcement of such regulations in that area of the high seas. He argued that the only issue in dispute:

> was whether Canada violated the rule of international law by claiming and exercising fisheries jurisdiction (namely, the prescribing of fishery regulations – including the exclusion of fishing vessels flying the Spanish flag –, the enforcement of those regulations by Canadian government authorities and the imposition of penal sanctions on a Spanish vessel and its master in an area of the high seas beyond the limit of its exclusive economic zone), or whether Canada was justified in exercising fisheries jurisdiction in that area, on the ground of its honestly held belief that the conservation of certain fish stocks was urgently required as a result of the fishery conservation crisis in the Northwest Atlantic – irrespective of the NAFO Convention, which neither provides for the unilateral adoption by coastal states of fishery regulations intended to apply in the Regulatory Area, nor entrusts coastal states with the enforcement of such regulations in that area of the high seas.[126]

Non appropriation of living resources on the high seas, however, does not exclude other stakeholder states from exercising their rights under section 2 of Part VII. The flag states' exclusive jurisdiction to choose which conservation measures they may adopt for their nationals fishing on the high seas is also subject to the other qualifications that allow coastal states[127] and other flag states who are participants in the fishery[128] to encroach upon the flag state's exclusive jurisdiction in its choice of conservation measures. This is how the balance of rights, duties and interests between stakeholder states is guaranteed. To harmonize conflicts that may arise out of unilateral conservation measures adopted on the strength of article 117, as opposed to the obligation to cooperate with other states in the taking of the same, it is more legally sound to argue that international law mandates the taking of necessary measures that also reflect the flag state's obligations towards others and that therefore certain minimum standards must be observed, rather than interpreting more recent regimes as an example of forced cooperation.

Another potential cause of conflict between UNCLOS and post UNCLOS treaties relates to what extent the flag state's regulatory jurisdiction may be encroached upon to include effective conservation measures that address both the species and their marine habitat. UNCLOS does not provide any cross reference between the provisions of section 2 of Part VII and its Part XII, 'Protection and the Preservation of the Marine Environment'.[129] This anomaly may allow states to argue that the two Parts are not interrelated and that UNCLOS does not require flag states to take conservation measures aimed at the protection of the marine habitat. In actual fact Part XII provides for the conservation of the marine habitat from anthropogenic sources of pollution; it does not refer to destruction and deterioration of the same habitat due to fishing effort or any other form of exploitation of living resources. Furthermore UNCLOS article 119 does not mention the conservation of the marine habitat itself but requires states to take 'comprehensive' conservation measures. Fisheries agreements and MEAs, which aim to prevent negative impacts on the marine habitat caused by all human activities[130] have met with severe opposition from some non parties who consider such measures as a harassment to the freedom of fishing and as discriminating between fisherman of various states.[131] Such a conflict arises, however, if one adopts a narrow-minded interpretation of Part VII and Part XII. It can be interpreted away[132] in the light of article 87(1), which obligates states to exercise the freedoms 'under the conditions laid down by the Convention and by other rules of International law'. Adopting a more holistic interpretation of the obligation to take conservation measures that also include the habitat has an impact on the exclusive jurisdiction of flag states, such as when regional treaties have encouraged states to establish marine conservation areas. For instance, Monaco, Italy and France have concluded a tri-partite agreement in pursuance of their obligations under the 1995 Protocol for Specially Protected Areas and Biological Diversity in the Mediterranean that establishes a marine conservation area, the Pelagos Sanctuary, which extends beyond maritime zones under their jurisdiction to the high seas. The flag vessels of other coastal states and distant water fishing states have adhered to stricter conservation measures delineated by these three states in accordance with the Mediterranean Protocol for Specially Protected Areas and Biological Diversity. None of these states have raised objections to date, indicating that for the purpose of this marine area beyond national jurisdiction in the Mediterranean, there is *prima facie* aquiescence to a form of encroachment upon flag state exclusive jurisdiction on the high seas. In other instances, fisheries treaties pursuant to UNCLOS article 119 have introduced conservation obligations such as more selective fishing gear, harnessing fishing effort and the prohibition of certain fishing methods. Such obligations aim to reduce bycatch and the negative impact on the marine environment and non harvestable marine species. Some of these measures have led to disputes between states[133] but as we shall see in the next three chapters, states have acquiesced to other examples of conservation measures such that they have crystallized into norms of customary law.

In the end, the inextricable link between the right of states to freedom of fishing and the provisions of section 2 in Part VII of UNCLOS emphasizes the strict interrelationship between its component articles, such that each provision cannot be interpreted separately from the rest. The section makes a number of cross references to the articles under the EEZ regime and refers to the obligation of states to negotiate cooperation agreements. This process of accretion of rules that states have generated to implement section 2, may in itself generate fragmentation. This is why various Parties to RFMOs and regional seas agreements have initiated a review exercise to scrutinize existing Agreements for possible harmonization with more recent developments in marine conservation brought about by post UNCLOS treaties. Unless there is compatibility between applicable norms, the balance of interests between the players that is essential both to the enjoyment of the freedoms and the sustainability of high seas living resources cannot be guaranteed. The provisions of section 2 and their legal implications will now be discussed individually.

(ii) Freedom of fishing subject to the treaty obligations of flag states

Freedom of fishing under UNCLOS is subject to any treaty obligations which flag states may have.[134] Treaties are a major source of international law and constitute the bulk of international norms for the conservation of high seas living resources. This qualification is a tautology because according to the doctrine of *pacta sunt servanda*[135] all states are bound by the treaty provisions to which they are Parties.[136] UNCLOS seems to emphasize two aspects here, which a number of provisions in Part VII already refer to. First, the duty of states to cooperate in implementing this part of the Convention by concluding other agreements[137] and secondly the exercise of the freedoms within the context of international law[138] and so as qualified by treaties each state has ratified. Parties to such treaties have qualified further their exclusive jurisdiction: they have to establish conservation measures for their nationals to comply with on the high seas that must comply with the provisions of these same treaties. This leads to the dilemma surrounding the position of non parties as to whether their non adherence bestows upon them more discretion on the high seas. If this is the case it would strongly prejudice the position of others that have chosen to adopt a more rigorous conservation regime in fulfilment of the UNCLOS provisions to cooperate when exploiting living resources on the high seas. It is not only the competitiveness of state parties which may suffer as a result of flag hopping but the 'opt out' strategy by some participants in the high seas fishery may destabilize the conservation status of the species in question. The major conflict surrounding this dilemma remains the issue of whether non parties can be subjected to either forced cooperation or else be excluded from participating in the fishery on the basis that they are adopting inferior conservation measures. As discussed above, international law does not admit forced cooperation to achieve uniform state practice in the conservation of living resources on the high seas. Therefore even in this case one may repropose the alternative techniques discussed above to harmonize the legal implications of international norms,[139] which apply both to parties and non parties. First and foremost non parties may still be bound if applicable treaties supplementing the UNCLOS provisions in section 2 Part VII either codify or generate customary international law. Where the norm-creating character of such treaties is uncertain, non parties may still be affected by the conservation measures and methodologies stipulated therein and can find themselves complying with them indirectly. This may happen when the nationals of non Parties exploit 'identical living resources or different living resources in the same area' of the high seas[140] with other participants in the fishery who may be parties to such treaties. In such cases, they have to conclude cooperation agreements with the latter for the conservation of the species that may incorporate the same measures stipulated in these treaties. Additionally, all flag states are obligated under article 116(b) to subject their nationals' freedom of fishing to the rights, duties and interests of those coastal states whose jurisdiction extends over marine areas adjacent to the high seas. If these coastal states are parties to such Conventions, they may set minimum conservation standards that comply with the more stringent treaties. The advantage of treaties is that the conservation obligations they establish upon state parties are more identifiable and usually more effective. If one takes verifiable catch quotas as a typical example, it would be hard to envisage a rule of customary international law that can match the certainty and the explicit nature which treaty provisions may achieve. Treaties must provide 'added value' if they are to encourage states to adhere to them; although the vast majority of states are genuinely interested in ensuring the sustainability of stocks, it is fundamentally important for treaties to be formulated in a way which would discourage states from preferring to 'opt out'. As we shall see in chapters 6 and 7 this can be done, for example, by requiring parties to take certain market-based measures as port states on all fish landings. Various multilateral, regional and sub-regional agreements[141] seek to implement this obligation to cooperate under article 118 and set out more detailed conditions to regulate the conservation and management of marine living resources. All these agreements endorse the flag state's exclusive jurisdiction but are more specific than UNCLOS in expressing its relative nature. They introduce various measures that serve to curtail the discretion of flag states not only by including more stringent conservation measures[142] but also by obligating them to develop administrative programmes and national legislation to ensure compliance by their fishing vessels on the high seas.[143] Some agreements also require parties to adopt enforcement regimes[144] and in a few cases to subject their fishing vessels to independent inspection.[145] The discussion in this part of Chapter 2 will identify how some conservation obligations occurring in these treaties impinge upon the exclusive jurisdiction of the flag state when its nationals fish on the high seas whilst the next chapter will expound upon the conservation measures introduced via these treaties. The effect of these treaties on enforcement jurisdiction, although referred to here, will be discussed in more detail in Chapters 6 and 7.

These treaties bind parties with new legal responsibilities, which they must implement as flag states, thus translating the qualifications to the freedom of fishing under UNCLOS into substantive obligations that encroach upon the flag state's exclusive jurisdiction. The 1946 Convention on the Regulation of Whaling, for example, imposes a moratorium on whaling. This is definitely the most drastic way of curtailing the flag state's exclusive jurisdiction.[146] The FSA[147] envisages cooperation through fisheries organizations and enhances monitoring, control and enforcement by flag states through international cooperation at the regional level. Its parties are to ensure that conservation measures are to be based on best scientific evidence. This leaves less discretion in the hands of the flag state parties particularly when they fish in an area governed by a regional fisheries agreement. The FSA obligates its parties not to authorize nationals to fish for stocks covered by these agreements unless their fishing vessels abide by the regulatory obligations[148] found therein, because it considers these agreements as laying down the minimum conservation standards for high seas living resources.[149] The FAO Compliance Agreement has been criticized for leaving flag states with too much discretion in their exercise of exclusive jurisdiction. It is less restrictive than the FSA but complements it by requiring flag states to ensure that their vessels comply with conservation and management measures established under regional agreements. The FAO Compliance Agreement provides that flag state parties are to ensure their vessels exercise restrictions when issuing authorizations to vessels that have undermined such measures. It impinges upon the exclusive jurisdiction of the flag state parties, by bestowing upon the port state the right to take investigatory measures and establish whether a vessel that voluntarily entered its port has violated conservation measures. Additionally, the flag state party must also maintain records of its vessels that are registered and authorized to fish on the high seas and must circulate this information to make it available to all parties. The flag state is required to cooperate and through the exchange of information identify its vessels defying international and regional conservation and management measures. The FAO established a high seas vessel authorization record to develop a comprehensive centralized database on vessels that fish in marine areas beyond national jurisdiction. The obligation to exchange information does not diminish exclusive flag state jurisdiction but serves to regulate it in a more specific manner, limiting its discretion whilst establishing the necessary controls whereby it can exercise its jurisdiction more effectively.

Fisheries agreements constitute valuable examples of regional state practice but they vary considerably in their obligations and therefore in the manner in which they restrict flag state regulatory jurisdiction. Some like NEAFC set a total allowable catch (TAC) for certain species. The stocks regulated by NEAFC are fully allocated and fishing opportunities are likely to be limited to new fisheries. New contracting parties will be able to participate on the same basis as existing contracting parties in future allocation of stocks that are unregulated at the time of application. New contracting parties, which were previously cooperating with non contracting parties, may request part of the relevant cooperative quota, whilst allocations are considered on a case by case basis. ICCAT controls access and fishing capacity by TACs, quotas and vessel effort limitations. The GFCM adheres also to the ICCAT recommendation on Blue Fin tuna quotas and on shark bycatch where the contracting parties must report on the implementation of mitigation measures. NAFO imposes a moratorium on certain species[150] and obligates parties to take conservation measures to reduce and mitigate bycatch, including the incidental catch of species subject to moratoria. NAFO establishes that stocks are fully allocated and fishing opportunities for new members are likely to be limited to new fisheries, shared quotas and stocks that are currently not yet allocated.[151] Under CCAMLR, parties must respect bycatch conservation guidelines[152] according to the ecosystem approach, setting benchmarks for other Conventions and fisheries organizations. All regulated fisheries in the areas under CCAMLR jurisdiction are subject to precautionary catch limits.[153] In fact state parties cannot develop new fisheries before the

CCAMLR Commission is able to evaluate their potential consequences. CCAMLR also requires parties to have an established registry of vessels permitted to fish. If bycatch limits are exceeded vessels must also cease to fish and must leave the area.

Jurisdictional issues over living resources on the high seas have been highly topical even in international environmental fora. Some environmental treaties like CITES and the 1979 Bonn Convention on the Conservation of Migratory Species of Wild Animals were concluded before UNCLOS and impose obligations upon state parties, to ensure that any nationals or vessels registered under their flag fishing outside their national jurisdiction should comply with conservation measures provided for under these treaties. The 1979 Convention on Migratory Species defines 'Range States' to include states whose vessels are engaged in taking the species beyond the limits of national jurisdiction and requires them to prohibit the taking of species listed in Appendix I, which are species in danger of extinction. This Convention also obligates parties to prevent or remove obstacles to migration and prevent and control factors that may endanger the species, even outside national jurisdiction. The relationship between CITES and the regional fisheries agreements has been characterized by intense (and acrimonious) discussions to find a solution agreeable to both sides regarding the application of trade restrictions imposed by CITES upon its parties with respect to species taken in the marine environment outside the jurisdiction of any state. Any species listed in CITES that are taken from maritime areas outside national jurisdiction, fall within the definition of 'introduction from the sea' and consequently their introduction and transportation into a state party is regulated by the CITES rules. This means that CITES further qualifies the regulatory jurisdiction of its state parties since prior consent, subject to the conditions listed in the Convention, must be given by the state party that imports or permits the transit of any marine species listed in its Annexes I and II. The inclusion of certain commercial fish species into these annexes such as the basking sharks, whale sharks, or bycatch such as the great white shark and the humphead wrasse has necessitated a call for a clarification of this definition as it imposes restrictions on flag state parties, which are not found under UNCLOS and most fisheries agreements.

Environmental law promotes the approach that the conservation of the environment, including its living components, need to be applied in a consistent manner across different jurisdictional systems. Many MEAs like the CBD attempt to implement a uniform set of conservation measures, which parties are bound to implement whether species are: within their territorial jurisdiction; subject to their sovereign rights; or under their control in areas outside national jurisdiction. Parties to the CBD for instance are required to implement its provisions consistently with rights and obligations which states have under UNCLOS. The CBD does not regulate the components of biodiversity in areas beyond national jurisdiction,[154] but it obligates parties to observe the provisions of the Convention in these areas in processes and activities carried out under a party's jurisdiction and control. It calls for cooperation for conservation and sustainable use of biodiversity beyond national jurisdiction either directly or through competent Intergovernmental Organizations.[155] Parties to the CBD also have various qualifications with respect to their exclusive jurisdiction since they are responsible for ensuring compliance with the CBD provisions whenever their fishing vessels[156] adversely impact biodiversity on the high seas. State parties are obligated to identify and monitor such activities and carry out environment impact assessments of proposed projects likely to have negative effects on the high seas. The Conference of the Parties[157] to the CBD recognized that parties must identify activities with impacts on species and deep sea bed ecosystems and that they are responsible for ensuring that activities do not cause damage beyond national jurisdiction. Parties are to promote reciprocal arrangements for notification, exchange of information and consultation on such adverse activities to notify potentially affected states in case of imminent danger.[158]

MEAs in fact have proliferated because widespread adherence to them promotes a uniform approach towards conservation and enables parties to bring forward international claims against other parties who fail to abide by such measures.[159] Since UNCLOS, various international Fisheries Conferences, together with the 1992 Earth Summit and Agenda 21, have been instrumental in enhancing the link between international fisheries and environmental fora. The conclusion of the FSA is seen as the culmination of this effort but the process is an ongoing and arduous one. The 2002 Johannesburg World Summit on Sustainable Development Plan of Implementation provides an international commitment to halt biodiversity loss by 2015, which has led to an increased impetus to revise fishing quotas and the adoption of stricter conservation measures under major fisheries agreements[160] but the targets are unlikely to be met by the stipulated deadline.

(iii) Freedom of fishing subject to the rights, duties and interests of the coastal states

The rights, duties and interests of coastal states are singled out in article 116(b) as one of the three major qualifications to the freedom of fishing under UNCLOS. Due to the cross-reference made to Part V of the 1982 Convention, the term 'coastal States' is not interpreted in a generic manner but is considered to refer to coastal states that have jurisdiction over maritime zones adjacent to the high seas. As discussed above, article 116(b) is the result of historical developments that have dominated the international regulation of marine living resources[161] and the freedom of fishing. UNCLOS' article 116(b) focuses mainly, but not exclusively,[162] on the coastal states' rights, duties and interests over catadromous and anadromous species, highly migratory species and straddling fish stocks as well as marine mammals that occur in the high seas adjacent to their EEZ.[163] The coastal states have a stronger legal standing than 'other States'[164] to challenge the flag state's exclusive regulatory jurisdiction on the type of 'necessary' conservation measures the same state has to take on the high seas with respect to these species. Coastal states also have sovereign rights to exploit sedentary species on their continental shelf even if the superjacent waters are part of the high seas. Article 116(b) highlights the relative nature of the flag state's jurisdiction linking it to its legal relationship with the coastal state, under whose jurisdiction these same particular species occur. UNCLOS stops short however of determining in substantive terms which conservation measures need to be adopted on the high seas with respect to these species. As a result, there are treaties and examples of state practice, particularly within the aegis of regional fisheries organizations, which have attempted to supplement UNCLOS in regulating the conservation of such species. Coastal states have played an influential role when it comes to the exploitation of such species on high seas fisheries, claiming preferential rights that have even been supported by international case law.[165] The tug of war between them and the distant water fishing states has dominated the legal debate with respect to the qualification to the freedom of fishing, as coastal states wanted to exercise jurisdiction over key fishing grounds adjacent to their coasts and the distant water fishing states wanted to preserve the status quo regarding the traditional interpretation of the freedom of fishing. UNCLOS codifying state practice did not derogate from the exclusive jurisdiction of flag states on the high seas but established a legal framework such that the two polarized positions may assume, via cooperation, regulatory functions that would address uncontrolled and unsustainable exploitation on the high seas.[166] The discussion below assesses state practice as it has evolved in treaties and customary law, since the conclusion of the 1982 Convention. The plurality of applicable international norms that regulate this balance of rights between high seas fishing states and the coastal states with an adjacent EEZ have developed sporadically and have been the root cause of fragmentation in the legal framework. This part of the chapter carries out a comparative analysis with the UNCLOS provisions to identify the current state of play so as to expose major inconsistencies or discrepancies in the interpretation of respective rights and duties of states under applicable legal instruments.

It will propose to what extent these may be harmonized via available legal techniques.

(a) Jurisdiction over the conservation of anadromous and catadromous species UNCLOS' article 66 establishes that states in whose rivers anadromous species[167] originate, shall have 'the primary interest in and responsibility for such stocks'. Article 67 provides that the coastal state in whose waters catadromous[168] species spend the greater part of their life-cycle shall have the responsibility for the management of these species and shall ensure the ingress and egress of the migrating fish. It is to be noted that the precise term to use in the case of anadromous species is 'state of origin' rather than coastal state since salmon originating in the rivers of one country may reach the sea via marine areas subject to the jurisdiction of another state. Due to their nature, it is impossible to adequately assess the impact of fisheries beyond national jurisdiction for these two types of species because stocks of anadromous or catadromous species from different points of origin intermingle with one another when they occur on the high seas. Under such circumstances the effective conservation of anadromous and catadromous species[169] requires control by the state of origin. On the basis of this particular requirement for the appropriate conservation of these species UNCLOS, codifying customary international law, prohibits fishing for them when they occur on the high seas.[170] It establishes that 'fisheries for anadromous stocks shall be conducted only in waters landward of the outer limits of the EEZ'.[171] The cross reference between article 116, which subjects the freedom of fishing to the rights, duties and interests of the coastal state and this article 66, not only qualifies it, as in the case of straddling stocks or HMS, but actually *restrains* the freedom of fishing for anadromous and catadromous species subject to some exceptional circumstances discussed further on. Access to such species on the high seas by flag states is curtailed, given that the right cannot be exercised once the obligation to conserve these resources on the high seas cannot be fulfilled. The norm that other states should refrain from fishing anadromous species on the high seas, whether as a direct harvest or a bycatch.[172] recurs in state practice and has been mainly agreed upon via cooperation agreements such as the 1985 Agreement on Fisheries Cooperation between Japan and the Soviet Union in the North West Pacific and the 1991 Convention on the Conservation of Anadromous Stocks in the North Pacific Ocean. There have been instances however where states, notably, the US and the Soviet Union at the time, acted unilaterally even if both never actually implemented their claims in this manner but managed to conclude agreements with the other distant water fishing states involved.[173] The rights of coastal states as states of origin

are by far the most extensive in encroaching upon the flag states' exclusive jurisdiction over these species on the high seas. States of origin have an interest in maximizing the return of stocks that commence their life cycle in their waters. UNCLOS refers to the 'primary interest' of states of origin. It waives the prohibition for flag states to fish for anadromous species on the high seas by allowing an exception when this would lead to

> economic dislocation for a state other than the state of origin. In such cases the states concerned shall maintain consultations with a view to achieving agreement on terms and conditions of such fishing giving due regard to the conservation requirements and the needs of the state of origin in respect of these stocks.[174]

These provisions reflect the claims made by high seas fishing states during UNCLOS negotiations, namely that anadromous species spend a considerable part of their lives on the high seas where they grow and therefore increase in value upon being harvested. So accordingly it is not only the state of origin which contributes to the anadromous stocks' growth and development but that part of the gains of the state of origin, when harvesting these species, that is attributable to the high seas marine environment and sometimes to other areas subject to other states' jurisdiction. Although it is the state of origin which has the primary interest, this is not the same as saying that its interest is exclusive. Apart from the state of origin's obligation to cooperate to minimize economic dislocation in other states fishing for these stocks, states which participate by agreement with the state of origin in measures to renew anadromous stocks particularly 'by expenditures for the purpose,' shall be given 'special consideration by the state of origin in the harvesting of stocks originating in its rivers'.[175]

The 1982 Convention reflects these trends in state practice at the time it was negotiated, influenced also by the changes which the extension of coastal state jurisdiction had brought about with respect to claims made by states of origin. Whenever fishing for anadromous species on the high seas is allowed in exceptional circumstances as specified under the 1982 Convention, it is subject to an agreement expressing fishing terms and conditions agreed upon with the state of origin, which has the authority to decide on the allowable catch.[176] This agreement is a precondition to fishing for anadromous species on the high seas; without it such an activity would be an in infringement of UNCLOS and customary international law. There is an obligation upon the state of origin and the other states to 'maintain consultation' to achieve agreement on terms and conditions 'giving due regard to conservation requirements and the needs of the state of origin with respect of these stocks'.[177] The words 'maintain consultation' suggest the need for continuous review of the terms and conditions agreed upon, which must be linked to the fishing cycle and adjusted accordingly. The parties concerned must agree to undertake periodic reviewing of the terms and conditions as they monitor changes and devise conservation requirements that vary according to the life cycle of the species and the fishing patterns. UNCLOS also requires enforcement of regulations regarding anadromous species beyond the EEZ to be 'by agreement' between the state of origin and the other states concerned. Although the state of origin has no exclusivity for enforcement purposes on the high seas, the wording of this provision does not leave enforcement exclusively up to the flag states either, constituting an exception to article 92.[178]

(b) Jurisdiction over Straddling Stocks and Highly Migratory Species (HMS) There have been a number of inter-State disputes[179] relating to the harvesting of straddling stocks and HMS due to their occurrence in areas both outside and within national jurisdiction. Coastal states have sovereign rights over these resources in their EEZ and therefore have a particular interest in their conservation even when they occur in the high seas. The difference between these two species, which both fall under the 'migratory species category', is in the distance they migrate. Whilst straddling stocks migrate for short distances within a particular maritime region, HMS span over much larger distances. Furthermore for the purpose of UNCLOS, only species listed in Annex I are considered as HMS. The distinction between the two species under the 1982 Convention was based on the premise that whilst the effective conservation of straddling stocks is regional in scope, HMS require a multilateral regime. Coastal states argue that according to UNCLOS article 116(b) and its cross reference to articles 63(2) and 64, flag states are obligated to ensure that their vessels on the high seas, fishing for straddling stocks and HMS outside their EEZ, should abide by the same conservation standards they apply within the areas subject to their jurisdiction, otherwise the flag states would be in breach of international law. Some flag states rebut this approach arguing that this interferes with their exclusive regulatory jurisdiction since they have the discretion to take unilateral measures under article 117 of UNCLOS. The coastal states' claims to limit exploitation of straddling stocks on the high seas (or in another coastal State's EEZ) is based on UNCLOS' article 63(2), which obligates the states fishing for such stocks and the coastal State, 'to seek either directly or through the appropriate regional or subregional organization to agree upon the measures necessary for the conservation of these stocks in the adjacent area'. The cross reference to this article in article 116 strengthens the legal status of the coastal state in requiring the flag state to adopt conservation measures which are acceptable to it. The subjection of the exercise of

freedom of fishing to article 63(2) implies that the flag state should only take conservation measures reached by agreement with the coastal state. In other words the flag state's jurisdictional rights under article 117 must be interpreted in the light of this obligation to agree with the coastal state on the conservation measures that need to be adopted, since its freedom of fishing is qualified by the rights, duties and interests of coastal states as expressed *inter alia* in article 63(2).

HMS are also species that transcend areas within and beyond national jurisdiction. Under UNCLOS, however, only HMS listed in Annex I of the Convention fall within the scope of the obligations imposed by article 64. Article 64 establishes that coastal state and other states, whose nationals fish in the region for HMS,

> shall cooperate directly or through appropriate international organizations with a view to ensuring conservation and promoting optimum utilization of such species throughout the region both within and beyond the EEZ.

Freedom of fishing is, as in the case of the straddling stocks, subject to the provisions of this article. This implies that the coastal state or the flag state, which takes unilateral conservation measures in the EEZ or the high seas respectively, without prior exchange of views,[180] is in breach of the UNCLOS provisions requiring both states to take collective conservation measures with respect to HMS. As in the case of straddling stocks, the flag state must subject its exclusive regulatory jurisdiction to adopt conservation measures for its vessels when harvesting HMS on the adjacent high seas that are compatible with the coastal state's allowable catch and conservation measures related thereto. It must also ensure that its vessels comply with such measures and failure to do so is subject to compulsory dispute settlement under the 1982 Convention.[181] Difficulties arise when there is no agreement and one has to interpret to what extent the coastal state may subject the flag state whose nationals fish on high seas adjacent to its EEZ to compliance with conservation measures. When the flag state's fishing vessels operate both in the EEZ and the high seas beyond it, there should be no particular difficulty as the coastal state shall apply the same conservation measures[182] and conditions. Neither should there be difficulties in the flag state adopting unilateral conservation measures that are not time dependent until an agreement is reached, even if these measures are different from those of the coastal state. Where the states involved fail to reach an agreement despite good faith on their part, it becomes essential to determine the rights and obligations of the flag state that decides to fish for HMS outside the EEZ, independent of the coastal state's control.

In sum, one must determine how the right of freedom of fishing must be interpreted in the light of the subjection to conservation measures imposed by the coastal states that fish for the same HMS. Any attempt to adopt a harmonized approach amongst the different legal arguments regarding the extent of jurisdiction which both coastal and high seas fishing states have over HMS on the high seas requires a proper understanding of the various modes of interpretation given to the applicable provisions of the 1982 Convention and the context within which they may be applied. There is a distinction between UNCLOS' article 63(2) and article 64 with respect to regulatory responsibility. In the case of straddling stocks, it is the flag state which must ensure that its conservation measures are compatible with those applied by the coastal state in its EEZ. On the other hand, the obligation to cooperate in establishing conservation measures for HMS is upon both states.[183] The obligation to cooperate in the conservation and optimum utilization of HMS is more mandatory under UNCLOS compared to straddling stocks.[184] Orrego Vicuna argues in this context that there has been a shift in the burden of proof and it is up to the distant water fishing states exploiting HMS on the high seas to prove that the conservation measures they have adopted are consistent with articles 87, 116 to 119 and article 64.[185] Should the straddling stocks fall under UNCLOS Appendix I species, it is article 64 which prevails. To eliminate this fragmented approach, the FSA has done away with this distinction between HMS and straddling stocks under UNCLOS and subjects them to a single regime based on article 64. The FSA, as UNCLOS' implementing agreement on the conservation of these two types of species, requires compatibility between the conservation measures taken by the flag state on the high seas and those taken by the coastal state within the maritime areas subject to its jurisdiction. Flag states and coastal states, parties to the FSA, are regulated by the more elaborate provisions of the Agreement addressing cooperation[186] that are discussed in the next chapter. It is, however, open to interpretation whether the FSA codifies customary international law in this respect, since there is no obligation upon UNCLOS parties to adhere to it. The normative character of the FSA is unclear vis-à-vis non parties, even if it is widely ratified[187] and its text was adopted by consensus. Although non parties may argue that species not listed in Appendix I are not subject to UNCLOS article 64, they may not have the same legal justification to reject the obligation to seek compatibility for Appendix I species since this obligation is also implied under article 64. The wording of article 64 also considers that the coastal state or the flag state, which takes unilateral conservation measures regarding HMS, without prior exchange of views with the other states fishing for them in the region,[188] is in breach of the obligation to cooperate. As already highlighted above however, the applicable UNCLOS provisions[189] are not very helpful in providing clear guidance as to what extent the states involved should agree, in order to be considered as having complied with Article 64.[190] It is often the uncertainty surrounding this issue which gives rise to conflicting interpretation and disputes between states. Under UNCLOS article 64, the flag state must subject its freedom of fishing over Appendix I species to the rights of the coastal state but the latter must in turn subject its exclusive sovereign rights to a preliminary obligation to agree to cooperate with the former. Provision for the conservation and the management of HMS under UNCLOS obligates states fishing for these species to adopt uniform conservation measures in order to safeguard the same political and commercial interests, as these species migrate through several zones subject to national jurisdiction and areas forming part of the high seas. Post UNCLOS developments, as is evident under the FSA, build upon the requirements of article 64. One can interpret the obligation to cooperate in the strictest sense possible to mean that unless states whose nationals fish for these HMS reach an agreement, other obligations must remain in abeyance. This would signify that until the states involved reach an agreement neither one can independently promulgate conservation measures or determine how to achieve optimum utilization regarding HMS. Such an interpretation is not in line with articles 64 and 116, which require both the coastal state and the flag state to take conservation measures. It also brings everything to a standstill, failing the conservation of HMS in the process. In other words, such an interpretation leaves HMS exploitation unregulated, upsetting the conservation and management programme both within and beyond the EEZ, when the Convention under article 64 prescribes that proper conservation and management measures must include the whole area where the stocks are harvested. Another interpretation relates to the wording 'with a view to achieve', as an indication that the conclusion of an agreement remains no longer a prerequisite before taking action. If despite good faith on the part of the states involved, negotiations are not successful either in whole or in part, it can be assumed perhaps that as long as there is good faith and continued dialogue, the states involved would be deemed as having cooperated 'with a view to' ensuring conservation, promoting optimum utilization and the setting up of an international organization to this effect, even if they are not entirely successful in concluding an exhaustive agreement on all of these measures. Lack of success in concluding an agreement should not inhibit the coastal state from taking conservation measures once it has, as a precondition, ensured that the negotiations were genuine. This line of interpretation is more consonant with articles 116 to 119, which seem to imply that the flag state on the high seas is to observe the allowable catch established by the coastal state and is required to take necessary measures to ensure compliance with article 64 when harvesting HMS on the high seas. The position of parties and non parties to UNCLOS is believed to be identical in this case, since both the conservation of high seas living resources and the EEZ regime under UNCLOS are considered to be a codification of customary international law.[191] The developments brought about by the FSA have helped to avoid situations where agreements between coastal and flag states remain in abeyance for a long time. As already observed in the previous part of this chapter, by ratifying the FSA, parties are agreeing to adopt such regional and subregional agreements and they must therefore abide by their conservation measures, otherwise they do not have the right of access over these resources on the high seas. The FSA also has an indirect effect on non parties as it elucidates the legal implications applicable to the UNCLOS provisions. The FSA in this regard has set specific standards, which states should find difficult to disregard or contradict and at the same time justify their position that they have sought to cooperate to enter into agreement in accordance with UNCLOS articles 63 or 64 or that they have adopted the 'necessary' conservation measures in accordance with article 117. The FSA conservation measures may be envisaged as *prima facie* the basis upon which non parties can negotiate an agreement. It has served to some extent to establish a point of reference and thus harmonize conflicting interests that would normally stall an agreement. The FSA also sets its own conservation and management measures that are discussed in the next chapters. Its provisions have also motivated the revision of many fisheries agreements to comply with it and they have shed new light on what kind of cooperation measures flag states and coastal states should abide by.

In essence, cooperation and decisions to conserve both straddling stocks and HMS would have to consider, and possibly agree upon, which state can take how many of the species targeted for harvesting. Upon determining allocation and rights relating thereto, the states concerned must identify conservation measures that specify where, when and how the fishing effort should take place. Whilst before the coming into force of the FSA, states may have not managed to reach an agreement on how they will cooperate with respect to all these issues because their views were miles apart, the FSA conservation and management provisions should serve to approximate their diverse social and political needs as well as the economics of the fishing industry to satisfy UNCLOS's basic obligations. In the end, unless the coastal state and the high seas fishing state are parties to the FSA or to a fisheries agreement that provides for an enforcement regime or dispute settlement mechanism, enforcing compatible measures beyond national jurisdiction remains at the discretion of the flag state. This is because even if the coastal state may allege that the flag state has ignored or defied its conservation measures and that it has breached international law, it cannot enforce its conservation measures outside its EEZ.[192]

(c) Jurisdiction over marine mammals Coastal states have jurisdiction over marine mammals in their territorial sea and EEZ. Some states have national legislation regulating the harvesting of cetaceans/marine mammals both in areas subject to their national jurisdiction and for nationals and vessels flying their flag wherever they may occur.[193] Article 65 in Part V of UNCLOS expresses both a right and a duty. It is one of the provisions, which article 116 of Part VII of the Convention includes in its list when referring to the coastal states' rights, duties and interests that qualify the freedom of fishing. It establishes that:

> Nothing in this Part *(Part V on the EEZ)* restricts the right of the coastal state or the competence of an International organization, as appropriate, to prohibit, limit or regulate the exploitation of marine mammals more strictly than provided for in this Part . . . states are to cooperate with a view to the conservation of marine mammals and in the case of cetaceans shall in particular work through the appropriate international organizations for their conservation, management and study.

Furthermore article 120 in Part VII provides that article 65 applies also to the conservation and management of marine mammals on the high seas. Article 120, through its cross reference to article 65, mentions, 'the right of a coastal state or the competence of an International organization, as appropriate to prohibit, limit or regulate the exploitation of marine mammals, more strictly than provided for in this Part'. The wording of article 65 however assumes different legal implications under Part VII. Only an international organization may impose stricter conservation measures[194] for the purpose of article 120 because no state can assert sovereignty over the resources of high seas. This line of interpretation, which seems the most plausible, still highlights the ambiguous nature of the first part of this provision particularly regarding the role and the juridical capacity of such an organization. The Convention does not use the same jargon for the conservation of marine mammals as it does with HMS[195] and straddling stocks[196] or when states participate in the same fishery.[197] Instead of obligating states to cooperate via regional and subregional organizations to take conservation measures, the wording of article 120 enables an international organization to take *stricter* measures than those prescribed by the provisions of UNCLOS Part VII.[198] It is unclear whether this means that the organization may provide a conservation regime that merely supplements the provisions of Part VII or whether it may go as far as to prohibit unilateral measures, obligating states to adopt only the conservation measures it proposes even upon non members. As already explained above, the obligation to take conservation measures via cooperation is incorporated in article 117 and 118 so article 120, which specifically singles out the conservation of marine mammals and of cetaceans in particular, must have an ulterior motive. If one adopts the widest interpretation that article 120 requires *all* states, whether members or not, to adhere only to conservation measures imposed by the 'appropriate organization', this would bestow upon marine mammals a *sui generis* status. In the sense that although marine mammals occurring in the high seas are a common resource, they would be subject to international management where an international entity has the power to restrict access to marine mammals by individual, or groups of, states. Such a concept is more akin to international management[199] rather than to the freedom of access, as qualified by the coastal state's encroachment upon the flag state's exclusive jurisdiction.

The subjection of marine mammals to international management cannot have been intended, particularly due to the specific exclusion of living resources and the superjacent waters of the deep seabed from the common heritage regime. International management of marine mammals, akin to the common heritage regime, has not happened even in post UNCLOS developments.[200] State practice shows that a group of states, albeit a very large group, chooses to adhere to the interpretation that stricter measures for the conservation of cetaceans than the ones included in Part VII may be imposed upon all states on the high seas via appropriate international organizations such as the ICRW and IWC. States that have opposed stricter measures have not changed their behaviour so the status of article 120 as a rule of customary international law remains applicable only vis-à-vis those states that have not persistently objected to a stricter conservation regime imposed by an appropriate organization. If one had to interpret the wording of article 120 in the less onerous manner possible, the provision obligates states that as a minimum they should cooperate with international organizations to ensure the conservation, management and study of cetaceans and other marine mammals rather than act unilaterally disregarding conservation measures agreed via cooperation. State practice however shows that dissenting states *have* refused to cooperate.[201] In the *JARPA II Whaling Case*,[202] Australia instituted legal proceedings against Japan before the ICJ, where it alleged that Japan has breached and is continuing to breach the obligation under paragraph 10(e) of the ICRW Schedule to observe the zero catch limit in relation to the killing of whales for commercial purposes, and its obligation under paragraph 7(b) to act in good faith and refrain from undertaking commercial whaling of humpback and fin whales in the Southern Ocean Sanctuary. Japan, as the respondent, claims that it is not breaching the moratorium but availing itself of whaling conducted under Article VIII, commonly referred to as 'special permit' or 'scientific' whaling.[203] Australia has rebutted these claims and additionally asserted that Japan has breached its obligations under CITES with respect to the proposed take of humpback whales under JARPA II and under the Convention on Biological Diversity, where it is required to ensure that activities under its jurisdiction and control do not cause damage to the environment of other states or areas beyond the limits of national jurisdiction. Australia has requested the ICJ to order Japan to cease the implementation of JARPA II, to revoke any authorizations, permits or licences, and provide assurances that it will guarantee that any further action under JARPA II or similar programmes be brought into conformity with international law. Eventually during the course of the proceedings Japan decided to stop its JARPA II programme in the Southern Ocean and so the case has been closed. The role played by Australia in this case is more akin to that of a state that commences proceedings on behalf of the international community as a whole, without having a direct interest. We will never know whether the ICJ would have accepted Australia's legal standing to institute such proceedings.

As in the case of post UNCLOS developments for HMS and straddling stocks, the application of conservation measures adopted via cooperation can be seen as constituting *prima facie* the 'necessary' conservation measures that all states fishing on the high seas are obligated to take. The relevance of such an interpretation for the high seas regime makes more sense, given that whilst article 62 under the EEZ regime in Part V lists specific conservation measures coastal states may adopt, article 119 under the high seas regime in Part VII provides only general obligations. Consequently coastal states, whose jurisdictional capacity within its EEZ is undisputed, may adopt stricter measures under article 65 than those established under article 62. Article 120 cannot on the other hand be compared to another provision in Part VII listing specific conservation measures for the high seas. So the interpretation of article 120 can be taken to mean that the flag states' freedom of fishing is subject to its vessels adopting a conservation regime for marine mammals that must be compatible with that of the coastal state, even if this is stricter than the flag state's national measures. This qualifies the flag state's prerogative to adopt unilateral measures under article 117 to the extent that it cannot adopt measures below the standards set by the coastal state or where applicable, those of an international organization, as these represent the rights, duties and interests of coastal states and other flag states. An organization's conservation measures may indirectly apply to non members, if the term 'necessary conservation measures' is interpreted by a majority or a large number of states as constituting the basic minimum standard of conservation in the case of marine mammals, although a state that is a persistent objector would not be considered as being bound by such a norm. This appears to be the most favoured legal interpretation of article 120 in the light of the other applicable UNCLOS provisions,[204] the 1946 IRCW and its compatibility[205] with post UNCLOS developments like the FSA, the CBD, CITES and the Bonn Convention on Migratory Species of Wild Animals.[206]

Certain geophysical circumstances provide coastal states with wider powers over marine living resources than they would normally enjoy under Part V and Part VII. A case in point is the extent and nature of coastal state jurisdiction in archipelagic waters.[207] State practice has shown that island states have claimed sovereign authority over marine mammals in inter-state waters considered part of EEZ. In case of archipelagic waters, coastal states would therefore have at least the same rights since living resources located therein are subject to the state's sovereignty and not only to its sovereign rights as is the case under the EEZ regime. In other words the coastal state's complete prohibition on the harvest of marine mammals within archipelagic waters is within the coastal state's authority under contemporary international law and this would also include the prohibition of the taking of other species when it leads to the incidental catch of marine mammals. This would affect the harvesting of such species in the adjacent high seas as discussed above, with the difference that the extent of areas subject to the coastal state's jurisdiction is more extensive. The higher the level of conservation adopted by the coastal states, the more qualified the high seas freedoms become with respect to the conservation of marine mammals. It would not only affect freedom of access to marine mammals themselves on the high seas but also introduce qualifications that restrict, or prohibit the use of fishing gear that leads to their incidental catch. The application of article 120 must also be considered within this context. It provides a stronger legal standing for the coastal states to impose upon flag states the adoption of conservation measures that are compatible with those adopted in areas subject to its jurisdiction. Such conservation measures may prohibit the taking of marine mammals both directly and as bycatch on the adjacent high seas. Having identified the legal complexities surrounding the interpretation of article 120, one may conclude that the article's main achievement is that it consolidates the legal standing of the coastal state and that of international organizations to encroach upon freedom of access to marine mammals on the high seas. The earliest dispute relating to conservation, the *Behring Fur Seals* case established that marine mammals on the high seas were in fact subject to freedom of fishing. The obligation to take the necessary conservation measures for marine mammals has undergone significant developments that acknowledge the special characteristics of these creatures and hence their need for a tailor-made conservation regime.[208] UNCLOS-related Agreements and the ICRW have confirmed this, subject to qualifications. They have also subjected fishing states to compulsory dispute settlement in case of conflicts relating to states' rights and obligations on the high seas.[209]

(d) Jurisdiction over sedentary species Coastal states have sovereign rights to exploit living resources of the sedentary kind on their continental shelf whether they declare an EEZ/EFZ or not. According to article 77 of UNCLOS the rights of the coastal state over the continental shelf are exclusive and do not depend on occupation or any express proclamation. Sedentary species remain subject to the continental shelf regime under Part VI of the 1982 Convention, where the coastal state has the exclusive right[210] to exercise sovereign rights for the purpose of exploring and exploiting such species defined as 'organisms, which at the harvestable stage either are immobile on or under the sea bed or unable to move except in constant physical contact with the seabed and the subsoil'.[211] In some cases because of the natural components of the continental margin, a coastal state may claim, as permitted by the 1982 Convention,[212] that its continental shelf exceeds the extent of 200 nautical miles from the baselines. The superjacent waters beyond the 200 nautical mile limit would also be subject to the high seas regime. Jurisdiction over sedentary species is clearly established once these occur on the seabed up to the delimitation of the coastal state's continental shelf. Such a delimitation may be disputed due to geophysical conditions, either because of opposite and adjacent states, or as mentioned above, when the coastal state claims a continental shelf that extends beyond 200 nautical miles.[213] Contentious debates regarding jurisdiction over sedentary species occurring on the deep seabed however are at present one of the issues dominating the meetings of the parties to the 1982 Convention and other fora discussing the conservation of living resources on the high seas. Since the 1982 Convention was negotiated and concluded, access to sedentary species on the outer limits of the continental shelf and on the deep seabed has become commercially important and viable, leading to a polarized debate in determining the rights of respective parties when bioprospecting for these species. At the heart of this contentious debate are two major jurisdictional issues. The first question is whether the regulatory jurisdictional rights of the coastal state to regulate bioprospecting on the outer continental shelf and to prohibit other states from having access to sedentary species occurring therein, conflicts with the high seas freedoms enjoyed by other states. The second

issue relates to what extent states have a right to carry out bioprospecting in areas of the deep sea bed falling outside national jurisdiction, on the pretext that this constitutes either freedom of conducting scientific research established under article 87(f), or freedom of fishing for sedentary species, or 'mining' for these living resources. UNCLOS bestows upon states different rights and obligations not only depending upon *where* their activities are undertaken but also depending upon the *kind* of activity undertaken. Consequently this debate on who has the capacity to do what, centres around whether one should classify bioprospecting activities as marine scientific research (MSR), as an extraction/mining operation or as a harvesting activity. It is essential to determine what kind of activity bioprospecting actually is and this is relevant both if it is carried out in areas within and beyond national jurisdiction. It is only the exercise of bioprospecting in areas falling outside national jurisdiction that will be tackled in this work.

The seabed beyond the continental shelf regime of the coastal states is regulated by Part XI entitled 'The Area'. All rights in the resources of the Area are vested in humankind as a whole on whose behalf the International Seabed Authority (ISBA) shall act.[214] It is the common heritage regime, which applies to the Area (also referred to as the deep seabed) and its mineral resources. No state, natural or juridical person may claim sovereignty or sovereign rights and hence have access or appropriate the Area's mineral resources. Conflicts of interpretation on bioprospecting arise because whilst for the purposes of Part XI 'resources', refers only to the exploitation of mineral resources excluding living ones,[215] the ISBA regulates MSR in the Area[216] without making such a distinction. The developing states therefore are keen to classify bioprospecting on the deep seabed as MSR, because in such a case it is the ISBA that would administer bioprospecting operations[217] and thus they may participate in the benefits derived from the genetic resources of sedentary species. Unlike mining for non living resources, however, MSR in the Area is also permitted by individual states who are obligated to promote international cooperation in MSR. At the other end of the spectrum, states carrying out bioprospecting argue that this activity is not MSR but falls either under the regime of the high seas either as a harvesting operation or under mining/extraction on the deep seabed, which is permitted because living resources are specifically excluded from the common heritage regime. They argue that the high seas freedoms apply in the absence of a specific international agreement.[218]

The situation is even more complex because UNCLOS fails to define MSR although it sets out the requirements for it. For instance MSR is to be conducted for peaceful purposes and the Authority or the individual states conducting it are to disseminate and publish information from

MSR. One argument is that commercial gain falls outside the interpretation of peaceful purposes and the involvement of confidentiality and property rights are incompatible with MSR under UNCLOS.[219] This had led to the argument that a distinction should be made between MSR used for commercial gain and MSR which entails pure scientific research. In practice, however, this distinction is difficult to make because prospecting may originate as searching for and sampling marine organisms and later on, when marine organisms are screened for useful compounds and tested, the activity becomes objectively distinguishable from pure research. The *ex post facto* test proposed by the United Nations University[220] shows how hard it is to determine whether a pure MSR activity would eventually be used for commercial gain since more often than not such activities are a public–private partnership, where it is difficult to determine the intent of commercial gain or otherwise. In other words, any MSR carried out to understand better the nature of the resources may eventually lead to financial gain.

Another jurisdictional issue that accentuates the reason for conflict is the role and the legal status of the Authority with respect to living resources in the Area. Whilst living organisms are clearly excluded from the definition of 'resources' under Part XI the Authority is obligated to take the necessary measures in accordance with the Convention with respect to 'activities in the Area' in order to ensure effective protection for the marine environment from harmful effects, which may arise from these activities. The Authority 'shall adopt rules regulations and procedures inter alia for the protection and conservation of the natural resources in the Area and the prevention of damage to flora and fauna of the marine environment'.[221] This implies that the Authority in fact does have the capacity to regulate any activity in the area whether it is termed as extractive, harvesting or MSR but only for the purpose of ensuring the conservation of these species. If bioprospecting occurs in the Area as MSR, it would be subject to the ISBA management and regulation even if carried out by individual states. If on the other hand it is classified as harvesting or extraction of living resources, it is the high seas regime which applies and it remains to be seen whether any patent rights derived from the research may exclude other states from exploitation and research for the same species. This in itself may be interpreted as going against the high seas freedoms themselves given that access to the living resources would be curtailed.

The status of bioprospecting has not been sufficiently addressed or resolved through state practice and negotiation. Coastal states would tend to favour classifying bioprospecting as a commercial extraction or harvesting activity rather than an MSR due to the fact that restrictions on MSR are limited under UNCLOS, contrary to other activities. Rather than harmonizing different sources of applicable norms, the regulation of bioprospecting on the high seas requires the negotiation of a new legal instrument, which would address in an appropriate manner an activity that was not even an issue when UNCLOS was negotiated and which remains distinct from other uses of the sea and its resources, contemplated under the 1982 Convention.

(iv) The duty to cooperate with other states fishing for the same species or in the same area of the high seas

Section 2 of Part VII of UNCLOS establishes two main interrelated obligations: the duty to take conservation measures and the duty to cooperate. Besides the obligation to cooperate with coastal states according to article 116(b), the regulatory jurisdiction of flag states on the high seas is further qualified by article 118, which requires them to cooperate and conclude agreements when participating in the same fishery.[222] UNCLOS does not qualify article 118 as being 'in addition to other articles' in section 2 of Part VII, as it does for example with article 64 and the rest of Part V on the EEZ regime. It establishes that, 'States shall enter into negotiations with a view to taking the measures necessary for the conservation of living resources concerned.' This wording implies that as a minimum, states are obligated to ensure compatibility with conservation measures taken by all flag states participating in the same fishery. The best way to ensure effective cooperation is definitely via a fisheries agreement. Article 118 however leaves this as an option to the discretion of flag states.[223]

The role of regional and subregional Fisheries Agreements and Organizations[224] is to ensure the sustainability of stocks. Most Agreements are concluded by participants in the same fishery in order to determine the permissible level of catch and fishing effort that would provide maximum net benefit for the fisheries involved, both with respect to target and also incidental species. Parties to these Agreements need to identify which species require a more stringent conservation regime due to their nature and vulnerability as well as the allocation of benefits and costs of high seas fishing. In the end, an Agreement needs to be supported by an effective organization that is endowed with the necessary powers and setup capable of coordinating and monitoring decisions regarding allocation and conservation of stocks as well as determining who bears the costs involved and which standards should be employed to reach its objectives. The success of a Fisheries Agreement depends upon transparency and this includes the provision of independent scientific advice on the status of the stocks and the standards/measures necessary to maintain their sustainability. Another advantage of having an Agreement that is backed up by an organization is flexibility. Parties may revise their objectives via the decisions that may be taken under the auspices of the organization rather than having to amend the Agreement every time. All of these functions, if applied in a consistent manner, leave a strong impact on the exclusive regulatory jurisdiction of the flag state parties. When choosing to cooperate in this manner, states would be consenting to waive their exclusive right to take any unilateral conservation measures for their nationals that fish in those areas of the high seas where such Agreements apply.[225]

As already observed, however, treaties that fulfil the obligations established by section 2 of Part VII may have repercussions beyond the parties themselves. All parties to the FSA are to comply with conservation measures established by fisheries organizations, whose geographical scope includes areas on the high seas where they fish for HMS or straddling fish stocks on the high seas. Additionally, even if not parties to the FSA or to any fisheries agreement, flag states are still required to subject their own nationals to conservation measures that safeguard the rights, duties and interests of coastal states and therefore they may still have to ensure compatibility with the coastal state's conservation measures according to these treaties if the latter are parties. State practice shows how certain agreements have forged ahead with imposing conservation measures applicable for the whole geographical area, despite rejection by non parties. Some of these conservation measures, such as establishment of an allowable catch and the classification of landings as IUU, if not accompanied with a certification of compliance applicable within the geographical scope of the agreement, have a crucial impact upon the regulatory jurisdiction of non parties.[226] Since members are normally, although not exclusively, the littoral states, the conservation measures imposed by the agreements can thus be seen as another form of encroachment by coastal state jurisdiction upon the freedom of fishing, albeit established via cooperation between a group of states. To understand better the complex conservation measures that may be applicable to flag states in the light of the above, this part will now examine how in contemporary state practice a number of fisheries agreements actually elaborate upon this obligation to take conservation measures.

The NEAFC promotes conservation and optimum utilization of fishery resources of the Convention Area within a framework appropriate to a regime of extended coastal state jurisdiction over fisheries and to encourage international cooperation and consultation with respect to these resources. NEAFC regulates certain species of straddling stocks as well as the rockall herring and since November 2004 even deep-sea species including the blue ling, black scabbard fish and the orange roughy. The NEAFC sets the TAC also for NAFO, besides its members, for the oceanic redfish, the Atlanto-Scandian herring in 1997 and for mackerel. It also implemented a Control and Enforcement Scheme and Non Compliant Parties Scheme in 1999. It introduced IUU lists for non contracting Parties in 2003. This identification of IUU non contracting parties' vessels has caused a decline in IUU landings in the contracting parties' ports. It also established a dispute settlement mechanism in 2004 by unanimously adopting amendments to the constituent convention establishing a fast track dispute settlement mechanism which is being carried out on a voluntary basis by the parties until amendments to the Convention come into force. It also established a very sophisticated VMS system and five areas with vulnerable habitats were closed to demersal fishing gear. Together with NAFO and CCAMLR, NEAFC attempts to secure common data communication and standards for vessel monitoring systems to engage other RFMOS to utilize the same format as a common global standard. NEAFC performance review is carried out by independent institutions like FAO. It is working for alignment with the FSA,[227] to modernize the Convention by introducing both the precautionary and the ecosystem approach as well as biodiversity protection. In November 2003 NEAFC agreed that the stocks it regulates are fully allocated and fishing opportunities are likely to be limited to new fisheries. New contracting parties will be able to participate on the same basis as existing contracting parties in future allocation of stocks that are unregulated at the time of application. New contracting parties that were previously cooperating with non contracting parties may request part of the relevant cooperative quota, whilst allocations are considered on a case-by-case basis. NEAFC is not considered as an open organization and new entrants' applications have been denied. The Agreement is currently developing guidelines for membership.

NAFO's objective is to contribute through consultation and cooperation to the optimum utilization, rational management and conservation of fishery resources of the North West Atlantic which is the NAFO Convention Area. It refers also to the 'Regulatory Area', which is the high seas component of the NAFO convention area. It addresses straddling stocks like cod, Greenland Halibut, redfish, skates, American plaice, yellowtail flounder, white hake, witch flounder, capelin, squid and shrimp. It also addresses discrete stocks and with respect to fishing gear, it regulates bottom trawling, mid-water trawls, longlines and gillnets. There is no cooperating status for non contracting parties. It has a General Council and a Fisheries Commission. Membership of the Fisheries Committee is only open for contracting parties, which are high seas fishing states in the NAFO Regulatory Area, whereas it is open to all parties in the Governing Council. A 1999 Resolution clarifies that stocks are fully allocated and fishing opportunities for new members are likely to be limited to new fisheries shared quotas and stocks that are currently not yet allocated. NAFO annually sets aside an allocation of regulated species called 'other' in part for states not included in the list of contracting parties allocations or for exceptional arrangements. Contracting parties are bound by Article XIX of the Convention to draw the attention of non contracting parties regarding fishing activities of nationals that may adversely effect NAFO conservation and management objectives.Vessels of non contracting parties that fish in the Regulatory Area are presumed to be IUU and undermining the effectiveness of NAFO measures. Major challenges for NAFO are avoiding overfishing, respecting pre-agreed TAC, rebuilding and maintaining fish stocks. This has proven to be difficult despite moratoria for nine stocks. Other challenges for NAFO include reducing and mitigating bycatch, as well as including incidental catch of moratoria species. Developing an ecosystem approach is also a challenge, which requires broadening the scope of the Convention to include marine biodiversity and habitat conservation concerns. The objection provisions are to be amended to ensure the conservation regime is respected. It is in the process of introducing effective deterrents for non compliance, requiring timely and effective follow up by flag states, as well as reducing and managing the fishing capacity.

ICCAT's objective is to maintain the population of tuna and tuna-like fisheries found in the Atlantic Ocean at levels that permit the maximum sustainable catch for food and other purposes. Besides regulating around 30 key HMS and fishing gear, it also regulates bycatch like seabirds, turtles, sharks and juveniles of target species. ICCAT implies that MSY is a target not a limit. Membership is open and highly encouraged even as cooperating non members. Flag states are to maintain vessel records to control those authorized to fish in the Area and ensure compliance with ICCAT measures. Contracting parties, fishing entities and cooperating non contracting parties (CPCs) are entitled to allocations using historical catch as a main criterion. ICCAT controls access and fishing capacity by TACs, quotas and vessel effort limitations. Some members are also seeking access to tuna stocks within the EEZ based on adjacency. Recommendations adopted by ICCAT apply throughout the Area and are implemented on a national level by the CPCs for fishing inside and outside their EEZ. The creation of CPC status enticed many non contracting parties that used to fish in the Area to abide by ICCAT's conservation measures. In 2001 ICCAT adopted criteria for the allocation of fishing possibilities to address new entrants and limit capacity. ICCAT has made use of trade measures to encourage compliance. Its main challenges remain overfishing due to the decline of the targeted species, reducing bycatch, addressing gear issues and dealing with overcapacity. It is also difficult for ICCAT to set limits based on the precautionary approach, given inadequacies in the data, in managing access, allocation and redistribution due to the expectations of large membership. ICCAT is working on improving upon the current enforcement system by increasing and standardizing observer coverage in the Area, standardizing and integrating catch and trade measures with other RFMOs, port states and CPCs. The GFCM's objective is to promote the conservation and management of living marine resources to formulate and recommend conservation measures and to encourage training in cooperative projects. It addresses both species of HMS like the Eastern Atlantic blue fin tuna, Albacore bonito and swordfish as well as straddling stocks like hake, red mullet, striped mullet, blue and red shrimp, Norway lobster, anchovy, sardine and dolphin fish. The members of the GFCM adhere also to ICCAT's recommendation on blue fin tuna quotas and on shark bycatch where the contracting parties must report on the implementation of mitigation measures. The GFCM's main challenges are overfishing and achieving sustainable fisheries. It requires internal strengthening to fulfil its functions and responsibilities. Another challenge is the control of IUU fishing and ensuring timely and reliable data on catch and effort which is communicated to the secretariat. Membership is more open and there is an increasing membership of states with 'real interest' including all Black Sea states. GFCM encourages states fishing in the area to become parties or cooperating non parties. It collaborates with ICCAT and has partnerships with IGOs such as UNEP, IUCN, ACCOBAMS and Tuna RFMOs. The GFCM has adopted an ecosystem approach to fisheries since 2004 and this includes establishing essential and sensitive habitats ecosystem indicators, gear selectivity for bycatch and vulnerable and protected species, gear prohibitions in specific areas established and a closed season from 1 January to 14 August for dolphin fish.

CCAMLR's key objective is to ensure the conservation, including rational use of the Antarctic living marine resources. The key species it targets are: the Antarctic krill, Patagonian Toothfish, Antarctic Toothfish, sub Antarctic Latern fish, mackerel icefish, seven star flying squid, Antarctic rock cod and crabs. There is currently no active crab or squid fishery. It regulates gear such as posts for crabs, bottom trawls, bottom long lines and squid gigs. Since 1992 CCAMLR has taken mitigation measures to address seabird bycatch as well as other bycatch. Its bycatch conservation guidelines and ecosystem approach principles have set benchmarks for other Conventions and fisheries organizations and include mesh size regulation and bottom trawl prohibition around some areas. Article II of the Convention has a management approach which regulates human activities to avoid degradation in the Antarctic ecosystem. It is the only RFMO to have fully incorporated the precautionary approach into stock assessment and decision-making measures. All regulated fisheries in areas under CCAMLR jurisdiction are subject to precautionary catch limits. New fisheries are not allowed to develop before the CCAMLR Commission has been able to evaluate their potential consequences. Membership is open but subject to criteria listed in its articles.[228] There are two categories of membership, members of the commission who pay dues and are involved in scientific research and/or fishing, subject to conservation measures. These have voting rights. Acceding states and REIOs are bound by the Convention and pay no dues and non parties can participate in the implementation. CCAMLR is actively involved with NEAFC and NAFO in developing common VMS reporting and monitoring standards. The Convention remains a leader in implementing both the precautionary and the ecosystem approach. It continues to develop precautionary approach reference points as a basis for decision rules. There is also an ecosystem approach for the management of the krill fishery. CCAMLR introduced comprehensive systems and mandatory VMS for the management of the toothfish fishery. There is an established registry of vessels permitted to fish. If bycatch limits are exceeded vessels must also cease to fish and must leave the area. A Scientific Observer Programme is mandatory for all fin fisheries. Major challenges are: to avoid and eliminate overfishing and rebuilding depleted stocks and doing away with IUU even in the adjacent Southern Indian Ocean, enhancing compliance even in the EEZ and controlling transshipment.

The IOTC[229] is to promote cooperation among member states with a view to ensuring, through appropriate management, the conservation and optimum utilization of stocks covered by the Agreement and encouraging sustainable development of fisheries based on such stocks. The IOTC has adopted a precautionary approach, recognizing the need to incorporate uncertainty in stock assessments. Membership is open to members of the FAO that are Indian Ocean Coastal states or whose vessels fish in the IOTC Agreement Area. Cooperating non contracting parties are referred to as CPCs together with the contracting Parties. The IOTC aims at improved enforcement through the establishment of the Compliance Committee to review the annual report of compliance by CPCs. It has a positive list and an IUU list of vessels fishing in the Area. It established statistical documentation scheme controls to regulate transshipment, address bycatch through its ecosystem approach and it requests data on non target associated or dependent species. The data available, the organizational capacity and research capacity of IOTC members are severely lacking. Challenges involve avoiding and reducing overfishing, reducing and eliminating IUU, addressing transshipment, reducing excess fishing capacity, implementing bycatch mitigation measures, improving upon the implementation of the precautionary and the ecosystem approach, establishing participation by fishing entities, and addressing the organizational capacity of CPCs, which was greatly deprived after the 2004 Tsunami devastation in the Indian Ocean.

2.3 CONCLUSION

The increasing scarcity of fish stocks has directed states to depart from the traditional perception that freedom of fishing[230] means unhindered access to a common resource without any form of control.[231] It can be said that the evolution of the law of the sea is characterized by three important and successive developments that are particular to the freedom of fishing, which have also demonstrated that the legal implications of this freedom are neither absolute nor immutable.[232] On the contrary, this principle of international law adapted to changes inspired by circumstances prevailing in different historical periods and has been qualified accordingly. The first phase was characterized by the principle as originally proposed by Grotius, namely, unrestricted freedom of fishing that is only qualified by the prohibition to allow equal access to these resources by other states. Despite the underlying requirement of reasonable use and non abuse of rights, this interpretation became ineffective when participants increased and the taking of such species was no longer via artisanal methods. The second phase was characterized by the coastal States' jurisdictional claims over maritime areas adjacent to their coasts who sought to gain exclusive jurisdiction over living marine resources occurring therein to the exclusion of access by third parties. This was an important phase whereby the coastal state assumed exclusive regulatory jurisdiction on what were previously resources subject to access by all states. In both these phases only such coastal states and distant water fishing states were seen as beneficiaries of the principle of freedom of fishing . The third and most recent phase widened this expression of interest over such resources and their sustainable use became a matter of international concern, whereby all states can be said to have a vested interest to ensure their conservation.[233] The applicable provisions of UNCLOS' article 87 and Section 2 of Part VII reflect these three phases: harvesting living resources beyond national jurisdiction is a right vested in all states but it is qualified by a number of conditions intended to curb abuse. The exclusive nature of the flag state's regulatory jurisdiction needs to be interpreted[234] with the element of relativity inherent to the applicable articles of the Convention, especially those stipulated in section 2 of Part VII.[235] To support and supplement the general provisions in this section, the Convention itself obligates states to cooperate and conclude Agreements that further regulate the exploitation of living resources on the high seas.[236] Since the 1982 Convention came into force, states have continued to generate new norms that seek to delineate in clearer, more substantive terms the rights and obligations of all states that are stakeholders in such operations. Subsequent and more specialized norms, however, do not necessarily supersede the previous and more general ones. Their incorporation in treaties renders them binding only upon the parties unless state practice provides evidence that even third parties acquiesce to them. As a result, the proliferation of new norms may have the opposite effect and could generate instead further confusion as to their interpretation vis-à-vis other applicable international regimes. In sum, a plurality of specialized norms does not necessarily address gaps or fine tune the position of international law if there is no attempt to integrate more recent legal developments within the general context of international law where they belong. This chapter has focused on three potential normative conflicts, which affect the flag state's exclusive regulatory jurisdiction and has proposed some legal techniques that may serve to facilitate harmonization amongst applicable norms. The three categories of conflicts in fact are closely related to the three different phases referred to above that have characterized the development of the jurisdictional implications of the freedom of fishing as a principle of international law.

The first type of conflict that may arise relates to the interpretation of the flag state's duty to take necessary conservation measures and how this may impinge upon its exclusive regulatory jurisdiction on the high seas. The taking of conservation measures[237] is only one of the qualifications to the freedom of fishing, but it is also inextricably linked to those referred to under article 116, namely, treaty obligations to which flag states are parties and the rights, duties and interests of coastal states[238] with a maritime zone adjacent to the high seas as well as the duty to cooperate with other participants in the high seas fishery found in article 118. Conflicting interpretation arises because UNCLOS' article 119 is directory and does not provide legal benchmarks against which, the conservation measures adopted by flag states may be assessed[239] and rated for their suitability. Neither does it establish what kind of juridical claims other stakeholder states may raise vis-à-vis flag states which take unilateral conservation measures that are less stringent than those adopted by other participants and coastal states, via treaties or independent therefrom. Flag states claim that any form of control by some states over marine species beyond national jurisdiction goes against the high seas freedoms where, 'no state may validly purport to subject any part of the high seas to its sovereignty.[240] Conversely other states raise the counterclaim that their rights and interests over these resources can only be guaranteed if a mandatory set of minimum conservation measures binds all states, as this ensures sustainability of stocks and the continued enjoyment of the freedom of fishing by all. States may also sometimes raise the same claim with respect to their own national interests over the harvestable stocks.[241] The strongest argument upon which other stakeholder states may base their legal claims against the flag state, would probably be the link between the obligation to take conservation measures and the enjoyment of the freedoms by all states. The fulfilment of a cardinal aspect of the high seas freedoms depends upon the flag state's compliance with conservation obligations as necessary, because in this manner it would also be contributing to the good governance of this common resource and safeguarding[242] the other states' enjoyment of the high seas freedoms.[243] These arguments are also applicable to the second normative conflict discussed in this chapter, which relates to the legal position of coastal states with maritime zones adjacent to the high seas and that of other flag states fishing in the same areas or for identical species. The chapter has examined whether the qualifications to the freedom of fishing bestow upon such states the capacity to encroach upon the flag state's exclusive jurisdiction to choose for itself which conservation measures it needs to adopt for its nationals on the high seas. From the discussion, it transpires that there is a discrepancy between the traditional interpretation of flag state regulatory jurisdiction that leaves conservation measures to the complete discretion of the flag state, as opposed to certain trends in current state practice. This is evident from the role, functions and objectives some fisheries agreements and organizations have assumed. For instance, NAFO classifies as IUU the harvesting of species by non contracting parties in the maritime area where the constituent treaty applies if nationals thereof cannot prove that they have abided by conservation measures according to the fisheries agreement. Sometimes the allocation of quotas for the harvesting of high seas living resources excludes new entrants to the fishery or limits access and allocation in one way or another. The best examples of conservation obligations that encroach upon the flag state's exclusive jurisdiction are those imposing restrictions for fishing certain species[244] and for prohibiting the use of types of fishing gear[245] on the high seas. Furthermore as the enforcement of such measures on the high seas can only be exercised by the flag state, parties to such agreements may adopt indirect compliance measures by prohibiting landings in their ports or by imposing other trade sanctions if non parties fail to demonstrate they have complied with the same conservation measures stipulated in the applicable treaty.

The qualification to the freedom of fishing in response to coastal states' rights, duties, is accepted in general terms but it is much more controversial when it comes to determine to what extent this qualification encroaches upon access to living resources on the high seas. Although the 1982 Convention regulates living resources according to a different legal regime depending upon where they occur,[246] it establishes through article 116(b) that the right to exploit high seas living resources cannot be considered in isolation from the same right, which the coastal state has within maritime areas falling under its jurisdiction. The successful conservation of marine living resources depends upon cooperation[247] between coastal states and high seas fishing states, particularly with respect to fish stocks that straddle or migrate between the high seas and areas subject to national jurisdiction[248]. Furthermore UNCLOS prohibits fishing for anadromous and catadromous species on the high seas except in limited circumstances.[249] These UNCLOS obligations are considered to codify custom and constitute examples of how the freedom of fishing may be qualified to different degrees depending on the circumstances and particularly upon the species being exploited. If a dispute between two states arises because they adopt different conservation measures and only one or neither of them are parties to an MEA or a fisheries agreement, the international adjudicating body must assess whether any conservation measures applied in that area of the high seas or with respect to those species, may have acquired the status of a customary rule of international law. The state (or group of states) that is alleging the crystallization of such conservation rules into customary international law must provide evidence that states have acquiesced to such rules and that there was no case of objection on the part of the other state disputing them.[250] However, the usual test for identifying the existence of a norm of customary international law would also need to be considered within the context of the applicable UNCLOS provisions. For instance, under article 118 , UNCLOS does not go as far as to impose forced cooperation but obligates states to enter into negotiations to agree upon conservation measures either between themselves or through fisheries organizations. Similarly and perhaps in a more onerous manner, UNCLOS subjects the exercise of freedom of fishing to articles 63(2) and 64, which in accordance with the wording of the Convention, identify the rights, duties and interests of coastal states.[251] Through these provisions, UNCLOS implies that the exploitation of high seas fisheries requires a common denominator type of conservation and should not be left to the complete discretion of the flag states themselves. UNCLOS also enables the adoption of a stricter regime for the conservation of marine mammals on the high seas[252] and various examples of state practice support these developments under international law such as the moratorium on whaling imposed by the IWC[253] and the conclusion of regional arrangements for the prohibition of sealing. The post UNCLOS treaties addressing fisheries or the conservation of living resources on the high seas, however, have not always been interpreted by flag states as the fulfilment of the obligation to cooperate and to further develop the 1982 Convention's provisions. The negotiation and coming into force of the FSA and the FAO Compliance Agreement, however, strengthened the role of regional and subregional fisheries agreements, because both treaties consider that these legal instruments establish the minimum conservation obligations which flag states must adopt for their nationals to comply with for particular species and/or the various areas of the high seas. This development is likely to affect international law in an unprecedented manner.[254] It may promote the harmonization of the legal position of flag states for the taking of conservation measures when they fulfil articles 116 to 119 of UNCLOS. The FSA was negotiated and adopted by consensus and has been adhered to by most major distant water and coastal fishing states. This may serve to provide sufficient *opinio juris* for an international adjudicating body to consider that when it comes to the interpretation of what are the 'necessary' conservation measures that flag states must adopt under article 117 of UNCLOS, these should not be less onerous than those found in applicable regional and subregional agreements. The FSA provisions help to circumvent the difficulties which emerge from the common resource status attributed to living resources beyond national jurisdiction.

The need for consensus by all states to establish a mandatory set of conservation measures that would be universally applicable is one of the major obstacles to achieving a common playing field amongst all flag states. The flag state's exclusivity in regulating its nationals fishing on the high seas may lead to the anomalous situation where states adopting stricter conservation measures would be at a disadvantage when their competitors adopt weaker ones. The latter states would jeopardize a more stringent conservation regime that would have been achieved via cooperation after arduous negotiations and discourage other flag states from adhering to more stringent obligations as this may trigger mass reflagging to other competitor states with more liberal registries. Non compliant states would still have access to the same fish stocks and although as discussed throughout the chapter, the legitimacy of fishing operations which disregard conservation measures adopted via a cooperation agreement may be challenged, it would be up to the applicant state to prove that such behaviour constitutes a breach of customary international law. Despite the achievements of the FSA, distant water fishing states often raise the common resource status as a defence when rebutting a claim that their conservation measures are below the standard set in a cooperation agreement they have not adhered to. Their argument is based on the premise that any imposition by other states runs counter to their juridical status as a common resource and the legal implications of freedom of access and non appropriation that are consequential to it. This position conflicts with the developments brought about by the FSA and current state practice on a regional and subregional basis as discussed above. Whilst the common resource status in terms of non appropriation has been upheld, parties to fisheries agreements are adopting obligations that approximate conservation for high seas living resources with those afforded to 'shared' resources. A shared resource is subject to the sovereignty or sovereign rights of two or more states, which would have the right to constrain third parties or one another to abide by certain practices when making use of it. Although some treaties do regulate the use of a shared resource, there is no authoritative and exhaustive list as to what are the general obligations of states vis-à-vis a shared resource in concrete legal terms and the position of international Law in this regard is unclear.[255] The UNEP Principles of Conduct in the Conservation and Harmonious Utilization of Natural Resources Shared by Two or More States[256] cannot be considered as a legal source but the United Nations General Assembly has called upon states to use these principles as guidelines and recommendations.[257] Their legal value may only be relied upon insofar as their provisions reflect international law and the practice of a significant number of states. It is interesting to note that many of the principles of the UNEP document on 'Shared Resources' refer to obligations that are already included in UNCLOS provisions, other applicable treaties and state practice regulating the conservation and exploitation of marine living resources on the high seas. These would include the need to resort to international cooperation and equitable utilization, to abide by the principle of non discrimination and equal access, to achieve a balance of interests between the parties concerned and to avoid or reduce to the maximum extent possible, adverse effects that may impinge upon the conservation status of the resources. In the 1974 *Icelandic Fisheries* cases, for instance the ICJ made significant observations on the character of high seas fishing resources as common property but highlighted that all states had an obligation of reasonable use which required them to take account of the needs of conservation and to allow coastal states preferential rights in the allocation of high seas stocks. The Court had asserted that there exists an obligation upon all parties to negotiate in good faith to reach an equitable solution.[258] This implies that species which have the status of a common resource would still require specific conservation measures that take into account the collective interest of the international community in ensuring their sustainable exploitation. This has been the trend shown in most post UNCLOS fisheries agreements and some MEAs that have mainly focused on the conservation of HMS, straddling fish stocks,[259] endangered species,[260] identical species that various states exploit on the high seas[261] or different species fished in the same areas.[262] In sum, the common resource status does not exclude a minimum standard of conservation that all states are bound to observe. More recently the FSA, the FAO Compliance Agreement and some MEAs such as the CBD have pushed for conservation via an ecosystem approach: an aspect that is implied even if not elaborated upon in UNCLOS' article 119. The link between the ecosystem approach and the vested interest of the international community is more evident in the CBD. Under the 1992 Convention, states have the obligation to take conservation measures whenever they conduct any operations beyond national jurisdiction that may affect components of biodiversity,[263] which the CBD in its preamble declares to be a common concern of humankind.

The third possible normative conflict derives from this link and revolves around the current uncertainty under international law, as to whether any state may have the legal standing to bring forward an international claim against another which allows its nationals to carry out illegal or unregulated exploitation of such species or to adopt conservation measures that do not meet with the necessary standards. It may be argued that if the common resource status represents an interest that is vested in the international community as a whole, any state may be eligible to raise a claim to safeguard this interest.[264] The increasing awareness on the part of states that activities beyond national jurisdiction should not prejudice the conservation of these species as a common, natural resource, which has an intrinsic value irrespective of whether its components are harvestable or not[265] is expressed in various treaties.[266] This is mainly due to the evolution of international environmental law, which promotes the conservation of living resources *per se*. This approach has been supported by state practice as a number of states have adopted conservation measures for high seas living resources on a national level even if they have no direct interest as a coastal state with an adjacent maritime zone or as a participant in a high seas fishery for the same stocks.[267] Doubtlessly, recent MEAs and soft law instruments have sought to strengthen the common interest that all states have to protect biological diversity. As we have seen above whether the position under UNCLOS and hence under customary international law is in harmony with this interpretation has not yet been put to test.[268] In order to harmonize the conflicting interpretation that may be attributed to the relationship between article 117 and the other UNCLOS articles in section 2 of Part VII as supported by more recent sources of international law, one can interpret article 117 as the *lex generalis* that allows for unilateral conservation measures to fulfil the general obligation to conserve living resources on the high seas and the rest as the *lex specialis* that further fine tune it. To overcome the sense of fragmentation arising from this plurality of norms, the obligations emerging from other provisions of UNCLOS and other applicable norms may be acknowledged as norms that further supplement and therefore are in harmony with the 1982 Convention.

As stocks continue to diminish and collapse, states will have no other option but to cooperate, to adopt all measures at their disposal to prevent this from happening and to restrict free riders from circumventing conservation measures. International law is not cast in stone and not even norm creating treaties like UNCLOS can resist state practice that inches its way around existing legal barriers that stand in the way of achieving better conservation. The discussion in this chapter demonstrates that there are a number of legal parameters that encroach upon a flag state's capacity to regulate its nationals for the taking of conservation measures when fishing on the high seas. As we shall see in Chapters 6 and 7, the same cannot be said with respect to enforcement jurisdiction. The problem of enforcement on the high seas remains a reality, inherent to international law as a whole. It can only be countered from a regulatory perspective to some extent, via port state measures, by means of trade sanctions imposed upon states that do not comply with minimum standards and through better monitoring.

The relationship between the way states implement the qualifications to the freedom of fishing and the impact this has on the development of the flag state's exclusive jurisdiction revolves around the evolution of the juridical capacity of the various stakeholders to bring forward international claims for the conservation of high seas living resources. When identifying which state has the capacity to make such claims, one is also specifying what kind of juridical authority a claimant state is asserting over an issue. The respondent state that answers with a counterclaim must also show it possesses the juridical capacity to rebut in whole or in part, the principal claim. The process of decision as a response to these claims invokes sources of international law pursuant to treaty provisions as well as independent thereof. This is the legal technique, which helps to establish the position under international law in the circumstances. Detecting trends in the behaviour of states when confronted with these issues gives an insight into their *opinio juris* but the more fragmented the sources of these norms are, the more difficult it is to ensure consistency and uniformity of state practice. This situation may generate inter state disputes, which serve as the appropriate testing ground for international adjudicators to assess the current position of international law with respect to the conflicting interpretation of applicable norms. The chances are, however, that in the face of uncertainty, states tend to opt for the least onerous obligations and they are more likely to persist in disregarding recurrent malpractice by their nationals, citing the ambivalent position of the law as a defence.

NOTES

1. See Shaw, M.N. (2003), *International Law*, 5th edn, Cambridge: Cambridge University Press, pp 572–4.
2. Jurisdiction under international law may be both concurrent with jurisdiction of other states or exclusive; see Harris, D.J. (2004), *Cases and Materials on International law*, 6th edn, London: Sweet and Maxwell, p 265.
3. UNCLOS article 87 reiterates article 2 of the 1958 Convention on the High Seas.
4. See ibid, article 89 which says, 'no state may validly purport to subject any part of the high seas to its sovereignty'.
5. For a brief historical account of the development of the law of the sea, see Brownlie, I. (2003), *Principles of International Law*', 6th edn, Oxford: Oxford University Press, pp 224–5; see also Birnie P., Boyle, A. and Redgwell, C. (2009), *International Law and the Environment*, 3rd edn, Oxford: Oxford University Press p 706.
6. Chapter V of *Mare Liberum,* 1609. The book was republished and edited with an introductory note by James Brown Scott (1916), Oxford: Oxford University Press, Oxford. See p 32 where Grotius says, 'the same principle which applies to navigation applies to fishing – namely it remains free and open to all'. In this manner the freedom of fishing came to be identified with the freedom of navigation and the freedom of utilization of resources of the high seas. Although Grotius did in fact later distinguish between navigation and fishing (at p 43) and says that, 'if it were possible to prohibit any of those things say for example fishing, for in a way it can be maintained that fish are exhaustible, it would still not be possible to prohibit freedom of navigation for the sea is not exhausted by that use'. See also below at note 7.
7. Even Grotius in his time had acknowledged that control becomes expedient when too many people hunt a common resource such as fish in a river; see Birnie, Boyle and Rodgwell (2009).
8. See Meltzer, E. (2009), *The Quest for Sustainable Fisheries*, Ottawa: NRC Research Press, pp 78–9 and generally Chapter 5; see also FAO, *World Fisheries Ten Years After the Adoption of the 1982 United Nations Convention on the Law of the Sea*, FAO Doc COFI/93/4 (Rome, 1992); FAO, *The state of the World Fisheries and Agriculture* (Rome, 2006) 5; Birnie, Boyle and Rodgwell (2009), pp 702–3.
9. Example: prohibition to board a foreign vessel and to search it; see Brownlie (2003) quoting Gidel (1932) *Le Droit International de la Mer en Temps de Paix*, p 225.
10. De Ferion, O. (1958), *Le Droit de la Mer*, Paris: Droz, p 73.
11. Gidel, G. (1932), 69, where the author refers to the fact that the First French Republic used to emblazon the slogan, '*Liberté des mers:égalité des droits pour toutes les nations*' which to a certain extent still demonstrates the basis of the legal status of the high seas; see also Dupuys, R.J., and Vignes, D. (1991), *A Handbook on the New Law of the Sea*, Volume I, The Hague: Hague Academy of International Law, Martinus Nijhoff Publishers, p 385.
12. See the *Lotus Case*, PCIJ Series A, No. 10, p 25.
13. See Rousseau, C. (1980) *Droit International Public*, Suey, p 277.
14. See Fauchille, P. (1925), *Traité de Droit International Public*, 8th edn, Paris, p 46 as quoted in Dupuy and Vignes (1991), at 11, p 402.
15. See Gidel (1932), p 224.
16. This norm of customary international law is codified under both the 1958 Geneva Convention on the High Seas under its article 10 and under UNCLOS in its article 94.
17. See UNCLOS articles 92 and 94.
18. See discussion by Brownlie (2003), p 226; see also the dissenting opinion in the *Anglo Norwegian Fisheries Case* by Judge Read, ICJ Reports (1951), 187–9; Lauterpacht (1958), '*The Development of International Law by the International Court*', London: Praeger, pp 190–19.
19. The right of the coastal state to claim an EEZ of 200 nautical miles from its baselines

referred to in UNCLOS under article 56 has been recognized as a rule of customary international law; see *Libya/Malta Continental Shelf* case, ICJ Reports, 1985, p 13; 81 ILR, p 238; see also below, note 23. The EEZ is optional and states may choose not to claim an EEZ or only claim it in part. Some states may also choose to claim an exclusive fishing zone (EFZ). The EEZ bestows other sovereign rights upon coastal states besides fishing, namely substantial jurisdiction over pollution by ships and more control in marine scientific research.

20. See Oxman, B. (1994–1995), 'International Maritime Boundaries: Political, Strategic and Historical Considerations', 26 U. Miami Inter-Am. L. Rev., 243.
21. *Icelandic Fisheries Cases (UK & Germany v Iceland)* ICJ Reports (1974).
22. The first UNCLOS session was held in Caracas in the summer of 1974. When the first draft proposals were tabled it was already clear how the issue would be resolved. Prior to this, although the extension of costal state jurisdiction was acceptable, there was no agreement on the limit.
23. See above at note 19; see also Tunisia–Libya Continental Shelf case, ICJ Reports (1982), 18 at 38, *Gulf of Maine* case, ICJ Reports (1984), 246 at 294–5, paras 94–6; *Libya–Malta Continental Shelf* case, ICJ Reports (1985), 13 at 32–4, paras 31–4.
24. For instance, it was only in August 1974 that the US accepted that the 200–mile limit on fisheries be incorporated in the draft negotiating text.
25. See discussion in Chapter 1 p 11–12.
26. *Pacta tertiis nec nocent nec prosunt.* The lack of consent by a given state means that it cannot be held to the rule in question; see VCLT articles 34–8.
27. See Riddle, K. (2006), 'Illegal, Unreported and Unregulated Fishing: Is International Cooperation Contagious?' ODIL, **37**, (3–4) 266.
28. In the *Fisheries Jurisdiction* cases, ICJ Reports, 1974, p 8, 175: 55 ILR 238, the ICJ stated that the concept of fishing zone as an area where the coastal state may claim exclusive jurisdiction for the purpose of fishing independently of its territorial sea had crystallized into customary international law and that the practice of extending this EFZ up to 12 nautical miles seems to be generally accepted. The dispute, however, related to a claim for an EFZ of 50 miles made by Iceland, which Germany and the UK were contesting as being contrary to international law. The Court did not give a decision which specifically answered this question but instead referred to the rule of customary international law which allowed for preferential rights, which according to it Iceland could claim because its economy was heavily dependent on fisheries. However, the developments at UNCLOS superseded this decision of the ICJ.
29. See UNCLOS article 56.
30. As established under Section Two of Part VII of UNCLOS.
31. Article 87 chapeau.
32. Article 87(2).
33. The most prominent is the 1993 Agreement to Promote Compliance with International Conservation and Management Measures by Fishing Vessels on the High Seas (FAO Compliance Agreement).
34. Examples include NAFO, ICCAT, GFCM, CCAMLR, NEAFC, IOTC, WCPFC, CCSBT; see discussion in Chapter 1 p 11–12.
35. There are 13 Regional Seas programmes established under the auspices of UNEP for the following regions: Black Sea, Wider Caribbean, East Asian Seas, Eastern Africa, South Asian Seas, ROPME (Kuwait Region) Sea Area, Mediterranean, North-East Pacific, North-West Pacific, Red Sea and Gulf of Aden, South-East Pacific, Pacific, and Western Africa. Each of these programmes has a legal component that includes a Convention and various Protocols issued thereunder such as, for example, the 1976 Barcelona Convention on the Protection of the Mediterranean Sea Against Pollution as amended in 1995, namely The Barcelona Convention for the Protection of the Marine Environment and the Coastal Region of the Mediterranean and its 1995 Protocol Concerning Specially Protected Areas and Biological Diversity in the Mediterranean. Six of these programmes are directly administered by UNEP. These

regional Agreements do not specifically regulate fisheries but address biodiversity issues.

36. The major ones are the Agreement for the Implementation of the Provisions of UNCLOS of 10 December 1982 Relating to the Conservation and Management of Straddling Fish Stocks and Highly Migratory Fish Stocks (FSA) and the 1979 Bonn Convention on Migratory Species, and the 1946 International Convention on the Regulation of Whaling (ICRW).
37. The 1973 Convention on International Trade in Endangered Species of Wild Flora and Fauna (CITES) and the 1992 United Nations Convention on Biological Diversity (CBD).
38. The 1946 International Convention on the Regulation of Whaling (ICRW), the 1957 North Pacific (Behring Sea) Fur Seals Convention (as amended), the 1998 Agreement on Conservation of the Cetaceans of the Baltic and Mediterranean Sea (ACCOBAMS), the 1999 Agreement on International Dolphin Conservation Programme.
39. The major objectives include catch quotas both with respect to target and incidental species, the provision of special conservation measures for species whose nature renders them particularly vulnerable, and institutional governance to coordinate and monitor data, assess costs, to determine which conservation standards are to be employed, and to provide independent scientific advice to maintain sustainability of stocks.
40. Examples include CITES, the Bonn Convention on Migratory Species and the CBD.
41. See above at note 26.
42. See Brownlie (2003), p 11; see also *Anglo-Norwegian Fisheries Case* 92 Hague *Receuil (1957, II)*.
43. See Brownlie (2003), 5, p 225 who quotes Gidel, ILC Yearbook (1950), ii. 68 and p 252.
44. See Orrego Vicuna, F. (1999), *The Changing International Law of Fisheries*, Cambridge: Cambridge Studies in International and Comparative Law, Cambridge University Press, pp 8–22.
45. See Brownlie (2003), pp 297–8 who argues that, under international law, sufficiency of grounds for jurisdiction is not merely a question of basic competence but is relative to the rights of other states; see also Shaw (2003).
46. *Behring Fur Seals Arbitration* Moore, Int Arb Awards, I (1989), reproduced in 1 IELR (2000) 43, *Icelandic Fisheries Cases (UK v Iceland) (Merits)* ICJ Reports (1974) 3 and *(FRG v Iceland) (Merits)* 175.
47. See Birnie and Boyle (2009), chapter 13; Orrego Vicuna (1999), pp 8–22.
48. See Brownlie (2003) p 252.
49. See Orrego Vicuna (1999), p 22.
50. UNCLOS article 92; see Brownlie (2003), p 297, who explains that jurisdiction is the central aspect of state sovereignty. In actual fact the two terms are often used interchangeably. Jurisdiction refers to the judicial, legislative and administrative competence of a state. In practice this entails the state's right to take decisions and to make, implement and enforce rules of law and the capacity to bring forward international claims.
51. UNCLOS article 87(1) which establishes that, 'Freedom of the high seas is exercised under the conditions laid down by this Convention'.
52. See Brownlie, I. (2003), p 298.
53. See UNCLOS article 87(2).
54. Ibid, para (7).
55. UNCLOS article 87(1) uses the words '*inter alia*' in the chapeau that precedes the list of freedoms, which all States, whether coastal or landlocked, may exercise on the high seas.
56. This contrasts with article 116(a), which qualifies the right of freedom of fishing with respect to those treaty provisions to which the states are parties.

57. For a discussion on the interrelationship between sources of international law see above Chapter 1, pp 6–10.
58. UNCLOS article 87(2) also establishes that the freedoms must be exercised with due regard for the rights under this Convention with respect to activities in the Area.
59. See below the discussion on pp 50–72.
60. The 1958 Convention on Fishing and the Conservation of Living Resources of the High Seas, the 1958 Convention on the Continental Shelf, the 1958 Convention on the High Seas, all done in Geneva, and the 1982 Convention on the Law of the Sea (UNCLOS) done at Montego Bay, Jamaica.
61. *Behring Sea Fur Seals Arbitration* (1898), 1 Moore's *International Arbitration Awards* 755, reproduced in 1 *International Environmental Law Reports* (1999).
62. Ibid, International Environmental Law Reports (1999), 43 and ICJ Reports (1974), 3, para 43.
63. See article 2 of the 1958 Convention on the High Seas which established that 'Freedom of the high seas is exercised under the conditions laid down by these articles and by other rules of International law and comprises inter alia both for coastal and non coastal states . . . the freedom of fishing'.
64. Article 1 of the 1958 Convention on Fishing and the Conservation of Living Resources on the High Seas, establishes that 'All states have the right for their nationals to engage in fishing on the high seas, subject (a) to their treaty obligations (b) to the interests and rights of coastal states as provided for in this Convention (c) to the provisions contained in the following Articles concerning conservation of the living resources of the high seas.'
65. *North Sea Continental Shelf Case*, ICJ Reports (1969).
66. Icelandic Fisheries Cases (UK v Iceland), and (FRG v Iceland), ICJ Rep (1974).
67. Ibid, at 200, para 64.
68. See also Orrego Vicuna (1999), p 10 and Shigeru Oda (1989), *International Control of Sea Resources*, Dordrecht: Martinus Nijhoff, p xxvi.
69. *North Sea Continental Shelf Case*, ICJ Reports (1969), 3.
70. See Birnie P., Boyle A. and Redgwell C. (2009), p 112–113. See also *Gabčikovo–Nagymaros Dam Case* (1997), ICJ Reports, 7, para. 140.
71. In some Conventions such as MARPOL 'due diligence' has been interpreted as requiring the establishment of a proper system of environment management that assesses and addresses foreseeable impacts and does not rely on uncertainty to postpone action on serious risks. This approach has also been criticized as offering little guidance on what type of controls or standards are required. Consequently various treaties have felt the need to agree upon minimum standards to facilitate compliance. See the annexes of the 1973 MARPOL Convention.
72. See Hey, E. (1989), *The Regime for the Exploitation of Transboundary Marine Fishery Resources*, Dordrecht: Martinus Nijhoff, pp 34–5. See also Birnie, Boyle and Redgwell (2009), p 652.
73. See Bierzaneek, R. 'La Nature Juridique de La Haute Mer', RGDIP, **2**, p 245. See also Burke, W.T. and McDougal, M.S. (1975), *The Public Order of the Oceans*, Yale 1975, pp 761–2. See also Dupuy and Vignes (1991), p 395.
74. See Orrego Vicuna (1999), p 14 and Birnie, Boyle and Redgwell (2009), pp 124–7.
75. See Orrego Vicuna (1999) who says that it is difficult to put these principles of customary international law into practice but it is wrong to assume that customary international law provides for unrestricted freedom of fishing. See also Birnie, Boyle and Redgwell (2009), p 495 who argue that the Tribunal in the *Behring Sea Fur Seals Arbitration* clearly recognized that the freedom of fishing was not absolute but had to be regulated to take reasonable account of the interests of other states.
76. See Dupuy and Vignes (1991), p 399.
77. UNCLOS article 87(1) provides an inclusive list and refers to the freedom of navigation, of overflight, to lay submarine cables and pipelines subject to Part VI, to construct artificial islands and under installations permitted under international law,

subject to Part VI, freedom of fishing subject to the conditions laid down in section 2 of Part VII and scientific research subject to Parts VI and XIII.

78. Ibid, article 87(2).
79. The chapeau of article 87 establishes, 'Freedom of the high seas must be exercised under the conditions laid down in the Convention and other rules of international law. . .'
80. See article 87(1)(e).
81. See article 2 of the 1958 Convention on Fish Conservation and Management in the High Seas which also says 'Conservation programmes should be formulated with a view to securing in the first place a supply of food for human consumption'.
82. See ibid, article 119.
83. See 1958 Convention on Fishing and the Conservation of Living Resources on the High Seas, article 2, which says, '"conservation of the living resources of the high seas" means the aggregate of the measures rendering possible the optimum sustainable yield from those resources so as to secure a maximum supply of food and other marine products. Conservation programmes should be formulated with a view to securing in the first place a supply of food for human consumption'.
84. See Chapter 5, pp 182–7.
85. Ibid.
86. The establishment of marine protected areas on the high seas, although still in an embryonic stage is a clear indication that states have come to acknowledge the importance of the conservation of the marine habitat for present and future generations. This development shows a clear departure from the perception that fishing on the high seas involves only distant water fishing states participants in the same fishery or coastal states that have jurisdiction over adjacent maritime areas.
87. UNCLOS article 116(b) which makes a cross-reference to article 63(2) referring to straddling fish stocks, 64 on highly migratory fish stocks, 66 and 67 on catadromous and anadromous species, and article 120 on marine mammals. The species based approach tends to highlight the vested interest of the international community in species which are more subject to over exploitation. Due to national interests over such species it is usually those states that are not directly involved in their exploitation that press for stricter conservation measures.
88. Coastal states may claim that that vessels fishing on the high seas high seas adjacent to maritime zones falling under their jurisdiction are subject to obligations emerging from article 116(b) especially with respect to articles 63(2), 64, 65, 66, 67, referred to in the said article whilst other flag states participants in the same high seas fishery may rely on article 118.
89. This is expressed in article 117 where the flag state may take conservation measures either by itself or in cooperation with others.
90. See above pp 33–4.
91. UNCLOS article 117 is taken as a legal basis that allows unilateral conservation measures as an alternative to cooperating with others.
92. This is due to conflicting interpretation which states give to the relationship between article 117 and 118 in UNCLOS.
93. This would include regional fisheries agreements concluded by various states to regulate high seas fisheries; for a list of these agreements see above note 35, and Chapter 1 pp 11–12.
94. See above at note 26.
95. Parties to fisheries agreements are bound to abide by these collective measures and, in the case of parties to the FSA, they are also obliged to observe them, even if they have not specifically adhered to them; see FSA article 8(3).
96. In fact this notion cannot be applicable to resources occurring within areas subject to state jurisdiction since the host state has sovereignty or sovereign rights over such resources.
97. See Kirgis, F.L., Jr (1990), 'Standing to challenge human endeavours that could

change the climate' Am. J. Int. L, Editorial Comment, **84** (2) 525, see also Boyle in Churchill R.R. and Freestone D. (1991), *International Law and Global Climate Change*, London: Graham & Trotman.

98. The concept originally put forward in UNGA Resolution 43/53 on Climate Change was then incorporated in the preambular paragraphs of both the United Nations Framework Convention on Climate Change and the United Nations Convention on Biological Diversity.
99. The concept was first proposed by Malta under UNGA resolution 43/53 as the first paragraph of this resolution that may be considered as the genesis of the UNFCCC. The legal implications of the phrase reported here were explained in the 2nd Committee by David Attard, chief legal adviser to the Malta delegation at the time. The same phrase was later adopted to define the status of biological diversity under CBD. See Birnie, Boyle and Redgwell, pp 128–30, 234, 657–59.
100. UNCLOS Part VII, Section 2, article 119.
101. *Barcelona Traction* case, ICJ Reports (1970), 3.
102. *Australia v France (Jurisdiction)* ICJ Reports (1974), 253 and *New Zealand v France (Jurisdiction)* ICJ Reports, 457.
103. ICJ Reports (1997), 7. See also Birnie, Boyle and Redgwell, p 131, footnote 153, who argue that the assumption that sustainable development is a legal obligation may be incorrect. Brownlie (2003) refers to sustainable development as an 'emergent principle of international law.'
104. See Birnie, Boyle and Redgwell, pp 232–3. See also below the discussion relating to Australia's international claim against Japan for exploiting whales on the high seas.
105. See Orrego Vicuna (1991) p 46.
106. See UN Doc. A/AC. 138/SC. 1/SR. 17, 9 August 1971.
107. See UN Doc. A/AC. 138/SC. II/SR. 30, 29 March 1972.
108. UNCLOS article 87 itself provides that the freedoms must be exercised under the conditions laid down in the Convention and other rules of international law and with '"due regard for the interests of other" in their exercise of the freedom of the high seas and with respect to activities in the Area'.
109. Ibid, article 116(a).
110. Ibid, article 116(b).
111. Ibid, article 118.
112. This provision refres to flag states that have competing interests over living resources on the high seas.
113. UNCLOS article 120.
114. See Orrego Vicuna (1991), p 27.
115. See ibid, p 42 et seq who comments on the status of these provisions as customary international law.
116. This refers to those coastal states with an adjacent EEZ to the high seas where fishing occurs for straddling stocks, highly migratory fish stocks, catadromous and anadromous species.
117. These include any distant water fishing states that fish in same area of the high seas and those that fish any where else for identical species.
118. See UNCLOS article 62.
119. Ibid, article 118 and in the case of marine mammals the last provision of section 2, namely article 120 establishes that Part VII of UNCLOS does not prejudice states from taking stricter measures addressing the conservation of marine mammals on the high seas, as adopted by international organizations.
120. This issue will be discussed in detail in the coming chapters on conservation; at this point this chapter serves to highlight the impact it may have upon the coastal state's exclusive jurisdiction.
121. See Orrego Vicuna (1991), p 42 regarding this shift in the burden of proof.
122. Under UNCLOS this is referred to as 'the Area' and is defined as including the seabed

and the subsoil thereof beyond the limits of national jurisdiction. See UNCLOS Article 1(1).

123. See Part XI, Section 1, article 135.
124. See Orrego Vicuna (1991), p 10 footnote 26 and footnote 27 where he quotes Shigeru Oda.
125. See the *Fisheries Jurisdiction Case (Estai Case) (Spain v Canada)*, ICJ General List No 96 (1998). On 3rd March 1995, Canada made certain amendments to its Coastal Fisheries Protection Regulations, the effect of which was that all foreign vessels were prohibited from fishing Greenland halibut in the NAFO Regulatory Area and that offenders were subject to arrest, seizure of vessel and catch and fines. The amendments were immediately notified to foreign fishing vessels by radio. The *Estai* incident took place less than a week later. The whole chain of events unfolded totally outside the framework of the NAFO Convention.
126. See ibid the final judgement of the *Fisheries Jurisdiction Case* (*Estai Case*), delivered on 4th December 1998, separate Opinion of Judge Shigenu Oda (para 7), p 478. The Fisheries Commission established under the framework of the NAFO Convention is responsible for the management and conservation of the fishery resources of the 'Regulatory Area'. This regional Fisheries Commission may adopt proposals for joint action by the Contracting Parties designed to achieve the optimum utilization of the fishery resources of the 'Regulatory Area'. It may also adopt proposals for international measures of control and enforcement within the 'Regulatory Area' for the purpose of ensuring within it the application of the Convention and the measures in force thereunder. Each proposal adopted by the Commission shall become a measure binding on all Contracting Parties and any Commission member may present to the Executive Secretary of NAFO an objection to a proposal by virtue of article XII, para 1. Within the framework of the NAFO Convention, the management and conservation of the fishery resources in the 'Regulatory Area', which is an area that lies beyond the fisheries jurisdiction of any coastal state, is the responsibility of the Fisheries Commission.
127. See UNCLOS article 116(b).
128. Ibid, article 118.
129. See ibid, article 197 which refers to cooperation on a global and regional basis, 'for the protection and preservation of the marine environment'. The UNEP regional seas programmes go beyond the regulation of marine pollution in scope and address also biodiversity issues and the marine habitat. Additionally under Part XII entitled the 'Protection and the Preservation of the Marine Environment', UNCLOS itself requires that, 'further global and regional standards, rules and practices will be adopted through appropriate bodies'.
130. Post UNCLOS treaties, particularly those involving the regional seas, even if they do not venture into the regulation of high seas fisheries, target the conservation of species and their habitat in their entirety.
131. US-Shrimp: *United States-Import Prohibition of Certain Shrimp and Shrimp Products*, complaints by India, Malaysia, Pakistan and Thailand (WT/DS58), panel and Appellate Body reports adopted on 6 November 1998.
132. See Birnie and Boyle (2009), p 384.
133. See above at note 126 and the *Estai* case at p 43.
134. UNCLOS article 116(a). See Oxman, B. (1994–1995).
135. Agreements must be honoured in good faith.
136. See VCLT article 26, which codifies the peremptory norm '*Pacta Sunt Servanda*', all agreements must be honoured in good faith.
137. This duty stems from their obligation to co-operate in the taking of conservation measures referred to in articles 117 and 118.
138. Article 87(1) chapeau, which says that, 'all freedoms are to be exercised under the conditions laid down by the Convention and other rules of International law'.
139. See discussion above at p 37 et seq.

140. See UNCLOS article 118.
141. See Moore, G. (1993), 'Enforcement without Force, New Techniques in Compliance Control for Foreign Fishing Operations based on Regional Cooperation', ODIL, **24** (2), pp 197–204.
142. Examples include the 1979 Bonn Convention on the Conservation of Migratory Species of Wild Animals, the 1992 Convention on Biological Diversity and the FSA.
143. Examples include the FAO Compliance Agreement and the FSA, NAFO and NEAFC.
144. Examples include ICCAT and CITES.
145. CCAMLR has a mutual inspection regime. See discussion in Chapters 6 and 7.
146. The IWC moratorium is contested for being inconsistent with the ICRW since it applies to entire species that are abundant and thus not in need of special protection measures.
147. The FSA was negotiated after considerable pressure to address the special situation of transboundary fish stocks, which is clearly expressed in Chapter 17 of Agenda 21 that called for the effective implementation of UNCLOS provisions relating to these types of fish stocks. Amongst other things this Agreement is the first and to date the only attempt to list a series of legal principles under its article 6 that apply re the management and conservation of these stocks in the high seas. These principles supplement and go beyond the obligations established under the corresponding UNCLOS provisions; for instance, article 6 of the FSA refers to the protection of biodiversity, the precautionary approach, the elimination or prevention of over-fishing long term sustainability and optimum utilization.
148. See FSA article 5.
149. See ibid. It provides also for measures on catch and effort, closed areas and seasons, selective gear controls over new or exploratory fisheries and introduces more conservation measures underlying the ecosystem approach.
150. There are nine species under moratoria, including capelin, cod, American plaice and the witch flounder.
151. NAFO annually sets aside an allocation of regulated species called 'other' in part for states not included in list of contracting parties, allocations or for exceptional arrangements. This was done via a Resolution taken in 1999.
152. Guidelines refer to mesh size regulation, bottom trawl prohibition around some areas.
153. CCAMLR does not define the precautionary approach but is a pioneer in efforts to manage marine ecosystems accordingly.
154. See CBD article 4 on the jurisdictional scope of the Convention, which establishes, 'subject to the rights of other States, and except as otherwise expressly provided in this Convention, the provisions of this Convention apply, in relation to each Contracting Party: (a) In the case of components of biological diversity, in areas within the limits of its national jurisdiction; and (b) In the case of processes and activities, regardless of where their effects occur, carried out under its jurisdiction or control, within the area of its national jurisdiction or beyond the limits of national jurisdiction.'
155. See CBD articles 3–5. Decision VII/5 para 30 of COP of the CBD addresses protected areas in marine areas beyond national jurisdiction where all parties agreed that urgent need for international cooperation and action was necessary to improve conservation and sustainable use of biodiversity in these areas. See also Molenaar, E.J. (2007), 'Managing Biodiversity Beyond National Jurisdiction', IJMC, **22** (1), pp 89–124; Juda, L., (1999) 'Considerations in Developing a Functional Approach to the Governance of Large Marine Eco Systems', ODIL, **30** (2) 89–126.
156. These fall within the scope of CBD article 4 as national activities or entities under the jurisdiction or control of a State, carrying out an activity outside national jurisdiction.
157. See CBD decision VII/5 para 56.
158. See CBD article 7(c) and 14(1)a–d.
159. This may occur if there is widespread adherence since the Statute of International Court of Justice, article 38(1), establishes that treaties to which states in the dispute are

parties is the first applicable legal source that will be considered to address the dispute or settle the claim made.

160. Cicin-Sain, B. and Knecht, R.W. (1993), 'Implications of the Earth Summit for Ocean and Coastal Governance', ODIL, **24** (4), 323–54; see also Orrego Vicuna, F. (1993), 'Towards an Effective Management of High Seas Fisheries and the Settlement of Pending Issues of the Law of the Sea', ODIL, **24** (1), 81–92.
161. See Oxman (1994–1995).
162. The term *inter alia* denotes that the flag state's exclusive jurisdiction on the high seas is not only relative to these particular species but to the entire range of coastal state's rights, duties and interests under the Convention.
163. Given the cross reference it makes to Part V on the EEZ, particularly to its articles 63(2), 64, 65, 66, 67.
164. This term emerges from the general qualification to the freedoms in article 87 (2) paying 'due regard for the interests of other States,' which addresses all states any time, whether they coastal or landlocked, whether directly affected or not.
165. *Icelandic Fisheries* cases; see discussion above p 27, 77. See also Orrego Vicuna (1991), p 16, who argues that in the *Icelandic Fisheries* cases, the ICJ acknowledged that freedom of fishing was made subject to the preferential rights of coastal states. This means that when states fish on the high seas they should adopt conservation measures as needed whilst seeking to accommodate the divergent interests of the states involved by referring to the substantive principles of 'reasonable use' and 'equitable arrangements' in resource allocation.
166. See Orrego Vicuna (1991), p 21
167. Such species reproduce and live for some time in fresh water but spend most of their lifespan in the ocean before they return to spawn in the state of origin. Examples include salmon, steelhead trout and some herring. Salmon stocks are by far the most commercially important on a global basis.
168. Anadromous and catadromous species are discussed in Chapter 4. Anadromous species are living marine resources whose life originates in fresh water and then they spend most of their life at sea, returning to the state of origin to spawn and die. Catadromous species are hatched at sea and spend most of their life cycle inland in fresh water bodies. The most well known anadromous species is salmon, whilst the eel is an example of a catadromous species.
169. See Burke W.T. (1994), *The New International Law of Fisheries, The 1982 UNCLOS and Beyond*', Oxford Monographs in International Law, Oxford: Clarendon Press, p 154 who argues that fishing on the high seas is inconsistent with conservation of these species.
170. See UNCLOS article 66(3)(a) for anadromous species and article 67(2) for catadromous species.
171. See ibid, article 66(3)(a).
172. For a detailed discussion, see Burke (1994) p 162. See also Orrego Vicuna (1991), p 34 and especially footnote 57.
173. Ibid, see also below discussion in Chapter 4, pp 140–43.
174. This means that only those states that are already involved in fishing for such stocks on the high seas can benefit from this exception, new entries are entirely excluded.
175. See UNCLOS article 66(3)(c).
176. Ibid, article 66(2).
177. Ibid, article 66(3)(a).
178. Article 92 establishes that, 'save in exceptional circumstances expressly provided for in International treaties and in this Convention' ships shall be subject to the exclusive jurisdiction of the flag state on the high seas.
179. Examples are many: in the Donut Hole in the Central Behring Sea over Pollock stocks, long distance fishing states have had various disputes with Russia and the US, which have an adjacent EEZ until late 1992, where by agreement the states involved agreed not to fish for two years. In the North West Atlantic the NAFO has had serious diffi-

culties in encouraging members to endorse and abide by its conservation measures for the high seas particularly with respect to the Grand Banks area. Canada has accused long distance fishing states of seriously jeopardizing its conservation and management measures for straddling stocks in its fishing zone. Claims made by Mexico over tuna fishing beyond its EEZ in the Eastern Tropical Pacific, linked its sovereign rights over tuna within 200 miles to an assertion of authority to establish the total allowable catch and entry fees for harvesting of tuna beyond its EEZ. See Miles and Burke (1989), 'Pressures on the United Nations Convention on the Law of the Sea of 1982 Arising from New Fisheries Conflicts: The Problem of Straddling Stock', ODIL, 20343, 344–9.

180. See Burke (1994), p 219, who argues that this does not only mean that parties exchange data and information but also concrete suggestions on specific conservation and optimum utilization measures that would eventually lead to an agreement as required under article 64.
181. See UNCLOS article 279 which provides for compulsory dispute settlement concerning disputes re the interpretation of an application of the Convention. The exception that fishing disputes arising from the interpretation and application of the coastal state's sovereign rights with respect to the living resources of the EEZ or the exercise of these rights does not apply because this applies only to those disputes in which only sovereign rights are at stake and not when both sovereign rights and high seas rights are in dispute. See also Burke (1994), p 223, footnote 64 and related text.
182. This is the case for instance with respect to tuna fishing in the central and western Pacific.
183. See Orrego Vicuna (1991), p 42 who argues that article 64 puts emphasis on cooperation between coastal and flag states for the conservation of HMS on the high seas. A development, he argues, that has been accepted even by distant water fishing states.
184. Ibid.
185. Ibid.
186. See FSA article 7; see also below the discussion in Chapter 4, pp 131 et seq.
187. To date the FSA has been ratified by 78 states up to 31 December 2008. It was agreed upon by consensus.
188. See Burke (1994), p 219 who argues that this does not only mean that parties exchange data and information but also concrete suggestions on specific conservation and optimum utilization measures that would eventually lead to an agreement as required under article 64.
189. See UNCLOS articles 64, 87, 116 and 119.
190. Ibid.
191. See for example the *Icelandic Fisheries Cases (UK & Germany v Iceland)* ICJ Reports (1974) which acknowledged that the conservation of living resources on the high seas is a rule of customary international law. The right of the coastal state to claim an EEZ of 200 nautical miles from its baselines referred to in UNCLOS under its article 56 has been recognized as a rule of customary International law: see *Libya/Malta Continental Shelf* case, ICJ Reports, 1985, p 13; 81 ILR 238.
192. See discussion in Chapters 6 and 7.
193. Under the nationality principle states can regulate certain activities performed by their nationals and hence even of vessels flying there flag. See Brownlie (2003), pp 301–2.
194. See Burke (1994), p 170, who argues that in the case of the high seas an international organization might completely prohibit the harvest of marine mammals or regulate them in a way that might be inconsistent with UNCLOS articles 64 and 65. See also McDorman, T.L. (1998), 'Canada and Whaling an Analysis of Article 65 of the Law of the Sea Convention', ODIL, **29** (2), pp 179–194; D'Amato, A. and Chopra, S. (1991), 'Whales: Their Emerging Right to Life', 85 Am. J. Int. L., 21–62. Morgera, E. (2004), 'Whale Sanctuaries: An Evolving Concept within the International Whaling Commission', ODIL, **35** (4), 319–338.
195. UNCLOS article 64.

196. Ibid, article 63(2).
197. Under the conditions envisaged in UNCLOS article 118.
198. Once article 120 establishes that article 65 is applicable to the high seas regime, article 65 must necessarily be applied *mutatis mutandis* and the reference to 'this Part' refers to Part VII and not to Part V on the EEZ regime.
199. The common heritage regime in Part XI, excludes living resources and any resources occurring in the superjacent waters.
200. See Birnie, Boyle and Redgwell (2009), pp 672–3.
201. Iceland officially withdrew from the IWC in 1992 because the IWC refused to lift the moratorium. A new Agreement namely the North Atlantic Marine Mammal Commission (NAMMCO) was set up between Iceland, Norway, Greenland and the Faroe Islands on 9 April 1992.
202. *Dispute Concerning Japan's JARPA II Program on 'Scientific Whaling' (Australia v. Japan) Application Instituting Proceedings* (31 May 2010) Available at: www.haguejusticeportal.net/Docs/Court Documents/ICJ/Australia against Japan_Applications instituting proceedings.pdf. See article by Rothwell, D.R., 'Australia v. Japan: JARPA II Whaling Case before the International Court of Justice' *Proceedings instituted by Australia against Japan: Application Instituting Proceedings, 31 May 2010,* the Hague Justice Portal.
203. Article VIII of the ICRW provides that: '. . . any Contracting Government may grant to any of its nationals a special permit authorizing that national to kill, take and treat whales for purposes of scientific research... and the killing, taking and treating of whales in accordance with the provisions of this Article shall be exempt from the operation of this Convention'.
204. Above all flag states are bound to cooperate with others in taking conservation measures particularly due to the HMS nature and the inclusion in Annex I of certain marine mammals as well as to negotiate and conduct scientific investigations.
205. The main issues that may affect compatibility between agreements and organizations addressing the conservation of cetaceans may be summed up as follows: open or closed membership, the scope of authority of the organizations/treaties including which species are affected, jurisdictional scope of the coastal state under the EEZ regime and the geographical scope, which activities are subject to scientific research, the competence of these international organizations/agreements to act and compatibility and consistency between their conservation objectives, methodologies adopted, particularly regarding scientific effort and understanding.
206. See Orrego Vicuna (1991), p 37, who argues that although there exist differing views on the interpretation of article 120 and its legal implications, its inclusion in this part of the 1982 Convention signifies that the conservation of marine mamals should be regulated more strictly under UNCLOS than if the provision was not included. See also Birnie, Boyle and Redgwell (2009) pp 533–4.
207. UNCLOS expressly states that sovereignty extends to resources within limits bounding the archipelagic water area so marine mammals would be considered wholly subject to archipelagic state authority when within the area.
208. See De Klemm C. (1989), 'Migratory species in international law', Natural Resources Journal, **29**, (73), pp 935–64.
209. See UNCLOS article 297(3).
210. See ibid article 77 which provides that the rights of the coastal state are exclusive, 'in the sense that if the coastal state does not explore the continental shelf or exploit its natural resources no one may undertake these activities without the express consent of the coastal State.'
211. Ibid.
212. See ibid, articles 76(4) (5) (6) (7).
213. See ibid, article 76(7) and also below the discussion in Chapter 4.
214. See UNCLOS articles 136 and 137.
215. See ibid, article 133.

216. Ibid. This includes encouraging international cooperation in research, ensuring that research programmes benefit developing countries and the dissemination of the research results.
217. Ibid and article 156.
218. UNCLOS article 86 establishes that the provisions of Part VII entitled 'High Seas' apply to 'all parts of the sea that are not included in the EEZ, in the territorial sea or in the internal waters of a State, or in the archipelagic waters of an archipelagic State'. Since the deep seabed does not fall under any of these maritime zones and since Part XI according to article 133 does not apply to non mineral resources, some states argue that by process of elimination living marine resources occurring on the deep sea bed are subject to the high seas regime.
219. See Tanaka, Y. (2008), 'Reflections on the Conservation and Sustainable Use of Genetic Resources in the Deep Sea Bed Beyond the Limits of National Jurisdiction', ODIL, **39** (2), pp 129–149.
220. Arico and Sapin (2005), *Bioprospecting of Genetic Resources in the Deep Seabed Scientific, Legal and Policy Aspects*, UNU-IAS Report.
221. UNCLOS article 145(b).
222. This is further explained as referring to a situation when its nationals fish for identical species or when they fish for different species but in the same region of the high seas.
223. Article 118 ends as follows, 'They shall, as appropriate, co-operate to establish subregional or regional fisheries organizations to this end.'
224. See discussion in Chapter 1 pp 11–12.
225. According to article 116(a) freedom of fishing is subject to the obligations it has under these treaties.
226. See discussion relating to the powers of the Port states in Chapter 7 p 247–9.
227. All Contracting Parties to NEAFC are Parties to the FSA.
228. See CCAMLR articles XXIX and VI.
229. IOTC has been established as an article XIV FAO body.
230. See Birnie, Boyle and Redgwell (2009) p 648.
231. In the mid nineteenth century in 1867, France and Great Britain concluded a bilateral agreement entitled the Convention relative to Fisheries. The Treaty for the Regulation of the Police of the North Sea Fisheries, better known as the Overfishing Convention, followed in 1882. Other examples of the earliest treaties regulating the exploitation of living resources on the High Seas are: The Agreement between the Government of the United states of America in 1891, the Treaty between Great Britain and the United states submitting to Arbitration the Questions relating to the Seal Fisheries in the Behring Sea, Washington, 1892, the Convention between the Government of the United states of America and the Government of Her Britannic Majesty for the Renewal of the Existing *Modus Vivendi* in the Behring Sea, Washington, 1892, the Convention between the United states of America, the United Kingdom of Great Britain and Northern Ireland, and Russia, for the Preservation and Protection of Fur Seals, Washington, 1911. Source: the 16th Report of the Select Committee on Environment Transport and Regional Affairs: www.parliament.uk and www.publications.parliament.uk/pa/cm199899/cmenvtra/307r/30702htm.
232. See Orrego Vicuna (1991), p 5.
233. Ibid, p 8.
234. The provisions of this section are considered to be both a codification of customary international law and norm-creating support with evidence.
235. See UNCLOS articles 87, 116, 117, 118, 119 and 120.
236. Ibid, articles 116(b) and the provisions referred to therein as well as article 117 and 118.
237. The obligation to take conservation measures is embodied in article 117, where the flag state is obligated to adopt the 'necessary' conservation measures for its nationals that fish on the high seas either unilaterally or via cooperation. Both article 87 and article

116(c) tie the freedom of fishing with the conditions of section 2 of Part VII, article 117 therefore must be interpreted also in the light of other provisions of this section.

238. Ibid, article 116 (a) and (b).
239. The legal interpretation of what constitutes conservation and necessary conservation measures as a general obligation intrinsic to the freedom of fishing is discussed in Chapter 3.
240. See Article 89 of 1982 UNCLOS.
241. For a discussion on this different interpretation of the term conservation see Chapter 3, particularly its implications for those participating in the same fishery and to the rights of the coastal states to exploit these resources within the maritime areas subject to their jurisdiction.
242. See pp 32–40
243. See article 87(2), which lays down that states shall exercise the high seas freedoms with due regard to other states in their exercise of the freedoms.
244. See below the discussion regarding jurisdiction over specific species in Chapter 5.
245. See Burke W.T., Freeberg, M., Miles, E.L. (1994), 'United Nations Resolution on Driftnet Fishing: An Unsustainable Precedent for High Seas and Coastal Fisheries Management' ODIL **25** (2) 127–86.
246. Part V regulates coastal states' rights and duties in the EEZ, Part VI regulates coastal states' rights over sedentary species on the continental shelf and Part VII, section 2 regulates the use of living resources on the high seas.
247. Ibid, article 117 establishes that, 'All states have the duty to take or to cooperate with other states in taking, such measures for their respective nationals as may be necessary for the conservation of living resources on the high seas'. This provision permits flag states to adopt unilateral conservation measures. Article 116(b) recognizes the duty of high seas fishing states to subject themselves to their rights, duties and interests particularly with respect to straddling fish stocks, HMS, marine mammals, catadromous and anadromous species. In the case of HMS and straddling stocks coastal states and high seas fishing states are to cooperate through a fisheries organization or directly.
248. See UNCLOS article 63(2). For instance, in the case of straddling stocks, both categories of states are to agree upon conservation measures necessary for these stocks in the adjacent areas of the high seas, article 64(1) Similarly coastal states and high seas fishing states are to cooperate with a view to ensure conservation and optimum utilization of HMS, listed in Annex I to the Convention, 'both within and beyond the exclusive economic zone'.
249. Ibid, article 66(3)(a) and 67(2).
250. If the adjudicating body finds for the crystallization of such a rule, the onus of proof is upon the state adopting different conservation measures on the High Seas to prove that it has persistently objected to it. See *Anglo-Norwegian Fisheries Cases,* ICJ Reports (1951), 131, re the persistent objector.
251. Ibid, article 116.
252. Ibid, article 120.
253. The moratorium started in 1983 a year after UNCLOS was concluded and before it came into force.
254. Some authors even suggest that it heralds a new generation of treaty obligations that favour a compulsory system of cooperation with respect to the conservation of marine living resources on the high seas. See Ellis, J. (2001), 'The Straddling Stocks Agreement and the Precautionary Principle: An Interpretative Device and Rule of Law', ODIL **32** (4) 289–312.
255. The term 'shared resources' and its legal implications remain controversial but there is agreement that certain basic obligations such as the duty to cooperate in avoiding negative effects through notification, consultation, negotiation and more recently impact assessment, have been endorsed by international bodies such as the ILC's Codification of the Law of Water Courses and quoted as examples of state practice in international case law such as the *Lac Lanoux Arbitration* 24 ILR (1957) and the

Nuclear Tests Cases (New Zealand v. France) (Interim Measures), ICJ Rep. (1973), 135; (Jurisdiction), ICJ Rep. (1974), 457. See Birnie, Boyle and Redgwell (2009), p 126 and footnote 341.

256. UNEP/IG/12/2 (1978).
257. UNGA Resolution. 34/186 (1979). The UNGA resolution states that these principles are 'without prejudice to the binding nature of those rules already recognized as such in International law.'
258. *Icelandic Fisheries Cases (UK & Germany v Iceland)* ICJ Reports (1974).
259. Examples include the FSA, the Bonn Convention on Migratory species of Wild Animals, ICCAT and SBSTA.
260. Examples include CITES and the Protocol to the Barcelona Convention on Biological Diversity and Specially Protected Areas.
261. Examples include the GFCM, NAFO and, NEAFC.
262. See UNCLOS article 118. CCAMLR is an example.
263. See CBD article 4.
264. The whole concept of Grotius' *Mare Liberum,* is based on the premise which promotes the free seas common property approach as an inclusive interest vested in the International community as a whole.
265. Also subject to freedom of fishing in accordance with section 2 of Part VII of UNCLOS, are those living resources occurring in the superjacent water column of the continental shelf (beyond the territorial sea) where the coastal state has not declared an EEZ or an EFZ. Unlike the mineral resources of the deep seabed, all states have access to high seas living resources as their governance is not subject to global management by a above national authority such as the ISBA.
266. Examples of such treaties include the 1992 UN Convention on Biological Diversity (CBD), the 1973 Convention on International Trade in Endangered Species of Wild Flora and Fauna (CITES), the 1979 Bonn Convention on Migratory Species of Wild Animals (CMS) and its Agreements as well as various other regional instruments such as the 1974 Convention on the Protection of the Marine Environment in the Baltic Sea Area, 1980 Convention on the Conservation of Antarctic Marine Living Resources (CCAMLR) and the 1995 Protocol Concerning Specially Protected Areas and Biological Diversity in the Mediterranean.
267. For instance states have prohibited fish landings or their placing on the market if sources cannot guarantee that there was no illegal, unregulated and unreported fishing or that certain conservation standards were abided by. These issues are examined in detail in Chapter 7, pp 247–9.
268. See discussion on the *Australian v Japan, JARPA II Whaling* Case, 2010 above.

3 The obligation to take conservation measures for living resources on the high seas

3.1 INTRODUCTION

By the late nineteenth and early twentieth centuries, fishing on the high seas had already generated sufficient political pressure to lead to the conclusion of various international agreements regulating the exploitation of seals and fisheries.[1] These treaties, which were mainly concerned with allocating national quotas influenced the manner in which states came to exercise their right to access and exploit these same resources. Conservation measures evolved as a means to control over-exploitation by a few states and so to guarantee the universal right of access[2] to these stocks. By the mid-twentieth century, advances in technology had led to a continuous increase in both fishing catches and the industry's capital costs. To cover these additional expenses and make up for the introduction of stricter conservation requirements such as fishing seasons and the use of more selective fishing gear,[3] the fishing industry intensified its efforts. Originally, the aim of these conservation measures was to secure the sustainability of stocks as a source of food for human consumption. As we have seen in the previous chapter, the perception that international regimes should aim at securing a sound conservation status for all species and their habitat by taking into account their special biological and behavioural characteristics is of more recent origin. The earliest fisheries treaties relied only marginally upon scientific advice and largely ignored other factors that negatively affect the conservation of stocks.[4] The international community did make some serious attempts to address these shortcomings over the years,[5] but even the extension of coastal state jurisdiction and the conclusion of the 1982 UNCLOS did not resolve these problems. Despite efforts in the 1970s and 1980s to regulate the situation in a more holistic manner,[6] the persistent, unsustainable exploitation of marine living resources led to the collapse of some major fisheries, with drastic socio-economic effects and, at times, irreparable ecological repercussions.[7] Efforts to reverse the situation intensified after UNCED[8] and the 1992

Cancun Conference on Responsible Fishing,[9] both held in 1992. Although the two Conferences manifested the international community's will to adopt an ecosystem and integrated approach for better conservation, they also exposed how complex and legally challenging it was for international law to implement these principles. For example, the ecosystem approach highlights the need to adopt conservation measures based on treating the oceans as one macro ecosystem whilst international law splits the oceans into jurisdictional zones where different legal regimes apply. Furthermore, even though some international treaties adopt a species-based approach, they mainly target only those living marine resources which have a high commercial value such as tuna. Other challenges include: poor coordination between different international institutions, the reluctance to address[10] the impacts of *all* anthropogenic uses[11] of the oceans and the piecemeal regulation of activities that have a negative impact upon the marine environment and its living resources, such as the introduction of alien species and climate change.

As highlighted in the previous chapters, this work focuses on conservation measures relating to the harvesting/exploitation of marine living resources on the high seas rather than on conservation in general. This chapter will examine how the applicable sources of international law interpret the meaning of conservation, its objectives and the methodologies associated with it. It aims to demonstrate whether the various regimes are coherent in this respect or are otherwise in need of harmonization to ensure legal certainty and consistency. The next chapter discusses the obligation to take conservation measures from a species-based approach and Chapter 5 elicits the most predominant constituent elements of the obligation to take conservation measures that are found in applicable regimes.

3.2 DEFINITION, GOALS AND TYPES OF CONSERVATION MEASURES[12]

A legal definition of the term conservation is hardly ever included in applicable treaties.[13] Conventions[14] and decisions[15] in international case law have opted, instead, for expressing the goals which conservation should aim for, whilst some legal sources have chosen to propose a legally binding methodology in order to achieve conservation objectives.[16] The legal implications of the term conservation with respect to high seas living resources will be primarily assessed according to treaty law because the international community has encouraged the progressive development and codification of the law of the sea, particularly through the organization of three plenipotentiary conferences which led to the 1958 Geneva

Conventions[17] and the 1982 UNCLOS. Treaty law is not the only applicable source of international law, however, and in the following chronological account, the decisions of international adjudicating bodies will be given particular prominence because, apart from applying treaty law, they seek evidence of other international norms as these emanate from custom and general principles of law that may be applied to settle such disputes.

3.2.1 Pre-UNCLOS Developments

The earliest attempt to regulate the conservation of living resources on the high seas via treaty law can be traced to 1882 with the conclusion of the North Seas Overfishing Convention.[18] This Convention did not define the term conservation but at the same time it established progressive measures to address the depletion of stocks harvested on the high seas. These included the harmonization of the registration and numbering of fishing vessels as well as the establishment of national authorities to supervise compliance with these obligations. It also imposed the use of certain types of fishing gear and the obligation to retrieve it when it becomes derelict. Following these legal developments, the scientific community deemed it necessary to establish a forum of scientists drawn from States bordering the North Sea, which eventually led to the setting up of the International Council for the Exploration of the Sea (ICES).[19] In sum, the Overfishing Convention implied that conservation required concerted effort to regulate exploitation, that it should be based on sound scientific advice, and that it necessitated an efficient control system to secure compliance on a national level. These regulatory measures remain the cornerstone for conservation principles under international fisheries law, as it subsequently developed via general state practice. They are regularly referred to when settling international fisheries disputes and are ubiquitous in treaties addressing the conservation of living marine resources.

Some years after the conclusion of the Overfishing Convention, the international tribunal presiding over the *Behring (Fur Seal) Arbitration*[20] did not define conservation in its decision but recommended instead the formulation of a methodology, namely a nine point Conservation Plan, to regulate exploitation such that the interests of both parties would be safeguarded. The Plan is considered to be the best attempt[21] ever to translate the term conservation into legal obligations. The decision of the tribunal serves to identify the point of departure on how international law originally perceived the obligation to take conservation measures whilst ensuring equality of access.[22] The decision in the *Behring Sea (Fur Seal) Arbitration* acknowledges the need to establish a balance between the unrestrained use of high seas living resources and the need to take measures to ensure their conservation. Conservation in this respect is envisaged as a guarantee to the right to exploit, which, although directed against the exclusiveness of use, must ensure equality of access.[23]

The decision of the Tribunal is considered as having laid down the foundations for international law as it developed in the subsequent years for the purpose of regulating access to living resources on the high seas. It also sheds light on why later developments introduced via treaty law and possibly customary international law are still contested by some states as going against the freedom of fishing. The Tribunal affirmed that the exploitation in maritime areas beyond national jurisdiction was based on the freedom of fishing, and so the need to take conservation measures in order to prevent the over-exploitation and decline of the species must depend on the express acceptance by participants in the fishery.[24] The Tribunal also disregarded the claim that marine mammals had to be treated differently from fish because of their diverse behaviour and characteristics. The nine-point Plan outlined basic conservation measures which reiterate those adopted by the Overfishing Convention and which are still resorted to in many fisheries agreements. These are: the establishment of a prohibited zone for exploitation, a closed season in a defined area of the high seas, limitations on the type of vessels used, a licensing system whereby governments would authorize vessels flying their flag to exploit living resources on the high seas, use of a special flag when sealing, the keeping of catch records, the exchange of data collected, responsibility on the part of the governments concerned for the selection of suitable crews, the transformation of these recommendations into national legislation of both parties in a uniform manner, and finally the adoption of national laws and national measures to ensure enforcement. The plan also highlighted the exceptional status of indigenous people who are allowed to exploit resources with traditional methods even in prohibited areas and closed seasons. Other procedural recommendations included in the plan and which are still availed of in contemporary conservation regimes are: the priority of national measures over international means for enforcement and a total ban on the exploitation of marine mammals for a period of time. The latter measure may be seen as constituting the foundation for the moratorium on whaling applied in current regimes for the conservation of cetaceans.[25] The tribunal's decision was not all positive. As noted above, it did not distinguish between the different conservation requirements of marine mammals from those of fish stocks. Neither did it base its decision on scientific information or make any reference to sustainability or catch quotas. It did, however, assert that the freedom of fishing is not an absolute right but must include the duty to conserve living resources over which other states have an interest. As pointed out above, the decision traced a link between the obligation of a flag state to conserve living resources on the high seas and the duty to ensure that its fishing operations would not impinge negatively on other states' right of access to the same resource or resources. The tribunal affirmed that freedom of fishing was supreme, and that conservation measures could only be binding upon the parties that consented to them. The indiscriminate application of freedom of fishing requires the involvement of all the participants[26] to ensure the successful conservation of the common resource. Consequently, non-compliance by some stakeholders leads to unfair competition at the expense of states that decide to adhere to a specific conservation regime.[27]

The 1955 UN International Technical Conference on the Conservation of the Living Resources of the Sea preceded the 1958 Geneva Convention on Fishing and the Conservation of Living Resources on the High Seas and established that the ultimate method to ensure conservation is to maintain the maximum sustainable yield (MSY). A commonly accepted working definition of MSY is: 'The largest average catch or yield that can continuously be taken from a stock under existing environmental conditions.'[28]

On the basis of this definition, the MSY is achieved when mortality through fishing and recruitment to the stock are maximized at the same time.[29] The main fault of the calculation of the MSY, as originally expressed, is its total reliance upon biological criteria, which is not only difficult to achieve but also unlikely to be accurate. Total reliance on the MSY ignores other factors such as economic interests and the relationship of the species with each other and their habitat. For many years international agreements on fisheries conservation relied on the MSY as the objective of conservation measures.[30] Nevertheless, scientists were, even at the time of the 1955 Conference, already proposing 'optimum fishing' as an alternative to MSY. They termed it as 'eumetric fishing' because it is a conservation method that takes into consideration biological, economic and social factors on an equal basis. This implied that an 'optimum yield' is set which is lower than the MSY.

As mentioned above, the 1958 Geneva Convention on Fishing and the Conservation of Living Resources on the High Seas provides one of the very few definitions of the term 'conservation' as 'the aggregate of measures rendering possible an optimum sustainable yield so as to serve a maximum supply of food and other marine products'.[31] It established that conservation programmes should be formulated with a view to securing, in the first place, a supply of food for human consumption.[32] The Convention reiterated the freedom to fish on the high seas without any specific reference to conservation, but it stipulated that such freedom is exercisable with 'reasonable regard'[33] to the interests of other states. The

1958 Convention preferred linking the term conservation to achieving the optimum sustainable yield instead of relying on the MSY. The insistence on the anthropocentric requirements as a basis for conservation constrained the legal development of the term from encompassing an ecocentric approach. There was a lack of widespread adherence to the 1958 Convention due to the fact that it did not reflect emerging trends such as the extension of coastal state jurisdiction. This situation stalled the further development of international conservation measures that aimed at achieving the optimum sustainable yield in the exploitation of living resources on the high seas.

The extension of coastal state jurisdiction brought about drastic changes in the interpretation of the obligation to take conservation measures. The 1945 Truman Proclamation[34] and the 200-mile claims of certain Latin American States in the late 1940s[35] to protect whaling and other fishing interests were unilateral measures that were considered as contrary to the established position under international law at the time. They may be envisaged as the precursor of the Exclusive Economic Zone (EEZ) regime[36] which has its roots in the development of the coastal states' claims to an exclusive fishing zone (EFZ) and to sovereign rights over the resources of the continental shelf. These events triggered a series of claims by various coastal states that sought exclusive jurisdiction over resources beyond their coast and their territorial sea.[37] The initial claims in the 1950s and the 1960s hardly had any impact on high seas fisheries, except to get the tuna industry agitated. Most extensions did not occur until after 1976, following the decision in the *Icelandic Fisheries Cases*, which recognized the legality of the 12-mile exclusive fishing zone. What coastal states did about conservation within areas of national jurisdiction varied a great deal in the initial years. In some cases, the extension of coastal State jurisdiction had virtually no impact on who harvested the living resources, and even less on how much was caught. For instance, to this very day it is still doubtful whether allocation and conservation in the Eastern Atlantic Ocean has been seriously affected by extended coastal state jurisdiction. The major negative impact on high seas fishing is perhaps the lack of effective control by states over their extended zones that has led to their being victimized for the past several decades by foreign fishermen that carry out illegal, unregulated and unreported (IUU) fishing. The extension of coastal state jurisdiction was initially referred to as the establishment of a fishery conservation zone. It was actually a measure whereby the coastal states could exclude other states from exploiting the living resources beyond their coast, previously subject to the high seas freedoms. It signifies that the decisions of the coastal states over living resources in their EEZ are plenary and that they have the final authority to determine access to and use of living resources in the EEZ.[38] The prospect of assuming exclusive jurisdiction for the exploitation and the conservation of living marine resources over vast maritime areas proved to be much more attractive and lucrative to coastal states than negotiating multilateral and regional agreements. For this reason, fisheries agreements were being undermined on the pretext that they were inadequate to provide the requisite conservation measures for marine living resources on the high seas. Instead, coastal states specified the type of conservation measures they wished to impose on the living resources over which they had an interest and proposed to extend their jurisdiction over them beyond their territorial sea.

On a more positive note, the extension of coastal state jurisdiction did spur the international community to a general acceptance of the obligation to conserve high seas living resources, so much so that under the 1982 Convention this obligation became a qualification to the freedom of fishing.[39] The negotiations leading to the 1982 UNCLOS provided ultimate evidence that there was increased impetus towards acknowledging conservation as a rule of customary international law. This trend emerged more clearly in the *Icelandic Fisheries Cases*.[40] The 1982 UNCLOS was still in the making, and the Court's decision, finding for the obligation of all states to conserve marine living resources on the high seas, was not based solely on the premise that this was a treaty obligation under the 1958 Convention, since Iceland, the respondent state, was not a party to it. Judge Dillard stated in his concurring opinion:

> . . . it is possible to surmise that in the light of practice of States and the widespread and insistent recognition of the need for conservation measures that the principle it announces may qualify as a norm of customary international law.[41]

Furthermore, the Court held that:

> It is one of the advances in maritime international law resulting from the intensification of fishing that the former laissez-faire treatment of living resources on the high seas has been replaced by the recognition of a duty to have due regard to the rights of other States and the needs of conservation for the benefit of all.[42]

The ICJ decision in the *Icelandic Fisheries Cases* accepted evidence of the crystallization of a customary obligation to conserve living resources on the high seas. Furthermore, the Court seems to acknowledge that this duty is towards the international community as a whole.[43]

Pre-UNCLOS developments in international law are particularly relevant to our discussion as they portray the underlying traditional legal principles that are either being challenged or elaborated upon by more recent legal instruments addressing the conservation of living resources on the high seas. Fragmentation of the law may occur whenever one or more states take unilateral decisions that are meant to supersede previous norms that may have become outdated, whilst other states remain reluctant to adhere to emerging norms. The legal interpretation of the obligation to take conservation measures as it evolved over the years before the conclusion of UNCLOS demonstrates that the law needs to be dynamic enough to adopt a different management approach or to take more stringent conservation measures as new political, scientific and technological developments unfold. The next part of this discussion examines the applicable UNCLOS provisions and their effect on the legal dimension of the obligation to take conservation measures on the high seas.

3.2.2 The Obligation to take Conservation Measures on the High Seas according to UNCLOS

Although UNCLOS provides for the conservation of living marine resources in various articles,[44] it avoided defining the term, leaving its meaning to be implied from the nature of measures presented.[45] This may mean that the international community already wanted to depart from the restricted interpretation expressed in the 1958 Geneva Convention on Fishing and the Conservation of Living Resources on the High Seas whereby conservation is merely used as a guarantee to satisfy the demand for human consumption of these resources.[46] Instead, the 1982 Convention has a whole section in its Part VII entitled the 'Conservation and Management of Living Resources on the High Seas'. According to UNCLOS, states must achieve the aims of conservation as expressed in the substantive articles[47] where it lays down certain conservation and management objectives to limit over-exploitation on the high seas. The 1982 Convention leaves it up to the states themselves to work out the methodology of how to attain these conservation goals.[48] The MSY as a conservation goal[49] is referred to under both articles 61(3)[50] and 119(1)(a) of the 1982 Convention, and these two provisions lay down almost identical[51] conservation objectives under both the high seas and the EEZ regimes. Otherwise section 2 of Part VII does not provide an elaborate list of conservation measures proper that could serve as a benchmarking exercise for flag states whose nationals fish on the high seas, as it does for instance with respect to the EEZ[52] in Part V. Article 119 is rather general in scope and establishes that:

> 1. In determining the allowable catch and establishing other conservation measure for the living resources in the high seas:

> (a) States shall take measures which are designed, on the best scientific evidence available to the States concerned, to maintain or restore populations of harvested species at levels which can produce the maximum sustainable yield, as qualified by relevant environmental and economic factors, including the special requirements of developing States, and taking into account fishing patterns, the interdependence of stocks and any generally recommended international minimum standards, whether subregional, regional or global.

States have the discretion to choose *how* to supplement the Convention's obligations under section 2 of Part VII by concluding cooperation agreements to determine 'the allowable catch and establishing other conservation measures on the high seas'[53] that would meet the particular conservation goals laid down in article 119. Furthermore, states shall aim at maintaining and restoring stock abundance in the case of target species, at levels producing the maximum sustainable yield (MSY), 'as qualified by economic and environmental factors'.[54] Even if the general nature of article 119 gives rise to conflicting interpretations on the legal meaning of its content, it is still considered as one of the major contributions made by the 1982 Convention.

Some States argue that, according to UNCLOS, the only acceptable conservation measures are those which aim to maximize the MSY, whilst others interpret it to mean that other conservation measures may be imposed to secure an optimum yield.[55] On the other hand, UNCLOS article 119 is also interpreted as being innovative from a conservation perspective,[56] permitting states to depart from the traditional MSY[57] as a goal for conservation measures. During the negotiations leading to UNCLOS the use of the MSY fishing mortality rate as a target reference point was heavily criticized for leading to serious miscalculations[58] that led to overfishing. The uncertainty surrounding the MSY, even when UNCLOS was negotiated, led to it being eventually supplemented by other reference points, which are deemed to be more sustainable as a management target. Under UNCLOS, states shall base their measures on the 'best scientific evidence available'. Article 119 therefore also establishes the standard of scientific evidence relating to conservation measures on the high seas. As in the case of the corresponding paragraph[59] under the EEZ regime, states are to employ the 'best scientific evidence available',[60] This standard is relative and imposes no obligation upon the states concerned to update or upgrade the scientific evidence that is available. Therefore conservation measures are not subject to the conclusion of intensive scientific research investigating cases of alleged overexploitation of particular fish stocks.[61] UNCLOS distinguishes between conservation goals for harvestable species as opposed to others applicable to dependant and associated species.[62] With respect to the latter, it obligates States whose nationals fish on the high seas:

> . . . to take into consideration the effects on species associated with or dependent upon harvested species with a view to maintaining or restoring populations of such associated or dependent species at levels that do not seriously threaten their reproduction.[63]

Furthermore, UNCLOS requires[64] states to make an effort to acquire information about associated and dependent species and to take into consideration effects upon them. This implies, for example, the promotion of selective fishing gear, although at times even non-selective gear may have little effect on incidentally caught species.[65] The conservation goal for associated and dependent species sets a very different standard than for target species. So, whatever measures are taken, these should be tailored to specific situations and could be used to prohibit various types of gear such as purse seines, trawls and driftnets that are non-selective and lead to the incidental catching of non-target species. This conservation goal is important for two major reasons: first because it evokes an ecosystem approach where conservation is no longer only directed towards harvestable species, and secondly, as will be discussed later, it also shows that the UNCLOS provisions support a species-based approach for more effective conservation results.[66]

Conservation of living resources under UNCLOS Part VII does not specifically mention the marine habitat and all the components of its biodiversity. In Part XII the Convention establishes that states have the obligation to protect and preserve the marine environment[67] and that they have the right to exploit their natural resources pursuant to their environmental policies and in accordance with this duty.[68] Furthermore, it lays down that measures taken in accordance with this Part shall include those necessary to protect and preserve rare or fragile ecosystems as well as the habitat of depleted, threatened or endangered species and other forms of marine life.[69] This paragraph was placed in an article dealing mainly with marine pollution control and it may be argued that it does not necessarily apply to the whole range of human activities, including fisheries, which may cause harm. However, if interpreted within the context of its opening provisions, Part XII deals with the protection and preservation of the marine environment and not only with the prevention of marine pollution. Article 196 in fact seems to adopt this wider view as it obligates states to take measures to prevent the introduction of new or alien species. Additionally, article 206, expressing the duty to assess potential effects of planned activities under the jurisdiction or control of a state, is to be invoked if a state has reasonable grounds to believe that such activities may cause substantial pollution 'or significant changes to the marine environment'. These provisions substantiate the view that Part XII is wider in scope and regulates other anthropogenic activities that may cause harm to the marine environment and consequently have a negative impact upon the conservation of its living resources. A specific link between Parts VII and XII (as there is between Part VII and Part V) would have been more appropriate to stress an ecosystem and integrated approach. However, under UNCLOS, states are to exercise the freedoms of the high seas subject to the provisions of the Convention and other rules of international law[70] so they are duty bound to observe Part XII in its entirety even when exercising their freedom of fishing. Similarly, the implementation of article 119 on conservation on the high seas cannot be isolated from the other provisions in section 2 of Part VII and the rest of the Convention. An assessment of the applicable UNCLOS provisions on conservation cannot be complete unless one discusses how the legal implications of the term and the methodology associated therewith further developed under the post-UNCLOS sources of international law and via the species-based approach which derives from the cross reference that article 116 of the 1982 Convention makes to the rights, duties and interests of coastal states with respect to certain species.

3.2.3 Conservation under Post-UNCLOS Developments

By the time UNCLOS was opened for signature, international law had evolved to bestow upon the coastal state an exclusive sovereign right to access, exploit and conserve living resources occurring within its declared EEZ.[71] The extension of coastal state jurisdiction relied on national self interest and, generally speaking, did not instil cooperation to ensure the rational and sustainable use of resources to secure their conservation. As a result, the 1982 Convention sought to establish a balance of rights between coastal and flag states in order to ensure that its provisions provide for the conservation of living resources both on the high seas and in marine areas subject to coastal state jurisdiction, particularly in the EFZ and the EEZ. UNCLOS emphasizes inter-state cooperation for the purpose of conservation since a long list of marine species[72] are shared across boundaries and international areas[73] and so are still subject to the high seas legal regime either because they occur outside national jurisdiction or because they migrate between areas within and outside the high seas.

In the years between the conclusion of UNCLOS and its coming into force[74] there was a new impetus to revive inter-state cooperation through fisheries agreements and organizations. Scientific and academic bodies like the IUCN, as well as NGOs, played a crucial role in increasing awareness on the precarious state of the marine environment. This spurred various intergovernmental fora to address conservation on the high seas more thoroughly and consistently. The IUCN work was rather influential in generating more ecocentric conservation principles whilst UNCLOS was in the making. The 1976 IUCN Resolution[75] on *Principles Replacing Maximum Sustainable Yield as a Basis for the Management of Wildlife Resources* requires that ecosystems should be maintained in such a manner that both consumptive and non-consumptive values could be realized on a continuing basis, ensuring maintenance of both present and future options. According to these non-legally binding principles, states should aim at minimizing the risk of irreversible change or long-term adverse effects whilst exercising caution to allow for limitation of knowledge and any shortcomings in management. Monitoring and assessment should be made both at the planning stage and during the use of a resource. The IUCN Principles also call for transparency and exchange of information with the general public. Furthermore, the IUCN World Conservation Strategy of 1980[76] drew attention to the urgent need of conservation of the world's ecosystem, including the marine ecosystem as an integral part of economic and social development to save diversity and the sustainable utilization of species and ecosystems. It did not suggest the prohibition of their use and exploitation but prescribed that states had to determine what form and level exploitation efforts had to abide by in order to meet these conservatory requirements. The 1980s were a crucial period in the development of international political awareness on sustainable resource management. The World Commission on Environment and Development (WCED) headed by Gro Harlem Brundtland, then prime Minister of Norway, was set up as an independent body in 1983 by the United Nations. It was asked to re-examine the state of the environment and development problems on the planet and to formulate realistic proposals to address these issues.[77] The legal experts of the WCED defined conservation in general terms as:

> . . . the management of human use of a natural resource or the environment in such a manner that may yield the greatest sustainable benefit to present generations while maintaining its potential to meet the needs and aspirations of future generations. It embraces the preservation, maintenance, sustainable utilization, restoration and enhancement of a natural resource or the environment.[78]

The WCED, however, did not provide a list of specific measures that are required to achieve this objective.

Any developments that occurred in the post UNCLOS era regarding the obligation to conserve living resources on the high seas need to be discussed also in the light of soft law instruments such as applicable General Assembly Resolutions, Agenda 21, the Johannesburg Programme of Implementation and the Cancun Conference on Responsible Fishing Process. These non-binding instruments have influenced the conclusion of major post UNCLOS treaties like the CBD, the FSA and the FAO Compliance Agreement. Most of the conservation principles, concepts and methodologies emerging from these sources of soft and hard law are included in the FAO Code of Conduct for Responsible Fisheries.[79] As its name indicates, the Code is a non-legally binding instrument which provides a list of conservation measures for living resources on the high seas that are considered by the drafters of the Code to constitute 'best practice'.[80]

3.2.4 The Post-UNCLOS Treaties

After UNCLOS, the conservation of marine living resources on the high seas was further elaborated upon in three major multilateral treaties, namely the CBD, the FSA and the FAO Compliance Agreement. Under these instruments conservation includes the sustainable use of the targeted stock, taking into consideration the incidental catch, the precautionary approach, the collection and exchange of scientific data, inter-state cooperation, the ecosystem approach to address the depletion of biodiversity, as well as the degradation of the marine ecosystem and the adoption of specific conservation measures according to the species-based approach. Under these conventions the interpretation of the term conservation is influenced by the concept of sustainable development which requires the integration of socio-economic and environmental concerns in all anthropogenic activities. In turn, regional fisheries agreements, regional seas agreements and other applicable conservation treaties have been reviewed to reflect these developments. The ultimate test, however, lies with state practice which determines whether there is acquiescence to these developments in the definition, goals and methodology of conservation. Although it can be assumed that conservation as an obligation has in fact been further elaborated upon since UNCLOS, one needs to evaluate whether the current regimes for the protection of living marine resources beyond national jurisdiction are more stringent in the sense of providing more effective legal conservation measures and goals than those established under the 1982 Convention. The trend in state practice has avoided the use of the word *preservation* and refers instead to the terms *conservation* and *sustainable use.* The related management concepts to achieve these aims have proved difficult to decipher and have not received universal endorsement. More elaborate legal obligations have not necessarily resulted in the achievement of more effective conservation goals because, in practice, competing states in a high seas fishery or coastal and distant water fishing states may not have necessarily adopted identical or at least compatible measures. The MSY, for instance, has been qualified under UNCLOS and disregarded in other Conventions[81] in favour of a more ecocentric conservation goal which also integrates other factors besides biological characteristics. Nevertheless, states still continue to disagree about catch level and, in practice, there has not been the improvement one expects given the advances in legal terminology embodied in treaties and soft law instruments.

(i) The CBD

The 1992 CBD was the first attempt to establish a more comprehensive and inclusive regime for the conservation of biodiversity *per se*.[82] It recognizes its intrinsic value but allows for sustainable use of biological resources. In its preamble the CBD acknowledges that the fundamental requirement for conservation of biodiversity is the conservation of ecosystems and natural habitats and the maintenance and recovery of viable populations of species in their natural surroundings. Integrated management and strengthening cooperation at all levels are key considerations in the CBD. Although it deals with biodiversity from all sources, the CBD Conference of the Parties singled out marine biodiversity as one of the main areas upon which the CBD Parties should focus.[83] The relevance of this Convention for the purpose of this book is that it incorporates emerging conservation principles and strategies that have evolved in the last decades of the twentieth century. The final text of the Convention was approved by consensus. The influence of the CBD[84] upon the obligations arising from UNCLOS is sometimes described as marginal, due to the fact that it expressly excludes components of biological diversity from its scope with respect to areas beyond national jurisdiction.[85] In such areas the CBD only provides for parties to regulate processes and activities carried out under their jurisdiction or control.[86] Parties to it therefore must regulate fishing activities carried out by vessels flying their flag and their nationals accordingly. As we shall see below, however, there are more subtle legal repercussions upon parties and in an indirect manner even upon non-parties.

The Convention[87] distinguishes between the application of its provisions upon the components of biodiversity found within the territory of a state party and between those activities carried out by parties under their jurisdiction or control regardless of where their effects occur. In the former case, parties are obligated to protect the components of biodiversity in the territory subject to their jurisdiction according to the obligations of the Convention, and in the latter case they are to comply with the provisions of the Convention when carrying out activities and processes under their jurisdiction and control even in areas beyond their jurisdiction.[88] Fishing on the high seas constitutes an example of the latter category. Therefore, a party must comply with the obligations of the CBD both as a coastal state and as a high seas fishing state, and must seek to achieve two of the main objectives of the CBD: the conservation of biodiversity and the sustainable use of its components.[89] The CBD's provisions, applicable within national jurisdictions, are highly relevant for the conservation of living resources on the high seas. These would impose binding obligations upon the coastal state parties with respect to the conservation and management of the living resources in their EEZ. The application of CBD obligations by its parties in their EEZ is influential in a species-specialized regime which requires compatibility and cooperation when states adopt conservation measures between areas subject to and beyond national jurisdiction, particularly in the case of anadromous and catadromous species, straddling stocks, HMS and sedentary species as well as marine mammals.

The CBD requires Parties to develop national strategies, plans or programmes for conservation and rational use of living resources. It also obligates them to adapt existing ones to reflect the Convention's objectives integrating conservation and sustainable use into relevant sectoral or cross-sectoral plans, programmes and policies.[90] Parties are to identify the components of biodiversity important for conservation and use, indicated generally in the list under Annex I.[91] These must be monitored, particularly those requiring urgent conservation measures and those having the greatest potential for sustainable use. The CBD recognizes:

> . . . the sovereign right of States to exploit their own resources within their territory, pursuant to their own environmental policies, subject to ensuring that activities within their jurisdiction or control do not cause harm to other States or areas beyond jurisdictional limits.[92]

In other words, state parties must use living resources in their EEZ and other areas, subject to national jurisdiction such as estuaries and archipelagic waters, in a manner which does not negatively affect the conservation of these resources on the high seas.[93] On the basis of this provision, failure to abide by these conservation measures should give rise to international legal responsibility for harm caused to the species in areas subject to the jurisdiction of other states and of global areas such as the high seas. Another way in which the CBD may influence the regime on the conservation of high seas living resources is via its interpretation of the term *sustainable use*.[94] As already pointed out, sustainable use has become synonymous with conservation ever since the conclusion of Agenda 21 at UNCED. The CBD establishes various legal obligations (albeit in generic terms) that parties must observe to ensure the sustainable use of the components of biodiversity. These include: monitoring of use, management of resources observing biological unity, adopting a holistic ecosystem approach, restoring depleted stocks, adopting a precautionary and integrated approach, ensuring inter-generational equity, and basing measures on scientific research.

Freedom of fishing under UNCLOS is subject to any treaty obligations high seas fishing states may have.[95] Both flag states and coastal states that are parties to the CBD would therefore be required to interpret their obligation to conserve living resources on the high seas or in their EEZ respectively in accordance with the parameters stipulated under the CBD, even if this means going beyond the standards of conservation laid down by UNCLOS. It is not clear to what extent current state practice has integrated the CBD's objectives when implementing the UNCLOS conservation regime, and so non-parties may not be bound by the more recent developments brought about by the 1992 Convention. Nevertheless, flag states which are not parties may still be indirectly affected by the CBD provisions if their nationals fish on the high seas adjacent to coastal states that are parties. This can happen because, when deciding on the conservation measures the flag states need to adopt under UNCLOS, they would need to cooperate with the coastal state or states particularly when they harvest HMS and straddling stocks. The CBD has 193 state parties, apart from the European Community.[96] On paper this should mean that states have acquiesced to the further elaboration of the obligation to conserve as introduced by the Convention. A constant overview of the integration of UNCLOS and the CBD provisions is essential, and to a certain extent it is being carried out by the United Nations Commission for Sustainable Development (UNCSD) which has an *ad hoc* working group on oceans and seas. This Commission assesses the implementation of the CBD indirectly since it is entrusted with the implementation of Agenda 21 whose requirements were addressed by the CBD. An *ad hoc* committee has also been set up by the Conference of the Parties of both Conventions to assess harmonization and integration between the two regimes. The work of the CBD Conference of the Parties and its Subsidiary Body on Scientific, Technical and Technological Advice (SBSTTA)[97] is a step in the right direction and constitutes evidence of the impetus to harmonize the compendium of obligations addressing the conservation of marine living resources emerging from various sources, in order to integrate them.

Apart from the CBD, the FSA is doubtlessly one of the most influential MEAs since UNCLOS when it comes to the conservation of living resources on the high seas but, since it relates to HMS and straddling stocks, it will be discussed further on in Chapter 4. The 1993 FAO Compliance Agreement[98] was formulated, as its name indicates, to ensure compliance with internationally-agreed conservation and management measures by fishing vessels on the high seas. This Agreement defines them as:

> . . . measures to conserve or manage one or more species of living marine resources that are adopted and applied in accordance with the relevant rules of international law as reflected in the 1982 United Nations Convention on the Law of the Sea. Such measures may be adopted either by global, regional, or subregional fisheries organizations subject to the rights and obligations of their members or by treaties or other International agreements.[99]

The Agreement sheds no light on what the specific content of these measures should be but only states that these must be *compatible* with relevant rules of international law as reflected in UNCLOS. This raises doubts as to whether the FAO Compliance Agreement includes emerging post-UNCLOS conservation management concepts, such as the precautionary approach, that were not considered in the 1982 Convention, even though it recalls Agenda 21 and the Declaration of Cancun on Responsible Fishing in its preamble. In actual fact, however, the Agreement is more oriented towards elaborating and promoting flag state responsibility over fishing vessels and the exchange of information on the high seas to address compliance with conservation and management measures rather than with conservation measures themselves. Its relevance to this discussion on the legal implications of conservation is therefore limited.

The complexities and the various polarized positions do not render the process of integrating and harmonizing the various conservation obligations in applicable treaties an easy task. Apart from various fisheries agreements protecting marine species, there are also MEAs such as CITES where all cetaceans and some other marine mammals are listed in CITES Appendix I and thus banned from trade. Some specific treaties like the Bonn and Berne Conventions, the Conventions on Antarctic Seals and Sea Turtles, list as protected various marine mammals and other marine species. So do various other treaties such as the African Convention on Conservation of Nature and Natural Resources in South East Area, the ASEAN Agreement,[100] and the UNEP Regional Seas Programmes, which have generated Protocols on the conservation of marine biodiversity that apply also to areas beyond national jurisdiction. Other examples include measures adopted by the IMO pursuant to Part XII of UNCLOS. The CBD is also influencing the IMO agenda. Amongst the subjects that IMO is addressing are over-exploitation of marine living resources and the destruction of the marine habitat. All these efforts in international fora demonstrate that the harmonization of the obligations in the CBD with those that already occur within the scope of existing conventions[101] enjoys widespread support by CBD state parties and the parties of other related Conventions. This is highly significant when assessing state practice, given the widespread adherence to these Conventions. It demonstrates that states consider it necessary to ensure better coordination and to avoid conflicting interpretation. The reason why these regimes evolved *ad hoc* and in parallel to one another is not incidental but is rather the effect of polarized political and commercial interests which unfortunately persist.[102] However, after decades of state practice, there is some genuine effort to integrate the various regimes to ensure stability and effective results when combating over-exploitation of marine living resources. This has been highlighted in the FAO's report on *Ecosystem-Based Management of Fisheries; Opportunities and Challenges for Coordination between Regional Fishery Bodies and Regional Seas Conventions*,[103] which proposed, amongst other things, an exercise where ecosystem objectives are defined in parallel to current conservation measures that are prevalent in the management of fisheries.

(ii) The FSA

The FSA is doubtlessly one of the most influential MEAs since UNCLOS. Although it is not compulsory for UNCLOS Parties to ratify the FSA, the treaty was concluded by consensus and its parties include both high seas fishing states and coastal states.[104] Whether the FSA provisions codify or generate norms of customary international law is open to interpretation. *Prima facie* it may be so, given that it is an 'Implementation Agreement' which gives substance to the UNCLOS provisions that require coastal states and flag states to enter into cooperation agreements.[105] The norm-creating status of the FSA, however, still needs to be tested. It has to be stressed, however, that the FSA conservation regime does not address *all* types of fisheries but only straddling stocks and HMS when these occur between the areas falling under the EEZ of coastal states and the adjacent high seas. Straddling stocks, however, may also include marine mammals, anadromous species or species listed as HMS[106] under UNCLOS. The FSA exempts stocks occurring in one EEZ and/or which straddle different EEZs. There are, in fact, only some obligations under the FSA that regulate stocks within the EEZ[107] and which, therefore, impose obligations upon the coastal state when adopting conservation and management measures. Consequently, any effect the FSA may have generated upon state practice cannot be automatically considered to apply to the conservation of living marine resources on the high seas in general. For this reason, its impact on the conservation of living resources on the high seas is discussed in detail in Chapter 4 which is dedicated to the species-based approach to conservation. The FSA has played a pivotal role even within the context of this general discussion on the juridical evolution of the obligation to take conservation measures on the high seas, as it refers to the MSY as a limit reference point.[108] The MSY, which under UNCLOS and other legal instruments serves as an internationally agreed benchmark that determines overfishing, is no longer a target reference point under the FSA, a management goal which serves as a limit that needs to be applied *together with* the precautionary approach, the minimization of waste and bycatch, the prevention of excess capacity and the protection of biodiversity.

(iii) The FAO Compliance Agreement

The 1993 FAO Compliance Agreement[109] was formulated, as its name indicates, to ensure compliance with internationally-agreed conservation and management measures by fishing vessels on the high seas. This Agreement defines them as:

> . . . measures to conserve or manage one or more species of living marine resources that are adopted and applied in accordance with the relevant rules of international law as reflected in the 1982 United Nations Convention on the Law of the Sea. Such measures may be adopted either by global, regional, or subregional fisheries organizations subject to the rights and obligations of their members or by treaties or other International agreements[110].

The Agreement sheds no light on what the specific content of these measures should be but only declares that these must be *compatible* with relevant rules of international law as reflected in UNCLOS. This raises doubts as to whether the FAO Compliance Agreement includes emerging post-UNCLOS conservation management concepts such as the precautionary approach that was not considered in the 1982 Convention, even though in its preamble it recalls Agenda 21 and the Declaration of Cancun on Responsible Fishing. In actual fact, however, the Agreement is more oriented towards elaborating and promoting flag state responsibility over fishing vessels and the exchange of information on the high seas to address compliance with conservation and management measures rather than with conservation measures themselves. Its relevance to this discussion on the legal implications of conservation is therefore limited.

3.2.5 The Effects of 'Soft Law'

In 1991 the FAO Committee on Fisheries (COFI), at its 19th session, referred to undeniable evidence that world fisheries had become a market-driven, dynamically developing sector which was leading to unsustainable and uncontrolled exploitation of these living resources. It called for the development of new concepts that would lead to responsible, sustainable fisheries in order to ensure their conservation and take stock of related environmental considerations. Following the COFI meeting, the Cancun International Conference on Responsible Fishing was held in 1992, before UNCED. The Cancun Conference requested the FAO to prepare an International Code of Conduct for Responsible Fisheries that would address these concerns. Via its Declaration, the Cancun Conference provided an important contribution to UNCED and Agenda 21, particularly with respect to Chapter 17 of the latter. The Code of Conduct was eventually developed and unanimously adopted by the 29th FAO General Conference on 31 October 1995 with the objective of providing the necessary framework for national and international efforts to ensure sustainable exploitation of aquatic living resources in harmony with the environment. The FAO committed itself to assist member states in the efficient implementation of the Code of Conduct for Responsible Fisheries, and to report upon progress achieved to the UN.

Agenda 21, in its Chapter 17,[111] asserts that the marine environment, including the oceans and all the seas and adjacent coastal areas, form an integrated whole that is an essential part of the global-life support system which also presents opportunities for sustainable development. The Agenda recognizes that UNCLOS serves as a basis to 'pursue protection and sustainable development of the marine and coastal environment'[112] but does not hesitate to 'require new approaches to marine and coastal management and development at the national, subregional and global levels that are integrated in content and are precautionary and anticipatory in ambit'. Agenda 21 affirms the inadequacy of the UNCLOS provisions to address sustainability of the high seas fisheries[113] and identifies sustainable use and conservation of high seas living resources as one of its Programme Areas. It sets various objectives[114] and lays down the methodology[115] to reach them. The UN Commission for Sustainable Development (CSD) was set up at UNCED to review progress in the implementation of Agenda 21 and consequently Chapter 17. It noted its relevance to marine biodiversity and reiterated the need of an integrated (ecosystem) and precautionary approach, taking into account the best available scientific knowledge while stressing the importance of international cooperation.

The Johannesburg Plan of Implementation[116] affirms that,

> Oceans, seas, islands and coastal areas form an integrated and essential component of the Earth's ecosystem and are critical for global food security and for sustaining economic prosperity and the well-being of many national economies, particularly in developing countries.[117]

It thereby adopts an integrated approach towards ensuring the sustainable development of the oceans and requires 'effective coordination and cooperation, including at the global and regional levels, between relevant bodies, and actions at all levels.'[118] It calls for the establishment of 'an effective, transparent and regular inter-agency coordination mechanism on ocean and coastal issues within the United Nations system.'[119]

To achieve sustainable fisheries, it requires states to maintain or restore stocks to levels that can produce the MSY with the aim of achieving these goals for depleted stocks on an urgent basis and, where possible, not later than 2015. It is rather surprising that the Johannesburg Plan of Implementation refers to the MSY as a means to achieve sustainable fisheries. It is retrogressive vis-à-vis UNCLOS because the 1982 Convention does not mandate the MSY in the same unqualified terms as does the 2002 Implementation Plan. The Johannesburg Plan calls upon States to ratify the FSA and the FAO Compliance Agreement as well as to endorse the Code of Conduct for Responsible Fisheries and the FAO Guidelines to develop and implement national and regional action plans.[120] It also urges states to establish effective monitoring, reporting and enforcement and control of fishing vessels even by flag states. The Johannesburg Plan of Action encourages relevant regional fisheries management organizations and arrangements to give due consideration to the rights, duties and interests of coastal states and the special requirements of developing states when addressing the issue of the allocation of shares of fishery resources for straddling stocks and highly migratory fish stocks. It invites states to do so:

> . . . mindful of the provisions of the United Nations Convention on the Law of the Sea and the Agreement for the Implementation of the Provisions of the United Nations Convention on the Law of the Sea of 10 December 1982 relating to the Conservation and Management of Straddling Fish Stocks and Highly Migratory Fish Stocks, on the high seas and within exclusive economic zones.[121]

The Johannesburg Plan of Action also requires that states eliminate subsidies that contribute to illegal, unreported and unregulated fishing and to over-capacity, and urges states to complete the efforts undertaken at the World Trade Organization to clarify and improve its disciplines on fisheries subsidies, taking into account the importance of this sector to developing countries.

The FAO Code of Conduct for Responsible Fisheries is voluntary and not a source of law *per se*. Although certain parts of it are based on relevant rules of international law, including those reflected under UNCLOS,[122] it cannot be considered as legally binding, and since it is a

Code of Practice it is at most an instrument of soft law. The FAO Code also has provisions that 'may be or have already been given binding effect by means of other obligatory legal instruments amongst the Parties', and as an example it quotes the FAO Compliance Agreement that forms an integral part of the Code.[123] However, the Code is definitely not a treaty, and so it cannot be said to be a codification exercise of existing sources of international law. It may be considered as a source of evidence of the predominant trends that are applied for the conservation of living resources, including those occurring on the high seas, especially as it incorporates under its provisions conservation and management concepts that emerge from other post-UNCLOS treaties such as the CBD and the FSA. When listing its objectives, the Code includes the establishment of principles 'in accordance with the relevant rules of International law for responsible fishing and fisheries activities'[124] and to serve as:

> . . . an instrument of reference to help States to establish and improve the legal and institutional framework for the exercise of responsible fisheries and the formulation and implementation of appropriate measures.[125]

Within this context the Code may be seen as the latest exercise in re-evaluating the international regime regulating fisheries law,[126] and its provisions may be perceived as a *resumé* of contemporary state practice in the field. Its non-normative nature is highlighted so much so that it refers to obligatory legal instruments 'amongst the Parties'[127] and adds that 'the Code is to be interpreted and applied in conformity with the relevant rules of International law as reflected by UNCLOS and that nothing in this code prejudices the rights, jurisdiction and duties of States under UNCLOS'.[128]

In the provisions addressing the relationship with other international instruments[129] the Code states that it relies on other sources of conservation law besides UNCLOS,[130] and refers to the *applicable rules* of international law and not only to treaty obligations of state parties. The general principles in fact reflect this integrated approach and include conservation measures that incorporate concepts from both UNCLOS and post-UNCLOS developments. For instance, the obligation to take conservation measures as a concomitant obligation to the right of freedom of fishing is followed by another provision which establishes that:

> . . . fisheries management should promote the maintenance of quality, diversity and availability of fisheries resources in sufficient quantities for present and future generations[131]

The term 'fisheries management' used in the Code clearly incorporates elements from the CBD and Agenda 21. The Code also refers to the prevention of overfishing and excess of fishing capacity, specifying that management measures should ensure that the effort is commensurate with the productive capacity of fishery resources and their sustainable utilization. The Code provides an example of how obligations emerging under UNCLOS may be harmonized with post-UNCLOS developments, as found in article 6(4) which lays down that conservation and management measures should be based on the best scientific evidence available taking into consideration economic, social and environmental factors. Furthermore, states, as well as regional and subregional fishery organizations, are to apply a precautionary approach widely to conservation, management and exploitation taking into account the best scientific evidence available to conserve target, associated, dependent and non-target species and their environment. The Code reiterates that absence of available scientific information should not be used as a reason to postpone the taking of such conservation measures. These provisions clearly reflect a merger between UNCLOS articles 61 and 119 as well as the FSA articles on the precautionary approach, and the wider ecosystem approach found under both the FSA and the CBD. The Code proposes habitat conservation as an intrinsic aspect of both conservation and management of these species. Specific reference is made to selective and environmentally safe fishing gear.[132] States are not only urged to develop such gear and to apply it to maintain biodiversity, but the Code also recommends that where such practices exist these should be recognized by states and accorded priority in establishing conservation and management measures for fisheries. The Code urges the minimization of waste, catch of non-target species both for fish and non-fish species, and impacts upon associated and dependent species.[133] In the articles on fisheries management[134] and fisheries operations,[135] the Code attempts to elaborate upon these general principles and identifies the need for long-term conservation and sustainable use of fisheries resources at levels which promote their optimum utilization and maintain their availability. Again, this is clearly an attempt to consider UNCLOS principles in the light of developments highlighted in another soft law instrument, namely Agenda 21. The Code paraphrases UNCLOS article 119(1)(a) on the qualified MSY and recommends that short term considerations should not compromise these objectives.[136] It also proposes that the long-term sustainable use of fisheries is the overriding objective of their conservation and management. The Code suggests an inclusive list of management measures meant to achieve a maximum sustainable yield as qualified under UNCLOS. It does so in a manner which reflects and incorporates more recent developments such as the integration of environmental, social and economic concerns. These include the avoidance of excess fishing capacity, the retaining of the economic viability of stock exploitation and the promotion of responsible fisheries under those economic conditions under which fisheries operate. The need to promote stakeholders' participation as an essential tool for sustainable development, as envisaged by Agenda 21, is also reflected in the Code's recommendation to take into account the interests of fishermen[137] when taking management measures. The Code also promotes the ecosystem approach addressing target, non-target, dependent and associated species, whether they are fish or non-fish. It also suggests an integrated approach since it provides that management measures should also aim for biodiversity conservation, the recovery and restoration of depleted stocks, and the minimization of other harmful anthropogenic activities.

The Code provides a detailed procedure and recommended approach:

> To be effective, fisheries management should be concerned with the whole stock unit over its entire area of distribution and take into account previously agreed management measures established and applied in the same region, all removals and biological unity and other biological characteristics of the stock. The best scientific evidence available should be used to determine, inter alia, the area of distribution of the resource and the area through which it migrates during its life cycle.[138]

Above all, this paragraph of the Code sheds light on how a controversial provision under UNCLOS could be interpreted, namely, that new entrants cannot use the freedom of fishing to disregard existing conservation and management measurements in a high seas fishery. Conservation measures can be used as a non-tariff trade barrier to trade or as an obstacle to the freedom of fishing in the sense of limiting access by a state or a handful of states. UNCLOS article 119(3) establishes that states shall ensure that conservation measures and their implementation do not discriminate in form or fact against fishermen of any state. This provision is often interpreted literally and can thus render null any conservation regime which imposes stricter measures than the general customary rule in order to take the necessary conservation measures on the high seas. The Code shows how it must also be interpreted in the light of the other provisions of UNCLOS.

The major cases of alleged *discrimination* on the high seas may arise as a result of straddling stocks, which involves the negotiation of a conservation regime with all states involved in the fishery, whether these be coastal or high seas fishing states. It may also occur in the case of an existing high seas conservation regime which has to deal with new entrants. In the case of straddling stocks, article 119(3) should be interpreted in the light of articles 63(2) and 116 that subject high seas fishing states to the rights of the coastal state. A new entrant is obligated to comply with the conservation measures deemed 'necessary' by the coastal states in whose EEZ the straddling stocks also occur. This conservation regime imposed on the new entrant cannot be termed as 'discriminatory' since it is imposed by the 1982 Convention itself. The entrant has a right for its nationals to fish, but, if it refuses to accept the existing regime and whatever quotas it allocates, the new entrant would inevitably diminish the share of the earlier participants upsetting the viability of the previously established regime. Discrimination cannot be used to challenge the fact that a new entrant must respect and accept previous arrangements among which are those involving allocation of catch. This provision of the Code is therefore proposing that, under the high seas regime, prior participants are to be allowed to impose certain burdens on the new entrant to reflect the fact that additional fishing imposes a cost on prior participants and further burdens on the stock; otherwise the conservation regime will collapse.[139]

The Code reflects the FSA and lays down that states fishing for straddling stocks, HMS and high seas fish stocks are to adopt compatible measures[140] throughout their range. It says that 'compatibility should be achieved in a manner consistent with the rights, competences and interests of the States concerned'.[141] It even goes beyond the FSA provisions and proposes such compatibility as a necessary conservation for *all* high seas fish stocks. However, it does not elaborate upon the role of the coastal state in ensuring compatibility as the FSA does in the case of straddling stocks and HMS. Despite its non-binding status, the Code remains a particularly useful instrument as it provides a harmonized outlook of the various legal implications of the term conservation that have evolved over time, as these were codified by UNCLOS, and how they continued to develop and to generate emerging management concepts since the 1982 Convention came into force. It managed to provide an *exposé* of the various elements that constitute a conservation regime in a harmonious manner and in specific terms.

3.3 CONCLUSION

This general overview on the legal implications of the term 'conservation', as applied generally to all living marine resources occurring beyond national jurisdiction, demonstrates that management measures must primarily devise guarantees for sustainable use to ensure that resources maintain a good conservation status. A sound conservation regime must also identify whoever bears responsibility through prescriptive and prohibitory rules to achieve this. Such measures are required to prevent a level of threat which endangers the survival of the species or otherwise depletes its stocks. Above all, conservation obligations should aim at ensuring the sustainability of a common resource. In the case of harvestable species, management measures should aim at equitable exploitation to achieve optimum utilization;[142] this is considered to be the best form of use in the interest of all participants. Conservation also aims at maintaining a favourable status with respect to all other species, whether they are dependent, associated or otherwise part of the marine ecosystem. The most recent developments since UNCED and the conclusion of the CBD portray the need for conservation of species for their own intrinsic value, and this as a duty pertaining to all states. Judging by the latest inclusion of this concept in treaties and in instruments of soft law like Ministerial Declarations, UN Resolutions and the FAO Code of Conduct for Responsible Fisheries, state practice indicates support for this integrated view in general terms but shows great caution when it comes to discerning the legal implications it would have upon other regimes such as freedom of fishing on the high seas. The situation becomes even more complex because conservation as an obligation has also been further developed from a species-based perspective, as will be discussed in the next chapter. International treaties elaborate upon the basic obligation for states to take conservation measures on the high seas. These treaties may be considered as the *lex posterior* that does away with the discretion that UNCLOS and customary international law allows to flag states. Instead, these treaties provide objectives, standards and methodologies that states must subscribe to, in order to fulfil their conservation obligations. The treaties aim to harmonize the legal implications of the obligation amongst parties and, as discussed above, may even influence indirectly the behaviour of non-parties. In this sense they are themselves an exercise in achieving better consistency and clarity when it comes to the interpretation of the general obligation to take conservation measures on the high seas. However, their success in facilitating harmonization depends upon their legal status, that is whether they are another source of international law or whether they have influenced it to the extent that states are legally obligated to go beyond unilateral acts solely dictated by their discretion and need instead of abiding by certain parameters. For this reason, any conflict in the interpretation of the obligation to take conservation measures and its application by flag states on the high seas is more likely to arise between different categories of sources under international law, namely between treaties and custom. The review of various fisheries agreements and the approximation of conservation measures referred to therein, along with the precautionary approach, the ecosystem approach and the integrated approach towards conservation, have indeed fine-tuned the general implications of the obligation to take conservation measures in such a way that parties to these treaties have little discretion in the manner they exercise this obligation. The effect of these legal sources as *lex posterior* may not yet be universally applied but, as their application may extend indirectly to non-parties, their impact upon state practice may be more far reaching than non-parties may wish to admit. Poor implementation is another matter, and it is intrinsic to the problem of compliance and enforcement that afflicts international law in general; in such cases the parties themselves may be as much to blame.

NOTES

1. Examples include the 1882 Convention on North Sea Overfishing and the 1911 Fur Seals Convention.
2. A definition of conservation measures was spelt out in article 2 of the 1958 Convention on Fishing and the Conservation of Living Resources on the High Seas; see below at note 14.
3. See Birnie, P., Boyle, A. and Redgwell, C. (2009), *International Law and the Environment*, 3rd edn, Oxford: Oxford University Press, p 647.
4. Multilateral agreements addressing marine pollution such as the International Convention for the Prevention of Pollution of the Sea by Oil, which was in force by 26 July 1958 (OILPOL) were negotiated separately from treaties addressing conservation of living resources on the high seas.
5. The three Geneva Conventions on the Law of the Sea, namely the Convention on Fishing and Living Resources of the High Seas, the Convention on the Continental Shelf and the Convention on the High Seas, all done in 1958, were a step in this direction. See Brownlie, I. (2003), *Principles of International Law*, 6th edn, Oxford: Oxford University Press, pp 223–45; Birnie, Boyle and Redgwell (2009), p 709 and Dupuys, R.J. and Vignes, D. (1991), *A Handbook on the New Law of the Sea*, Volume I, The Hague: Hague Academy of International Law, Martinus Nijhoff, p 385.
6. Examples of these efforts include: the 1972 Stockholm United Nations Conference on the Human Environment, the drawing up of the 1980 Earth Charter and the conclusion of some MEAs such as the 1973 Convention on International Trade in Endangered Species of Wild Fauna and Flora (CITES), the 1979 Bonn Convention on the Conservation of Migratory Species of Wild Animals, and the 1979 Berne Convention on the Conservation of European Wildlife and Natural Habitats; see also Birnie, Boyle and Redgwell (2009), pp 1–12.
7. See FAO *Review of the State of World Marine Fishery Resources*, FAO Fisheries Technical Paper No. 457 (Rome: FAO, 2005); see also Meltzer, E. (2009), *The Quest for Sustainable Fisheries*, Ottawa: NRC Research Press, pp 77–82.
8. UNCED was held from June 3 to June 14 1992, in Rio de Janeiro, Brazil. The conference was the culmination of two years of negotiations by the Preparatory Committees. Five major agreements on global environmental issues were signed. These included the Convention on Biological Diversity (CBD) and other agreements namely Agenda 21 and the Rio Declaration which were non-binding statements on the relationship between sustainable environmental practices and the pursuit of socio-economic development. Agenda 21 is a wide-ranging assessment of social and economic sectors with goals for improving environmental and developmental impact of each sector. The Rio Declaration summarizes the consensus achieved on principles of sustainable development.
9. In the early 1990s, disputes between states over certain valuable fish stocks were leading to various dramatic conflicts and inhibiting effective conservation. The 1992 Cancun Conference on Responsible Fishing, like the 1992 UNCED, was held to give a new boost to the international community's efforts to address the coordination of

conservation measures. At the multilateral level these efforts included the negotiation of two new treaties to regulate ocean fisheries, namely the 1993 FAO Compliance Agreement and the 1995 FSA. The FAO also adopted a comprehensive non-binding instrument, the 1995 Code of Conduct for Responsible Fisheries. The United Nations General Assembly established a moratorium on the use of large-scale driftnets on the high seas; this became effective in 1993. Other global instruments included, among others, four International Plans of Action (IPOAs) negotiated and adopted under FAO auspices dealing with fishing capacity, conservation and management of sharks, seabird bycatch and illegal, unreported and unregulated (IUU) fishing. See also Balton, D.A., *Managing Living Resources Multilaterally: Some Threshold Questions,* Conference on the Governance and Management of Deep Sea Fisheries, 1–5 December 2003, Queenstown, New Zealand, Part I, Conference reports (Ross Shotton, (ed)), FAO Rome, 2005.

10. Orrego Vicuna, F. (2003), *Le Droit de la Pêche en Haute Mer: Développement et Conservation des Resources, La Mer et Son Droit, Mélanges Offerts á Laurent Lucchini et Jean Pierre Quéneudec*, Paris: Pedone.
11. Directive 2008/56/EC of the European Parliament and of the Council of 17 June 2008 establishing a framework for community action in the field of marine environmental policy (Marine Strategy Directive) attempts to provide integrated marine spatial planning ensuring an ecosystem approach. See Juda, L. (2007), 'The European Union and ocean use management: The marine strategy and the marine policy', ODIL, **38** (3), 259–82.
12. These include management concepts and specific examples of conservation measures.
13. See Birnie, Boyle and Redgwell (2009), p 550.
14. See, however, article 2 of the 1958 Convention on Fishing and the Conservation of Living Resources on the High Seas, namely, 'the aggregate of the measures rendering possible the optimum sustainable yield from those resources so as to secure a maximum supply of food and other marine products. Conservation programmes should be formulated with a view to securing in the first place a supply of food for human consumption'. The definition is discussed above at. See also CCAMLR, which does not define the term but whose meaning is implied from the measures intended to achieve conservation. See also the 1979 Bonn Convention on the Conservation of Migratory Species of Wild Animals, Article 1, paras (b), (c), (d), which defines the conservation status of a migratory species as 'the sum of the influences acting on the migratory species that may affect its long-term distribution and abundance.' According to the Convention the 'Conservation status' will be taken as 'favourable' when '(1) population dynamics data indicate that the migratory species is maintaining itself on a long-term basis as a viable component of its ecosystems; (2) the range of the migratory species is neither currently being reduced, nor is likely to be reduced, on a long-term basis; (3) there is, and will be in the foreseeable future, sufficient habitat to maintain the population of the migratory species on a long-term basis; and (4) the distribution and abundance of the migratory species approach historic coverage and levels to the extent that potentially suitable ecosystems exist and to the extent consistent with wise wildlife management; and (d) 'Conservation status' will be taken as 'unfavourable' if any of the conditions set out in sub-paragraph (c) of this paragraph is not met.'
15. See below *Behring Sea (Fur Seal) Arbitration*, p 96 and the *Icelandic Fisheries Jurisdiction Cases*, pp 100–101. In both cases the adjudicating bodies refrained from defining the term although they acknowledged conservation as a concomitant obligation to fishing on the high seas.
16. See above at note 14. The 1982 UNCLOS does not define conservation and does not provide for specific conservation measures for the high seas regime as it does for instance under the EEZ regime where in article 62 it lists conservation measures that may be imposed by coastal states for vessels fishing in their EEZ. Part VII, however, prescribes the methodology that may be used for the utilization of living resources on the high seas in article 119.

17. See above at note 5.
18. Actually the term had been used even earlier. See Van Heijnsbergen (1997), *International Protection of Wild Flora and Fauna,* Thesis Universiteit van Amsterdam, Amsterdam: Asd. IOS Press, p 45, which refers to the use of the term 'conservation' in a treaty dating to 1781 between the King of France and the Prince Bishop of Basel.
19. Set up in 1902 and established by treaty since 1967, ICES is open to any state which is approved by its members. Although its scope is limited to the Atlantic Ocean and the adjacent seas, its aim is to promote and organize research for the study of living marine resources (as well as marine pollution) and then disseminate the results. It has acquired a reputation of offering independent and sound scientific advice that is sought by UN organizations such as FAO, IMO, UNEP and UNESCO.
20. See the *Behring Sea (Fur Seal) Arbitration* (1898), Moore's *International Arbitration Awards*, 1, 755 reproduced in *International Environmental Law Reports* (1999), 1, 43.
21. See Birnie, Boyle and Redgwell (2009), p 707, who affirm that the nine point plan is still a model for many fishery commissions.
22. See Gidel, G. (1932), *Le Droit International de la Mer en Temps de Paix,* Paris, p 69, who argues that directed against the exclusiveness of use the freedom of fishing on the high seas necessitates and resolves itself in equality of use. See also De Ferion, O. (1958), *'Le Droit de la Mer',* Paris: Droz, p 73, who notes the change in the perception of states with respect to the high seas freedoms in what was originally an attitude of abstention towards one another but that was to become an approach that ensures reasonable use of resources without compromising the right of access by all.
23. Dupuys and Vignes (1991), p 385; see also Orrego Vicuna, F. (2003).
24. Birnie, Boyle and Redgwell (2009), p 707.
25. See discussion in Chapter 4, p 146.
26. The decision and recommendations of the tribunal involved only two of the four states participating in sealing, and therefore Canadian and US vessel owners simply reflagged to the other two states, namely Japan and Russia, to avoid stricter conservation measures. Consequently, the depletion of the seal stocks continued until the situation became so drastic that a treaty was concluded between these four states in 1911 entitled the *Convention on Bering Sea Fur Seals*; 104 British and Foreign State Papers (1911) based on the arbitral award. In 1957, a new Convention, entitled the *Interim Convention on the North Pacific Fur Seals* replaced the 1911 treaty.
27. This aspect is discussed in detail in Chapter 6; see also Kwiatkowska, B. (1993), 'The High Seas Fisheries Regime: at a Point of No Return?', IJMC, 8(3), 327–58.
28. From http://www.st.nmfs.noaa.gov/st4/documents/FishGlossary.pdf. See also the OECD definition of MSY as 'the maximum use that a renewable resource can sustain without impairing its renewability through natural growth and replenishment'. Meltzer (2009), p 105 endnote 43 quotes a definition of the FAO on MSY as 'the highest theoretical equilibrium that can be continuously taken (on average) from a stock under existing (average) environmental conditions without significantly affecting reproductive success'. See Birnie, Boyle and Redgwell (2009), p 551 footnote 29, quoting a definition of MSY from Holt and Talbot (eds), *The Conservation of Wild Living Resources*, as, 'the greatest harvest that can be taken from a self-generating stock of animals year after year while maintaining the average size of the stock'.
29. See definition found at http://www.st.nmfs.noaa.gov/st4/documents/FishGlossary.pdf.
30. See De Klemm, C., in Johnson, D.M. (ed) (1981), *The Environmental Law of the Sea*, Berlin: IUCN Environmental Policy Paper No. 18, p 118, who remarks that it is ironic that international law insisted on relying on the MSY despite the scepticism surrounding the validity and accuracy of the concept for achieving a favourable conservation status. See also Burke, W.T, (1994), *The New International Law of Fisheries, UNCLOS and Beyond*, Oxford: Clarendon Press, pp 45–55.
31. See the 1958 Geneva Convention on Fishing and the Conservation of Living Resources on the High Seas, article 2.

32. Ibid.
33. The exercise of the high seas freedoms, which includes the freedom of fishing, were qualified in article 2 of the 1958 Geneva Convention on the High Seas and not in the 1958 Geneva Convention on Fishing and the Conservation of Living Resources on the High Seas.
34. Proclamation No. 2667 10, Federal Registry. 12, 303 (1945) established that the USA asserted jurisdiction and control over the resources located in maritime zones contiguous to the coast of the USA in order to ensure their conservation.
35. See O' Connell, D.P. (1983), *International Law of the Sea*, Vol I, Oxford: Oxford University Press, ch 14. See also Brownlie I. (2003), p 252, footnote 22.
36. See Harris, D.J. (2004), *Cases and Materials on International Law*, 6th edn, London: Sweet and Maxwell, p 466; Burke, W.T. (1994), p 31 et seq.; Attard, D.J. (1987), *The Exclusive Economic Zone in International Law*, Oxford: Oxford University Press, pp 1–3; Grzybowski, D.M. et al (ed), (1995), 'A Historical Perspective Leading Up To and Including the UN Convention on Straddling Fish Stocks and Highly Migratory Fish Stocks', *Pace Environmental Law Review*, **13** (1), Pace University School of Law, New York.
37. See UK Hydrographic Office Notice, January 1 2002 UK MIL, (2001) referred to in *The British Year Book of International Law*, p 634. In 1978, 23 states claimed a 200-mile EFZ and another 38 claimed EEZs. By 2002, 111 states, from various political groups, claimed a 200-mile EEZ without protest from other states.
38. See Burke (1994), p 39 who affirms that it is not inconsistent with the notion of sovereign rights that the coastal state has duties and obligations to their exercise and has the final right to exercise a claim.
39. See UNCLOS whose article 87(1)(e) identifies fishing as one of the freedoms on the high seas subject to the conditions laid down in section two of Part VII entitled *Conservation and Management of the Living Resources of the High Seas*. In its articles 117 to 119 it lays down further obligations addressing conservation on the high seas. In article 116 it subjects the freedom of fishing to the rights, duties and interests of coastal states, as embodied in articles 63(2), 64, 65, 66 and 67, which are also obligated under the Convention to conserve living resources in their EEZ.
40. See above at note 15.
41. Ibid. *Icelandic Fisheries Cases (UK v Iceland)*, ICJ Rep. (1974), at 31, para 72 and *Icelandic Fisheries Cases (Germany v Iceland)* ICJ Rep. (1974), at 200, para 64.
42. Ibid.
43. See Chapter 2 p 43 et seq; see also Byers, M. (1997), 'Conceptualizing the Relationship Between *Jus Cogens* and *Erga Omnes* Rules', *Nordic Journal of International Law*, 66, p 211.
44. See UNCLOS articles 61 and 62 under the EEZ regime (Part V) and articles 118 and 119 under the high seas regime (Part VII).
45. See UNCLOS article 119.
46. The anthropocentric approach persists to this day under the guise of developmental or commercial interests.
47. Particularly in articles 61 in respect of the EEZ regime and 119 in respect of the high seas regime.
48. In article 116 UNCLOS establishes that states have an obligation to adopt conservation measures, either unilaterally or via cooperation, when their nationals fish on the high seas. Additionally, in article 118 it establishes that states must cooperate in the conservation and management of living resources when their nationals harvest the same species or different species in the same area of the high seas.
49. See discussion above at p 104 et seq.
50. The problem for the coastal state is to decide what are safe limits on catch, who should get access and on what terms and the conditions upon which access should be granted. The obligation to establish an allowable catch by the coastal state in the EEZ is more apparent than real. See Burke (1994), pp 44–55. UNCLOS leaves it up to the

coastal state's discretion to determine the reference to declare a surplus and whether to allow foreign fishing in its EEZ. Regulating allowable catch is only one means of managing fishery exploitation; it is a method which encounters and creates serious problems.

51. *Almost* identical because whilst under the EEZ regime the coastal state must establish TAC, the wording under article 119 may be interpreted to make this an optional measure under the high seas regime.
52. See UNCLOS article 62(4).
53. See ibid, chapeau to article 119(1).
54. See ibid, article 119(1)(a).
55. This is defined as maintaining abundance at higher level than that associated with MSY; see below at note 58.
56. See Burke (1994), p 53. He quotes Ambassador McKernan of the USA who had written that the new concept 'requires the adjustment of the conservation regulations, seeking the average MSY so as to take into account environmental and economical factors as well as special requirements of developing countries (which represent the social aspect). In a practical sense this leads to a reduction in the total fishing effort on a particular stock of fish and maintaining on average a higher level of stock size with a reduced average annual yield from a fishery'.
57. See above p 104 et seq for a discussion on the definition of MSY as it originated in the 1955 UN International Technical Conference on the Conservation of the Living Resources of the Sea and how the term *optimum yield* was considered as more of a conservation goal since it integrated in its allowable catch a variety of other factors affecting the conservation status of the species.
58. See Meltzer (2009) p 84 who lists the following shortcomings: 'errors in estimation; uncertainty surrounding its exact value; its year to year variability; its negative properties in terms of stock stability and resilience and its lack of reference to the state of associated or dependent species or the resource habitat; its lack of relation to the cost of fishing and the inability to effectively implement the harvesting strategies based on FMSY'.
59. See UNCLOS article 61(2).
60. Ibid, article 119(1)(a).
61. This involves intensive investment in obtaining data and information on catch statistics, characteristics of the life history of the species, abundance, interrelationship with other species and with the entire ecosystem. Data of this sort is not easily obtained and it is often not comparable; it is also subject to different interpretations.
62. See UNCLOS article 119(2).
63. Ibid.
64. Ibid.
65. Fishing for tuna on the high seas, for example, has a relatively minor bycatch in the central and western Pacific whilst the bycatch in the eastern tropical Pacific was considerably minimized by changes in the trawl gear in that fishery.
66. See Oxman, B. (1995), 'Coastal states' competences over high seas fisheries and the changing role of international law comment,' *Zeitxhrift Fur Auslandisches Offentliches Recht Und Volkerrecht* **55**, 536.
67. See UNCLOS article 192.
68. Ibid, article 193.
69. Ibid, article 194(5).
70. Ibid, article 87.
71. The right of the coastal state to claim an EEZ of 200 nautical miles from its baselines referred to in UNCLOS under article 56 has been recognized as a rule of customary international law; see *Libya/Malta Continental Shelf*, ICJ Reports, 1985, p 13; 81 ILR, p 238. The EEZ is optional. States may choose not to claim an EEZ or only claim it in part; see Brownlie (2003), p 214.
72. Vide Burke (1994), p 83. There is a short list of species that are primarily found in the

high seas, such as cetaceans, seals, tuna, swordfish, billfish, horse mackerel, squid, pomfret, sharks and krill. A much longer list of species, however, move between the high seas and the coastal waters; examples include cod, salmon and tuna.

73. Hey, E. (1987), *The Regime for the Exploitation of Transboundary Marine Fisheries Resources*, Dordrecht: Martinus Nijhoff, p 77.
74. UNCLOS was concluded in 1982 and came into force in 1994.
75. IUCN Resolution No 8, 12th General Assembly of the IUCN, 1976.
76. Entitled *Caring for the Earth a Strategy for Sustainable Living* (Gland 1991). The Strategy was revised in 1991 to take into account developmental implications of environmental measures within the context of sustainable development according to Agenda 21 and related instruments.
77. The report produced by the WCED entitled '*Our Common Future*' was hailed as the most important document of the decade and paved the way for the organization of UNCED and the formulation of Agenda 21.
78. Munro and Lammers, Legal Experts Group Report (1986), *Environmental Protection and Sustainable Development*, London: Graham & Trotman/Dordrecht: Martinus Nijhoff.
79. The FAO Code of Conduct is not a legally binding instrument but includes various rules of international law.
80. The Code was unanimously adopted by the FAO Conference on 31 October 1995.
81. See discussion on CCAMLR below, Chapter 4 at p 178 et seq.
82. Zoi Varfis, C. (1994), 'La Conservation et l'Exploitation des Resources Biologiques Marins', in Dommen, C. and Cullet, P. (eds), *General Convention des nations Uniés sur le Droit de la Mer et la Conservation et l'Exploitation des Resources Biologiques Marines*, The Hague : Kluwer Law International, pp 95–122.
83. The Subsidiary Body on Scientific Technical and Technological (SBSTTA) is to advise it on aspects of conservation and sustainable use of biodiversity.
84. Negotiations for the CBD started in 1988 and were concluded in time for the document to be open for signature at UNCED in June 2008. It entered into force in December 1993. It is one of the most widely ratified of all the environmental conventions, with 191 ratifications by 31 December 2008. It can be defined as a framework Convention laying down various conservation principles on an international level. State parties can use these principles as a basis to adopt national law and policy whilst at the same time protocols may be added to it to substantiate its general obligations. In article 28 it specifically establishes that parties must cooperate in formulating protocols and then adopting them at a Conference of the parties.
85. See below at note 87.
86. Ibid.
87. See CBD article 4, on jurisdictional scope, which provides: 'Subject to the rights of other States, and except as otherwise expressly provided in this Convention, the provisions of this Convention apply, in relation to each Contracting Party: (a) In the case of components of biological diversity, in areas within the limits of its national jurisdiction; and (b) In the case of processes and activities, regardless of where their effects occur, carried out under its jurisdiction or control, within the area of its national jurisdiction or beyond the limits of national jurisdiction.'
88. Oxman, B. (1997), 'The International Commons, the International Public Interest and New Modes of International Law Making', in J. Delbrück, *New Trends in International Lawmaking: International 'Legislation' in the Public Interest*, Berlin: Ducker & Humblot, p 21.
89. The CBD in article 1 sets its three main objectives: the conservation of biodiversity, the sustainable use of its components, and the fair and equitable sharing of benefits arising from the utilization of genetic resources.
90. See CBD article 6 which is, however, qualified by the phrase 'only to the extent of their capabilities'.
91. Ibid, article 7.

92. Ibid, article 3.
93. It reiterates the wording of Principle 21 of the Stockholm Declaration at the 1972 UNCHE. The Rio Declaration further qualifies Principle 21 by including the State's right to use its natural resources in accordance with its developmental, besides environmental, policies. The CBD, however, followed the earlier version as expressed in Principle 21 of the Stockholm Declaration.
94. Defined in article 2 of the CBD as requiring, 'the use of biological diversity in a way that maintains its potential to meet the needs and aspirations of present and future generations'.
95. This obligation is clearly established under UNCLOS article 116(a).
96. As per information on http://www.cbd.int/ on 4 April 2012.
97. The SBSTTA is established under article 25 of the CBD as an open-ended intergovernmental scientific advisory body to provide the Conference of the Parties (COP) and, as appropriate, its other subsidiary bodies with timely advice relating to the implementation of the Convention. As a subsidiary body of the COP, SBSTTA is to report regularly to the COP on all aspects of its work. Multidisciplinary and open to participation by all parties, the SBSTTA comprises government representatives competent in the relevant field of expertise. Its functions include: providing assessments of the status of biological diversity; providing assessments of the types of measures taken in accordance with the provisions of the Convention; and responding to questions that the COP may put to the body. See also Annex 1 of Decision IV as amended by Decision V/20 and Annex III of Decision VIII/10, which provide its consolidated *modus operandi*.
98. The Agreement to Promote Compliance with International Conservation and Management Measures by Fishing Vessels on the High Seas was adopted at the Twenty-seventh Session of the FAO Conference (Annex 1) in November 1993.
99. FAO Compliance Agreement article 1(b).
100. The ASEAN (Association of South East Asian Nations) Ministers responsible for Environment in November 2002 agreed to further synergise the regional environmental cooperation by identifying ten priority areas based on the World Summit on Sustainable Development Plan of Implementation, marine and coastal issues is one of these priority areas.
101. See Gillespie, A., (2002), 'Forum shopping in international environmental law: The IWC, CITES and the management of cetaceans', ODIL, **33** (1), 17–56.
102. Despite concerted efforts to improve conservation of high seas living resources, uneconomic fisheries continue to be subsidized, fishing vessels are on the increase, and advanced technology continues to facilitate tracking of such resources.
103. RFB/II/2001/7, Rome, February 2001.
104. See Birnie,Boyle and Redgwell (2009), p 673.
105. See UNCLOS articles 63(2) and 64.
106. For the purpose of the Convention, HMS are those species listed in Appendix I. Only these are subject to article 64 which lays down more onerous obligations upon coastal and high seas fishing states.
107. See FSA article 3 which provides that 'Unless otherwise provided, this Agreement applies to conservation and management of straddling stocks and HMS beyond areas under national jurisdiction except that articles 6 and 7 apply also to the conservation and management of such stocks within areas within national jurisdiction, subject to the different legal regimes that apply within areas under national jurisdiction and in areas beyond national jurisdiction as provided for in the Convention (i.e UNCLOS)'. Article 6 relates to the application of the precautionary approach, and article 7 to the compatibility of conservation and management measures.
108. See Meltzer (2009), pp 84 and 85; see also Garcia, S. and Staples, D. (2000), 'Sustainability Reference Systems and Indicators for Responsible Marine Capture Fisheries: A Review of Concepts and Elements for a Set of Guidelines', *Marine and Freshwater Research*, 51, 385–426 at p 410.

109. The Agreement to Promote Compliance with International Conservation and Management Measures by Fishing Vessels on the High Seas was adopted at the Twenty-seventh Session of the FAO Conference (Annex 1) in November 1993.
110. FAO Compliance Agreement article 1(b).
111. Chapter 17 of Agenda 21, entitled *Protecting the Oceans*, is divided into seven programme areas. Area C, relates to the sustainable use and conservation of living marine resources on the high seas.
112. Ibid, para 44.
113. Ibid, para 45.
114. Ibid, para 46: 'States are to: (a) develop and increase the potential of marine living resources to meet human nutritional needs, as well as social, economic and development goals; (b) Maintain or restore populations of marine species at levels that can produce the maximum sustainable yield as qualified by relevant environmental and economic factors, taking into consideration relationships among species; (c) Promote the development and use of selective fishing gear and practices that minimize waste in the catch of target species and minimize by-catch of non-target species; (d) Ensure effective monitoring and enforcement with respect to fishing activities; (e) Protect and restore endangered marine species; (f) Preserve habitats and other ecologically sensitive areas; (g) Promote scientific research with respect to the marine living resources in the high seas'; see also Grzybowski (1995).
115. Ibid, para 49 which establishes the following subheadings for implementation: 'a) Management-related activities, b) Data and Information and International and regional Cooperation and Coordination. As means of implementation Chapter 17 identifies a) Financing and Cost Evaluation, b) Scientific and Technical Means, Human Resources Development, c) Capacity Building.'
116. The World Summit on Sustainable Development (WSSD), also referred to as Rio+10, was held in Johannesburg, South Africa, between 26 August and 6 September 2002 to undertake a review of the progress registered to implement Agenda 21. It produced an Action Plan, entitled the Johannesburg Plan of Implementation which sought to provide targets and time frames for the implementation of Agenda 21.
117. The Johannesburg Plan of Implementation, para 30.
118. Ibid.
119. Ibid. subpara (c).
120. FAO International Plan of Action for the Management of Fishing Capacity by 2005 and the FAO International Plan of Action to Prevent, Deter and Eliminate Illegal, Unreported and Unregulated Fishing.
121. Johannesburg Plan of Implementation, para 30 subpara (e).
122. See FAO Code of Conduct for Responsible Fisheries article 1.1.
123. FAO Conference Resolution 15/93 paragraph 3.
124. See FAO Code of Conduct for Responsible Fisheries article 2(a).
125. Ibid, article 2(c).
126. The FAO Committee on Fisheries (COFI) called for the development of new concepts, which would lead to responsible, sustained fisheries, at its Nineteenth Session in March 1991. Subsequently, the International Conference on Responsible Fishing held in 1992 in Cancun (Mexico) further requested FAO to prepare an international Code of Conduct to address these concerns. The Code, which was unanimously adopted on 31 October 1995 by the FAO Conference, provides a necessary framework for national and international efforts to ensure sustainable exploitation of aquatic living resources in harmony with the environment (Annex 2). The FAO Governing Bodies recommended the formulation of a global Code of Conduct for Responsible Fisheries which would be consistent with important developments in world fisheries and related instruments such as Agenda 21, the FSA and the FAO Compliance Agreement. The Code is intended to establish, in a non-mandatory manner, principles and standards applicable to the conservation, management and development of all fisheries.

127. See FAO Code of Conduct for Responsible Fisheries article 3.2(a). This refers to the treaties to which the parties to the FAO Code of Conduct have adhered.
128. See Code article 3.1.
129. See ibid, article 3.
130. Ibid, paragraph 3.2 provides: 'The Code is also to be interpreted and applied,' consistently with the FSA, 'in accordance with other applicable rules of International law including obligations of State Parties' and 'in the light of' the Cancun and Rio Declarations, Agenda 21 and other relevant instruments.
131. Ibid, article 6.2.
132. Ibid, article 6.6.
133. Ibid.
134. Ibid, article 7.
135. Ibid, article 8.
136. Ibid, article 7.1.1.
137. Ibid, article 7.2.1.
138. Ibid, article 7.2.2.
139. See Burke (1994), p 131.
140. See FAO Code, article 7.3.2.
141. Ibid.
142. Vide Molenaar, E.J., (2003), 'Participation, allocation and unregulated fishing; the practice of regional fisheries management organizations', IJMC, **8** (4), 457–480.

4 Specialized conservation measures for particular species on the high seas

4.1 INTRODUCTION

Although most conservation obligations under UNCLOS were organized on the basis of jurisdictional zones,[1] the 1982 Convention and other international regimes devise norms that target the conservation of particular species which, at some point during their life cycle, may occur on the high seas. This reflects the recent trend for international regimes to adopt measures based on an ecosystem approach,[2] which UNCLOS supports under its articles 61 and 119. A conservation regime that is tailor-made to address particular species is essential for a number of reasons. States have diverse interests over different species; these are dictated by national socio-economic needs and cultural attitudes. Some species have a higher commercial value and are therefore more subject to over-exploitation, whilst others are more vulnerable to over-harvesting or for being taken as bycatch because of their behavioural characteristics. All these realities have influenced the evolution of international law to develop conservation norms from a species-based perspective. In this context, UNCLOS distinguishes between the following different types of living marine resources: straddling,[3] highly migratory,[4] anadromous,[5] catadromous[6] species, and marine mammals.[7] All of these species may occur on the high seas and hence they are subject to the freedom of fishing. Another separate group of living marine resources that are referred to under UNCLOS are the sedentary species, which are considered to be an integral part of the resources of the continental shelf[8] and are specifically excluded from the EEZ regime.[9] There is no mention of sedentary species under the UNCLOS high seas regime.[10] As discussed in Chapter 2,[11] the uncertainties surrounding jurisdictional claims over sedentary species, when they occur on the deep seabed,[12] are hindering the development of an effective regime for their conservation.

Apart from these different categories of species, UNCLOS also refers to the conservation of 'associated and dependant species' on the high seas.[13]

Both the coastal states and the flag states[14] have conservation obligations in this respect. Contention as a result of bycatch, notably with respect to dolphins and turtles, has resulted in states concluding agreements affording particular attention to fishing gear in tuna and shrimp fisheries.[15] States which disregard the taking of conservation measures to prevent associated or dependent species from being caught as bycatch may be breaching article 119 and if this is the case, they would be subject to compulsory dispute settlement between the parties to UNCLOS. It is mainly the methodology and the fishing gear utilized which need to be addressed when attempting to eliminate or reduce bycatch.

Chapter 2 has already highlighted the jurisdictional issues affecting particular species and how the states' capacity to take conservation measures in their regard is inextricably linked to their jurisdictional rights, duties and interests over them. For example, Mexico linked the exercise of its sovereign rights as a coastal state within its EEZ to establishing its authority in establishing the TACs and entry fees for harvesting by foreign vessels in the adjacent high seas areas. The US contested this claim, especially as at that time it rejected sovereign rights by coastal states over tuna in their EEZ. It was only in 1990, when the *Magnuson Fishery Conservation and Management Act*[16] asserted US jurisdiction over tuna in its EEZ that the US withdrew from its original position. Another case in point is Chile's doctrine of '*mar presencial*' which it applies beyond the 200 nautical miles. It includes surveillance without affecting other states' exercise of the high seas regime. In the *mar presencial* Chile affirms that it can adopt conservation measures for straddling stocks occurring therein, and if fishing vessels fail to comply with them it would ban the landing of their catches and deny such vessels port facilities. This chapter will focus on conservation measures proper and discuss the tailor-made regimes that international law has developed with respect to particular species and which supplement the general obligations to safeguard a favourable conservation status for living resources on the high seas, discussed in the previous chapter.

4.2 THE CONSERVATION OF STRADDLING STOCKS AND HIGHLY MIGRATORY SPECIES ON THE HIGH SEAS

Apart from the controversies surrounding the UNCLOS common heritage regime, the most disputed provisions of the 1982 Convention[17] were those relating to the conservation of straddling stocks and HMS.[18] States held disparate views as to how these provisions should be applied and implemented. This situation led to some highly emotional fisheries disputes[19] that threatened to upset the delicate balance of interests between coastal and high seas fishing states established under the Convention.[20] They also hampered the ultimate goal of ensuring adequate conservation for straddling stocks and HMS. Amongst these disputes the most notorious was perhaps the *Estai* case,[21] already discussed in Chapter 2, which demonstrated the dire need for an effective implementation agreement of those provisions under UNCLOS addressing straddling fish stocks and HMS. The legal challenges involved could not simply be resolved by agreeing upon the allocation of jurisdiction over stocks between vessels fishing for them in the EEZ and on the high seas but also required concerted action to ensure at least a compatible, if not a uniform approach, towards the conservation of such species wherever they occurred.[22] In the case of straddling stocks and HMS, the applicable international regime must provide for coordination amongst stakeholder states such that measures adopted in one zone would not be undermined by the mismanagement of these species in another. This premise holds true for the appropriate conservation of *all* marine living resources and for obvious political and commercial reasons, it is even more urgent for the international community to adopt such an approach when regulating the conservation of harvestable stocks that transcend maritime areas.

As already highlighted in Chapter 2, the FSA was a reaction to the difficulties exposed by states' practice in trying to rely on the UNCLOS regime that left too much discretion in the hands of the stakeholders.[23] To resolve the issue, Agenda 21 proposed[24] a multilateral agreement to promote the effective implementation of the applicable UNCLOS provisions on straddling stocks and HMS; this was later endorsed by a United Nations General Assembly Resolution.[25] The FSA, which adopts many of the sustainability objectives established under Chapter 17 of Agenda 21,[26] seeks to establish specific rules to address the conservation of straddling stocks and HMS that migrate across maritime areas, subject to coastal state jurisdiction and the high seas. It is in fact termed to be an 'implementation agreement' meant to supplement the UNCLOS legal framework by introducing new conservation concepts such as sustainable use, the precautionary approach, a broadened application of an ecosystem approach, compatibility between EEZ and high seas conservation measures, and placing additional weight upon the duty to cooperate.[27] It provides the conservation measures which need to be taken[28] if high seas fishing states and coastal states fail to reach an agreement, as required by UNCLOS, to regulate the management and conservation of such stocks. The FSA also amplifies the conservation and management regime of the 1982 Convention[29] and other regional fisheries agreements addressing straddling stocks and HMS.

Under UNCLOS, only those species listed in its Annex I[30] are considered to be HMS. The FSA on the other hand does not distinguish between straddling stocks and HMS nor does it define them.[31] It addresses simultaneously the conservation of both types of species because they share important characteristics and are also similarly regulated under UNCLOS.[32] For instance, UNCLOS calls upon states to cooperate in the conservation of stocks that cross in and out of the EEZ; it envisages that such cooperation is best carried out via regional fishery organizations and with respect to both types of species, but the Convention does not provide a solution when cooperation is not forthcoming. At the same time, the UNCLOS articles on straddling stocks[33] and HMS[34] differ slightly. Whilst under the 1982 Convention states are to work multilaterally to develop new conservation measures on the high seas, adjacent to the EEZ, for straddling stocks, UNCLOS proposes multilaterally agreed measures for HMS that apply throughout the region within and beyond the EEZ and the area of the high seas adjacent to it. The reason for adopting this different approach is based on biological differences between the two categories of living marine resources. Straddling stocks occur primarily in the EEZ of a few coastal states and are harvested in some areas of the adjacent high seas.[35] It is therefore justifiable and reasonable for the coastal state to unilaterally determine conservation measures applicable in its EEZ, and for both the flag states and the coastal state to jointly develop such measures applicable on the adjacent high seas. On the other hand, HMS migrate longer distances across maritime regions both outside and within national jurisdictions. Consequently, international cooperation is necessary for the development and application of compatible conservation measures throughout their range for the effective conservation measures of HMS as a whole. State practice has, generally speaking, followed this distinction.[36] For instance, ICCAT rules apply to tuna as a highly migratory species both within the EEZ and on the high seas. Parties' obligations condition and limit the rights of their nationals and vessels to fish beyond national jurisdiction in marine areas falling within the jurisdictional scope of the constituent Convention. Similarly, the WCPFC's objective is to ensure, through effective management, the long term conservation and sustainable use of HMS[37] in accordance with both UNCLOS and the FSA.

The salient characteristics of the conservation obligations imposed by the FSA upon its parties are: the application of the principles of sustainable use,[38] the adoption of the precautionary approach,[39] and ensuring the compatibility[40] of conservation measures adopted by the coastal and flag states whose nationals fish in the adjacent high seas.[41] In its general principles on the conservation and management of straddling stocks and HMS, the FSA replicates article 119(1)(a) of UNCLOS but it also specifies that these conservation principles are envisaged as 'giving effect to the duty to cooperate in accordance with the Convention (UNCLOS)'.[42] It further supplements the UNCLOS conservation regime by specifying that parties shall adopt these measures 'to ensure long-term sustainability' and 'promote the objective of their optimum utilization'.[43] In so doing, it requires parties to apply the precautionary approach in accordance with its article 6.[44] A detailed discussion on the precautionary approach is found in the next chapter, where it is identified as one of the major constituent elements of a harmonized conservation regime for the high seas. The general principles on conservation expand upon UNCLOS article 119 by requiring parties to assess the impact of fishing and other anthropogenic activities on the target, as well as on the dependent and associated species. The principles obligate parties to minimize pollution, waste, discards, bycatch, lost or abandoned gear, catch of non-target species, which includes both fish and non-fish species, and impact on associated or dependent species, particularly endangered types. State parties are obligated, to the extent practicable, to develop and make use of selective, environmentally safe and cost effective fishing gear and techniques.

The FSA provides a direct reference to the protection of biodiversity in the marine environment as well as to the prevention and elimination of overfishing and excess fishing capacity. Parties shall ensure that their level of fishing effort 'does not exceed those commensurate with the sustainable use of fishery resources'.[45] Other conservation obligations also additional to UNCLOS article 119 are: the consideration of the interests of artisanal and subsistence fishers; the accurate, timely and complete collection and sharing of data concerning fisheries activities on '*inter alia* vessel position, catch of target and non-target species and fishing effort as set out in Annex I of the Agreement'; and information on national and international research programs.[46] Intrinsic to these conservation measures are compliance and enforcement through effective monitoring, control and surveillance, the promotion and the conduction of scientific research as well as the adoption of appropriate technologies in support of fisheries conservation and management.[47]

The FSA is the first multilateral treaty to translate into substantive obligations, albeit in mild language, the precautionary approach. The legal status of its article 6, vis-à-vis the provisions of UNCLOS, is open to interpretation since the Agreement is venturing into uncharted legal ground, not only with respect to UNCLOS, but also regarding conservation law in general. This is because, until the conclusion of the FSA, the precautionary approach had never been expressed in terms of specific legal rights and duties. Although it is included in other treaties as a legal principle,[48] the extent of precaution required has always been left to the discretion of states. Through its list of implementation measures the FSA specifies which are the precautionary steps to take and when parties should take them. The FSA requires states to implement the precautionary approach by taking into account uncertainties relating to stock size and productivity, as well as stock conditions with respect to the reference points. Other factors that are taken into consideration are: levels and distribution of fish mortality; oceanic, environmental and socio-economic conditions; and the impact on non-target, associated or dependent species. With respect to the latter, parties are required to develop data collection and research programmes to assess the impact of fishing on such species and to adopt plans which are necessary to ensure both their conservation as well as the protection of habitats of special concern.[49] Where the status of target stocks, non-target stocks, associated or dependant species is 'of concern', states shall subject such stocks and species to enhanced monitoring in order to review both their status and the efficacy of the conservation and management measures which will be revised 'regularly in the light of new information'.[50]

Every implementing measure under article 6 of the FSA is precautionary because it pre-empts negative effects by including in-built conservation measures that apply as soon as the conservation status of *all* species is under threat. The threshold in the case of the target species is pegged to approaching the reference points,[51] whereas for the other species it is less specific. In both cases, it is closely linked to scientific information such that it must be reviewed in accordance with it. This interpretation of the precautionary approach and its transposition into substantive norms differs from the way it was interpreted by the international community when the Driftnet Resolutions[52] were adopted by the United Nations General Assembly. These Resolutions, which eventually led to the 1989 Convention for the Prohibition of Fishing with Long Drift Nets in the South Pacific, proposed a moratorium based on the argument that science could not provide evidence that drift net fishing is *not* harmful. The FSA underpins the review of any conservation measures to emerging scientific information.[53] Even when venturing into new and exploratory fisheries, state parties are obligated to 'adopt as soon as possible cautious conservation and management measures'.[54] The FSA curbs the discretion of the parties to decide which precautionary measures to take, and instead makes it mandatory upon them to include catch and effort limits that shall remain in force:

> until there is sufficient data to allow assessment of the impact of fisheries on long term sustainability of the stocks, whereupon conservation and management measures based on that assessment shall be implemented.[55]

The effects of these developments on non-parties may still be considerable since the FSA provisions were negotiated by consensus and although, for example, the legal implications of the precautionary approach are still open to interpretation, the concept itself as a management tool enjoys widespread support. As highlighted above, state practice demonstrates observance of the ban on drift nets even by non-parties to the 1989 Convention for the Prohibition of Fishing with Long Drift Nets in the South Pacific,[56] with the result that it appears that their prohibition has crystallized into a rule of customary international law. A similar stand is being currently taken against purse-seine tuna fishing.[57]

The FSA's precautionary approach extends to adverse impacts on the status of straddling fish stocks and HMS in the case of a natural phenomenon. In such circumstances, state parties are to adopt conservation and management measures on an emergency basis wherever fishing activity presents a serious threat to the sustainability of such stocks. Nevertheless, the FSA still specifies that such emergency measures shall be temporary and must be based on the best scientific evidence available. In sum, even if the FSA adopts a wide precautionary approach that includes not only targeted species but marine biodiversity in general, it is always precautionary as far as available scientific evidence warrants. Its interpretation of the precautionary approach focuses on an ecosystem approach that must be constantly fine-tuned to conservation needs prescribed by emerging scientific information.

Article 7 of the FSA clarifies what the UNCLOS provisions imply regarding the compatibility of conservation and management measures in areas subject to national jurisdiction and beyond; that is, as an *essential* conservation measure for both straddling fish stocks and HMS.[58] The coastal states and states fishing on the high seas for the same straddling stocks or HMS in the EEZ and adjacent areas outside national jurisdiction are basically bound by the same corresponding obligations included under UNCLOS articles 63(2) and 64. The only additional requirement imposed by the FSA is that if they seek agreement via cooperation they would do so through appropriate mechanisms provided in its Part III. However, in line with UNCLOS, the parties still have the option to cooperate directly.[59] The FSA goes one step further and makes it mandatory for the parties to adopt *compatible* conservation and management measures in respect of such stocks.[60] Unlike UNCLOS, the FSA provides an exclusive list of basic parameters that both categories of States must 'take into account' when determining compatible conservation and management measures.[61] Some of these parameters are based on conservation and management obligations that the parties have already adopted and applied under UNCLOS[62] and other RFMOs or fisheries agreements. The state parties are to ensure that measures established with respect to straddling stocks and HMS on the high seas 'do not undermine the effectiveness' of any measures taken by the coastal states in accordance with UNCLOS article 61 with respect to the same species.[63] Furthermore, the FSA establishes that states shall take into account 'previously agreed measures established and applied for the high seas in accordance with the convention in respect of the same stocks' by relevant coastal and high seas fishing states or by an agreement, whereas *any* conservation and management measures adopted and applied by the coastal state in accordance with article 61 in its EEZ must be taken into account.[64] The FSA introduces new parameters that must be taken into consideration when determining compatible measures over and above any existing conservation measures the parties would already have taken. These new additions evolved in the post-UNCLOS era and constitute parameters which the 1982 Convention, at most, merely refers to. These are: the biological unity and other biological characteristics of the stocks, and the relationships between the distribution of stocks. Others are: the fisheries and geographical particularities of the region concerned, including the occurrence of the stocks and to what extent they are harvested in the areas under national jurisdiction; the respective dependence of the coastal states and the high seas fishing states on the stocks concerned; as well as ensuring that measures adopted do not result in a harmful impact on the living marine resources as a whole. If states are unable to reach agreement on compatible measures within a reasonable time, the FSA provides for provisional obligations and dispute settlement measures.[65]

Apart from the FSA, one can trace other salient examples of state practice which indicate further developments that supplement and bridge the legal gap left by UNCLOS on the kind of conservation measures coastal states and flag states are obligated to adopt for straddling stocks and HMS. The unilateralism[66] that led to various fisheries disputes also motivated the reform of various regional agreements like the NAFO Convention and the Convention on the Conservation and Management of Pollock Resources in the Central Behring Sea, commonly known as the Donut Hole Convention. The objective of NAFO to coordinate and to seek consistency in the conservation and management measures for straddling stocks was repeatedly disregarded by parties through the unilateral setting of quotas as well as by the evasion of controls through flags of convenience, thereby forsaking compatibility and consequently undermining the effectiveness of conservation measures. This is in fact was what had triggered the dispute between Canada and Spain, both NAFO parties, in the *Estai* case. Canada argued before the ICJ that it arrested the Spanish-flagged vessel because it had breached its national laws on conservation of straddling stocks. The settlement of the dispute, however, did not occur via the decision of the ICJ, which eventually turned down the dispute, but was resolved by agreement whereby the two sides pledged cooperation; the agreement remained applicable insofar as both sides honoured their obligations. In 2005 the NAFO Annual Meeting of the Conference of the Parties adopted an EU/Canada proposal for NAFO reform which sought to overhaul conservation and enforcement measures to render NAFO consistent with the FSA provisions in this regard. The Donut Hole Convention[67] also provides elaborate fallback measures for determining the allowable harvest level when agreement on straddling stocks cannot be reached. This reform was prompted by many disputes over the catch of pollock because of the allegedly negative impacts which catches on the high seas by vessels of various flags were leaving upon the abundance of the same stocks in the US and Russian EEZ. The suspension of the fishery in the US EEZ led US fishing vessels to exploit the same stocks in the adjacent high seas until, by agreement in 1992, several states fishing in the Donut agreed upon a two-year moratorium. The Convention that was concluded thereafter does not permit parties to opt out of any conservation measures they disagree with.[68] Besides the Behring Sea and the North West Atlantic disputes, others over straddling stocks occurred between Mexico and the United States in the Eastern Tropical Pacific over tuna which is also listed as an HMS.[69]

The FSA provisions have also influenced many regional agreements regulating the harvesting of tuna,[70] which is the most commercially important exploitable species[71] of all the HMS listed in UNCLOS Annex I. Regulating the conservation of tuna is usually the biggest bone of contention between coastal and fishing states. As with other HMS, the highly migratory nature of tuna requires that its management is subject to international or, at least, regional regulation meant to lead to successful results.[72] The range of movement throughout the life cycle of tuna significantly affects the distribution of benefits since the economic demands of the industry play a fundamental role.

As in the case of the 1982 Convention and the FSA, regional fisheries agreements on tuna and other HMS, such as ICCAT, avoid defining conservation but set general goals to achieve it and to promote optimum utilization.[73] These goals can be summed up as: establishing the Total Allowable Catch (TAC) in the EEZ, or the Maximum Sustainable Yield (MSY) in the case of the high seas, as qualified by environmental and economic factors. These targets should be based on the best scientific evidence available, adopting proper conservation measures to prevent overexploitation, considering effects on associated and dependent species, and contributing to the exchange of data and information. The coastal state has to determine its harvesting capacity as well as the terms and conditions of any access to the surplus that may be identified and declared. In its turn, this will affect even flag states whose nationals operate in the region since these decisions and related functions would impinge on any cooperation agreement to ensure tuna conservation and its optimum utilization.[74]

ICCAT has launched a 15-Year Recovery Plan to ensure recovery of bluefin tuna stocks. It has fixed quotas for its parties and, at long last, the EU took drastic action to honour its obligations and avoid exceeding its quotas for the tuna fishing season in 2008 both in the Mediterranean and the East Atlantic. As a result, EU Regulation 530/2008 banned with immediate effect the taking of bluefin tuna by purse-seines fleets as soon as its monitoring agency noted enforcement deficiencies in the member states that grossly under-reported catches. The Commission decided to ban purse-seine fishing for tuna because, according to its statistics, EU member states had already almost exhausted its quotas. The EU Regulation also prohibits EU operators from accepting landings, placing in cages, fattening or farming, and the transhipment of bluefin tuna caught by purse-seines, whether they fly flags of EU member states or those of third parties. The Commission based its decision on evidence that showed that the EU purse-seines fleet could actually catch 10 per cent of the total EU quota in three days. However, it allows traditional fishing gear for fishing bluefin tuna. One may interpret article 64 as allowing the coastal states to establish an allowable catch for each EEZ by determining each state's harvesting capacity and by taking into account all fishing in the region. If the collective capacity of all the coastal states involved leaves a surplus due to insufficient harvesting of the allowable catch, the high seas fishing states may harvest the remaining HMS until the allowable catch permits. If the coastal states' harvesting of HMS within the various EEZ exhausts the quota permitted in the allowable catch, as a conservation measure no high seas fisheries of the same HMS may be allowed. In the case of straddling stocks, scientific evidence obtained from the region where the species occur may be sufficient to formulate adequate conservation measures. However, the highly migratory nature of HMS necessitates the taking of measures that are not solely based on scientific information derived from the area where exploitation occurs. When no agreement is reached regarding the harvesting of HMS within and beyond the areas subject to the coastal state's jurisdiction, nothing prevents the coastal state from implementing conservation measures based on its own allowable catch.

When determining the allowable catch, which entails taking into account the stock's accessibility in both areas subject to coastal state jurisdiction and beyond, the migratory characteristics of these species render the timing factor particularly relevant. Lack of cooperation on the part of the flag state whose nationals fish in the adjacent high seas may leave no option for the coastal state but to adopt unilateral conservation measures. On the basis of the applicable UNCLOS and FSA provisions referred to above,[75] these may be obligatory even for the high seas fishing states. The same migratory nature may also affect the type of conservation measures that need to be implemented to safeguard over-exploitation, particularly in the case of deciding on fishing seasons, size limits, area closures and the type of gear to be used. It particularly affects the coastal state in determining its environmental and economic factors which would qualify its operations 'to maintain or restore populations of harvested species at levels, which can produce the maximum sustainable yield.' The coastal state may thus adjust these qualifying factors to reflect the effects which the exploitation of HMS by other coastal and flag states would have upon its economic and environmental interests.[76] If conservation for high seas fishing states is interpreted to be synonymous with observing the allowable catch established by the coastal states in the absence of an agreement, then the fishing state is required to harvest any HMS on the high seas while respecting the coastal states' collective allowable catch. This interpretation, however, bestows enough discretion upon the coastal states to interpret their allowable catch in a manner which deliberately excludes the harvesting of any HMS on the high seas. Allowing such discretion in the hands of the coastal state seems to contradict the notion of freedom of fishing which, although subject to article 64, must also ensure, according to this same article, that conservation measures are reached via cooperation. A failed agreement cannot prejudice conservation measures, but it cannot be interpreted by the coastal state in such a manner as to permit the unilateral determination of the permissible allowable catch without taking into account other states' rights of freedom of fishing in accordance with the 1982 Convention.

Post-UNCLOS developments, therefore, further elaborated upon the UNCLOS provisions by requiring states to take collective conservation measures with respect to HMS and straddling fish stocks. As already mentioned above, this would mean that the fishing state whose nationals disregard the coastal state's allowable catch and its conservation measures for straddling stocks when fishing on the high seas adjacent to its EEZ, or if either state harvesting HMS fails to cooperate in good faith or to implement cooperation agreements, would be subject to compulsory dispute settlement under the 1982 Convention.[77] Although the coastal state may allege that the flag state, ignoring or defying its conservation measures, has breached international law, it cannot enforce its conservation measures outside its EEZ.[78] The coastal state can exercise its enforcement powers only if the flag state explicitly consents to the coastal state's extension of enforcement powers on its vessels when these fish on the high seas. The coastal state's lack of legal standing to take enforcement action on the high seas weakens its position to ensure the implementation of its conservation measures for straddling stocks and HMS beyond its national jurisdiction. On the other hand, the coastal state has some leverage in prodding flag states to reach an agreement because of its discretion when establishing an allowable catch. Despite the discussion above, when parties fail to reach agreement the interpretation of the legal relationship between articles 64 and 116 remains unclear for states that have failed to ratify the CBD and the FSA. The norm-creating character of the provisions of these two treaties remains untested, although adherence to them is very strong. The coastal state with an adjacent EEZ has some advantage over the flag states, but it is also obliged to exercise its discretion reasonably, that is without abusing its rights.[79]

4.3 THE CONSERVATION OF ANADROMOUS AND CATADROMOUS SPECIES ON THE HIGH SEAS

The successful conservation of anadromous and catadromous species is intrinsically linked to the role which the state of origin assumes in their regard.[80] The life cycle of these species places such states in a unique position to determine and implement the necessary conservation measures. UNCLOS regulates the conservation of both species in the same manner. This discussion, however, will focus on anadromous species; unless otherwise specified, the same conservation requirements are applicable to catadromous species. In Chapter 2 we have seen how UNCLOS bestows upon the states of origin of anadromous species a primary interest over them as well as responsibility for their conservation and management[81] to 'ensure their (anadromous species) conservation by the establishment of appropriate regulatory measures for fishing in all waters landward of the outer limits of its exclusive economic zone'.[82] It does the same with catadromous species.[83] If one takes salmon as an example (which is the most commercially exploited anadromous fish), different stocks originating from various continents intermingle with one another when they migrate beyond national jurisdiction, making it impossible to assess in an adequate manner the impact of high seas fisheries upon specific stocks. Consequently, any attempt to formulate and implement meaningful conservation measures beyond the jurisdiction of the state of origin is both impractical and futile. The behavioural characteristics of these species constrain states to adopt a unique conservation regime for anadromous fish stocks, which requires a specific type of management during exploitation, namely targeting specific species, their age groups and individual runs. To fulfil the obligations referred to above, the state of origin shall establish regulatory measures[84] for fishing landward of the outer limits of its EEZ. It remains in the discretion of the state of origin to establish the total allowable catch (TAC)[85] *after*[86] consultations with other states suffering economic dislocation or where stocks migrate into another state's EEZ.[87] This entails that the TAC should allow for high seas catch allowances given by way of exception and interceptions in the jurisdictional waters of other states. Furthermore, the use of the term 'after' and not of 'in' consultation with, implies that the state of origin should lead this process of consultation.[88] The words 'maintain consultation' suggest the need of continuous review of the terms and conditions agreed upon, which must be linked to the fishing cycle and adjusted accordingly.[89] The parties concerned must agree to undertake periodic reviewing of the terms and conditions as they monitor changes and devise conservation requirements that vary according to the life cycle of the species and the fishing patterns. UNCLOS is not specific as to what the conservation requirements and the needs of the state of origin should be. The term 'conservation requirements' may include the provision of data regarding the components of the fishery, but the word 'needs' has a wider meaning and may include even environmental and socio-economic requirements, which the state of origin wishes to take into consideration when fixing the TAC and proposing the terms of agreement with other states in respect of the anadromous stocks.

UNCLOS establishes that states of origin and other states participating in the fishery are to implement article 66 via regional organizations where appropriate[90] even with respect to anadromous species. Coastal states are also obligated to cooperate with the state of origin when anadromous stocks migrate into or through their jurisdictional waters. Nevertheless, as discussed above, despite this obligation to cooperate, it is possible for the state of origin to take adequate conservation and management measures that are not otherwise possible on the high seas. The 1982 Convention took several years to come into force, and in the meantime various states of origin took unilateral action to halt the taking without permission of anadromous species originating in their rivers beyond the 200 nautical mile limit from their shores. This in fact triggered a process of international negotiations between flag states and states of origin and brought about various institutional changes with the setting up of agreements for the North West and the North East Pacific, and the Atlantic. The most salient developments from a conservation point of view have occurred whilst UNCLOS was being negotiated and after its coming into force. These are embodied in the few treaties regulating anadromous species, namely the 1982 Reykjavik Convention for the Conservation of

Salmon in the North Atlantic Ocean (NASCO) and the 1992 Convention for the Conservation of Anadromous Stocks in the North Pacific.[91] Both Conventions ban exploitation of anadromous species on the high seas. From these treaties one can elicit certain conservation and management features which predominate and recur. The most salient of these is the use of such agreements to set up institutions that are responsible for a regime governing the use and management of anadromous species. In this manner it becomes possible to agree upon the conservation and allocation of these species on a bilateral or multilateral level. They purport that other states should refrain from fishing anadromous species on the high seas, whether as a direct harvest or a bycatch.[92] This is considered to be in conformity with article 66, which implies the prohibition of the *incidental* catch of anadromous species. At least with respect to salmon caught incidentally in the North East Pacific this appears to be the case, since the primary issue in regulating Japanese high seas fisheries in the area has been organized around efforts to minimize and avoid the incidental catch of North American salmon when Japan targeted catching salmon originating in Asia. Annex II of the 1991 Convention on North Pacific Anadromous Stocks also provides for reducing incidental catching of anadromous stocks to the extent that if this is not addressed it can trigger off the suspension of the fishery. Another salient conservation measure emerging from these treaties is the development of data on the stocks being harvested. The North Atlantic Salmon Convention provides[93] that its Council must establish working arrangements with ICES. The importance of independent and objective scientific data is undisputed since management issues depend upon the assessment of the state of stocks, identification of the state of origin, estimates of abundance and migratory behaviour and patterns. The more autonomous the data is, the more likely it is to ensure adherence when it comes to taking difficult political decisions. There are, however, wide disparities between fishery organizations in this respect. The Fraser River Panel of the Pacific Salmon Commission, for example, may authorize immediate regulatory measures as necessary during the fishing season when variations in anticipated conditions occur.[94] These agreements have developed and adopted conservation principles that emerged since UNCED, particularly with respect to conservation of biodiversity and salmon habitats by adopting a precautionary approach as an essential tool to secure their sustainable use.

More than anything, these treaties embody general state practice and support the view that UNCLOS article 66 is a codification of international law relating to the conservation of anadromous species.[95] It appears that customary international law is supportive of the legal standing of the state of origin to lawfully control access wherever the anadromous species occur, to prescribe conditions for their exploitation, and to invoke and apply conservation regulations relating thereto. Post-UNCLOS state practice, including treaty law, is generally in harmony with article 66 of the Convention and allows high seas fishing for anadromous species only by agreement with the state of origin. However, there are exceptions. For instance, under the 1982 Convention a fishing state other than the state of origin is to be allowed to fish for anadromous species on the high seas by agreement with the latter only in cases where it suffers an economic dislocation.[96] Japan's fishery for salmon originating in US rivers, in the high seas area of the Eastern Pacific authorized by the US as a state of origin under the North Pacific Fisheries Convention, does not necessarily satisfy this condition since Japan's salmon fishery in this area of the high seas has never been significant. It is unlikely, therefore, that Japan can claim that it is entitled to fish anadromous species on the basis that prohibition would lead to it suffering economic dislocation. Furthermore, in the North Pacific, regulations addressing high seas fishing of anadromous species have been formulated by negotiating agreements between the high seas fishing state (Japan) and the states of origin (Canada and the US); so it is not wholly prescribed by the state of origin. The US as a state of origin has not always adopted regulations pertaining to fishing for anadromous species. This has been left to the agreement with Japan via the North Pacific Anadromous Fish Convention which has the authority to recommend conservation measures for salmon and ecologically related species in the convention area.

The term 'minimize economic dislocation'[97] admits that some loss is inevitable, but also that high seas fishing, being an exception, should be eventually phased out. The state of origin may continue to restrict the level of effort until it becomes no longer commercially viable for the other states to pursue fishing by agreement for anadromous stocks.[98] The state of origin is obligated to give special consideration to states which, by agreement with it, are establishing measures to renew anadromous stocks originating in its rivers, particularly with respect to 'expenditures for that purpose'.[99] This article promotes the arrangement of allowing high seas fishing states to share in the benefits of the taking of anadromous species by the state of origin or other coastal states. Various examples of state practice, such as the 1911 North Pacific Fur Seals Convention and later the North Atlantic Salmon Agreements, have been successful examples of benefit-sharing amongst states participants in a fishery. Article 66(3)(b) of UNCLOS also further emphasizes the need of agreements to allow the state of origin to defray costs for supporting conservation measures and, unless the other states contribute, the state of origin may opt out of concluding an agreement which allows them to participate in the fishery.[100] The CBD, as referred to in the previous chapter, may also have an impact in constraining states of origin to ensure sustainable conservation of anadromous stocks whether or not fishing for such stocks remains commercially viable. Apart from management concepts, the CBD also sheds more light on an issue that has been ignored by UNCLOS article 66, namely the vested interest the international community may have in benefit sharing from the exploitation of such species and their sustainable conservation. This relates mainly to the unaccounted role of the international community's interests in the marine environment of the high seas, which also contributes to the anadromous stocks' growth and development during a substantial part of its life cycle. The success of aquaculture such as salmon farming and salmon ranching has brought to the fore competition issues with wild salmon, liability issues for the degradation of the marine environment via pollution, and the introduction of alien species. This raised further conflicting claims regarding the marine environment itself as a source, which sustains the enhancement of anadromous species and which therefore should be conserved from an overall input of organisms that exceed its carrying capacity as a healthy and sustainable habitat. Addressing this issue inevitably calls into question issues of allocation of anadromous resources, and the cost of using the marine environment within the context of article 66 has to be taken into account. No weight was given to this issue at the time of negotiating article 66 because related problems were not evident. The degradation of habitats, including marine habitats, is addressed by the CBD and other MEAs as well as by other treaties relating to the conservation of anadromous species in general, but it remains to be seen to what extent the discretion on the part of the state of origin to conserve anadromous resources has given way to an obligation to protect anadromous species *in situ* as an accepted rule of customary international law. It is also unclear if this issue could fall within the scope of the CBD provisions on fair and equitable sharing of benefits, since anadromous species are harvested by the state of origin. The CBD establishes that parties are required[101] to take measures aimed at sharing, in a fair and equitable way, not only with respect to the results of research and development but also regarding the benefits arising from commercial and other uses of these resources, with the party providing them upon mutually agreed terms. Balancing things out is subject to further negotiation and discretion in the hands of the provider to facilitate access for sound use and to minimize access contrary to the Convention's aims. The CBD Conference of the Parties has appointed a regionally balanced expert panel to work on a common understanding of basic concepts and options for access and benefit sharing in mutually agreed terms. These include guiding principles, guidelines and codes of best practice for access and benefit-sharing that may address requirements for prior informed consent in provider states. The CBD approach as it emerged is concerned with regulating foreign access to each state's biodiversity. Although the CBD recognizes state sovereignty,[102] the use and terms of access of the components of biodiversity as a threat to their conservation remain a common concern of humankind, and contracting parties must represent this interest. Sovereignty and sovereign rights are tempered by the requirements governing access policies. The situation is still under review at the CBD, and any guiding principles produced could be an important means of achievement of required balancing of interests involved in qualifying sovereign rights over access to genetic resources and sharing benefits of their use. This is, however, still unchartered territory and, given the controversies surrounding equitable sharing of benefits under the CBD, it can be ascertained that at this point in time the influence of the CBD on marine biodiversity is limited to the implementation of its conservation and management obligations examined above and in the previous chapters.

4.4 THE CONSERVATION OF MARINE MAMMALS ON THE HIGH SEAS

Despite the conclusions of the *Behring Fur Seals Arbitration*,[103] where the adjudicating tribunal held that there was no distinction between marine mammals and fish and that both were subject to the freedom of fishing, there are various reasons why marine mammals require a *sui generis* conservation regime in marine areas beyond national jurisdiction.[104] Their migratory behaviour, general distribution, abundance status, low reproduction rates and capacities,[105] mortality rates and other behavioural and biological characteristics[106] distinguish them from other marine living resources. These traits render marine mammals more vulnerable to recuperation from over-exploitation, and therefore any conservation measures to ensure the sustainability of stocks need to be more rigorous than those of other species which are more resilient. A number of marine mammals are highly migratory species,[107] and so their conservation can only be satisfactorily regulated from a multilateral perspective. Other species remain within national jurisdiction, but even in such cases treaty law can qualify the coastal state's obligations in addressing their conservation.[108] An ever increasing number of MEAs[109] provide for the conservation of marine mammals, such that parties may prohibit their harvesting, incidental catch and even maltreatment within their own jurisdiction or by their nationals or flag vessels when on the high seas. Although the regulation of marine mammals has always generated a certain degree of conflict, as is evident from the *Behring Fur Seals* case,[110] it is mainly the conservation of cetaceans that nowadays causes most contention amongst states. For this reason, the discussion below focuses mainly upon the position of international regimes regulating their conservation. International law addresses the conservation of marine mammals on the high seas under two main aspects: norms which regulate the exploitation of the marine mammals themselves, and others that aim to prevent their incidental catch during fishing operations and other anthropogenic activities.

There are wide differences between international treaty law, which provides for the strict conservation of cetaceans on the high seas, and the position of some states that consider these species subject to the freedom of fishing.[111] This rift is caused by divergent views that result both from jurisdictional claims over cetaceans, which were discussed in Chapter 2,[112] as well as the *extent* of conservation requirements relating thereto. The conservation of marine mammals under international law is a mix of traditional legal principles influenced by various multilateral and regional treaties and the position of a number of states that insist that such species on the high seas are still subject to the freedom of fishing. The MEAs obligate parties to adopt more stringent conservation measures based on emergent principles of international law,[113] such as the ecosystem approach, sustainable use and the precautionary approach.

There seems to be consensus, at least in principle, that the taking of preliminary stock assessments to allow harvesting of cetaceans on the high seas may be considered as a 'necessary' conservation measure, although the existence of such a norm under customary international law has not yet been tested. Scientific information on cetaceans is not easily forthcoming. There exist major obstacles in determining abundance, hampering stock assessment and the obtaining of adequate data such as inability to delineate the boundaries of a stock, inadequate understanding of reproduction rates, unknown conditions and rates of natural mortality, ascertaining discrete stocks and determining the boundaries between separate populations, and remote distance from human activity hampering the obtaining of adequate data. Given this state of affairs, a controversial issue[114] surrounding the exploitation of marine mammals concerns the methodology states use to determine the abundance of stocks since this impinges directly upon the capacity of states to harvest the surplus. This is a common problem with respect to the exploitation of all species taken from the wild, especially in the case of living marine resources. However, the very nature and special characteristics of marine mammals generate a certain amount of disagreement among states as to whether it is sustainable to harvest stocks of marine mammals based upon estimates of abundance.[115] This is the general trend amongst those states that support a total ban on harvesting.[116] They base their position upon emerging information that exposes these species' vulnerability to natural mortality and their slow reproduction. This measure is severely contested and defied by major whaling states, and there is no agreement between the two factions on how the data should be collected or on the extent of precaution required when taking conservation measures. These two major issues are the crux of the discrepancy between treaty law and customary international law, or rather between states who support harvesting and those which insist on banning it. States that support the ban adopt the run-of-the-mill application of the precautionary approach: lack of available scientific data should not be used to delay measures preventing harvesting, since to postpone action until such data is acquired may be detrimental to the sustainability of stocks in the meantime. Some states extend this interpretation arguing that, even if scientific data shows that harvesting may be allowed, it is still necessary to take precaution and keep the ban, because it is difficult, if not near to impossible, to guarantee compliance with strict measures allowing only the harvesting of targeted marine mammals on the high seas. This type of reasoning from states supporting the ban contrasts with the traditional approach which provides for the conservation of species on the high seas only when the best available scientific information indicates such a need. This is the counter claim made by states at the other end of the spectrum, that is those that favour the harvesting of cetaceans.

The successful regulation of the conservation of cetaceans depends upon acquiring more awareness about their migratory behaviour and specific routes.[117] Furthermore, conservation measures must not only address the species themselves but also the breeding stocks. This is, in fact, the major flaw which has hampered the international regulation of whaling since for many years there was not even an attempt to distinguish between different species.[118] It is of vital importance to understand which stocks occupy which maritime areas, and during which periods, in order to formulate adequate conservation measures that are both time- and space-based. The varied behaviour of marine mammals also depends upon their feeding and reproductive patterns. Regulatory measures therefore must be based on scientific information on these aspects that may lead states and international organizations to devise regulatory measures that support the non-disturbance of these vital processes. Conservation law in general quantifies the permissible taking of a particular stock from the surplus on the basis of its rate of reproduction and loss through natural causes.[119] For these reasons, the regulation of marine mammals has always been extremely controversial and highly emotional, especially since some states also perceive marine mammals, especially cetaceans, as species which should be exempt from human exploitation and intentional harm due to moral reasons. Pro-whaling states allege that available scientific information shows the abundance of certain stocks and argue that justification of non-harvesting should not be based on moral considerations. It must be noted, however, that the majority of states supporting a ban on harvesting of cetaceans and other marine mammals do so on the basis of lack of available information on their conservation status as well as the more stringent application of the precautionary approach and not for moral considerations. The issue of treating marine mammals differently because they are termed as megafauna by humans goes against the ecosystem approach which does not distinguish between species on the basis of their charisma. It should be the different biological nature of such species that warrants the need for special conservation measures based on scientific advice, and not otherwise.

Other disputes between states concerning the conservation of marine mammals relate to the introduction of regulatory measures that would prevent the incidental catch of such species during fisheries operations on the high seas. The use of non-selective fishing gear such as purse-seines and drift nets leads to the unintentional taking of various species, notably dolphins and porpoises. This has led some states to prohibit the use of such fishing gear for their nationals, and to ban fish imports that were caught via their use by other states. Such a ban has given rise to acrimonious trade disputes, the most infamous being the Tuna–Dolphin disputes between the US and Mexico.[120] The World Trade Organization's Dispute Settlement Unit ruled that such a ban constituted a trade barrier, and did not accept that conservation measures justified it. However, within the General Assembly, as recalled above, there was a call for a total ban on drift net fishing. UNCLOS article 119(1)(b) requires states fishing on the high seas to take into consideration the effects on species associated with or dependent upon harvested species. This argument, in fact, provided a legal basis for states to oppose the use of drift nets because of the negative impacts such fishing gear had on marine mammals.[121] Prohibiting the taking of marine mammals as bycatch seems to have acquired more support since the banning of drift net fishing[122]. This applies also to fur seals and smaller cetaceans which are more likely to be killed due to bycatch rather than due to direct harvesting on the high seas.

Some authors criticize the manner in which the prohibition of drift net fishing came about, namely without first determining whether there are any conservation and management measures that can actually be designed and turn out to be effective, as is the norm.[123] While it is laudable that the international community saw fit to address a problem that was causing indiscriminate exploitation of high seas living resources, it is not legally sound to assume that a remedy is not possible without first conducting an inquiry. In fact, the same 1989 Resolution proposed a moratorium on the use of drift nets 'unless effective conservation measures were in force by 30th June 1992'. A ban is more than justified by law if exploitation does not respect the parameters of conservation specific to the species concerned.

The implementation of the precautionary approach is closely linked to scientific information, which also gives rise to discord amongst states as they seek to harmonize international regimes for the conservation of marine living resources. The importance of adequate scientific data is even more sensitive when formulating a conservation regime for marine mammals, as was explained in the beginning of this part. In such cases the margin of error permitted in conservation measures should be extremely narrow, and the precautionary principle has been proved to be the means to deal with such uncertainty. However, decision making requires specific direction and not an overarching hypothetical principle; certain measures cannot be swept aside on the pretext of the precautionary principle. On the contrary, every effort should be made to identify specifically the impacts of an activity that may cause harm, estimating the chances of probability for such harm and what are the risks which may occur unless measures to avoid or control such harm are taken. It is also essential to examine the risk of harm from actions caused by precautionary measures and the alternative costs of precautionary measures including enforcement, displacing, and moving an affected activity. Precautionary measures would be the best option where the risks of long-term substantial harm are high. On the other hand, when upon estimating the degree of risk and the extent of harm avoided it may be evident that the probability of harm is not high, or when duration of the impacts is doubtful, it would be a better option to take less drastic measures. The FSA article 7 discussed in Chapter 4, which establishes implementing measures on the basis of the precautionary approach, follows this approach albeit in more general terms.

UNCLOS article 120 establishes that article 65 applies also to the conservation and management of marine mammals on the high seas. This is interpreted to mean that an international organization (because no state can assert sovereignty over the resources of high seas) may regulate high seas exploitation for its parties or impose conservation measures.[124] Although UNCLOS confirmed this in accordance with the qualifications discussed above, the 1982 Convention also subjects disputes about states' rights and obligations on the high seas to compulsory dispute settlement.[125] Some claims made by coastal states arise from agreements affecting marine mammals' harvests on the high seas and the conservation of marine mammals under international, regional and subregional agreements. Apart from the ICRW and the FSA, there are other multilateral treaties such as CBD and CITES, and regional conventions such as ACCOBAMS, that impose stricter conservation measures for marine living resources in general or cetaceans in particular.

These legal instruments tend to contribute towards the harmonization of applicable international rules addressing the conservation of cetaceans, at least among the faction of states that oppose the harvesting of cetaceans. Claims made by parties to such treaties emerge from their obligations under them, which they must apply as coastal states within areas subject to their jurisdiction. The strongest claim to prohibit harvesting of marine mammals on the basis of a treaty is made by states parties to the ICRW that oppose whaling. The IWC established a zero quota for commercial exploitation of all stocks of whales subject to its authority.[126] Since there is no permissible commercial catch, the reversed burden of proof means that the proposed harvester has the burden of showing that it is safe for the zero quota to be changed to allow a catch. Although this moratorium arises as a treaty obligation, which in itself permits some exception,[127] some states contend and act as if it were an obligation upon all states whether parties to ICRW or not. In other words, they argue that the conservation measure requiring flag states to refrain from whaling on the high seas has a basis under customary international law.[128] US Legislation, for instance, provides for economic sanctions against any state acting contrary to the IWC moratorium on whales whether or not it is a party to ICRW.[129] Pro-whaling states argue that any conservation obligations states may be bound to take when exercising freedom of fishing apply also for marine mammals, although they do acknowledge that such species, particularly cetaceans, have different and more stringent conservation requirements than other marine species. Given the controversies surrounding the interpretation of article 120, it is important to assess the conservation obligations under the 1946 ICRW and its compatibility with other treaties. The main issues that may affect compatibility between agreements and organizations addressing the conservation of cetaceans may be summed up as follows: open or closed membership; the scope of authority of the organizations/treaties including which species are affected; jurisdictional scope of the coastal state under the EEZ regime and the geographical scope; which activities are subject to scientific research; the competence of these international organizations/agreements to act; and compatibility and consistency between their conservation objectives and methodologies adopted, particularly regarding scientific effort and understanding.

4.5 THE CONSERVATION OF SEDENTARY SPECIES IN MARINE AREAS BEYOND NATIONAL JURISDICTION

The regulation of sedentary species was first addressed at the 1958 Convention on the Continental Shelf.[130] Certain lucrative offshore fisheries of sedentary species prompted coastal States to avail themselves of the opportunity to claim sovereign rights over these species.[131] UNCLOS defines sedentary species as:

> organisms which, at the harvestable stage, either are immobile on or under the sea-bed or are unable to move except in constant physical contact with the sea-bed and the subsoil.[132]

Originally, there was an attempt to include, as part of the continental shelf regime, all bottom-dwelling fishes on the basis that their existence and survival were intimately associated with the seabed. This was rejected to include only species which when harvestable lived in connection with the seafloor, drawing upon an analogous interpretation that sedentary species are like crops to a field. This interpretation has been criticized as legal fiction since such species, contrary to crops, are not growths of the soil. Furthermore, some species such as corals[133] are made up of both living and non-living organisms and therefore fall outside the scope of the definition found under both the 1958 Convention and UNCLOS.[134] In contemporary legal and scientific fora, this definition continues to be seen as particularly narrow when it comes to identifying the demarcation line between sedentary species and other fish; so much so, that this ambiguity has led to various international disputes.[135]

Apart from this anomaly, article 77 of the 1982 Convention does not impose any obligations upon the coastal state to take conservation measures for sedentary species subject to its jurisdiction. It only mentions that the coastal state has sovereign rights for the purpose of exploring or exploiting its natural resources on the continental shelf. UNCLOS does not refer anywhere to sedentary species on the deep seabed, that is in areas beyond the continental shelf. The International Seabed Authority (ISBA) has no responsibility relating to benthic marine life of the area. It is therefore unclear who is responsible for the conservation of sedentary species that occur beyond the continental shelf. This was not an issue when UNCLOS was being negotiated, but it is of particular relevance in this day and age due to bioprospecting. This activity involves collecting samples of marine species from the ocean bed to screen them for genetic materials and other properties that may be of commercial value. Although such species are not taken in large numbers, exploitation, even for research purposes, may be carried out in a non-sustainable manner. Terrestrial species have suffered from threats to their survival due to uncontrolled exploitation to support the commercial need for genetic material; the risk is even greater for marine sedentary species beyond national jurisdiction. As long as bioprospecting remains unregulated it continues to pose severe risks for the marine environment of the deep seabed.

Bioprospecting raises a number of questions that challenge UNCLOS regulation and conservation of sedentary species. The most contentious and fundamental issue that needs to be addressed is whether bioprospecting can be classified as a harvesting or an extraction activity or marine scientific research (MSR). If it is interpreted as harvesting, bioprospecting outside the jurisdiction of the coastal state is subject to the high seas regime of freedom of fishing as qualified by the 1982 Convention. If it is extraction outside national jurisdiction, it is not regulated at all, given that the Common Heritage regime applies only to mineral resources on the deep seabed.[136] If it is MSR the activity is regulated by Part XIII of the Convention.[137] Another challenging question that UNCLOS does not address is: 'at what point do sedentary species become harvestable?'[138] since they qualify as being such when they occur on the seabed at 'the harvestable age', and until they reach this stage can they be subject to another regime besides that of the continental shelf such as that of the EEZ or the high seas. These legal ambiguities and lacunae raise particular difficulties when it comes to determining whether and to what extent, if at all, there exists an obligation under international law for the conservation of these unique living resources when they occur on or under the deep seabed.

There is no ambiguity or uncertainty in applicable regimes for the coastal state's rights to exploit the sedentary species on its continental shelf located up to 200 miles. UNCLOS also provides for the possibility of a state's continental shelf being extended even further, but it does not regulate what is the coastal state's position regarding sedentary species beyond the 200 miles 'outer continental shelf'.[139] If beyond these 200 miles there are seamounts supporting sedentary species, these are not regulated by the 1982 Convention. Originally thought to be inaccessible or not feasible to exploit, species have been discovered on seamounts and around deep sea hydro thermal vents, not only on the outer continental shelf, but also on other parts of the deep sea bed. Apart from bioprospecting, high seas fishing operations using bottom trawl nets destroy corals and associated species, including sedentary species, to the detriment of the sustainability of such resources. This may happen incidentally when various commercially valuable species such as the Orange Roughy may be targeted for exploitation via bottom trawling. Under current technology, trawling to depths of 1200 metres is possible, but limited to slopes less than 30 degrees.[140] In practice, bottom trawling practised outside and within the EEZ not only leads to the incidental catch but also to the destruction of sedentary species and their benthic habitat.

The legal difficulties highlighted above hamper the right of the coastal state or the international community in general to regulate the conservation of sedentary species. Various anthropogenic activities may be directed towards the exploitation of living resources on the continental shelf[141] or the deep sea bed. States have explored various ways in which to protect rare and fragile ecosystems, both within and beyond national jurisdiction, under UNCLOS. One of the most common suggestions endorsed even by the WSSD[142] is the creation of marine protected areas.[143] It can be said that, under UNCLOS, states have a general obligation to protect and preserve the marine environment[144] and to protect rare and fragile ecosystems. It remains unclear, however, whether this obligation by itself can actually constrain states whose nationals exploit sedentary species beyond national jurisdiction to take the necessary conservation measures. Another possible UNCLOS provision that may be applicable is article 119 which establishes that states exercising the freedom of fishing are to consider the effects on associated and dependent species. Such an obligation also emerges under other MEAs, such as the CBD, where there is a general duty for states to take steps to conserve marine biodiversity. A corollary to the exclusive right to exploit sedentary species on the shelf is that the coastal state should have the right to protect those resources from actions by other states that would damage or prevent the coastal state from exercising its rights. The distinction between regulating for a purpose of conservation and protecting a resource to allow for future exploitation is not easily distinguishable, but it is important to draw when it comes to determining on what basis the coastal state may refuse a flag state permission to carry out MSR with significance to the exploitation of marine living resources.

The conservation of sedentary species does not fall within the scope of other treaties, although the CBD bestows upon its parties the obligation *inter alia* of managing biological resources located within national jurisdictions to ensure their conservation and sustainable use *in situ*. The coastal state party would be obligated to take conservation measures when exploiting sedentary species on the continental shelf, an obligation it does not have under UNCLOS, whilst the flag state party would be bound to regulate the conservation of sedentary species according to the provisions of the CBD when its nationals exploit them on the deep seabed. The CBD states that its obligations must be applied consistently with the obligations under UNCLOS, but the former treaty offers more impetus and legal comfort to preserve areas of significant biodiversity on the continental shelf and the deep seabed. Furthermore, the CBD provides a number of principles that address access and benefit-sharing arrangements for genetic resources. The CBD recognizes states' rights to determine access by other nations to the genetic resources within a state's jurisdiction. States are instructed to endeavour to create conditions to facilitate access to genetic resources by other states, the establishment of mutually agreed terms for access, as well as the transfer of technology under favourable terms, and exchange of information. The expectation is that, where states obtain benefits from the exploitation of biodiversity, they will be encouraged to ensure sustainable use of its components. Under the auspices of the CBD, states have continued to develop principles and guidelines to assist states and private companies in negotiating access and benefit-sharing arrangements.

The CBD sought to clarify that genetic resources are subject to the sovereignty of the state where they are located, and thus are subject to the state's right to exploit them in the pursuit of its environmental policies.[145] States are to endeavour to create conditions that facilitate access to genetic resources and are not to impose unnecessary restrictions.[146] In practice, it is difficult for a coastal state to monitor what happens on the outer limits of its continental shelf; it may therefore be more beneficial to enter into agreements with foreign and local companies involved in research to participate, promote capacity building and be in a position to assert its rights when it has better scientific knowledge. Apart from the difficulty of monitoring activities by other states on its outer continental shelf, the coastal state cannot exercise enforcement upon vessels acting illegally in marine areas beyond its national jurisdiction, because this can only be carried out by the flag state. Although this issue was raised in the Canada–US Scallops dispute, the debate during the dispute settlement negotiations centred more around whether scallops were sedentary species rather than on whether Canada was acting in conformity with UNCLOS and international customary law regarding the legality of arrest of a ship. Coastal states would be in a better position working with RFMOs when negotiating conservation and management measures designed to protect their sedentary species on the outer continental shelf below superjacent waters subject to the high seas regime. This would avoid accusations that the coastal state is undertaking unilateral conservation measures which hamper high seas freedoms. In the absence of an RFMO, or where the RFMO has no mandate over such species, the other possibility is to agree with the same fishing states in negotiating bilateral agreements.

4.6 CONCLUSION

There appears to be general acquiescence amongst members of the international community regarding the need to apply specific conservation measures for particular species on the high seas. These norms emanate mainly from treaties, although certain customary rules of international law do support important qualifications to the freedom of fishing as we have seen, for instance, in the case of anadromous and catadromous species. In the case of the other species, notably HMS and straddling stocks, it would be erroneous to assume that customary international law has kept pace with the progress registered via treaty law. The FSA may have more or less harmonized the interpretation of the general nature of UNCLOS provisions relating to HMS and straddling stocks, or at least set certain management concepts like compatibility that may have acquired the requisite *opinio juris* as benchmarks in conservation law. Widespread acquiescence to these concepts is perhaps mostly evident by the review process the FSA has triggered with respect to other fisheries agreements, whereby parties to the latter have sought to approximate the provisions of such agreements with those of the FSA.

The situation is different when it comes to the allocation of quotas. In this case, the position of customary international law cannot be expected to assimilate itself with that of treaty law, where the parties spend endless hours of negotiations to agree (if they ever manage to do so) upon catch quotas and effort levels. The situation may be different in the case of other treaty obligations imposing restrictions on the freedom of fishing via the prohibition of certain fishing gear, for example. If it is proved that these treaty provisions have a norm-creating character, then they may be considered as the *lex specialis* which further elaborates upon the general obligation to take conservation measures on the high seas, especially if states acquiesce to these norms as being necessary for the conservation of the same species. There are various examples as to how the position under international law between treaty and custom has been harmonized in this manner; the prohibition of access to anadromous and catadromous species on the high seas other than by the state of origin is perhaps the best manifestation of how a restriction on the freedom of fishing becomes justified when the link between certain activities and the very survival of the species is what is at stake. Other examples include: the moratoria on drift net fishing and the establishment of certain high seas areas as specially protected areas or sanctuaries where fishing or any form of taking of the species is prohibited. In all of these cases, however, the harmonization of the position under treaty law and customary international law depended upon the acquiescence by states to these treaty norms. There are other examples where the rift between treaty law and customary international law remains wide open, even if it is only a small number of states that persistently refuse to adhere to the treaty provisions or to acknowledge that they have generated custom. These would usually be the same states that have particular interests in the species concerned. The refusal by some states to adhere to the moratorium on whaling is a classic example. In the case of marine mammals, there have been various attempts to harmonize conflicting interests, and in so doing it is easy to express desirable policy measures without, however, offering advice on choices required to be made when preferences and interests conflict. Perhaps the wisest approach is to ensure that any harvesting of marine mammals would only be permitted within the limits imposed by conservation measures guaranteeing sustainability. It is on this premise that UNCLOS, for instance, prohibits access to anadromous and catadromous species on the high seas. Those states that want to adopt stricter measures, including the prohibition of any form of harvesting, even incidental, should be allowed to do so within their own jurisdiction or upon nationals and legal entities who are subject to their jurisdiction or control such as vessels flying their flags, wherever these may occur. Adherence to treaties which address marine mammals would bind flag state parties to comply with conservation measures emerging therefrom in accordance with UNCLOS article 116(a). If the coastal state is a party and the flag state is not, the latter may still be required to indirectly apply conservation measures emerging from such treaties, since it must ensure that it takes compatible conservation measures in the adjacent high seas areas. The legal grounds justifying this obligation upon flag states whose nationals fish on the high seas do not therefore emerge from imposing upon third parties international rules to which they have not given their consent and whose status as customary rules of international law is dubious, but from their exercising the freedom of fishing as qualified by the rights, duties and interests of the coastal state on the strength of UNCLOS article 116(b) and article 120 as well as the special position of archipelagic states under article 51 and coastal states in semi-enclosed seas under article 123, as discussed in Chapter 2.[147]

In the case of sedentary species, it is clear that the UNCLOS provisions leave gaps in international law that have not been addressed by other legal instruments. Rights and obligations of both coastal states and high seas fishing states with respect to sedentary species occurring beyond the continental shelf are unclear. The restrictions on coastal states are mainly due to the fact that the UNCLOS regime for the continental shelf was formulated with the intention of regulating mining and extraction of non-living resources. The commercial importance of sedentary species when UNCLOS was negotiated was certainly not the same as it is today. Furthermore, the international community needs to determine whether bioprospecting should be classified as a harvesting activity, an extracting activity or even an MSR. Perhaps the best option is that international law would regulate the conservation of sedentary species beyond national jurisdiction and particularly bioprospecting as a *sui generis* activity possibly via a new treaty. International cooperation lessens the potential for conflict. It is the best solution to avoid problems with monitoring, compliance and enforcement, to facilitate exchange of information, inspection of vessels, scientific research and capacity building on a national level.

NOTES

1. UNCLOS is arranged in Parts, some of which related to the various maritime jurisdictional zones; these include Part II *Territorial Sea and Contiguous Zone*, Part V *Exclusive Economic Zone*, Part VI *Continental Shelf*, Part VII *High Seas* and Part XI *The Area*. Different regimes apply in these jurisdictional zones which bestow diverse rights and obligations upon flag states and coastal states that vary from one zone to the other. See Chapter 2 for a general discussion.
2. The ecosystem approach requires conservation measures that are based on a proper understanding of the way the whole marine ecosystem functions and the adoption of conservation measures reflecting an ecosystem approach. See discussion on the ecosystem approach, Chapter 5, p 182 et seq.
3. See UNCLOS article 63.
4. Ibid, article 64.
5. Ibid, article 66.
6. Ibid, article 67.
7. Ibid, article 65.
8. Ibid, article 76(1) which defines the continental shelf of a coastal state to 'comprise the sea-bed and subsoil of the submarine areas that extend beyond its territorial sea throughout the natural prolongation of its land territory to the outer edge of the continental margin, or to a distance of 200 nautical miles from the baselines from which the breadth of the territorial sea is measured where the outer edge of the continental margin does not extend up to that distance.' Article 77 then provides that the coastal state 'exercises over the continental shelf sovereign rights for the purpose of exploring and exploiting its natural resources' and further specifies that these rights are exclusive such that no one may undertake these activities without the express consent of the coastal state. Nor do these rights depend upon any occupation or express proclamation. The natural resources include mineral and other non-living resources as well as 'living organisms belonging to sedentary species'.
9. See ibid, article 51.
10. See discussion below, p 172 et seq.
11. See above at p 63.
12. Their conservation is currently at the centre of a polarized political controversy since they are harvested for their genetic material in marine bioprospecting operations. As living resources in marine areas falling outside national jurisdiction, access to these resources and their conservation should, *prima facie*, fall under the high seas regime given that only mineral resources are subject to the global management and non-appropriation under the common heritage regime under Part XI of UNCLOS; see UNCLOS article 133.

13. See ibid, article 119; see also article 61(4): associated or dependent species are also subject to conservation measures in the EEZ.
14. Both articles 61 and 119 have identical provisions.
15. See, for instance, the report of the National Research Council Dolphins and the Tuna Industry (1992); see also Burke W.T. (1984), 'Highly Migratory Species and the New Law of the Sea', ODIL **14**, 273.
16. US Public Law No. 101-627, 101(b) (I), 103 (a)–(c). See Burke, W.T. (1994), *The New International Law of Fisheries, UNCLOS and Beyond*, Oxford: Clarendon Press, p 85, footnote 6.
17. UNCLOS leaves it up to the state parties themselves to cooperate and reach agreement on adequate conservation measures with respect to straddling fish stocks and does not provide any kind of interim conservation and management in case of a lack of agreement. Neither does it *specifically* require states to ensure compatibility between conservation measures to be adopted by the coastal state in its EEZ and those that are taken by states fishing for the same species on the adjacent high seas. See Burke W.T. (1996), 'Introduction' to ODIL, **27** (1) (2) who argues that at the time it was envisaged that the international community would witness a further round of extended jurisdiction on the part of coastal states which were dissatisfied with foreign fishing efforts on straddling stocks that could not be brought under control either by international means or through directly agreed conservation measures between themselves.
18. UNCLOS articles 63(2), 64 and the cross reference to these articles in article 116(b).
19. Examples are many: in the Donut Hole in the Central Behring Sea over Pollock stocks, long distance fishing states have had various disputes with Russia and the US, which have an adjacent EEZ, until late 1992 when by agreement the states involved agreed not to fish for two years. In the North West Atlantic the NAFO has had serious difficulties in encouraging members to endorse and abide by its conservation measures for the high seas, particularly with respect to the Grand Banks area. Canada has accused long distance fishing states of seriously jeopardizing its conservation and management measures for straddling stocks in its fishing zone. Claims made by Mexico over tuna fishing beyond its EEZ in the Eastern Tropical Pacific linked its sovereign rights over tuna within 200 miles to an assertion of authority to establish the total allowable catch and entry fees for harvesting of tuna beyond its EEZ. See Miles, E.L. and Burke, W.T. (1989), 'Pressures on the United Nations Convention on the Law of the Sea of 1982 Arising From New Fisheries Conflicts: The Problem of Straddling Stock', ODIL **20**, 343, 344–9.
20. See Freestone, D. (1995), 'The 1995 Agreement between Canada and the EU over Fishery Control and Enforcement in the NAFO Regulatory Area', *The European Environmental Law Review*, **4** (10), 270–272. See also Sullivan, M.S., (1997), 'The Case in International Law for Canada's Extension of Fisheries Jurisdiction Beyond 200 miles', ODIL, **28** (3), 203–68.
21. Involved Canada as the coastal state and Spain, later on represented by the EU, as the high seas fishing state, *Fisheries Jurisdiction Case (Spain v Canada)*, ICJ General List No. 96, 1998.
22. See Grzybowski, D.M., et al, (ed), (1995) 'A Historical Perspective Leading Up To and Including the UN Convention on Straddling Fish Stocks and Highly Migratory Fish Stocks', *Pace Environmental Law Review*, **13** (1).
23. See Edrson, W., Freestone, D. and Gudmundsdottir, E. (2000), 'Legiferer pour Une Gestione Durable des Pecheries, Guide de l'Accord de Conformite de la FAO de 1993 et de l'accord de l'ONU de 1995 sur les Stocks Chevauchants,' Collection Droit, Justice et development, Washington: Banque Mondiale, pp 72–74.
24. See Agenda 21, chapter 17, para 50. Agenda 21 is a non-legally binding document, but its unanimous endorsement at UNCED as an action plan regarding collective decisions that must be taken by states to attain and maintain sustainable development could be interpreted as expressing state practice or acquiescence by the international community on how to achieve sustainable development. See also *Gabčikovo–Nagymaros*

Dam Case, ICJ Rep (1997), 7, at para 140 where the ICJ referred for the first time to 'this need to reconcile economic development with the protection of the environment, aptly expressed in the concept of sustainable development.' See also the Johannesburg Plan of Implementation, which sets specific, non-legally binding, targets relating to sustainable development that states must achieve.

25. UNGA Resolution 47/192 endorsed the call for the negotiation of such an agreement, which was done between 1993 and 1995.
26. See Grzybowski et al. (1995), p 61.
27. In fact the FSA stipulates that, if no such agreement is reached due to lack of good faith, states may lose access to the right to fish on the high seas for straddling stocks and HMS.
28. See articles 5, 6 of the FSA and the two annexes where it sets more specific rules for their conservation and management.
29. The FSA provides guidance on the meaning of articles 63, 64 and 116–119 of UNCLOS.
30. This should mean that Annex I species only are considered to be HMS for the FSA, given that its article 4 establishes that 'This Agreement shall be interpreted and applied in the context of and in a manner consistent with the Convention'.
31. Only fish is defined as 'including molluscs and crustaceans except those belonging to sedentary species as defined by Article 77 of the Convention (UNCLOS)'.
32. See UNCLOS articles 63 and 64.
33. See ibid, article 63(2).
34. Ibid, article 64.
35. Under the FSA article 7(1), in the case of straddling stocks the high seas fishing states are obligated to take compatible conservation measures on the high seas adjacent to the EEZ.
36. Balton, D.A. (1996), 'Strengthening the CLOS: The New Agreement on Straddling Fish Stocks and Highly Migratory Fish Stocks', ODIL, **27** (1–2).
37. Annex I species and others which the Commission may determine.
38. Listed in FSA article 5.
39. Ibid, as provided for under article 6.
40. Ibid, as laid down in article 7.
41. These three predominant obligations under the FSA can be said to represent the developments generated by the international community through state practice and international fora in the post-UNCLOS era. For instance, the interpretation of the precautionary approach under the FSA, as explained below, is the one which enjoys more support than the more restrictive interpretation attributed to this term under the UN Resolutions banning drift net fishing. See Ellis, J. (2001), 'The Straddling Stocks Agreement and the Precautionary Principle: An Interpretative Device and Rule of Law', ODIL, **32** (4), 289–312.
42. See FSA, article 5 chapeau.
43. Ibid, para (a).
44. See discussion below at p 34.
45. See FSA, article 5 para (h).
46. Ibid, paras (i) (j).
47. Ibid, paras (k) and (l).
48. For example article 3(3) of the United Nations Framework Convention on Climate Change provides, 'The Parties should take precautionary measures to anticipate, prevent or minimize the causes of climate change and mitigate its adverse effects'.
49. See FSA article 6(3)(d).
50. Ibid, article 6(5).
51. Reference points are originally conceptual criteria which encompass in broad terms the management objective for a fishery. To implement the management of a fishery, it must be possible to convert the conceptual reference point into a technical reference point, which can be calculated or quantified on the basis of biological or economic

characteristics of the fishery as well as societal and ecological objectives. In fisheries management there are two typres of reference points that are recognized: target reference points (TRPs) and limit reference points (LRPs). See Caddy, J.F. and Mahon, R. (1995), 'Reference Points for Fisheries Management', FAO Fisheries Technical Paper. No. 347, Rome, FAO.

52. UNGA resolutions 44/225 of 22 December 1989, 45/197 of 21 December 1990 and 46/215 of 20 December 1991, as well as its decisions 47/443 of 22 December 1992, 48/445 of 21 December 1993 and 49/436 of 19 December 1994, on large-scale pelagic drift-net fishing and its impact on the living marine resources of the world's oceans and seas.
53. See FSA article 6(5) which provides that parties shall revise measures 'regularly in the light of new information'.
54. Ibid, article 6(6).
55. Ibid.
56. This convention bans the use of drift-nets over 2.5 metres long in the South Pacific, and paved the way for a global moratorium on drift-net fishing on the high seas agreed by the United Nations in 1991.
57. See below note 121.
58. The chapeau in this article asserts that the article is without prejudice to the rights of coastal states in their EEZ and the freedom of fishing of all states for their nationals. This seems to imply that this article should not be interpreted as an encroachment upon either of these two rights under these separate regimes. At the same time it creates some doubt as to what extent this article on the rule of compatibility is representative of states' general acquiescence.
59. In the case of straddling stocks, the obligation for both categories of states is to 'seek to agree upon' conservation measures whilst, in the case of HMS, the obligation is to 'cooperate with a view to ensuring conservation and promote the optimum utilization of such stocks throughout the region both within and beyond the areas under national jurisdiction.' Furthermore, under the UNCLOS high seas regime, states are obligated to cooperate for the conservation and management of living resources when they fish for the same species or for different species in the same area. UNCLOS article 118 stresses the obligation to cooperate in such circumstances over and above the general obligation to conserve and manage such resources either unilaterally or via cooperation as in article 117.
60. See FSA article 7(2).
61. Ibid.
62. See ibid at article 7(2)(a), (b) and (c).
63. Ibid article 7(2)(a). Under article 61, UNCLOS lays down the rights and obligations of the coastal state with respect to the conservation of living marine resources in its EEZ. Flag states whose nationals fish on the high seas have almost identical obligations under article 119.
64. Ibid FSA article 7(2)(a).
65. See below Chapter 7, p 250 et seq.
66. Both Chile and Canada have enacted legislation to regulate straddling stocks beyond 200 nautical miles from their coasts. Canada's extension of jurisdiction to conserve straddling stocks beyond 200 nautical miles resulted in the notorious *Estai* case and to a great emotional dispute with the EU, eventually settled within NAFO when both Canada and the EU worked together on a proposal for reform referred to above. See above at p 136.
67. 1995 Convention for the Conservation and Management of Pollock Resources in the Central Behring Sea.
68. It also provides for flag state enforcement and, if requested, the vessel may carry an observer from another state to monitor or allow other parties to board vessels and carry out inspections. However, only flag states can undertake criminal proceedings resulting from infringement of the Convention's obligations. Parties are to encourage

non-parties to respect the Convention's provisions and, where this is not sufficient, parties are to take measures, both individually and collectively, that are consistent with international law in order to deter adverse operations of non-parties. Parties are also to seek to prevent fishing vessels from transferring registration to avoid non-compliance.

69. UNCLOS does *imply* compatibility under article 64 since it requires high seas fishing states to subject freedom of fishing to the coastal states rights, duties and interests. See Meltzer, E. (1994), 'Global Overview of Straddling and HMS: The Non Sustainable Nature of High Seas Fisheries', ODIL, **25** (3), 255–344. See also Miles, and Burke (1989).
70. There are more than a dozen types of tuna species that are harvested commercially, the most popular ones being skipjack, yellowfin tuna, bluefin tuna and albacore. The latter two sub-species migrate most and occur mainly in temperate zones, whilst yellowfin tuna and skipjack, although less mobile, constitute the bigger share of the global catch.
71. Although it is the most important HMS species from a commercial point of view, tuna is also harvested for recreational purposes, and there are also artisanal fisheries targeting smaller tuna species closer to shore.
72. Recent scientific evidence does not corroborate this overriding assumption. Although this is not the norm, there may be instances where some species of tuna, even if listed as HMS, may never actually leave the jurisdictional waters of the coastal state and may be successfully managed by it, because most of the stock is harvested within its jurisdiction and high seas fishing does not affect it. See Burke (1994), p 203.
73. See UNCLOS article 61 for the coastal state, and article 119 for the high seas fishing state.
74. Most states that have vessels fishing for tuna, including Japan, regard HMS in their EEZ as subject to their sovereign rights but until 1990 the US persistently objected to this position arguing that it perceives customary law as excluding tuna from being subjected to the EEZ regime and that the coastal states could not assert sovereign rights over them. The US based its legal position upon the long standing view that, since tuna does not reside in the EEZ, it cannot therefore be effectively managed by the coastal state. By agreement, the US had *only* recognized the jurisdiction of Pacific Island States over tuna in their EEZ, before it reversed its position. This position was reversed when, in the President's statement upon signing the amendments to the *Magnuson Fishery Conservation and Management Act*, it was held that with immediate effect the US would recognize similar assertions by coastal states regarding their EEZ.
75. See above, p 135 et seq.
76. The social element, although not mentioned, is inherent to these economic and environmental interests. The notion of sustainable development, which is nowadays recognized as the objective of any conservation regime, does not admit separation of the social aspects from the economic and environmental concerns.
77. See UNCLOS article 279 which provides for compulsory dispute settlement concerning disputes re the interpretation of an application of the Convention's provisions. The exception that fishing disputes arising from the interpretation and application of the coastal state's sovereign rights with respect to the living resources of the EEZ or the exercise of these rights does not apply here because this refers only to those disputes where sovereign rights are at stake and not when both sovereign rights and high seas rights are in dispute. See also Burke (1994), p 223, footnote 64, and related text; see also Miles and Burke (1989).
78. See discussion in Chapters 6 and 7.
79. See discussion on due regard in Chapter 2, p 34 et seq.
80. See Burke (1994), p 154 who argues that fishing on the high seas is inconsistent with conservation of these species; see also De Reynier, Y.L. (1998), 'Evolving Principles of International Fisheries Law and the North Pacific Anadromous Fish Commission', ODIL, **29** (2), 147–178.
81. States of origin have an interest to maximize the return of stocks that originate in their waters, and so their claims go beyond simply requiring other states to adopt

compatible conservation measures as in the case of straddling stocks and HMS, since this would not lead to effective results.

82. UNCLOS article 66(2).
83. Ibid, article 67(1).
84. Besides the TAC, other regulatory measures would include measures required for maintaining stocks and runs and, depending on the outcome, whether fishing would be allowed.
85. See UNCLOS article 66 para 3(b). The provision refers to the obligation of the state of origin to cooperate to put this obligation into effect as much as it should cooperate to minimize negative economic repercussions upon other states fishing for these stocks.
86. See article 66(2).
87. The use of the plural in article 66(3)(a) when referring to EEZs implies that coastal states are not prohibited from taking anadromous stocks originating from another state, and that such catches may occur within the jurisdictional limit of states other than the state of origin; but the coastal state is duty bound to cooperate with the state of origin in the conservation and management of such stocks.
88. Article 66(2) under UNCLOS, qualifies the other provisions of this same article. It mainly determines the conditions under which high seas fishing for anadromous species may be allowed but whether and how this should be done is to be determined by the state of origin. Even if article 66 requires the state of origin to accommodate the interests of other states fishing for anadromous stocks, it has the right under the Convention to allow its interests to prevail.
89. See UNCLOS article 66(3)(a). There is an obligation upon the state of origin and the other states to 'maintain consultation' to achieve agreement on terms and conditions, 'giving due regard to conservation requirements and the needs of the State of origin with respect of these stocks'.
90. UNCLOS article 66(5).
91. Four international fishery bodies regulate salmon harvesting. Apart from NASCO and the North Pacific Anadromous Stocks Commission, there is also the Japan–Soviet Fisheries Joint Commission and the US–Canada Pacific Salmon Commission.
92. This has mainly been agreed upon via cooperation agreements, but there have instances where states, notably the US and the Soviet Union at the time, acted unilaterally even if both never actually implemented their claims in this manner but managed to conclude agreements with the other distant water fishing state involved.
93. See North Atlantic Salmon Convention article 4(1)(d). ICES is a long established organization with expertise on scientific information for fish management. The Fraser River Commission also has its own scientific staff.
94. Pacific Salmon Treaty; see Article IV(7).
95. See Sohn (1985), 'The Law of the Sea: Customary International Law Developments', Am. UL Rev., **34**, 271, 278–9. See also Burke (1994), p 194, and related footnote at 161, who opines, 'Regarding access to anadromous species on the high seas, it is fair to conclude that the customary international law of freedom of fishing no longer affords any right to harvest without the agreement of the State of origin. All of the Salmon-producing and fishing States of the world are agreed that fishing for anadromous species on the high seas is no longer a right.'
96. By way of exception, UNCLOS allows fishing for anadromous species beyond the EEZ of the state of origin when exclusion would result in economic dislocation in such other states fishing these stocks. This means that only those states that are already involved in fishing for such stocks on the high seas can benefit from this exception; new entries are entirely excluded. Fishing for anadromous species on the high seas is subject to an agreement expressing fishing terms and conditions agreed upon with the state of origin, which decides on the allowable catch. This agreement is a precondition to fishing for anadromous species on the high seas. Without such an agreement such an activity would be in infringement of UNCLOS and customary international law.
97. UNCLOS, article 66(3)(b).

98. See Burke (1994), p 170.
99. See UNCLOS article 66(3)(c).
100. See Burke (1994), p 171.
101. See CBD article 15(7).
102. See ibid, article 15.
103. See discussion above, Chapter 3, p 96 et seq.
104. UNCLOS, for example, distinguishes between fish and marine mammals specifically in article 65 and provides that cetaceans on the high seas may be subject to stricter conservation measures. The special conservation measures applicable for marine mammals under CITES, the Bonn Convention on the Conservation of Migratory Species of Wild Animals which has generated the ACCOBAMS Agreement on cetaceans of the Mediterranean Sea, the Black Sea and the Contiguous Atlantic Area, and the Agreement on the 1999 International Dolphin Conservation Programme, are all examples of how states recognize the special conservation needs of marine mammals. The ICRW itself regulates the exploitation of cetaceans in a manner which encroaches upon the freedom of fishing with respect to these species.
105. Apart from low reproduction rates, marine mammals reach sexual maturity late and they do not copulate as frequently as other marine creatures.
106. This includes the age when they reach puberty, the means of respiration, gender characteristics, for example, size and appearance, differences in anatomy, feeding habits, temporal and area segregation, migratory patterns, reproductive and rearing characteristics.
107. Listed in Annex I to UNCLOS are dolphins namely *Coryphaena hippurus; Coryphaena equiselis* and cetaceans: Family *Physeteridae*, Family *Balaenopteridae*; Family *Balaenidae*; Family *Eschrichtiidae*; Family *Monodontidae*; Family *Ziphiidae*; Family *Delphinidae.*
108. See, for example, ACCOBAMS, The Bonn Convention on Migratory Species and the Biodiversity Protocol to the Barcelona Convention on The Protection of the Mediterranean Sea.
109. See above at note 104.
110. The earliest international dispute regarding conservation did not in fact regard cetaceans but pinnipeds under the *Behring Fur Seals Arbitration* (1989), 1 Moore's International Arbitration awards 755, reproduced in 1 *International Environmental Law Reports* (1999), 43.
111. Ibid. This case is actually related to the arrest by the US of a Canadian vessel on the high seas that was harvesting such species. The US argued that the seals' breeding grounds were situated in its territory and it had enacted laws to protect them as well as their habitat that were being undermined by over-exploitation on the high seas. As a result, it claimed, it had every right to protect its interests even beyond its national jurisdiction. The Court, however, dismissed the claim made by the US and asserted that freedom of fishing was the prevailing doctrine.
112. See Chapter 2, p 59 et seq.
113. See Brownlie, I. (2003), *Principles of International Law*, 6th edn, Oxford: Oxford University Press, p 276.
114. This controversy is mainly linked to the low reproductive rates of cetaceans.
115. This stems from the fact that conservation for fish entails the fullest sustainable use of particular stocks that is consistent with the maintenance of other stocks, the ecosystem in general and meeting the objectives of the entity managing the fishery as acceptable to the international community and in accordance with the obligation to meet other States interests in the same fishery.
116. See Birnie, P. (1985), *International Regulation of Whaling*, 2 volumes, New York: Oceana Publications, p 27.
117. For instance, despite the wide distribution of various species of marine mammals throughout the world's maritime areas, discrete populations and stock must be identified for management purposes since the depletion of a population of such marine mammals cannot be sustained by immigration from surrounding stocks.

118. The management unit of whales was, until 1972, expressed in blue whale units to determine in a comparative manner oil production from various species against the blue whale stocks, but ditching this system did not render it any easier to separate stocks for regulation purposes.
119. See discussion on MSY and Optimum utilization, Chapter 3, pp 98 and 102; see also the Bonn Convention and its definition of conservation status in article 1(b) '"Conservation status of a migratory species" means the sum of the influences acting on the migratory species that may affect its long-term distribution and abundance; (c) "Conservation status" will be taken as "favourable" when: (1) population dynamics data indicate that the migratory species is maintaining itself on a long-term basis as a viable component of its ecosystems; (2) the range of the migratory species is neither currently being reduced, nor is likely to be reduced, on a long-term basis; (3) there is, and will be in the foreseeable future, sufficient habitat to maintain the population of the migratory species on a long-term basis; and (4) the distribution and abundance of the migratory species approach, historic coverage and levels to the extent that potentially suitable ecosystems exist and to the extent consistent with wise wildlife management; d) "Conservation status" will be taken as "unfavourable" if any of the conditions set out in sub-paragraph (c) of this paragraph is not met.'
120. WTO Dispute Settlement Unit Cases 58 and 61 brought against the USA in 1996 by Thailand, Pakistan, Malaysia, India and the Philippines respectively regarding the Prohibition of Certain Shrimp and Shrimp Products by Thailand and various other States and under GATT, Environment Dispute 4 and Environment Dispute 5 brought against the US by Mexico in 1991 and the EU in 1994 respectively relating to restrictions on Imports of Tuna. See also Joyner, C.C. and Taylor, Z. (2000), 'Marine Conservation Versus International Free Trade: Reconciling Dolphins with Tuna and Sea Turtles with Shrimp', ODIL, **31** (1–2), 127–50.
121. Some states have also opposed the use of other fishing gear such as purse-seines and trawls. The US Marine Mammal Protection Act was a reaction to US concern over the take of dolphins by the tuna seine fishery in the Eastern tropical Pacific ocean and provides for the goal that incidental killing or injury of marine mammals in commercial fishing operations is reduced to insignificant levels approaching zero mortality and serious injury; Art 101, 16 USC 1371. Trawl bycatch in shrimp fishing did not involve marine mammals but turtles.
122. The General Assembly Resolution in itself is not a binding legal instrument, and acquiescence to this prohibitory rule expressed in the Drift Net Resolutions is to be interpreted as an example of 'instant' customary international law rather than as giving a legally binding character to a soft law instrument. The 1989 Convention for the Prohibition of Fishing with Long Drift Nets in the South Pacific brought about by the Resolutions served to codify this customary international rule supported by a moratorium from using drift nets anywhere in maritime areas beyond national jurisdiction. The use of the General Assembly to press action on living resource management is not common, but this event was not the first of its kind with respect to a moratorium approach to activities beyond national jurisdiction. The 1969 Deep Seabed Mining Moratorium Resolution regarding exploitation of the deep seabed beyond national jurisdiction was the first of its kind in establishing a moratorium upon activities previously considered as legitimate under the high seas freedoms.
123. See Burke (1994), p 266 who says that precautionary measures prohibiting drift net use may well be justified for some drift net fishing activities but may not be so for other cases.
124. Burke (1994), p 170 who says that, in the case of the high seas, an international organization might completely prohibit the harvesting of marine mammals or regulate them in a way that might be inconsistent with articles 64 and 65.
125. See UNCLOS article 297(3).
126. See 33 IWC report pp 21–2 (1981–2).
127. One of these exceptions is whaling for scientific research that is availed of by Japan.

128. See Gillespie, A., (2002), 'Forum Shopping in International Environmental Law: The IWC, CITES and the Management of Cetaceans', ODIL, **33** (1), 17–56.
129. See above at note 121.
130. Article 2(4) of 1958 Convention on the Continental Shelf.
131. See Mossop J. (2007), 'Protecting Marine Biodiversity on the Continental Shelf beyond 200 Nautical Miles', ODIL, **38** (3), 291, footnote 89.
132. UNCLOS article 77(4).
133. Long and Grehan (2002), 'Marine Habitats', 17 *International Journal of Marine and Coastal Law* 237–8.
134. Ibid at footnotes 90 and 91.
135. See Von Zharen, W.M. (1999), 'An Ecopolicy Perspective for Sustainable Living Marine Species', 30 *Ocean Development and International Law*, 1; Roach J.A. (1995), 'Dispute Settlement in Specific Situations', 7 Geo Int'l Envtl L Rev 775, 784. See also Goldie, L.F.E. (1969) 'Sedentary Species and art 2(4) of the 1958 Convention on the Continental Shelf: A Plea for a Separate Regime', *American Journal of International Law* 86; Harris, D.J. (2004) *Cases and Materials in International Law*, 6th edn, London: Sweet & Maxwell, p 483.
136. See UNCLOS definition of resources under article 133.
137. The ISBA does impose restrictions on MSR without distinguishing whether this relates to living or non-living resources. These include: encouraging international cooperation in research, ensuring research programmes benefiting developing countries, and dissemination of the results of the research.
138. See Craig, A. (2001), 'Protecting the Oceanic Gardens of Eden: International Law Issues in Deep-sea Vent Resource Conservation and Management', 13 Geo Int'l Envtl L Rev 563, 584.
139. See Mossop (2007); see also *Barbados v Trinidad and Tobago*, Permanent Court of Arbitration, 11 April 2006, note 4, available at www.pca-cpa.org.
140. See Mossop (2007).
141. The extent of the continental shelf depends on geological characteristics, but for the purposes of UNCLOS each coastal state possesses the associated sovereign rights up to 200nm whether geologically it exists or not, such that the continental coexists with continental shelf limits. When the continental shelf extends beyond 200nm there is a complicated formula whereby states can estimate their outer limits and submit their estimate to the Commission on the Limits of the Continental Shelf (CLCS); see UNCLOS article 76. The following countries have been identified as possibly having outer continental shelves: Angola, Argentina, Australia, Brazil, Canada, Denmark, Ecuador, Fiji, France, Guinea, Guyana, Iceland, India, Indonesia, Ireland, Japan, Madagascar, Mauritius, Mexico, Micronesia, Myanmar, Namibia, New Zealand, Norway, Portugal, the Russian Federation, the Seychelles, South Africa, Spain, Suriname, the United Kingdom, the United States and Uruguay. Up to June 2006 some countries, namely Russia, Australia, Brazil, Ireland and New Zealand, had made submissions to the CLCS.
142. Johannesburg Plan of Implementation recommended the establishment of representative networks of marine protected areas 'consistent with International law and based on scientific information by 2012', para 31(c). See also Eichenberg, T. and Shapson, M. (2004) 'The Promise of Johannesburg Fisheries and the WSSD', 34 Golden Gate UL Rev 587, 638.
143. See CBD COP December II/10. In 1995 the Jakarta Mandate on Marine Coastal Biodiversity created a programme of work to consider the conservation of protection of marine biodiversity, including the establishment of MPAs.
144. See UNCLOS article 192.
145. See CBD article 3.
146. See ibid, article 15.
147. See above, p 50 et seq.

5 The main constituent elements of conservation regimes for living resources on the high seas

5.1 INTRODUCTION

Chapters 3 and 4 demonstrate that the obligation to conserve living resources on the high seas has generated a cohort of international norms which take into account a number of variables. These include diverse geophysical and ecological characteristics of the oceans as well as disparities in fishing and fishing efforts between one area of the high seas and another. Additionally, the applicable norms address both marine biodiversity in general, and the diverse needs of particular species, because of behavioural and biological characteristics, their commercial value or other considerations.[1] The discussion in the previous chapters highlights the importance of the dynamic nature of the law that led to an intensive build-up of treaty norms intended to fine-tune the general obligation for states to take conservation measures. We have seen that these treaties enjoy wide membership and so they have influenced state practice but that some states have continued to persist in their objections regarding certain conservation measures and methods adopted by the international community at large. Furthermore, gaps in international law still exist, as in the case of the conservation of sedentary species beyond national jurisdiction. This successive accretion of rules may leave the user baffled by the complex nature of the applicable international legal framework. Systematic integration of this plurality of general and specialized norms indicates the need for a harmonization exercise, which elicits the major constituent elements emerging therefrom. These elements would serve to establish a common denominator: a set of legally binding methodologies and management principles that guide states on how they may fulfil their conservation obligations. The overlap between methodologies and management principles is inevitable; the distinction made here is just for better organization, as these two facets of the same obligation are interdependent and cannot be isolated. Whilst methodologies relate mainly to procedures, the principles serve as the underlying aim and purpose for the formulation of substantive norms.

The constituent elements referred to below should not be considered as an exhaustive list, but as the most common conservation methodologies and principles referred to in applicable treaties. They are also acclaimed under soft law, which may be an indication that they are supported by general state practice. Although controversy exists as to what is the extent of their scope and their legal standing outside treaty law, they appear to represent the most dominant parameters used by states when setting legal obligations to address conservation on the high seas.

5.2 THE LEGAL METHODOLOGIES

Legal methodologies include the duty to cooperate, compatibility in the taking of conservation measures, linkages with science and technology, and compliance and enforcement mechanisms.

5.2.1 The Duty to Cooperate

The duty to cooperate is discussed throughout this book as a basic, legally-binding methodology, which is indispensible for states to fulfil conservation obligations when a resource is subject to freedom of access by all. To recapitulate, UNCLOS provides that this is particularly the case when the same kind of species are exploited or when different species are harvested in the same area of the high seas.[2] Cooperation is also required between states under the species-based approach[3] both amongst high seas fishing states and in the case of coastal states in whose EEZ the exploited species may migrate. Under the post UNCLOS treaties, both the FSA and the CBD[4] provide that their parties are to cooperate directly or through international organizations concerning areas beyond national jurisdiction and other matters of mutual interest for conservation and sustainable use of biological diversity[5]. Cooperation as an obligation for the conservation of living resources on the high seas has also been singled out as a rule of customary international law in the *Icelandic Fisheries Jurisdiction* cases.[6]

Throughout the various chapters we have seen that the best way to fulfil the duty to cooperate is via its institutionalization. This approach is supported by most states because fisheries Commissions and regional agreements appear to provide the most effective institutional capacity for conservation purposes. Both UNCLOS and the FSA refer to RFMOs as the main drivers for successful conservation methodologies since they provide the required institutional capacity to enhance cooperation. For instance, the FSA establishes that right of access to straddling stocks and HMS is linked to compliance with applicable RFMOs conservation measures. This obligation, however, is binding only upon the FSA's parties. The CBD on the other hand leaves the obligation to cooperate for the conservation and sustainable use of biological diversity in areas beyond national jurisdiction at the discretion of the state parties.[7]

It has also been pointed out however, that institutions may themselves be hampered by lack of internal cooperation due to weaknesses inherent to their constituent treaty. In practice, RFMOs have encountered great difficulties in leading states to reduce catch to levels that can sustain exploitation on a continuing basis. But, despite their shortcomings, they provide the best possible forum for constructive and efficient international cooperation to safeguard stocks in their entirety and in the interest of the stakeholder parties. For example, one form of cooperation adopted by RFMOs is a legal framework where decisions at the Conference of the parties that amend regulations governing catch, gear, seasons and so on, are not included in the substantive text of the constituent agreements but in an appendix or annex that can be amended by a two-thirds or three-fourths majority on an annual basis.[8] This provides flexibility but has also the disadvantage that the state parties may choose to opt out. The Canada–Spain dispute over turbot, caused by the inability of the Northwest Atlantic Fisheries Commission to control over-fishing by Spain, is a good example of how this problem[9] can reduce a conservation agreement to a stalemate situation, even if it was actually under the aegis of NAFO that the deadlock between the two states in relation to the *Estai* dispute was resolved. There have been various successful examples of institutionalized cooperation. Under CCAMLR, closed seasons have been adopted to avoid bycatch of seabirds or fish by particular fisheries. Fixing catch quotas also stands out as a common element in various MEAs and fisheries agreements. For example, under ICCAT, parties fix quotas for catch in relation to particular stocks or groups of stocks or catch per vessel over a period of time or to the catch by nationals of any state during a specific period. Other regional agreements also regulate the size of species that can be caught and fix closed seasons.[10] These conservation measures would not be able to come into effect if cooperation was not institutionalized. The regional approach is also another frequently adopted form of cooperation and most RFMOs have generally opted for fisheries agreements addressing smaller geographical areas or zones, where specific conservation measures are applicable only to these subdivisions. In this manner, it is easier to apply methodologies such as closed areas and seasons for some or for all target species, either temporarily or until studies are concluded so as to allow stocks to recover. Some RFMOs provide for the designation of special areas for protection and scientific study. For example, under

CCAMLR two marine sites have been designated as part of its ecosystem monitoring programme.

International cooperation has been used by states as a means of harmonizing various conflicting interests involved in fisheries,[11] overcoming disparate interpretation of conservation obligations by individual states that usually generate gaps and conflicts in international law. Inevitably, the more members join an international organization, the more difficult it is to move forward and achieve consensus; but the fact remains that international organizations still offer the most appropriate fora to overcome differences.

Different international organizations also need to ensure that as fora where international negotiations unfold, they must cooperate to ensure coherence with other international organizations that play a similar role. Such a form of external cooperation is even more difficult to achieve and given the autonomy of most international institutions it is highly likely that the work of one does not relate to that of others that share the same objectives. The lack of cooperation amongst international institutions and fora has in fact been identified throughout the various chapters of this book as the root cause of fragmentation in the applicable international regime for conservation of living resources on the high seas. This issue has been a recurrent problem and various publicists have sought to provide a solution by proposing the establishment of one single institution with overarching powers. Alvarez and Colombos in 1924 proposed the establishment of an 'International Commission' with some management powers over some activities on the high seas, including the prohibition of fishing if conservation so requires and the imposition of sanctions upon those states who violated rules issued by the said authority.[12] Later on Gidel would build upon this idea to suggest that this proposed international commission would be empowered to prevent abuses on the high seas.[13] The FAO has been set up with the specific role of promoting collaborative regulation of high seas fisheries. It is the principal intergovernmental organization dedicated to fisheries and since its inception in 1945 it has sought to coordinate and promote cooperation amongst the various fisheries institutions and also has, under articles VI and XIV of its Constitution, enabling powers to establish regional fisheries commissions open to both coastal and distant water fishing states. The problem of lack of cooperation on an internal level, discussed above, led to the extension of coastal state jurisdiction as fisheries organizations were often not allowed to work effectively by their constituent members. In the post UNCLOS era, the problem of lack of external cooperation between such organizations and MEAs led to fragmented institutionalization that generated an accretion of international norms, which were neither interpreted nor applied in a coherent manner by these different entities and their member states. The FSA has served to further strengthen the role of fisheries organizations by providing that conservation norms, addressing straddling stocks and HMS which were concluded under their auspices, would prevail precisely because they were concluded via a cooperation agreement. For this reason, the FSA is seen by some experts in the field as the lifeline for collaborative regulation and governance of high seas fisheries that should serve to improve consistency and clarity in the development of a conservation regime for the high seas.[14] It is hailed by various publicists as the current legal benchmark, which defines what the duty to cooperate entails.[15] Only time will tell, but the effectiveness of an international organization, especially one regulating a common resource like high seas fisheries, depends upon the goodwill of the stakeholder states. The separate juridical personality of an international organization does not entirely shield it from the whims of its constituent members but under the system of state sovereignty, such bodies provide the best means of cooperation. In the words of Evelyn Meltzer, 'RFMOs are not perfect constructs but are essential in the development of a coherent global management regime for responsible regulation of high seas fisheries'.

5.2.2 Promoting Compatibility between Conservation Measures Adopted by Various States

RFMOs are also instrumental in promoting compatibility between conservation methodologies as well as management principles and concepts. The FSA requires compatibility in respect of its parties amongst the different participants to a fishery in such a way that both catch and effort limitations are applied in an equitable manner. Furthermore, it also establishes that any conservation measures adopted by existing fisheries agreements are legally binding upon their parties. Under the FSA, it is also an obligation for high seas fishing states parties to adopt measures which are compatible with those of the coastal state when fishing for straddling stocks in the adjacent high seas. Compatibility is essential not only amongst participants of the same fishery on the high seas but also *vis-à-vis* conservation regimes applied in areas subject to national jurisdiction. Compatibility is interpreted to be an implied legal requirement under UNCLOS with respect to HMS and is a specific obligation under the FSA when state parties fish on the high seas adjacent to the EEZ both for straddling stocks and for HMS.[16] The FSA reiterates the need for states to ensure cooperation via RFMOs that would 'take into account the characteristics of the region or subregion'.[17] To ensure compatibility and fill in the lacuna left by UNCLOS, the FSA also regulates the situation when an agreement between states fishing for straddling stocks and HMS has not yet been concluded. In this manner it harmonizes the position adopted by different states. The FSA requires states either to become members of the RFMO that has the competence to establish conservation measures for particular fish stocks and HMS, or else apply the same conservation measures. The FSA prohibits access to living resources in the applicable area of the high seas if the conservation measures adopted by a State with respect to the resources harvested are not the same as those of the RFMO regulating the same. The FSA interprets the principle of non-discrimination under UNCLOS[18] in a manner which prohibits RFMOs from precluding any state that has 'a real interest in the fishery'[19] from becoming a member. The FSA also requires states to take conservation measures 'where such action would have a significant effect on conservation and management measures already established by a competent sub regional or regional fisheries management organization or arrangement' to consult through the RFMO with its members or participants prior to submitting the proposal to the RFMO to the extent that it is practicable.[20] The FSA lists the issues states are to agree upon when establishing an RFMO[21] and which functions such an organization should have,[22] the nature and extent of new members' participatory rights,[23] as well as the conditions relating to the exchange of data and information on scientific research.[24] In sum, the FSA provisions attempt to exclude any form of unilateralism to ensure compatibility and, although these provisions are only binding on FSA parties, the wide adherence to this Agreement and the adoption of these provisions by consensus may be considered to express general state practice as to what the obligation to cooperate in order to ensure compatibility entails.

To what extent the high seas fishing state must ensure compatibility remains, however, subject to interpretation because if a state party to the CBD assumes a certain level of conservation and sustainable use of its fisheries within its national jurisdiction, would it expect, on the basis of compatibility, that high seas fishing states need to respect such measures and adopt the same conservation standards? If both the coastal state and the flag state concerned are parties to the FSA and the CBD, the answer in accordance with UNCLOS article 116(a) and especially due to the application of *pacta sunt servanda* is in the affirmative. If the flag state is not a party to the two treaties, the status of compatibility as a rule of customary international law must be proved by the coastal state. As highlighted above, UNCLOS provisions regarding such species already imply compatibility and, at the very least, cooperation. Furthermore, the CBD's SBSTTA put forward a three-year programme[25] that includes as one of its thematic areas integrated marine and coastal protected areas, thereby highlighting the fact that state parties acknowledge the need to ensure compatibility between conservation measures taken within and beyond national jurisdiction.

5.2.3 Linkages with Science and Technology

International regimes for the conservation of high seas living resources underline the symbiosis between the development of effective conservation methodologies and cooperation in the exchange of scientific knowledge and technological information.[26] Scientific information, if it is compiled via transparent and comparable assessment methods, would provide an invaluable tool to ensure responsible decision making that is not only dictated by the socio-economic needs and political priorities of the individual states. The availability of scientific data on the conservation status of species usually generates enough pressure at grass roots level that constrains states to adopt a position that integrates socio-economic and envi-romental requirements rather than one that defends only the interests of the commercial sector. Reliance on scientific advice is a dominant feature in all RFMOs that aim to develop gradually sufficient information to make good judgments on the potential sustainable yield and the possible impact of the fishery on other ecosystem components, using data collection plans prepared by their scientific committees. CCAMLR provides for the identification of the necessary information for well-founded advice on appropriate catch and effort limits as well as on any gear restrictions. A catch limit is set which is not substantially above that necessary to obtain the required information, and a scientific observer is required on each vessel. This allows parties to review restrictions on catch, fishing location and fishing effort, to test different fishing models like particular gear and practices, or to explore the need of establishing closed areas and seasons. Scientific bodies exist under:

- NAFO, which primarily provides advice on stock assessment and serves to assist the fisheries commission to set the TAC for different species, national quota allocations and advice on conservation measures that need to be adopted;
- SEAFO, which has a scientific committee that collects and analyses catch and environmental data;
- the Central Behring Sea Donut Hole Convention, which has a Scientific and Technical Committee to compile data and facilitate exchange of information between the parties;
- ICCAT which has its own permanent scientific staff but its Standing Committee on Research and Statistics also provides advice on conservation and management measures and coordinates data and

research is made up of representatives from parties, cooperating non contracting parties and fishing entities;

- the GFCM has a scientific advisory committee, which also carries out stocks assessment in collaboration with ICCAT;
- IATTC has permanent scientific advisors in major fishing ports and has a scientific advisory committee to review research programmes and assessments; and
- the CCSBT has an independent scientific body to provide advice to national representatives on stock assessment and the processing of relevant data.[27]

The scientific bodies are not always independent and not all RFMOs have permanent staff but the RFMOs' reliance on scientific advice, which dates back to the setting up of ICES[28], highlights the role of scientific advice as a basis for informed decision making as an underlying principle to apply necessary conservation measures and also an essential constituent element which promotes the effectiveness of environmental protection.[29]

5.2.4 Compliance and Enforcement Measures

Compliance and enforcement measures such as observer programmes, monitoring and surveillance requirements, port state controls, trade restrictions with non-parties that do not adopt the same conservation measures and dispute settlement mechanisms, are all essential methodological tools to ensure effective conservation. However, none of these compliance and enforcement measures can be said to be legally binding unless they are specifically consented to by states. Although this aspect is discussed in much more detail in the next two chapters, it is necessary to refer to it here in order to complete the inclusive list of legal methodologies that are most commonly applied for the purpose of implementing the obligation to take conservation measures on the high seas. A common legal methodology that is adopted by RFMOs to ensure compliance is the adoption of standardized authorization and licensing measures whereby flag state parties can secure better compliance over vessels flying their flag[30] in a uniform manner. Standardization will only be discussed briefly here because it is also tackled within chapters 6 and 7 on enforcement. The standardization of fishing/fishing effort conditions is also common practice and some RFMOs[31] obligate state parties to include specific conditions on the prohibition or limited use of certain fishing gear and methods for ensuring sustainable use such as catch and effort levels whilst some MEAs also control the exploitation of certain species such as marine mammals.[32] RFMOs allow parties to take such measures as part of a conservation regime via a bilateral, subregional or regional agreement. The application of standardized conservation measures implemented across a region, and ideally also multilaterally, ensures compatibility and limits flag-hopping, offering a better safeguard to the competitiveness of the flag state. Within this context it is pertinent to examine to what extent liability issues have come to be considered as an intrinsic requisite in compliance and enforcement measures found in treaties for the conservation of living resources on the high seas. Liability is not referred to under UNCLOS Part VII as it is, for instance, under Part XII where the 1982 Convention lays down that,

> States are responsible for the fulfilment of their international obligations concerning the protection and preservation of the marine environment. They shall be liable in accordance with international law.[33]

This does not, however, mean that states breaching any of UNCLOS provisions under Part VII are exempt from responsibility under international law. The legal implications of this type of *responsibility* are rather obscure, even if the responsibility for harm in areas beyond national jurisdiction, caused by a state within its territory or carried out under its control, is an application of the maxim *sic utero tuo alienum non laedas* referred to under the *Corfu Channel* Case.[34] At the very least, states are obligated to notify and consult affected states if activities carried out by an entity falling within their jurisdiction result, or are likely to result, in transboundary harm; they are also to cooperate for the good of the international community as a whole.[35] No guidelines regarding the extent of legal responsibility are provided under the CBD either, but parties need to identify processes and categories of activities which have or are likely to have significant adverse impacts on conservation and sustainable use of biodiversity, to monitor their effects and to maintain and organize the data derived therefrom. The CBD requires[36] parties to introduce 'appropriate procedures' requiring environment impact assessments of proposed projects:

> 'likely to have significant adverse impacts on biological diversity with a view to avoiding or minimizing such effects and to introduce appropriate arrangements to ensure that the environmental consequences of its programmes and policies that are likely to have significant adverse impacts on biological diversity are duly taken into account.[37]

Liability does not need to be spelt out in an agreement for it to ensue, since the breach of a treaty gives rise to international responsibility. An international adjudicating body can settle claims of international liability for harm, and any breach of international law after the states involved in the dispute consent to such form of settlement. Under customary international law, states have the discretion to refuse. UNCLOS[38] and other applicable treaties[39] have surpassed this impasse and specifically provide for compulsory dispute settlement for their parties. However, the applicable UNCLOS provision on compulsory dispute settlement cannot be considered to codify customary international law because a state needs to have given its specific consent, such as by adhering to a treaty, in order to be bound by compulsory dispute settlement procedures.

5.3 THE MANAGEMENT PRINCIPLES AND CONCEPTS

The various management tools used by states to achieve conservation can be grouped under four main categories, namely: harvesting targets and methods, which include the establishment of fishing seasons and the prohibition to use certain fishing gear, catch limitations, effort level constraints and conservation measures which aim at the protection of the marine habitat. The latter category falls outside the scope of this work, but in brief it can be said that conservation of the habitat in general imposes obligations upon other anthropogenic activities besides the exploitation of living resources on the high seas. The most recent efforts in marine habitat conservation have been directed towards the establishment of specially protected areas that may span from areas subject to coastal state jurisdiction to areas falling under the definition of the high seas.[40] The methodologies mentioned earlier establish how these conservation measures are best implemented. The management principles that also recur in most conservation treaties[41] and major soft law sources are: sustainable use, the precautionary approach and the ecosystem approach. They have been termed by international publicists as emergent principles of international law whilst others consider them to be more established,[42] referred to in international case law; the FAO has published Technical Guidelines on the Ecosystem Approach,[43] the Precautionary Approach[44] and Sustainable Development Indicators.[45] As in the case of the methodologies, these three principles are not the only ones that may be considered as constituent elements for a conservation regime on the high seas but they are definitely the most dominant principles emerging from applicable treaties.

5.3.1 Sustainable Use of Marine Living Resources on the High Seas

Sustainable use, like sustainable development, is identified as a constituent element because it serves as a basis for determining and establishing permissible quotas that aim to prevent over-exploitation, namely the maximum sustainable yield as qualified by UNCLOS, optimum sustainable yield and optimum utilization. There exists no specific definition of sustainable use. Indeed sustainable use of common property, given the history of high seas fisheries,[46] is even viewed as an oxymoron according to Hardin's theory in his work *The Tragedy of the Commons*.[47] Living resources occurring on the high seas are subject to an open access regime where there is no overarching authority to govern and represent the interests of the stakeholders, namely the members of the international community. This in itself is not conducive to a situation where use of a common resource is sustainable. It is this need to regulate access to the common resource in order to ensure its sustainability that usually triggers the process for a fisheries agreement or any other legal instrument that regulates the conservation of living resources in areas outside national jurisdiction. A large number of instruments set certain standards of conduct to regulate fishing activities on the high seas fisheries, but these are binding only upon the parties, and even in such cases effective compliance and enforcement depends upon the exclusive authority of the flag state.

It appears, however, that there is acquiescence on the part of states in approximating conservation with sustainable use, even if there is no universal agreement on what this would imply in terms of specific legal rights and duties. Sustainable use requires a particular type of management which should lead to the species concerned achieving and maintaining a favourable conservation status both at present and in the long term. Although this book focuses on aspects of conservation addressing exploitation, this is only one of the many reasons for the dwindling of stocks, and therefore an effective conservation regime aiming at the sustainability of stocks must go beyond the regulation of harvesting species. Current developments, as they are expressed in UNCLOS, in post-UNCLOS treaties, general state practice and in international fora, tend to favour adopting a list of objectives that must be reached[48] to ensure sustainable use and avoid highly specific prohibitions of various fishing techniques. As discussed above, treaties also provide legally-binding methodologies to achieve these goals.

One of the most controversial ways of ensuring sustainable use is the control of access of living resources on the high seas. Almost all fisheries agreements require parties to control access to high seas living resources by establishing quotas and/or prohibiting the harvesting of certain species in order to ensure the sustainability of stocks. Fishing quotas and targets on the high seas are closely related to jurisdictional issues and to the qualifications to the freedom of fishing, since the setting of quotas imposes limitations on access to a common resource.[49] The jurisdictional developments under international law relating to access and limiting access were dealt with in the Chapter 2. As a conservation measure, limiting access allows the stocks to recover or, as in the case of anadromous and catadromous species, ensures that exploitation does not take place where appropriate conservation measures cannot be taken. In turn, the process of setting quotas and harvesting targets requires cooperation and can only be negotiated within the context of a fisheries agreement or by a fisheries body. It is only in the case of anadromous and catadromous species that international customary law unequivocally supports the prohibition of access to high seas, allowing restricted access by way of exception under limited circumstances.[50] The limitations on access to species agreed upon within a fisheries agreement applicable in a specific area on the high seas have also been subject to controversial debate as to whether they can be imposed on new entrants and non-parties. The FSA, as supported by the FAO Compliance Agreement,[51] establishes that conservation measures established by fisheries organizations on the high seas, and therefore including limitations on access imposed by fishing quotas, are directly applicable upon its parties. It also establishes various obligations on new entrants that are parties to it.[52]

The setting of limitations on access to high seas living resources requires reliable and objective scientific data on the abundance of stock. This allows states participating in a fishery to set the MSY which acts as a threshold determining allocation rights and harvesting targets. However, it has to be said that the condition to take conservation measures based on reliable and objective scientific data[53] is not always observed.

Under UNCLOS, the MSY is to include environmental and economic factors in order to determine the level of abundance that needs to be maintained in a fishery. This enables the possible adoption of measures that provide for higher abundance of stocks than may have to be maintained to produce the *unqualified* MSY. The increased stocks resulting from adopting this approach allow for a higher catch per unit of effort, translating into lower costs and greater net returns to fishing states. To achieve this, the total catch must be lowered and so less fish are shared among fishing states participating in the high seas fishery. Although the overall returns may be higher, the net returns might be lower to some participants.

The inclusion of biological, economic and social factors on an equal basis in establishing the MSY extended the assimilation of conservation from maintaining the MSY to establishing an optimum yield or optimum sustainable yield. This integrated approach in assessing the MSY is fundamentally different from the way the MSY concept originated, since the more recent interpretation supports a conservation goal allowing fishing at $F_{0.1}$ rather than at F_{max}. These alternative measures of abundance, allowed by UNCLOS article 119, may however lead to conflicts amongst states if each adopts a different approach in calculating the Total Allowable Catch (TAC) when deciding on which stock level to choose. This is what happened in the dispute between Canada and the European Community regarding fishing for straddling stocks in the North West Atlantic when Canada sought to maintain a higher level of abundance than the European Community. Canada used $F_{0.1}$ to calculate the TAC, while the European Community used F_{max} which yields a noticeably higher allowable catch.[54] The words 'in determining the allowable catch and other conservation measures',[55] can be, and in fact they have been, interpreted to mean that article 119 does not require states fishing on the high seas to compulsorily determine an allowable catch. It leaves it up to the states themselves to adopt alternative conservation measures[56] as necessary for the fishery.

In other words, fine-tuning the definition of the MSY to support an integrated approach may reflect the very essence of sustainability but it has failed to bring harmonization in estimating stock levels that are permissible for exploitation. UNCLOS and fisheries law in general distinguish between the conservation measures that aim for sustainable use of target species as opposed to those for associated and dependent species. The obligation to take conservation measures was previously limited to harvestable species. The 1958 Geneva Convention on Fishing and the Conservation of Living Resources on the High Seas defined conservation[57] as the aggregate of measures rendering possible an 'optimum sustainable yield' for these resources, so as to serve a maximum supply of food and other marine products. Under UNCLOS and other treaties that succeeded it, the conservation of non-harvestable species remains a separate issue. These are not subject to an MSY, but states are to take into consideration impacts upon them to maintain or restore their populations above levels where their reproduction does not become seriously threatened. This is because originally conservation programmes were formulated with a view to securing in the first place a supply of food for human consumption.

CCAMLR does away with this distinction and more recently the FAO Code of Conduct for Responsible Fisheries seems to imply that conservation measures should apply towards *all* species.[58] However, state practice has shown that doing away with the distinction may not necessarily and realistically contribute to the adoption of an ecosystem approach which, as we shall see below, is another principle that is a constituent element of the contemporary conservation regime for the high seas living resources. The distinction proves to be an important requirement to ensure the effectiveness of conservation measures since the underlying motive for the conservation and exploitation of harvestable and non-harvestable species is dictated by different interests and motives. Ignoring such a reality would only complicate matters to the extent that it becomes impossible to regulate exploitation effectively. This is, in fact, what has happened in CCAMLR, which has had considerable difficulties in establishing quotas for harvestable species as a result.

State practice in recent decades has assimilated conservation with sustainable use, at least as a guiding principle to achieve conservation as a general obligation. The phrase itself was considered as the most acceptable to the negotiating parties to the CBD since it allowed enough flexibility whilst representing an agreed guiding principle.[59] This is indicative of widespread acquiescence of the term itself, even if there is no universal agreement on what the coined phrase implies in terms of substantive legal obligations. The Conference of the Parties of the CBD at its very first session requested its Subsidiary Body on Scientific Technical and Technological Advice (SBSTTA) to advise it on aspects of conservation and sustainable use of marine biodiversity.[60] At its second session the Conference of the Parties of the CBD adopted an important decision, based on SBSTTA advice, which proposed the development of a work programme on marine biodiversity and cooperation with related conventions and relevant international and regional organizations. The Ministerial Declaration referred to as the Jakarta Mandate on Marine and Coastal Biological Diversity[61] constitutes evidence that there is global consensus, albeit not legally-binding, on the need for the CBD Conference of the Parties to address conservation and sustainable use of marine and coastal biodiversity. The CBD SBSTTA forwarded a three-year programme[62] whose basic principles include the ecosystem and precautionary approaches, the importance of scientific advice, the need for primary action at local and national level, and strong coordination between the CBD and other relevant bodies. Since UNCED, many RFMOs have reviewed the constituent treaty to reflect these recent developments.[63]

5.3.2 The Precautionary Approach

The general wording of UNCLOS article 119 requiring the taking of measures 'designed on the best scientific evidence available' is essential to prevent the taking of conservation measures from being stalled on the pretext that an 'absolute standard' of scientific knowledge is required before taking any action. The term 'best available' allows states to pursue more detailed scientific research and imposes upon them a legal obligation to act on the basis of some scientific evidence. The need for available scientific evidence as a prerequisite to the taking of conservation measures has been the subject of controversial debates in post UNCLOS fora because of its alleged incompatibility with a strict interpretation of the precautionary approach[64] which encourages states to take measures even when scientific information is not available. The precautionary approach is usually interpreted to mean that available scientific information indicates a certain element of risk whereby harm would ensue if particular anthropogenic activities are carried out. The uncertainty relates more to the *extent* of that risk and/or harm rather than to whether there exists a risk or not.

As already mentioned in the previous chapters, an important, albeit controversial, development was the restrictive interpretation[65] of the precautionary approach that led to the banning of drift net fishing by the United Nations General Assembly in 1989 and 1991 and by the corresponding treaty, which prohibited large-scale drift net fishing in the South Pacific.[66] The interpretation of the precautionary approach adopted in this case inverted the onus of proof for the taking of conservation measures as established under UNCLOS. UNCLOS requires the taking of necessary conservation measures in accordance with the best available scientific evidence and article 119 also implies that there is a requirement upon fishing states to act not only on the basis of such scientific evidence but also upon other factors that may qualify the conservation measures they would take, which emerge from 'relevant economic and environmental factors'. The ban on drift nets under the said Resolutions, and eventually under the the Drift Nets treaty, was based on the presumption that it was necessary because there is no scientific certainty that such type of fishing gear does *not* cause harm.

There is no doubt that states have acquiesced to the prohibition of drift net fishing, but it is doubtful whether this strict interpretation has affected the application of the precautionary approach in other contexts with respect to fisheries on the high seas. The FSA, which was negotiated and came into force after the Resolutions, does not appear to adopt this same restricted interpretation of the precautionary approach.[67] The FSA, as we have seen in the previous chapter, provides a list of substantive obligations on how to implement it with respect to HMS and straddling fish stocks. However, the FSA's articles on the precautionary approach do not require states to take fishery management standards and obligations unless these are positively required according to supportive and significant best available scientific evidence.[68] This may mean that the traditional interpretation of the precautionary approach, as a constituent element for the conservation of living resources on the high seas, even if not referred to in UNCLOS, enjoys acquiescence by states. Although all the post-UNCLOS treaties adopted the precautionary approach as an underlying principle of their conservation regime, they appear to adopt the wider rather than the restricted interpretation favoured by the drift net resolutions and treaty.

The FSA establishes that states are to apply the precautionary approach 'widely' for the purpose of:

> conservation, management and exploitation of straddling fish stocks and highly migratory fish stocks in order to protect the living marine resources and preserve the marine environment.[69]

The FSA however mandates that states shall not use the absence of adequate scientific information as a reason for postponing or failing to take conservation and management measures.[70] It says nothing about taking precautionary measures once there is scientific uncertainty about the negative impacts of an activity as the Drift Net Resolutions have in fact done. The FSA lists[71] various mandatory obligations upon parties under the heading 'In implementing the precautionary approach' all of which are based upon scientific information. As a first obligation, in fact, parties are required to obtain and share the 'best scientific data available', to improve decision making for fishery resources. This Agreement sets guidelines in Annex II such that stock-specific reference points may be determined on the basis of the best scientific information available. The precautionary approach is therefore implemented by setting these reference points which, if approached, will trigger off another obligation where states must determine what action should then be taken such that they are not exceeded[72] and, if they are, take any necessary action to restore stocks.[73] The FSA approach, even if applicable only with respect to HMS and straddling stocks, seems to reflect general state practice and according to the manner in which UNCLOS interprets the link between conservation measures and reliance upon scientific information in article 119. CCAMLR, which predates the FSA, is the only RFMO that applies and incorporates the precautionary approach as a conservation principle into stock assessment and decision making. Catch limits for fisheries under the CCAMLR regime are precautionary and it aims to manage marine ecosystems from a precautionary approach perspective. CCAMLR takes into consideration all the gaps and uncertainties in data collection before taking decisions that relate to the management of fisheries within its jurisdictional scope. The Convention refers to its precautionary objective in its article II, without defining it as such, but explains that its aim is to ensure that any management measures it adopts serve to avoid the risks and long-term negative effects of decision making that would not be based upon precaution. It therefore incorporates uncertainty in its management strategy and it has been successful in achieving scientific consensus on risk avoidance conservation measures despite gaps in data available to it. Basically the precautionary approach adopted by CCAMLR is more akin to that which steered the abolition of drift net fishing, as its scientists achieve consensus on the basis that certain risks cannot be ruled out rather and not because they agree that certain negative effects may or may not occur.[74] CCAMLR then develops biological reference points to help it base its decisions accordingly both on target species and any new fisheries.

Even within the realm of MEAs where the concept originated, however, the legal implications of the precautionary approach under international law remain shrouded in controversy, but its validity as a management concept in conservation has acquired widespread endorsement,[75] albeit more often in rhetoric than in practice.

5.3.3 The Ecosystem Approach

As already mentioned, under UNCLOS there is a distinction between the objectives for the conservation of non-harvestable species when compared to that for harvested species. In the case of associated and dependent species, the objective is to maintain or restore populations above levels at which their reproduction may be seriously threatened. This obligation requires in-depth research effort even if it permits also substantial takings. The obligation to ensure the conservation of associated and dependent species was something relatively new to fisheries law at the time and caused UNCLOS section 2 of Part VII to be considered as adopting an ecosystem approach. This view is also supported by the fact that the UNCLOS negotiators did not limit the scope of conservation measures to ensure only food security. Although article 119 of UNCLOS presented a conservation regime that was wider in scope, the interpretation of the terms 'associated and dependant species' would not have been interpreted to suggest an ecosystem approach that addresses the conservation of biological diversity in its entirety. The acknowledgment that ultimately all species are associated with and dependent upon one another and their habitat may have been obvious in scientific fora during UNCLOS negotiations but did not receive the necessary acquiescence in the legal-political sphere at the time. In 1976, the IUCN[76] in its document 'Principles Replacing Maximum Sustainable Yield as a Basis for Management of Wildlife Resources', referred to the maintenance of ecosystems in a state that ensures that both consumptive and non-consumptive values could be realized on a continuing basis. Another common conservation method is levelled towards the use of fishing gear meant to eliminate or reduce incidental catch, non-target fish and other non-fish species. Both CCAMLR and the IATTC propose to reduce and ultimately eliminate dolphin bycatch in purse seine fisheries and other bycatch such as sharks and turtles. ICCAT has taken measures to prevent bycatch of seabirds and marine turtles. CCAMLR forbids the use of bottom trawls in demersal fisheries whilst NEAFC closed five seamounts and a section of the ocean ridge on the high seas to bottom trawling and other types of bottom fishing for three years.

Similarly, in 1980, CCAMLR extended its scope to all marine living resources in the area within the whole Antarctic ecosystem. It allows rational use of species, but harvesting must be based on ecological principles with the aim of avoiding reduction of a population below those which ensure its stable recruitment. It refers to the stock level to be maintained close to that which ensures the greatest net annual recruitment. In practice, however, the development of conservation from an ecosystem approach has not registered much progress even under CCAMLR, despite it being supported by an active Commission and Scientific Committee. This is mainly because the multi-species management promoted by the CCAMLR regime, despite its value from a conservation perspective, remains too highly complex to readily translate into concrete measures regulating exploitation.[77] The CBD negotiated under the auspices of the United Nations Environment Programme (UNEP) was adopted in 1992 and came into force as of 1993; to date it has been endorsed by 190 state parties, apart from the EU. It defines biological diversity as:

> the variability among living organisms from all sources including, inter alia, terrestrial, marine and other aquatic ecosystems and the ecological complexes of which they are part; this includes diversity within species, between species and of ecosystems.[78]

As discussed above, even if its article 119 may have been innovative at the time, UNCLOS does not adopt an ecosystem approach as this is intended under the CBD[79] or the FSA. UNCLOS provisions, although general, cannot be interpreted to provide for strategic environment assessments, representative networks of marine protected areas or modern governance norms such as transparency, accountability and inclusiveness. These were conservation concepts that developed later and are found in more recent post-UNCLOS treaties. These concepts are also likely to be more adequate and appropriate in regional fisheries agreements and regional seas agreements.

An ecosystem approach and a species-based approach are not mutually exclusive. UNCLOS introduced a conservation regime which is also species-based and particularly relevant from an ecological point of view as it acknowledged that the biological and behavioural characteristics of certain species necessitated a specialized regime that was applicable both to coastal and high seas fishing states. It was mainly intended as a balancing act to the drastic changes in jurisdictional powers assumed by coastal states and hence to the sudden shift in the legal status of various marine stocks, but it was also an important step in the right direction towards sustainable harvesting of marine living resources. Success has been far from overwhelming, as was explained in Chapters 2 and 3, but the UNCLOS species-based approach, together with its provisions on the conservation of associated and dependent species, served to codify issues of responsibility and jurisdiction tailor-made for specific types of marine living resources to ensure effective conservation of such stocks and to highlight the need for cooperation between all participants in a fishery. It also served to fine-tune the traditional interpretation of freedom of fishing by qualifying it according to a species-based conservation regime applicable on the high seas. This emerges from article 116, which subjects the freedom of fishing to the rights, duties and interests of the coastal states, particularly with respect to these species. Besides referring to the conservation of associated and dependent species, UNCLOS qualifies the MSY to reflect other aspects, besides maximizing on exploitation, which are more based on the eumetric optimum yield. This is in itself more compatible with the ecosystem approach. The best proof, however, that trends in state practice acknowledge the ecosystem approach as a constituent element of the conservation regime for high seas living resources are those RFMOs and Regional Seas Agreements which have adopted this concept. The following are a few examples.

One of the regional treaties concluded whilst UNCLOS was being negotiated was CCAMLR.[80] It is, in fact, a pre-UNCLOS rather than a post-UNCLOS treaty, establishing conservation obligations that already went beyond those of the 1982 Convention even before the latter treaty was concluded. CCAMLR adopted conservation measures based on an ecosystem approach for parties harvesting and carrying out associated activities in the CCAMLR area. Its substantive articles extend its scope to all marine living resources in the area within the whole Antarctic ecosystem. However, the negotiating parties to CCAMLR did not succeed in introducing comparative provisions under UNCLOS.[81] CCAMLR remains to date one of the Conventions dealing with the conservation of marine living resources with the broadest ecosystem approach. The substantive articles extend its scope to all marine living resources in the area within the whole Antarctic ecosystem, which it defines as 'the complex of relationships of Antarctic marine living resources with each other and with their physical environment'.[82] It refers to conservation as including 'rational use',[83] but harvesting must be based on ecological principles to avoid reduction of the population level below those ensuring stable recruitment. The stock level must be maintained to the closest level, ensuring the greatest net annual recruitment. Although it avoided relying on MSY to overcome difficulties associated therewith, it has still registered slow progress and has encountered various problems in determining what this catch level should be. This is because, in practice, the national interests still dominate, especially since third parties are not bound by the obligations of the Convention. Furthermore, adopting a wide ecosystem approach involving all living resources has rendered matters very complex when it comes to setting harvesting targets.

Most Regional Seas Agreements developed in environmental fora[84] and therefore they evolved distinctly from fisheries agreements applying in the same region. They reflect the concerns and needs of littoral states to address environment issues in a maritime area to which they are bound by proximity, through land and sea configuration and, more often than not, even by political affinity. Each Regional Seas Agreement establishes, through annexes or protocols, a series of conservation measures applicable in defined maritime geographic areas, which may include areas beyond national jurisdiction.[85] They increasingly strive to incorporate an ecosystem approach, but all specify that the types of activities subject to regulation under them shall not affect the rights of other parties or third states under international law. In other words, any conservation measures that the parties to Regional Seas Agreements may take, and which are applicable beyond national jurisdiction, must be consistent with the UNCLOS regime. The more recent protocols in some of the regional seas agreements incorporate many elements present in the CBD, thereby supporting better regional implementation of the conservation obligations of the Convention regarding marine biodiversity. The geographical scope of the 1986 Convention for the Protection of Natural Resources and Environment of the South Pacific region includes certain areas beyond national jurisdiction that are completely enclosed by a 200 nautical mile EEZ. The Convention provides for the establishment of specially protected areas and protection of wild flora and fauna either via individual or via joint conservation measures taken by the parties, which are to prohibit or regulate any activity likely to have adverse effects on the species, ecosystems or biological processes that such areas are designed to protect.[86]

The 1992 Convention for the Protection of Marine Environment of the North East Atlantic, commonly known as the OSPAR Convention, adopted Annex V on ecosystems and biodiversity in 1998. Annex V mainly calls upon parties to take the necessary measures, either individually or jointly, to protect and conserve the ecosystems and biodiversity of the OSPAR maritime area including the seabed, which extends from the shores of contracting parties to a substantial adjacent area on the high seas. It specifies that no measures relating to fisheries management may be adopted pursuant to it, but draws attention to relevant actions needed in the competent international fisheries body.[87] In 2004 the OSPAR working *Group on Marine Protected Areas, Species and Habitats* referred to a scoping study on how the protection of high seas and deep ocean biodiversity could best be achieved. In the short term it recommended that, in order to reduce impacts on biodiversity, attention could focus on the identification of the sensitivity and vulnerability of marine biodiversity in the maritime region to human induced impacts. It also recommended the taking of necessary management measures to address these impacts, including possible revisions to the mandates of relevant authorities The OSPAR Commission wrote to NEAFC drawing attention to the need to protect the biodiversity of cold water coral reefs on the western slopes of the Rockall Bank. In turn, OSPAR parties agreed to provide data on the distribution of lophelia reefs in order to produce an up-to-date distribution of these habitats in the OSPAR region and had to provide this map to the fisheries management authorities.

The 1976 Barcelona Convention was amended in 1995 and applies throughout the Mediterranean. Its Protocol concerning Specially Protected Areas and Biological Diversity is applicable to the sea, the seabed and subsoil, and even provides for listing of endangered species, species whose exploitation is regulated and criteria for the establishment of specially protected areas even in areas outside national jurisdiction that are deemed to be of Mediterranean interest (SPAMI).[88] Once species are listed, parties to the Protocol cannot engage in activities that are contrary to the objectives of the Protocol with respect to these species. In addressing the relationship with third countries, the Protocol invites non-parties and international organizations to cooperate in the implementation of the Protocol's obligations.[89] The Pelagos Sanctuary for marine mammals, which forms 53 per cent of one SPAMI, lies in areas subject to the high seas regime. Originally established via a tripartite agreement between Italy, France and Monaco, it was recognized as a SPAMI under the Barcelona Convention in 2001. Under the designation agreement these three countries claim the right to enforce the sanctuary's regulations on the high seas even with respect to third party states, within the limits of the rules established under international law. No formal prosecution of high seas violation in this sanctuary has tested the legality of this arrangement, and to date third parties have not objected to its establishment. This may be interpreted to mean that non-parties recognize the establishment of this MPA, most of which extends to the high seas. If these three coastal states were to establish an EEZ in the region, the sanctuary would be completely within their EEZ, but they have opted not to do so and consequently the status of the waters in the Pelagos sanctuary falls within the scope of the high seas regime. The management of the MPA according to the tripartite agreement lies with the three nations.

There are 15 RFMOs in all with responsibility to agree on binding conservation and management measures with respect to stocks and species concerned in a given geographic range where each fisheries agreement applies.[90] The scope and conservation responsibilities vary with the each agreement. Some, like CCAMLR, mandate an ecosystem approach;[91] others focus only on managing target fisheries since their mandate does not provide them with responsibility to consider effects on non-target species and habitat conservation; neither do they address other negative impacts on marine resources in general. The more recently concluded agreements, like those for highly migratory species in the western and central Pacific Ocean, are influenced by the FSA and tend to adopt both an ecosystem and also a precautionary approach. The Agreements predating UNCLOS, however, do not even possess the incipient ecosystem approach of UNCLOS, let alone the precautionary approach of FSA.[92] The following RFMOs have adopted an ecosystem approach: NEAFC, for example, is examining how to strengthen its role in adopting more holistic conservation measures; the Parties to SEAFO may adopt conservation measures for associated and dependent species of target species; the GFCM established an ecosystem approach *ad hoc* working group to assess habitats, ecosystem indicators, gear selectivity and bycatch and the impact of target fisheries on dependent or related species; under the IATTC the ecosystem approach is provided for under article II and also in article VII of the Antigua Convention, which amended the constituent instrument under which the parties have agreed to develop ecosystem models; IOTC exercises an ecosystem approach in its quest for the collection of data on non target associated and dependant species.[93]

5.4 CONCLUSION

This discussion on legal methodologies and legal concepts common to most treaties on the conservation of living resources on the high seas is meant to provide an inclusive list of elements that form the basis of conservation regimes for living marine resources occurring beyond national jurisdiction. This chapter has attempted to draw attention to the state of play with respect to their interpretation and application by states. It has sought to identify where states have managed to apply these methodologies and concepts in a consistent and harmonious manner, as well as the uncertainties that still persist. This discussion also shows that, although these concepts and methodologies form an integral part of the legal toolbox, states do not always apply them in a consistent manner. The nexus between fragmentation and diversification lies not so much in the plurality of laws that aim to address so many different requirements that emerge with the passage of time, but rather in the lack of coordination amongst the promoters and users of the applicable regimes. As international law continues to evolve it is evident that certain underlying concepts and methods that are identified as essential for the purpose of regulating the conservation of living resources on the high seas withstand the test of time. There have also been important changes such as, for example, the acknowledgment that marine mammals should have a different conservation regime from fish, a position that differs from that taken by the judges in the *Behring Fur Seals* arbitration.[94] Similarly, the ecosystem approach as a basis for conservation is wider in scope than the perception of conservation as defined by the 1958 Geneva Convention on the High Seas. Those methods and principles that have remained the same have become more complex since they were adapted to suit modern times and to reflect more recent scientific and technological discoveries. State practice via treaties and other norms has continued to develop and demonstrate acquiescence to the exercise of freedom of fishing as being subject to a set of legal obligations which aim to achieve a sound conservation status for living marine resources. Despite attempts for their harmonization, the interpretation and application of these obligations will always vary as long as it remains subject to political manoevering to suit the whims and national interests of the individual members of the international community. These legal methodologies and concepts will only be effective in so far as they are interpreted and applied within the context of the legal framework where they coexist and interrelate with each other.

NOTES

1. See Birnie, P. (1985), *International Regulation of Whaling* New York: Oceana Publications; D'Amato, A. and Chopra, S. (1991), 'Whales: Their Emerging Right to Life', Am. J. Int. L., **85,** 21–62.
2. See UNCLOS article 118.
3. See also ibid article 116 and articles 63(2), 64, 65, 66 and 67.
4. See CBD article 5.
5. The obligation is worded in a generic manner without clarifying issues concerning liability for harm.
6. See *Icelandic Fisheries Cases (UK v Iceland)*, at 31, para 72; *(FRG v Iceland)*, at 200, para 64.
7. See CBD article 5.
8. Most fisheries organizations reach decisions by consensus, but examples where a two-thirds majority binding decision is taken and which binds only those parties that voted for it include the IOTC, ICCAT and NEAFC. Some other organizations rely only on consensus; examples include CCAMLR, The Donut Hole Convention, the CCSBT and the WCPFC. Still others, like the NAFO and the GFCM, use simple majority for decision making once there is a quorum, but are still entitled to object within a

stipulated time period. The right to vote is often forfeited if the member states fall into arrears.

9. See Koers (1973), *The International Regime of Marine Fisheries,* London: *West Byfleet Fishing News*; see also Davis Redgwell (1996), 67 BYBIL, 199–217.
10. For example NAFO regulates the taking of non target species by introducing bycatch mitigation measures that include gear mesh size, establishes minimum fish size as well as prescribing areas and time periods where and when fishing cannot take place. NEAFC has since 2001 closed the area round Rockall Bank for trawling. The GFCM establishes minimum size for landed fish. See Meltzer, E. (2009), *The Quest for Sustainable Fisheries*, Ottawa: NRC Research Press, pp 271, 273 and 282.
11. See Orrego Vicuna, F. (1999), *The Changing International Law of Fisheries*, Cambridge Studies in International and Comparative Law, Cambridge: Cambridge University Press, p 36.
12. See ibid, p 17.
13. Ibid, p 18.
14. See Meltzer, E. (2009), p 54 et seq.
15. Ibid, p 67 where Meltzer says, 'Under the UNFSA, States are obliged to join RFMOs or must agree to comply with or not undermine conservation measures; arguably, such an obligation is now part of customary international law independent of the provisions of the UNFSA'.
16. See discussion referred to above at 10; see also Balton, D.A. (1996), 'Strengthening the CLOS: the new agreement on straddling fish stocks and highly migratory fish stocks', ODIL, **27** (1–2), 125–152.
17. See FSA article 8(1).
18. See UNCLOS article 119(3) which establishes that 'States concerned shall ensure that conservation measures and their implementation do not discriminate in form or in fact against fishermen of any State'.
19. See FSA article 8(3).
20. Ibid, article 8(6).
21. Ibid, article 9.
22. Ibid, article 10.
23. Ibid, article 11.
24. Ibid, article 1.
25. SBSTTA, Recommendation III/2; amended by COP III, adopted at the fourth session of the Conference of the Parties by Decision IV/5 and Annex. It includes basic principles that include the ecosystem and precautionary approaches, the importance of scientific advice, the need for primary action at local and national level, and strong coordination between the CBD and other relevant bodies.
26. See Orrego Vicuna (1999), p 165.
27. For a thorough exposition on the scientific component of RFMOs see Meltzer (2009), pp 270–91.
28. See Chapter 3, p 96.
29. See Orrego Vicuna (1999), p 14.
30. See discussion in Chapter 7, p 218 et seq.
31. See Meltzer (2009), pp 270–91 for a thorough overview of how major RFMOs establish conservation measures via the regulation of fisheries for key species and the use of fishing gear.
32. Examples include the 1979 Bonn Convention on the Conservation of Migratory Species and Wild Animals and its ACCOBAMS, CITES and the CBD.
33. See UNCLOS article 235(1) on responsibility and liability.
34. *Corfu Channel Case,* ICJ Rep. (1949), 1.
35. See Birnie, P., Boyle, A. and Redgwell, C. (2009), *International Law and the Environment,* 3rd edn, Oxford: Oxford University Press, p 575 and Handl (1990), 1 *YbIEL*, 32. Nevertheless, in its interpretative declaration, the UK stated that this Principle in the Convention was intended to apply only to the adverse impacts on biological diversity

that are duly taken into account in programmes and policies as impacts that are likely to have significant adverse effects. Acquiescence to Principle 21 of the 1972 Stockholm Declaration is evident as it has been reproduced in many treaties and referred to in innumerable Resolutions and Declarations since UNCHE.

36. See CBD article 14.
37. The innovative character of the CBD's article 14 is the introduction of this obligation to apply, whether negative effects are transboundary or are restricted to national territory. The 1991 Environmental Impact Assessment Convention applies only when transboundary harm is likely to result.
38. See UNCLOS Part XV particularly article 286.
39. The FSA is another treaty which provides for dispute settlement procedures. See also the discussion below in Chapter 7, p 249 et seq.
40. See page 186.
41. Examples include the FSA, the CBD and CCAMLR.
42. See Orrego Vicuna (1999), pp 145–56 and Meltzer (2009), pp 115–85.
43. FAO Technical Guidelines series No. 4, Supplement 2 (2003).
44. Ibid, No. 2 (1996).
45. Ibid, No. 8 (1999).
46. See Birnie, Boyle and Redgwell (2009), at pp 26, 647.
47. Quoted in ibid as 'Individual exploitation of the common resources provides little incentive for the individual to preserve the commons since there is an underlying understanding that if the individual does not exploit the resource on an immediate basis someone else would.'
48. See Cicin-Sain, B. and Knecht, R.W. (1993), 'Implications of the Earth Summit for Ocean and Coastal Governance', ODIL, **24** (4), 323–54.
49. See Brownlie, I. (2003), *Principles of Public International Law*, 6th edn, Oxford: Oxford University Press, pp 252 and 253.
50. See UNCLOS articles 66 and 67.
51. The FAO Compliance Agreement defines conservation and management measures as those measures set by the fisheries organizations in article 1(b).
52. See FSA article 11.
53. See ibid, article 10(d) and article 14.
54. See Burke, W.T. (1994), *The New International Law of Fisheries, UNCLOS 1982 and Beyond, Oxford Monographs in International Law*, Oxford: Clarendon Press p 113.
55. See the chapeau to paragraph 1 of article 119.
56. See ibid at article 113.
57. See the 1958 Geneva Convention on Fishing and the Conservation of Living Resources on the High Seas, article 2.
58. See Joyner, C.C. (1995), 'The Antarctic Treaty System and the Law of the Sea – Competing Regimes in the Southern Ocean?', IJMC, **10** (2), 301–31; Molenaar, E.J. (2007) 'Managing Biodiversity Beyond National Jurisdiction,' IJMC, **22** (1), 89–124.
59. See Birnie, Boyle and Redgwell (2009), p 576.
60. It can do so on the strength of article 25 of the CBD.
61. CBD, Conference of the Parties, Decision II/10.
62. SBSTTA, Recommendation III/2; amended by COP III, adopted at the fourth session of the Conference of the Parties by Decision IV/5 and Annex.
63. See Sydnes, A.K. (2001), 'Regional Fishery Organizations: How and Why Organizational Diversity Matters', ODIL, **32** (4), 349–72.; Von Zharen M.W. (1999), 'An Ecopolicy Perspective for Sustainable Living Marine Species', ODIL, **30** (1), 1–42.
64. See Burke (1994).
65. See UNGA Resolutions 44/225 and 46/215 UNGA resolutions 44/225 of 22 December 1989, 45/197 of 21 December 1990 and later 46/215 of 20 December 1991, as well as its decisions 47/443 of 22 December 1992, 48/445 of 21 December 1993 and 49/436 of 19 December 1994, on large-scale pelagic drift net fishing and its impact on the living marine resources of the world's oceans and seas.

66. The 1989 Convention for the Prohibition of Fishing with Long Drift Nets in the South Pacific. This Convention bans the use of drift nets over 2.5 metres long in the South Pacific, and paved the way for a global moratorium on drift net fishing on the high seas to be agreed by the United Nations in 1991.
67. See Burke (1994).
68. See Ellis, J., (2001), 'The Straddling Stocks Agreement and the Precautionary Principle as an Interpretative Device and Rule of Law', ODIL **32** (4), 289–312.; Hewison, G.J. (1996), 'The Precautionary Approach to Fisheries Management: An Environmental Perspective', IJMC, **11** (3), 301–32.
69. See FSA article 6(1).
70. Ibid, article 6(2).
71. Ibid, article 6(3).
72. Ibid, article 6(4).
73. Ibid, article 6(3)(b).
74. See Meltzer (2009), pp 122–3.
75. Examples of RFMOs that have made an effort to assume a precautionary approach include NAFO, which adopted a precautionary approach framework in 2004; NEAFC which requested ICES to incorporate the precautionary approach in its scientific advice to the Commission; GFCM which in its article III.2 refers to implementing the precautionary approach; IATTC has applied the precautionary approach in the absence of scientific information when assessing impacts of fisheries on stocks since 1980 and included it, in line with the FSA position in article IV of the Antigua Convention of 2003, which amended the original constituent treaty of 1949; WCPFC adopted the precautionary approach in article 5(c), and its article 6 refers to the precautionary approach in accordance with the FSA and the IOTC has adopted the precautionary approach recognizing the need to incorporate scientific uncertainty when compiling stock assessments. See Meltzer (2009), pp 121–9.
76. See IUCN Resolution No. 8, 12th General Assembly of IUCN, 1976. The IUCN is a federative membership organization consisting primarily of governments, their agencies, and scientific, professional and conservation bodies. It is a unique hybrid organization, neither entirely intergovernmental nor wholly non-governmental.
77. See Burke (1994), footnote 86 on p 115 and Birnie, Boyle and Redgwell (2009), p 672.
78. See CBD article 2.
79. In its preamble the CBD acknowledges that the fundamental requirement for conservation of biodiversity is the conservation of ecosystems and natural habitats, and the maintenance and recovery of viable populations of species in their natural surroundings.
80. Negotiations that eventually led to CCAMLR commenced when UNCLOS was already in the making and were concluded two years earlier.
81. See Burke (1994), p 114 et seq.; see also ibid, footnote 86 on p 115. According to Burke, CCAMLR conservation objectives are impossible to achieve in a fishery harvesting more than one species since not to allow all populations of harvested species to fall below a level close to that which ensures the greatest net annual increment cannot be realized in a multi-species fishery. He maintains that it is not possible to maintain all affected components of an ecosystem at a uniform maximum level. See also Birnie, Boyle and Redgwell (2009), who affirm the difficulties in adopting such an approach, pp 552–3.
82. See article I (3). Article VI however establishes that nothing in CCAMLR shall derogate from the rights and obligations of the ICRW and the Convention on the Conservation of Antarctic Seals.
83. See CCAMLR article II(2).
84. For a detailed account see *The International Legal Regime of the High Seas and the Seabed beyond the Limits of National Jurisdiction and Options for Cooperation for the Establishment of Marine Protected Areas in Marine Areas Beyond National Jurisdiction*, CBD Technical Series No. 19, November 2005.

85. The UNEP regional seas conventions address areas beyond national jurisdiction with respect to the protection of marine biodiversity and deep-sea biodiversity at the regional scale. These regional seas conventions also promote cooperation with FAO and RFMOs to address environmental impacts of fisheries and promote an ecosystem management approach.
86. 1986 Convention for the Protection of Natural Resources and Environment of the South Pacific region, article 14.
87. It does the same with maritime transport, which is also outside its scope making the same call to IMO.
88. Specially Protected Areas in the SPAMI list are distinct from those specially protected areas subject to national jurisdiction. These shall include sites that are important for conserving the components of biodiversity in the Mediterranean. The Protocol specifies in detail procedures for establishment of SPAMIs; the decision to include an area in the SPAMI list is to be taken by consensus.
89. See the 1996 Protocol concerning Specially Protected Areas and Biological Diversity to the Barcelona Convention article 28(1).
90. Most agreements cover only areas beyond national jurisdiction, few cover both, and three cover only areas within national jurisdiction. Five of these bodies have competence over most or all living resources within their area of application, while others have competence only with respect to certain species like tuna and salmon. There are high seas areas where there are no fisheries agreements or organizations, for example, the South West Indian Ocean.
91. See CCAMLR, Art II.3. This establishes certain principles whereby harvesting and associated activities within the Convention area must be in accordance with one another. The Agreement lays down examples of how this can be done: maintaining ecological relationships between harvested, dependent and related populations of Antarctic marine living resources, restoring depleted populations and preventing changes in the marine ecosystem which are not potentially reversible over two to three decades. These measures should be adopted, taking into account the state of available knowledge of the direct and indirect impact of harvesting, and the effects of alien species introduction, of associated activities in the marine ecosystem and of environmental changes.
92. This notwithstanding that some of these agreements, like the IATTC and the GFCM, were revised in 2003 and 1997 respectively in the light of the UNFSA precisely to include the precautionary approach.
93. See Meltzer (2009) pp 143–72.
94. See above, Chapter 4, p 145 et seq.

6 Enforcement jurisdiction on the high seas and the conservation of living resources

6.1 INTRODUCTION

Chapter 5 identified compliance and enforcement measures as one of the constituent elements which states consider to be essential for an effective conservation regime. State practice shows that despite this consensus these provisions remain the toughest to negotiate in any agreement on the subject.[1] Enforcement under international law is, generally speaking, both difficult to agree upon and to implement. It is particularly challenging with respect to the conservation of living resources on the high seas, due to their vast expanses, which hamper thorough and effective enforcement. Apart from these geophysical reasons, there are also various legal stumbling blocks. UNCLOS does not establish what kind of compliance and enforcement measures should be taken by states to fulfil their obligation to adopt the 'necessary' conservation measures when fishing on the high seas.[2] Furthermore, despite the qualifications to the freedom of fishing imposed upon the flag state, compliance and enforcement obligations on the high seas remain entrenched within its exclusive jurisdiction, unless the flag state specifically agrees otherwise. This gives rise to contrasting legal arguments as to what extent, if at all, other entities may be responsible for and allowed to secure compliance with conservation measures, when the flag state fails to do so. Responsibility for compliance depends upon whether the conservation measures were breached in a maritime zone subject to a coastal state or a flag state jurisdiction.[3] In fact, enforcement provisions under UNCLOS[4] and other related multilateral, regional and bilateral legal instruments operate within a complex scenario of conflicting interests between flag states, coastal states and the international community as a whole. Since this study focuses on conservation on the high seas, it will address only enforcement and compliance in areas outside national jurisdiction.

The success of a conservation regime for living resources on the high seas depends upon its ability and flexibility to strike a balance between the need to establish procedures and measures that enable states to enforce conservation obligations whilst guaranteeing that this will not interfere with the rights of coastal states and other states in their exercise of the high seas freedoms. Secondly, it must also essentially address practical and legal difficulties that hinder compliance and enforcement to restrain abusers and free riders that may thwart an otherwise successful conservation regime. Apart from identifying these difficulties, this chapter will examine whether any new legal rules addressing enforcement and compliance of the obligation to conserve marine living resources have evolved under post-UNCLOS instruments, and whether they strengthen, supplement or are potentially in conflict with any UNCLOS provisions.

6.2 LEGAL OBSTACLES TO THE APPLICATION OF COMPLIANCE AND ENFORCEMENT MEASURES ON THE HIGH SEAS

There is a great deal of uncertainty when it comes to the applicable international regime for compliance and enforcement on the high seas. The 1982 Convention establishes exclusive flag state jurisdiction on the high seas[5] and imposes upon flag states the obligation to conserve living resources when exercising their freedom of fishing by either cooperating with others or taking unilateral measures.[6] Any emerging rules have to be assessed within this context, namely: to what extent has exclusive jurisdiction for compliance and enforcement been upheld, how post-UNCLOS agreements have developed compliance and enforcement tools, as well as how states deal with non-compliance and address the main obstacles that prevent them from fulfilling their conservation obligations. However, assessing an enforcement regime for the conservation and management of living resources on the high seas does not only entail an examination of the monitoring and compliance tools to determine their value as a deterrent or their efficiency in identifying and applying sanctions to any entity that breaches these same measures. There are other issues particular to the high seas which any international regime must take into consideration in order to be as effective as possible. These obstacles may be practical, such as the physical difficulties in conducting enforcement over vast areas[7] of the high seas or in monitoring transshipment, which allows defaulters to remain undetected because they avoid being subjected to any port state controls.[8] More importantly from a legal perspective, the main difficulties revolve around the abuse of the exclusivity of flag state jurisdiction or the incapacity or inertia on the part of flag states to exercise control over their vessels on the high seas, as well as reflagging.

The lack of commitment or the incapability of the flag state to exercise control over its vessels inevitably leads to non-compliance and abuse. This anomalous situation is further exacerbated because there is no universal agreement as to what constitutes the link between a ship and the nationality it assumes. Since a vessel is free to choose its nationality, vessel owners can simply reflag to other states when they feel that conditions imposed upon them by their flag state have become too onerous. This is known as flag hopping or reflagging. This is possible because of lax conditions for ship registration offered by some states that are commonly referred to as flags of convenience. And since the implementation of the enforcement regime on the high seas is intrinsically dependent on flag state jurisdiction, it is pertinent to examine any developments since UNCLOS that attempt to address these two major obstacles.

6.2.1 The Exclusivity of Flag State Jurisdiction and its Abuse

Access to living resources on the high seas revolves around the system of nationality of vessels precisely because it is the flag state that has exclusive jurisdiction over the vessel flying its flag on the high seas. Article 116 of UNCLOS establishes that 'All States have the right for their nationals to engage in fishing on the high seas.' This provision implies that freedom of fishing under the Convention is a state right and not a private fishing right, and that the exploitation and the conservation of marine living resources is subject to flag state jurisdiction on the high seas. Consequently, flag states have complete authority over all vessels under their registry[9] in maritime areas outside national jurisdiction. Any other enforcement authority on the high seas is not permissible unless, as we shall see,[10] the flag state specifically agrees to entrust enforcement measures in certain circumstances to the coastal state. Post-UNCLOS agreements do not contest the exclusive jurisdiction of the flag state; this is a long established customary rule of international law reiterated under UNCLOS.[11] These agreements generally seek to ensure that vessels on the high seas adopt a certain code of behaviour. In very limited cases, some fisheries agreements such as CCAMLR and the Donut Hole Convention bestow limited powers upon the coastal state or other inspecting states to intervene or to exercise pressure on the flag state to take action in the absence of any form of control or in case of complete inertia on the part of the flag state.[12] These agreements cannot, however, be considered norm-creating. They are only binding on their parties.

UNCLOS article 94 specifies in legal terms the duties of the flag state on the high seas. The applicable provisions[13] refer to measures that must be taken by the flag state to ensure safety at sea, maintain communications and prevent, reduce and control marine pollution. However, UNCLOS does not refer to any duties flag states may impose upon their fishing vessels to put into effect their obligation to take conservation measures.[14] For instance, the 1982 Convention does not require the flag state to initiate an inquiry when its vessels do not observe these conservation measures, as it does in the case of marine pollution.[15] Although the same provision allows for an inquiry in the case of 'serious damage caused to the marine environment',[16] it appears that in practice states adopt a restrictive interpretation of this clause in article 94 and have never applied it to also include grounds for a compulsory inquiry if a flag state is accused of breaching conservation measures on the high seas. At the time of the negotiations leading to UNCLOS, issues relating to the conservation of marine living resources and the threat to the marine environment caused by pollution from ships were seen as separate issues. It was only after UNCED that a comprehensive approach became more widely accepted. It is therefore debatable whether the list of flag state duties under UNCLOS, imposing upon them certain measures to ensure the protection of the marine environment, can be interpreted to include these same measures to implement the obligation states have to conserve living marine resources on the high seas.[17] UNCLOS does not specifically exclude marine living resources from Part XII, but the vast majority of the substantive obligations,[18] including those on enforcement, all refer to pollution and discharges into the marine environment. There is no specific provision under UNCLOS that sheds light upon how states are to enforce their obligation to conserve living resources on the high seas, and this lacuna is an obstacle to determine which enforcement tools should be applied to secure compliance by flag states. This situation necessitated the conclusion of agreements that seek to supplement UNCLOS in this respect. Post-UNCLOS multilateral agreements have in fact superseded the need for such a debate and have assimilated enforcement obligations for the conservation of marine living resources with the same responsibilities flag states have in this respect for marine pollution offences[19] under the 1982 Convention. For instance, flag state responsibility with respect to fishing vessels is regulated by the FAO Compliance Agreement.[20] Article 18 of the FSA expands upon flag state responsibilities and duties, whilst all of Part VI of the same Agreement is entirely dedicated to compliance and enforcement.[21]

The FAO Compliance Agreement is the first multilateral legal agreement that deals directly with compliance and enforcement relating to conservation of living resources on the high seas.[22] The Agreement's main objective is securing compliance and, if fishing vessels do not comply, it obligates flag state parties to resort to enforcement. It seeks to overcome the problem of lack of compliance on the part of flag states by strengthening their duties. In this respect it establishes two main obligations. First, parties are to exercise control over fishing vessels flying their flag, ensuring that these vessels do not undermine international fishery conservation and management measures. The Compliance Agreement obligates parties to take such measures 'as may be necessary' to ensure that fishing vessels flying their flag 'do not engage in any activity that undermines the effectiveness of international conservation and management measures'.[23] It does not provide any indication as to what these conservation measures should actually consist of, but makes a cross reference to other legal sources.[24] Secondly, it establishes that it is the duty of the flag state to submit information about its vessels fishing on the high seas. The FAO Compliance Agreement's rationale is therefore the identification of flag states' duties and the type of control they should exercise over fishing vessels flying their flag. It fills a lacuna which UNCLOS left unaddressed in its Article 94.[25] It does so in three practical ways. First, it obligates state parties to authorize fishing operations and subjects such an authorization to the flag state's capacity to ensure that fishing vessels bearing its flag comply with conservation and management measures on the high seas. This is in line with the predominant interpretation of the term 'genuine link' according to current state practice.[26] Secondly, the Agreement strengthens international cooperation. And thirdly, it increases transparency in the exchange of information between state parties regarding high seas fisheries. These two measures serve to render more accessible information about the level of enforcement that is undertaken by flag states with respect to their vessels. In turn, state parties would feel the pressure to remain compliant and to exercise appropriate controls on their vessels.

The Compliance Agreement provides a specific methodology regarding how flag States should effectively exercise their duty to ensure the conservation of high seas living resources.[27] The system of authorizations required by the Agreement seeks to guarantee that flag states would honour their commitment to secure the vessels' compliance with the applicable conservation measures, because the Agreement prohibits state parties from granting an authorization for fishing on the high seas when they cannot exercise such control. The responsibility to ensure compliance with conservation measures lies with the flag state even with respect to vessels that fall outside the scope of the Agreement.[28] In such cases the flag state can only exempt them where they would not undermine the 'object and purpose of the Agreement'.[29] At any rate, a flag state's decision to bind its nationals by a system of authorizations in order to be able to exercise the freedom of fishing is a treaty obligation that also arises under other regional legal instruments and the FSA. Nothing, however, prohibits non-parties from exercising the freedom of fishing anywhere on the high seas if they do not have a system of authorizations.

The authorization system is an expression of the state's vested right to the freedom of fishing that is being bestowed upon its nationals.[30] It is an important compliance tool in the hands of flag states, involving them more directly and hence imposing more responsibility upon them in fulfilling their obligation to conserve high seas living resources. Subjecting the exercise of freedom of fishing to an authorization with conditions that reflect multilateral conservation and management measures is a useful way of helping flag states not to abdicate their responsibility or take advantage of more conservation conscious states by luring to their register fishing vessels that ride roughshod over multilateral conservation measures without the risk of having to face enforcement measures. It is, however, also true to say that authorization as a compliance tool is only obligatory upon parties to the Agreement, the FSA and other regional and subregional agreements. Non-parties can still attract fishing vessel registrations and bestow the right to fish upon vessels flying their flag without adopting such stringent measures. Furthermore, since the Agreement does not define which conservation measures are obligatory, parties under the Compliance Agreement can adopt different conditions to implement conservation measures when granting an authorization.

The Compliance Agreement tried to overcome the issue of the flag state's inability or reluctance to comply with conservation measures by requiring port state parties to intervene[31] and 'promptly notify the flag State' that it has 'reasonable grounds for believing that the fishing vessel has been used for an activity that undermines the effectiveness of international conservation and management measures'. The Agreement even provides for parties to:

> make arrangements regarding the undertaking by Port States of such investigatory measures as may be necessary to establish whether the fishing vessel has indeed been used contrary to the provisions of this Agreement.[32]

Under the Agreement, therefore, flag states may choose to concede to port states the authority to collect evidence and inspect the fishing vessel.[33] This can be seen as an important legal development, but it is entirely dependent on the flag state's consent in order to be put into effect even when the flag state is a party to the Agreement. It must be stressed, however, that once a fishing vessel voluntarily enters the port of a foreign state it would anyway be subject to the regulations of that port state. The Compliance Agreement is hereby attempting to encourage cooperation instead of restricting the exclusive jurisdiction of the flag state. Cooperation facilitates compliance and, if adhered to by all states, it would also curb unfair competition and restrain flag hopping which would prejudice those flag states that conscientiously take enforcement measures to secure compliance with conservation and management measures.

The FSA also seeks to retain the exclusivity of flag state jurisdiction, but elaborates even further upon flag states' duties in its article 18 than the Compliance Agreement does. Like the latter, it requires flag state parties to ensure that their vessels comply with subregional and regional conservation and management measures, and that they do not engage in any activity that undermines the effectiveness of these measures. More importantly, the FSA establishes that:

> A State shall authorize the use of vessels flying its flag for fishing on the high seas only where it is able to exercise effectively its responsibilities in respect of such vessels under the Convention (UNCLOS) and this Agreement.[34]

This is more elaborate than the corresponding provision under UNCLOS.[35]

The FSA uses authorization as a compliance tool to compel flag states to exercise control over their fishing vessels, thereby enhancing compliance with conservation measures. This is because the system of authorization is linked to the nationality of the ship in two ways. First, it can only be granted by the flag state if the latter is 'able to exercise effectively its responsibilities in respect of such vessels' under UNCLOS and the FSA. Conversely the authorization is forfeited once the fishing vessel ceases to be entitled to fly the flag of the state where it was registered. This may occur, for example, when the flag state is no longer in a position to ensure that the fishing vessel is complying with the conservation and management obligations it has as a party to the FSA. In such cases the fishing vessel would cease to be entitled to the nationality of the flag state, and hence to the authorization to fish. Secondly, as discussed already under the Compliance Agreement, the authorization is a direct consequence of the flag state's responsibility to exercise effectively its jurisdiction over the fishing vessel by taking measures via conditions stipulated in the authorization granted to it.

The authorization procedure is strongly recommended by the FAO IPOA-IUU, and it is an enforcement tool adopted by many other regional and subregional fisheries agreements. Nevertheless, as in the case of the Compliance Agreement, it must be pointed out that a system of authorization as envisaged under the FSA does not bind non-parties. States have a right under UNCLOS to bestow upon their fishing vessels their public right to fish on the high seas, but UNCLOS stops at that and does not specify how this may be done. Doubtlessly, the ambiguous wording under

UNCLOS facilitates reflagging to states that are not parties to FSA that adopt weaker conservation measures for fishing operations carried out on the high seas by vessels flying their flag.

The FSA also attempts to deal with the abuse of the exclusivity of flag state jurisdiction by doing away with the flag state's discretion to determine the measures that may be necessary to ensure control over fishing vessels.[36] It obligates the flag state parties to follow a specific procedure in exercising their exclusive jurisdiction. The FSA, in fact, lays down specific obligations relating to flag state duties that are not found in UNCLOS. An inclusive list of compliance measures under article 18 of the FSA is mandatory upon flag state parties.[37] Furthermore, as is the case under the Compliance Agreement, state parties are to ensure that the measures they impose on fishing vessels flying their flag are to be compatible with any regional and globally-agreed conservation measure that is in effect.[38] Another encroachment upon the discretion of the flag state when exercising its exclusive jurisdiction relates to the investigation of infringements. Under the FSA, flag states must investigate 'immediately and fully' alleged violations by their vessels.

The FSA leaves it up to the flag state concerned to decide whether to inspect the vessel physically, but it makes it mandatory for the flag state to report on the progress of the investigation both to the state alleging the violation as well as to the applicable subregional or regional organization or arrangement. In other words, under the FSA a flag state party becomes answerable to other parties as to whether it has exercised control over its fishing vessels accused of infringing conservation measures on the high seas. This obligation upon flag states who are parties to the FSA is more onerous than the corresponding provisions under UNCLOS, which says that:

> a State which has clear grounds to believe that proper jurisdiction and control with respect to a ship have not been exercised may report the facts to the Flag State.[39]

When receiving the report the flag state shall investigate and 'if appropriate, take any necessary action to remedy situation'.[40] Under the FSA, flag state parties must report to other states and regional Fisheries Organizations whether they have fulfilled their investigative obligations in order to ensure compliance with conservation measures on the high seas by their vessels. It is also mandatory for the flag state to require its vessels to give information to the investigating authority on their position, their catches, fishing gear, fishing operations and related activities in the area of the alleged violation.[41] Furthermore, contrary to the corresponding

UNCLOS provision referred to above, parties to the FSA are to take legal action against vessels flying their flag if evidence sufficiently indicates that a violation has in fact occurred. Unlike UNCLOS, the FSA does not leave it up to the flag state to decide whether it is appropriate or not to take any action to remedy the situation.[42] The FSA provisions bestow upon the port state, coastal or other inspecting state these powers to supplement the flag state's responsibilities in this regard.

The sanctions to be imposed by the flag state and applicable in the case of violations under the FSA 'shall be adequate in severity to be effective in securing compliance and to discourage violations and shall deprive offenders of the benefits accruing from their illegal activities'.[43] This is also reminiscent of the corresponding provision under Part XII of UNCLOS.[44] The FSA gives directions on the nature of the sanctions that are to be applied with respect to the masters and officers of fishing vessels. Although the use of the words 'shall include provisions' gives one the first impression that these obligations are mandatory upon flag states, the term 'which may permit *inter alia*' exonerates flag state parties from necessarily adopting the suggested sanctions, namely the withdrawal, refusal or suspension of authorizations and to serve as masters or officers on such vessels.[45]

The jurisdictional scope of the CBD in areas beyond national jurisdiction applies only to processes and activities carried out under a party's jurisdiction or control which may have an adverse impact on biodiversity.[46] CBD parties whose fishing vessels exploit marine living resources on the high seas fall within the scope of its conservation and enforcement regime. The CBD upholds the exclusivity of flag state's jurisdiction on the high seas but also refers to the need for cooperation among parties in these areas to safeguard the conservation and sustainable use of biodiversity. This cooperation can be achieved either directly or through competent international organizations.[47] Every party to the CBD is responsible for monitoring processes and activities carried out by its nationals or entities under its jurisdiction or control, for securing their compliance with the provisions of the Convention, and for enforcing under its national laws any infringement committed. Parties are to promote reciprocal arrangements for notification, exchange of information and consultation on any activity likely to have significant adverse effects on biodiversity in areas beyond national jurisdiction and to notify potentially affected states in cases of grave or imminent danger.[48] The provisions outlining state responsibility with respect to compliance elaborate upon the UNCLOS provisions on the obligation states have towards the conservation of high seas living resources. The obligation under the CBD to assess state activities outside national jurisdiction further supplements the UNCLOS obligation to cooperate when exploiting marine living resources. It also implements the obligation to pay 'due regard to the interests of other States'. In many ways the CBD re-echoes the FSA and FAO Compliance Agreement and UNCLOS itself. It considers the flag state to be responsible for monitoring compliance and, although the flag state can do so directly, it favours cooperation as the means to secure enforcement particularly through competent international organizations.

States have taken certain measures under these post-UNCLOS international legal agreements to ensure more effective enforcement on the high seas, such as authorization, notification, information and better accountability by flag states through their reporting obligations. However, none of these enforcement tools challenge the exclusivity of flag state jurisdiction on the high seas, and state practice does not imply that such tools have become customary rules of international law.[49] Other enforcement tools adopted, such as surveillance and inspection carried out by the coastal state, always depend on the flag state's express consent. All these post-UNCLOS legal instruments provide enforcement regimes which acknowledge that the flag state jurisdiction is exclusive but it may allow other parties to investigate and inspect fishing vessels that are not registered under their flag, both at sea and in port.

There is however a fundamental difference between the controls that coastal states may exercise qua coastal states on vessels on the high seas because they are part of a fisheries agreement and the controls the coastal state may exercise as a port state, if the same vessel enters its ports voluntarily. Coastal states exercising enforcement measures on the high seas may do so only with respect to vessels whose flag state consents via an agreement to this effect. In such cases, the flag state always retains the priority to exercise enforcement itself. On the other hand, since no vessel has an automatic right of access to ports, any conditions on port access imposed by coastal states are an effective way to regulate fishing vessels registered in states that do not adopt the same conservation measures or which do not exercise sufficient control over their vessels or else which are states that are not even parties to an agreement. All these compliance and enforcement measures introduced by the FSA, the Compliance Agreement and the CBD attempt to address the abuse and inability of the flag state to exercise its exclusive jurisdiction. They impose measures upon the flag state party regarding how it must exercise certain aspects of its exclusive jurisdiction. They may also give other state parties alleging the violation, either individually or through regional fisheries organizations, the ability to intervene under certain circumstances. The exclusivity of flag state jurisdiction subsists, and states that are not parties to these Agreements continue to enjoy absolute discretion to decide what conditions to impose upon ships registering under their flag.

The post-UNCLOS legal instruments have sought to further expound upon[50] the introduction of new obligations which are inherent to parties as their flag state duties. There is no imposition upon UNCLOS state parties to adhere to these Agreements, even if they were specifically negotiated to supplement this lacuna by elaborating upon the type of control flag states are supposed to exercise on fishing vessels flying their flag. Both the CBD and the FSA have been widely adhered to, and so these Agreements may also *prima facie* represent what general state practice perceives to be the legal duties of flag States *vis-à-vis* their vessels when fishing on the high seas. Their crystallization into customary rules of international law can only be determined if raised in a dispute before an international tribunal and the adjudicating body accepts it as such. Until this is ascertained, this lack of coherence between treaty law and customary international law continues to generate uncertainty and thus tends to favour non-compliance.

6.2.2 Reflagging of Fishing Vessels

Another major obstacle to securing compliance with and enforcement of international law on the high seas and which arises as a result of the exclusive nature of flag state jurisdiction, is the reflagging of vessels (including fishing vessels) from one state to another. States bestow nationality to ships flying their flag, but not all states adopt the same standards when registering vessels. The problem of reflagging is not unique to the conservation and management of marine living resources, but it hampers all types of enforcement attempts to maintain the rule of law on the high seas. However, in the case of enforcement of conservation obligations it has two major implications that further exacerbate fragmentation. First, changing the flag of a fishing vessel may signify subjecting fishing operations to different obligations that may be either more onerous or less stringent. Secondly, the issue of nationality poses a particular difficulty to fisheries law enforcement with respect to allocation rights. Problems relating to allocation and access to resources are often resolved by distinguishing harvesting vessels according to their registration or nationality. Consequently, certain harvesting restrictions may apply to certain vessels and not others, as enforcement with respect to quotas and management in general is closely linked to the nationality of fishing vessel. In other words, certain ship registries therefore become more attractive than others for the wrong reasons, namely lax conservation and management measures and lack of allocation quotas due to non-adherence to cooperation agreements.

Some states actually consider this situation as an opportunity that gives them a better competitive edge, and they take the opportunity to make registration easier and at least as obliging as possible. Flag hopping or reflagging may thus occur when vessel owners desert or avoid registries of states which adhere to more stringent conservation obligations; this is done in order to avoid enforcement measures relating thereto and to seek better or unlimited allocation rights. The negotiation of adequate conservation measures and equitable allocation rights in accordance with the UNCLOS provisions is, in practice, at the mercy of those states which adopt the bare minimum standards of conservation or which simply do not have the means to control compliance with conservation measures on the high seas, as owners of fishing vessels would reflag to their registers. This rampant abuse is therefore directly linked to the continued practice of illegal, unreported and unregulated fishing leading to unsustainable exploitation. It also jeopardizes the equitable distribution of allocation quotas. In sum, access itself and the enforcement measures necessary to regulate it revolve around the registration of ships and the obligations of the flag states under international law. UNCLOS tried to address the issue by inserting a clear, albeit generic, obligation upon states with respect to ship registration and provides[51] that 'There must be a genuine link between the State and the ship', but it does not define the term in more precise legal language.

Since its inception in the 1950s,[52] the legal interpretation of the term 'genuine link' has been riddled with controversy. During UNCLOS negotiations the genuine link was not discussed at great length,[53] and the states' perception of its legal interpretation, at the time, reflected article 5 of the High Seas Convention as well as the advisory opinion of the ICJ in the *Constitution of the Maritime Safety Committee of the IMCO* case.[54] There are, in fact, two main schools of legal thought under maritime international law which have tried to define the meaning of 'genuine link'. The restricted approach interprets the term to require that its nationals are either the owners or are part of the crew of those ships flying its flag. This approach has had limited success, mainly as a result of opposition from the traditional maritime states and states with open registries. Another interpretation examines the genuine link within its broader context, prescribing it for the sole purpose of safeguarding the necessary authority of the flag state in the best possible manner. According to the latter approach, without this requirement of necessary authority the concept of nationality of ships is futile and leads to anarchy on the high seas.[55] This latter interpretation embodies, in a better manner, the concomitant duties which flag states have with respect to ships flying their flags. Ultimately, it is the lack of control over vessels flying their flag which leads to the flag states' failure in securing compliance and enforcement of their international obligations during the exercise of their high seas freedoms.

Since UNCLOS, there have been various developments that shed further light on how the interpretation of the concept of genuine link as well as the effective jurisdiction and control over ships have evolved. These developments occurred mainly as a result of the Convention on Conditions for Registration of Ships, commonly referred to as the Registration Convention, and the work of the International Maritime Organization (IMO) on flag state implementation of obligations under international law. The Registration Convention[56] does not, however, apply to fishing vessels. Nonetheless, for the purpose of our discussion it is still useful because the Convention recognizes the close connection between the genuine link and effective control and jurisdiction of the flag state over ships flying its flag. It goes, however, beyond both the 1958 High Seas Convention and UNCLOS as it defines the requirements concerning the nationality of ownership and the manning of ships in connection with their registration by a state.[57] The Registration Convention[58] establishes a link between nationality issues and effective jurisdiction, and lays down that the level of national participation in ownership 'should be sufficient to permit the flag state to exercise effectively its jurisdiction and control over ships flying its flag.'[59] Since the conclusion of the Registration Convention, which is still not in force, the trend in maritime merchant shipping law has leant more towards the elaboration of effective flag state jurisdiction and control rather than towards expanding the definition of genuine link itself. Nevertheless, the Registration Convention shows that the two issues are intrinsically interlinked.

The interpretation of a genuine link entailing effectiveness to secure compliance is also present in legal instruments regulating fishing vessels on the high seas where the debate on the meaning of 'genuine link' has also proved to be controversial. This was all too evident during the negotiations that led to the conclusion of the FAO Compliance Agreement.[60] The Agreement did not adopt the wording of the Registration Convention with respect to the interpretation of the term.[61] Neither did it include its qualification as to what the level of national participation in ownership should be in order to ascertain this genuine link. This demonstrates that states, in general, do not endorse the legal argument that *sufficient* national participation is an essential requirement to guarantee effective jurisdiction and control by flag states over their vessels fishing on the high seas. The rejection of the Registration Convention's approach by the negotiators of the FAO Compliance Agreement highlights a discrepancy between these two international legal instruments which have adopted a different yardstick when determining the legal implications of the same term, albeit for vessels which carry out different operations on the high seas. Consequently, if the Registration Convention comes into force, the legal meaning of what constitutes a genuine link, at least with respect to merchant shipping vessels belonging to its state parties, would vary depending upon the nature of a vessel's activity on the high seas. In this sense, unlike the Registration Convention, the FAO Compliance Agreement has remained in line with UNCLOS. The UNCLOS provision on genuine link neither refers to national participation nor does it distinguish between vessels used for fishing and other forms of shipping vessels. Therefore, despite the Registration Convention, the main trend is to interpret the term 'genuine link' as the flag state's capacity to control and exercise jurisdiction on the high seas, without going into the issue of 'sufficient national participation'.

State practice appears to prefer the wider interpretation as adopted by UNCLOS and the FSA. This is evident in a number of cases before the Court of Justice of the European Union which examined the imposition of nationality requirements as an essential condition to guarantee a genuine link. In one set of cases the European Court of Justice addressed the question of whether member states of the European Communities can maintain nationality requirements in respect of the registration of ships, as this would in turn discriminate against the freedom of movement of citizens of other member states. On the other hand, member states have alleged that the imposition of such nationality requirements is an important instrument to ensure the existence of a genuine link between the state and the ship.[62] The European Court of Justice has rejected this argument and held that, under international law, member states are not obliged to implement the genuine link concept by imposing nationality requirements. In one particular case[63] the European Court of Justice examined not only the genuine link concept in the context of the legal order of the European Communities but the genuine link concept under international law, where it held that a member state may not treat a vessel which is already registered in a non-member country and therefore has the nationality of that country, as a vessel flying the flag of that member state. The fact that the sole link between a vessel and the flag state is the administrative formality of registration cannot prevent the application of that rule. The Court held that it was for the state that conferred its nationality in the first place to determine, at its absolute discretion, the conditions on which it would grant its nationality.[64] This judgment of the Court confirms that, under international law, states have absolute discretion to establish the conditions for granting their nationality to ships. Various international legal sources and general state practice therefore accept that the flag state's genuine link with the vessel manifests itself in its obligation to ensure effective jurisdiction and control over its vessels in order to secure compliance with conservation measures on the high seas. This is, after all, the real crunch issue given that it is the *absence* of such control which leads to non-compliance and poor enforcement, and which stultifies regional cooperation for the conservation and management of marine living resources. Although admittedly national participation in ownership is an advantage for securing compliance, this does not necessarily mean that to improve enforcement and eliminate illegal, unregulated and unrecorded fishing the international community should rely upon nationality as a guarantee to better enforcement, and to this effect it is futile for it to waste more effort to elaborate upon the definition of the term 'genuine link'. State practice therefore has steered away from a more restrictive definition of 'genuine link', particularly by avoiding linking it with ownership nationality requirements. These post-UNCLOS Agreements chose instead to focus upon measures which in themselves ameliorate the flag states' effective jurisdiction and control over their vessels fishing on the high seas. Apart from this, they have supplemented the flag states' capacity to control their vessels by bestowing a monitoring role that can be exercised by port states and, to a more limited extent, by coastal states when in the latter case the flag state explicitly consents. This approach is reflected both in the FSA and in the FAO Compliance Agreement.[65] States negotiating the FAO Compliance Agreement in fact worked their way out of this obstacle, and instead of addressing the legal act of flagging and vessel registration they shifted their attention to the act of requiring states to adopt an authorization system for their vessels to fish on the high seas.

For instance, in order to discourage reflagging, the FSA provides that 'the vessel shall not engage in fishing operations on the High Seas until such time as all outstanding sanctions imposed by the Flag State in respect of the violation have been complied with'.[66] The wording of this provision, however, makes it unclear as to who is to fulfil this obligation, as the provision does not explicitly say so. If it is directed only to the flag state, it would be futile because it would not stop other state parties from accepting it under their register as the vessel owners opt to reflag. In this way it will only prejudice those flag states which would take sanctions seriously. If it is intended as a measure to avoid reflagging, it must be directed to all state parties; but the provision does not say so and the way it is worded seems to impose the obligation also upon the private owners of the vessel. This is unlikely because the freedom of fishing on the high seas is not a private right but is vested in the state under whose flag the vessel is registered.[67] It is not impossible either, because even UNCLOS itself has provisions on ship nationality directed at ships themselves,[68] imposing therefore an international obligation upon private individuals. The most plausible and effective way of interpreting this provision so that it achieves its objective would be to consider that it is imposing this obligation upon *all* state parties and the vessel owners. This would ensure that the flag state takes and implements sanctions against the vessel that has violated conservation measures on the high seas. Similarly, by imposing this obligation upon all other state parties, the owners of the vessel would be unable to avoid sanctions imposed by the original flag state by registering under another flag. Furthermore, if this provision imposes an international obligation upon the private owners of the vessel it would also prevent reflagging to non-parties.

The FSA and various regional agreements[69] propose other measures to secure compliance with and implementation of international conservation regimes. Devising legal mechanisms to guarantee the effective exercise of jurisdiction and control over fishing vessels helps one to avoid entering into the controversy raised by the genuine link concept. This approach is not only a safer alternative, politically speaking, but also allows for more legal and practical flexibility. Compliance measures can be varied to address the very different exigencies posed by fishing on the high seas. More importantly, widespread adherence to the FSA encourages port states to adopt strict sanctions on vessels with fish landings that have not been harvested on the high seas according to the Convention's conservation regime. Similarly, coastal states (with the flag state's consent) may be allowed to exercise their enforcement powers upon foreign flag vessels. This would not only assist or supplement compliance by the flag state but may also help to discourage reflagging since fewer states would be in a position to offer a less rigorous conservation regime than the one imposed by the FSA. Even flag states which are reluctant to authorize port and coastal states to exercise controls over vessels flying their flag would at least be legally bound to act. At any rate, once the vessel voluntarily enters port it will be subject to the port state's regulations. It is only with respect to the exercise of criminal jurisdiction against the owners and the master of the vessel that the port state remains dependent on the flag state's consent.[70]

On the other hand, bypassing the lack of presence and control of the flag state over its vessels by bestowing rights on the coastal state is not a right that the latter can assume without the consent of the flag state. In the *M/V Saiga* case,[71] the tribunal found that the absence of a genuine link does not give another state additional possibilities to take measures against a ship violating international standards. States cannot, on the basis of proving that there is no genuine link between the flag state and the vessel infringing international obligations, exercise control themselves. Therefore the option of enhancing jurisdiction and control over fishing vessels by other interested parties can *only* apply when the flag state specifically consents to such an intervention by third parties. Since the flag state enjoys exclusive jurisdiction[72] on the high seas, the possibility of adopting flags of convenience and the promotion of open registries remains one of the major hurdles for ensuring compliance with and the enforcement of conservation obligations in maritime areas falling outside national jurisdiction. This practice of changing from one state registry to another has a tremendous impact on competitiveness and discourages states from taking strict conservation measures, as this usually triggers the reflagging of vessels from the ship registries of parties to conservation agreements to those of non-parties. It remains perhaps the main reason why illegal, unregulated and unrecorded fishing continues to jeopardize innumerable attempts to establish effective conservation regimes on the high seas. To counter this situation states can always apply the active nationality principle, also recommended in the FAO IPOA-IUU,[73] which under international law enables states to exercise criminal jurisdiction over nationals wherever they fish, even if their fishing vessel is registered in another state. Despite national legislation that inflicts criminal punishment upon the owners and crew of ships that permit and use illegal fishing gear, exploit protected species or carry out any other illegal activity related to fishing on the high seas, enforcement in such cases remains however unlikely due to this lack of 'presence'. Furthermore, the way states apply the active nationality principle varies, and is often limited in many ways. Few states have a legal framework that bestows upon them jurisdiction over their nationals under any circumstances, wherever these nationals would be.[74] It is therefore unlikely that this legal remedy would spur flag states that do not have the will or the capacity to control their vessels to take action.

6.3 CONCLUSION

RFMOs and multilateral agreements have attempted to overcome the two major legal obstacles, namely abuse of the exclusivity of flag state jurisdiction and reflagging that had been left open to interpretation under UNCLOS. They have done so by elaborating upon this obligation, that is, defining in substantive terms the responsibility of the flag state. Mandatory measures to improve control on the high seas were included in these instruments, and treaty provisions established a procedure that renders the flag state accountable towards the RFMO and interested state parties. The flag state is obligated to explain and defend its position with respect to enforcement measures taken against vessels flying their flag that have been in breach of conservation measures. Primarily, states have opted to cooperate rather than to resort to judicial settlement when obstacles arise. They have also further developed compliance and enforcement measures under both multilateral as well as regional and subregional agreements. They have intensified the involvement of the port state, cooperating non-parties, fishing entities and to a limited extent even enhanced the role of the coastal state which is responsible for compliance and enforcement in the EEZ.

The need for better compliance measures was the major reason behind the conclusion of the FAO Compliance Agreement[75] which conforms to the FSA's provisions on the same subject.[76] Both international Agreements came about as a reaction to various major Fisheries Conferences and Agenda 21.[77] There is no sufficient evidence to support the view that any of the compliance and enforcement provisions in the FSA and the Compliance Agreement as well as the regional fisheries agreements have crystallized into customary international law. States that are not parties to these two multilateral Agreements are still regulated by UNCLOS, which gives them the option to adopt unilateral conservation measures,[78] instead of concluding agreements with other states to this effect. On this basis, non-party flag states[79] taking unilateral conservation measures for their fishing vessels that are less onerous than those found in the post-UNCLOS legal instruments or the subregional and regional agreements, argue that they cannot be deemed to be guilty of breaching conservation obligations agreed upon via cooperation.[80] Non-parties claim that specific conservation measures applicable on the high seas, and the compliance and enforcement obligations related thereto, need to be specifically acquiesced to in order to be applicable and opposable to them. Consequently, they argue, they cannot be constrained to obligate their vessels to comply with conservation measures which they do not adhere to or to subject their vessels to the compliance and enforcement of these same obligations. Under UNCLOS, however, all states must subject their freedom of fishing to the rights, the duties as well as the interests of coastal states and to the provisions of section two of its Part VII. On this basis, the major counter argument some states make when negotiating legal instruments on the subject is that compliance and enforcement measures are essential tools for the conservation of high seas living resources; they are part and parcel of the same obligation, which is a qualification to the freedom of fishing and which cannot be perceived as further restricting it.[81] In other words, conservation measures adopted by coastal states via multilateral, regional and subregional fisheries agreements may still be binding upon non-parties fishing on the high seas because they express those measures the coastal states have taken to safeguard their interests, rights and duties and which flag states whose nationals fish on the high seas must subject their operations to in accordance with UNCLOS article 116(b).[82] The argument made above may be easier to support when one refers to conservation measures in general and, to a certain extent, even with respect to compliance. It is somewhat more difficult to argue in favour of it in matters relating to enforcement, which is exclusively within the hands of the flag state. The effect of these Agreements upon non-parties must be seen in the light of their position as third parties under international law. To date there are no norms relating to conservation that qualify as *jus cogens*,[83] so the balance would definitely tilt in favour of a restrictive interpretation to the qualification to the freedom of fishing. States are also bound by customary international law rules, unless they have persistently objected to such norms whilst they have been in the making.[84] International law is by its very nature dynamic, and no treaty provisions, not even those of a norm making-treaty like UNCLOS, are resistant to change. In the end, the UNCLOS provisions on the subject are very general and were negotiated with the intention that further legal developments through cooperation between states would elaborate upon the 1982 Convention. The harmonization of the applicable international regimes for the conservation of marine living resources highlights the need to assess whether post-UNCLOS Agreements[85] may have introduced more detailed compliance and enforcement regimes that may be considered as common, minimum measures required by international fisheries law to ensure the conservation and management of high seas living resources and to safeguard the rights, duties and interests of coastal States. This will be discussed in the next chapter.

NOTES

1. See Gillespie, A. (2003), 'The Search for a New Compliance Mechanism within the International Whaling Commission', ODIL, **34**, (3–4), 349–68.
2. UNCLOS article 117 refers to living resources on the high seas and does not enter into any detail. Article 61 refers to living resources in the EEZ; it is more elaborate than article 117 but still leaves the specific details regarding conservation measures to be determined by the coastal state.
3. See Burke W.T. (1994), *The International Law of Fisheries UNCLOS and Beyond*, Oxford: Clarendon Press, pp 303–47.
4. Few provisions refer specifically to enforcement under UNCLOS. Nevertheless, those provisions establishing rights and freedoms of those entities using the marine environment both within and outside national jurisdiction, namely articles 17, 21, 24, 25, 36, 38, 39, 45, 51, 56–68, 73, 110, 111 and 116, may all affect the development of enforcement measures in multilateral agreements regulating the conservation of living marine resources. From these, articles 21, 25, 49, 73 refer to enforcement and fishing within national jurisdiction. With respect to provisions applicable on the high seas, article 66 relates to the enforcement of regulations re anadromous stocks beyond EEZ and articles 110 and 111 refer to enforcement with respect to the right of visit and hot pursuit. There are no provisions dealing directly with enforcement and fishing on the high seas, although article 116 implies some enforcement authority.
5. See UNCLOS article 92.
6. Ibid, article 117.

7. See Riddle, K. (2003), 'Illegal, Unreported and Unregulated Fishing: Is International Cooperation Contagious?' ODIL, **37** (3–4), 267 on the challenges CCAMLR faces with respect to IUU fishing of the Patagonian toothfish due to the monitoring and surveillance difficulties because of the remote areas where it is carried out.
8. A state has the jurisdiction to impose upon vessels that voluntarily enter its ports any controls on fish landings it may deem necessary, irrespective of where the fish were harvested.
9. See Shearer, I.A. (1986) 'Problems of Jurisdiction and Law Enforcement Against Delinquent Vessels' *International and Comparative Law Quarterly* **35**, 320–43.
10. See discussion below at pp 198 et seq.
11. See UNCLOS articles 91 and 92.
12. Ibid.
13. Article 94 of UNCLOS lists the duties of the flag state.
14. Article 117 establishes this duty upon states to take conservation measures on the high seas.
15. UNCLOS does obligate state parties to carry out an inquiry in case of an incident on the high seas involving a ship flying their flag and causing serious damage to the marine environment. For instance, in case of prevention, reduction and control of pollution of the marine environment from vessels, UNCLOS establishes that the flag state, 'shall provide for immediate investigation and, where appropriate, institute proceedings in respect of the alleged violation', irrespective of where the incident occurred or where pollution occurred or was spotted. Furthermore, it obligates states to investigate, at the written request of any state, any alleged violation deemed to have been committed by a vessel flying their flag. States shall institute proceedings without delay if satisfied that sufficient evidence is available to enable proceedings to be brought in respect to any alleged violation. States shall also promptly inform the requesting state and the competent international organization of the action taken and of the outcome. Such information shall be available to all states.
16. See UNCLOS articles 94(4)(c) and (7).
17. See UNCLOS article 217(1); the specific wording under Part XIII on enforcement by flag states excludes the regime therein from applying to anything but pollution prevention, reduction and control.
18. Only ibid, article 192 which sets down the general obligation, article 193 that reiterates Principle 21 of the Stockholm Declaration at the UNCHE, and article 196 which addresses the accidental introduction of alien species, refer to the marine environment in a more general sense and hence may be interpreted to include the regulation of conservation on the high seas; otherwise the provisions are only applicable in the case of pollution as this is specifically referred to.
19. See UNCLOS article 217.
20. FAO Compliance Agreement article III. See also paragraphs 6.11 and 8.2. of the non-legally binding Code of Conduct for Responsible Fisheries adopted on 31 October 1995.
21. Article 19 of the Code relates to enforcement by the flag state, article 20 deals with international cooperation and enforcement, and article 21 with sub-regional and regional cooperation and enforcement. Article 22 lays down the basic procedure for boarding and inspection, and article 23 the measures to be taken by a port state.
22. Its success, however, has been limited due to lack of ratification particularly by states that are renowned to represent flags of convenience.
23. FAO Compliance Agreement article III 1(a).
24. Under the FAO Compliance Agreement these conservation measures are not specifically defined, but the agreement says that they mean, 'international conservation and management measures to conserve or manage one or more species of living marine resources that are adopted and applied in accordance with the relevant rules of international law as reflected in the 1982 United Nations Convention on the Law of the Sea and that such measures may be adopted either by global, regional or subregional fisher-

ies organizations, subject to the rights and obligations of their members, or by treaties or other international agreements'.
25. This section lists the duties of the flag states on the high seas.
26. See discussion below at pp 205 et seq. on the genuine link and the nationality of ships. See also Oude Elferink, A. (1999) 'The Genuine Link Concept: Time for a Post Mortem?', Netherlands Institute for the Law of the Sea, Utrecht: Utrecht University (available at http://www.uu.nl/faculty/leg/NL/organisatie/departementen/departemen trechtsgeleerdheid/organisatie/onderdelen/NetherlandsInstitutefortheLawoftheSea/pub lications/onlinepapers/Documents/genuine%20link.pdf).
27. UNCLOS article 117.
28. Only fishing vessels that are 24 metres in length and over are subject to the Compliance Agreement.
29. See article II(2). There are also other grounds when exemptions do not apply; See article II 2(a), (b). In these cases the Agreement allows bordering coastal states that have not as yet declared an EEZ/EFZ to agree directly or through regional fisheries organizations on a minimum length of fishing vessels below which the Agreement would not apply.
30. See UNCLOS article 116.
31. When a fishing vessel 'is voluntarily in the port of a Party other than the flag State'.
32. Article V (2).
33. Ibid.
34. See FSA article 18(1), (2).
35. Se UNCLOS article 116 which lays down that all states have the right for their nationals to engage in fishing on the high seas subject to their treaty obligations, the rights, duties and interests of the coastal States (*inter alia* under articles 63(2) and 64 to 67) and the provisions of section 2 Part V.
36. See FSA article 18(3).
37. Ibid.
38. Ibid, article 18(4).
39. UNCLOS article 94(6).
40. See however UNCLOS article 217(4), re enforcement by flag states in case of prevention, reduction and control of marine pollution of the marine environment from vessels, which says that the flag state 'shall provide for immediate investigation and where appropriate institute proceedings in respect of the alleged violation' irrespectively of where it occurred or where pollution occurred or was spotted. Furthermore, under article 217(6) states are obliged to investigate any alleged violation deemed to have been committed by a vessel flying their flag, at the written request of any state. States shall institute proceedings without delay if satisfied that sufficient evidence is available to enable proceedings to be brought in respect to alleged violation. States shall also promptly inform the requesting state and the competent international organization of the action taken and the outcome. Such information shall be available to all states.
41. Ibid, article 19(1)(c). The flag state is required to demand all these details; the wording of the FSA is clearly mandatory.
42. Ibid.
43. See FSA article 19(2).
44. See UNCLOS article 217(7); the FSA article 19(2) is identical to it except in the last part, where it establishes 'and shall deprive offenders of the benefits accruing from their illegal activities', which is not found in UNCLOS article 217(7).
45. FSA article 19(2).
46. In areas falling under a party's national jurisdiction it applies to the components of biodiversity *per se*.
47. See para 30 of decision VII/5 of the CBD Conference of the Parties, addressing marine areas beyond national jurisdiction.
48. CBD articles 7(c) and 14(1)(a–d).
49. See Moore, G. (1993) 'Enforcement Without Force: New Techniques in Compliance

Control for Foreign Fishing Operations based on Regional Cooperation', ODIL, **24**, (2), 197–204.
50. UNCLOS article 94 lists the duties of the flag state.
51. See UNCLOS article 91.
52. Included as article 5 of the 1958 United Nations Convention on the High Seas.
53. The paragraph in the Main Trends Working Paper during the UNCLOS negotiations had adopted verbatim article 5 of the 1958 Convention and there were no proposals for an alternative text.
54. The advisory opinion of the ICJ in the *Constitution of the Maritime Safety Committee of the IMCO case, ICJ Reports, (1960)*, 23 has contributed to the shifting away from attempts to use the genuine link so as to limit reflagging of ships to open registries. It leans towards the need to ensure a genuine link by calling for the adoption of more stringent international norms for safety of ships and vessel-source pollution.
55. See Meyers, H. (1967), *The Nationality of Ships*, The Hague: Martinus Nijhoff.
56. Negotiated between 1984 and 1986, this IMO Convention attempted to elaborate the genuine link concept even further.
57. The possibility of introducing such requirements was considered by article 8 of the Registration Convention; it lays down conditions with respect to the nationality of ownership of ships and article 9 with respect to the nationality of crews. One important restriction on the obligations under these articles is that parties can choose to implement either the provisions concerning nationality of ownership or those concerning nationality of crews.
58. See Registration Convention, article 8.
59. Ibid.
60. The FAO Compliance Agreement was concluded on 24 November 1993, and so it was negotiated later than the Registration Convention. A provision on the 'genuine link' was originally included in a draft, but it was deleted when it became clear that its inclusion would jeopardize the timely finalization of the whole agreement.
61. The FAO Compliance Agreement had attempted to address the act of reflagging. A draft of the agreement provided that parties to it should refuse to register fishing vessels unless 'they had sufficient grounds to believe that the vessel would not be used to undermine the effectiveness of internationally agreed conservation and management measures.' In addition, the original draft agreement contained a provision on the Allocation of the Flag (Art IV) on the genuine link which read: '1. No Party shall accord any fishing vessel to which the Agreement applies the right to fly its flag unless it is satisfied, in accordance with its own national legislation, that there exists a genuine link between the vessel and the Party concerned. 2 (a) in determining whether or not there exists a genuine link for the purposes of paragraph 1, each Party shall give due weight to all relevant factors, including in particular: (i) the nationality or the permanent residence of the beneficial owner or owners of the vessel in accordance with their national law; (ii) where the effective control over activities of the vessel is exercised.' Despite the latitude of discretion, which this draft article left to the decision of the parties, it still managed to be considered too restricted and controversial, and was left out from the final text.
62. This case examined whether a vessel registered in a non-member country of the European Community may be treated, for the purpose of article 6(1)(b) of Council Regulation (EEC) 3094/86 of 7 October 1986 as a vessel with the nationality of a member state on the grounds that there is a genuine link between it and the member state. The vessel concerned was owned and manned by Danish nationals and effectively operated from Denmark, and had previously been registered in Denmark. In answering this third question the Court held that, under international law, a vessel in principle has only one nationality, that of the state in which it is registered (see in particular articles 5 and 6 of the Geneva Convention on the High Seas of 29 April 1958 and articles 91 and 92 of the 1982 UNCLOS).
63. *Anklagemyndigheden v Poulsen and Diva Navigation Corp.* (C-286/90) [1992] E.C.R. I-6019, ECJ.

64. The Court held that it follows from these considerations that the answer to the question must be that a vessel registered in a non-member country may not be treated, for the purpose of article 6(1)(b) of Council Regulation (EEC) No 3094/86 of 7 October 1986, as a vessel with the nationality of a member state on the ground that it has a genuine link with that member state.
65. Also found in the FAO Code of Conduct for Responsible Fisheries which is not a legally binding document.
66. Article 19(1)(e).
67. See UNCLOS article 116.
68. Ibid, article 92 on the status of ships.
69. See the ISM code. The success of regional cooperation in controlling and enforcing maritime Conventions under the Paris Memorandum of Port State Control has led to the adoption of this approach for other regions in recent years. The Paris Memorandum itself has been amended several times to enhance its effectiveness.
70. In the case of marine pollution, a European Union legal instrument has done away with the exclusivity of flag state jurisdiction on criminal proceedings. The EU Directive 2005/35/EC on ship-source pollution and on the introduction of penalties for infringements, as amended by Directive 2009/123/EC, applies to all types of vessels, irrespective of their flag. On the strength of this directive EU member states can initiate criminal proceedings for polluting discharges in the internal waters, including ports, the territorial waters, the exclusive economic zone (EEZ) of an EU member state and straits used for international navigation subject to the regime of transit passage, as laid down in the 1982 United Nations Convention on the Law of the Sea, as well as on the high seas.
71. M/V Saiga (Application for Provisional Measures), ITLOS No. 1(1997); 37 ILM (1998), 360. See also Kwiatkowska, B. (1999), 'Inauguration of the ITLOS jurisprudence: The Saint Vincent and the Grenadines v Guinea M/V Saiga Cases', ODIL, **30**, (1), 43–78.
72. See however Chapter 7 pp 237 et seq which discusses how the FSA, the Compliance Agreement and RFMOs have introduced limited jurisdiction to the 'inspecting state' and the port state that can intervene immediately and which may act in the absence of any measures that flag states should take but do not do so.
73. See FAO IPOA-IUU p 6 under 'Responsibilities of all States'; the IPOA refers to controls over nationals and national legislation providing for enforcement in the case of IUU.
74. This is in fact what the US can do under the Lacey Act, which provides US enforcement officials with authority to prosecute vessels and fishermen in the US for violating any fishery regulations of any state wherever the vessel is and wherever the offence was committed. See also Riddle, K. (2003).
75. The FAO Compliance Agreement provides that 'Parties shall, when and as appropriate, enter into cooperative agreements or arrangements of mutual assistance on a global, regional, subregional or bilateral basis so as to promote the achievement of the objectives of this Agreement.'
76. See FSA articles 20 and 21 where it obligates states to cooperate either directly or through subregional or regional fisheries management organizations or arrangements in order to ensure compliance with and enforcement of such conservation measures established therein.
77. Agenda 21 in chapter 17 called upon states to take effective action, consistent with international law, to deter reflagging of vessels as a means of avoiding compliance, to commit themselves to the conservation and sustainable use of high seas living resources, and to acknowledge that the flag state shall to this end exercise effectively its jurisdiction and control over vessels flying its flag.
78. UNCLOS article 117.
79. That is to states which are not parties to FSA and the Compliance Agreement, or to any of the subregional or regional agreements.
80. Fishing vessels of flag states not parties to these Agreements, which harvest fish on the

high seas and take conservation measures that fall short of those reached via a cooperation agreement, are deemed to be 'unregulated'. See definition of unregulated fishing in FAO IPOA-IUU, 2001 at 3.3.1 which says, 'unregulated fishing refers to fishing activities that are conducted by vessels . . . flying the flag of a State not party to that organization or by a fishing entity, in a manner that is not consistent with or contravenes the conservation and management measures of that organization or in areas or for fish stocks in relation to which there are no applicable conservation or management measures and where such fishing activities are conducted in a manner inconsistent with State responsibilities for the conservation of living marine resources under international law.'

81. See UNCLOS article 116.
82. Ibid, article 116(b).
83. Under the VCLT, norms of *jus cogens* are binding on all states whether they have specifically consented to them or not.
84. See *Anglo-Norwegian Fisheries* case, ICJ Reports (1951), 131; See also Brownlie I. (2003), *Principles of Public International Law*, 6th edn, Oxford: Oxford University Press, p 11.
85. See Moore (1993). See also Balton, D.A. (1996), 'Strengthening the CLOS: The New Agreement on Straddling Fish Stocks and Highly Migratory Fish Stocks,' ODIL, **27**, (1–2), 125–52.

7 The conservation of living resources on the high seas: constituent elements for compliance and enforcement

7.1 INTRODUCTION

As we have seen in Chapters 3 and 5, states may disagree on the constituent parameters of sustainability on any issue involving the exploitation of natural resources,[1] but state practice endorses 'sustainable use'[2] as the rationale of the law in regulating the conservation of natural resources. Therefore, the qualification to the freedom of fishing entails that any conservation measures that flag states may take should be conducive to sustainable exploitation[3] of marine living resources.

As discussed in the previous chapter, both compliance and enforcement measures are essential for conservation regimes to achieve their objectives and to remain effective. The major acts that breach the obligation to conserve living resources on the high seas[4] can be summed up as follows: fishing for protected species, exceeding fishing quotas, under-reporting of catches, using illegal fishing gear, fishing in marine protected areas, fishing in closed seasons, fishing without authorization or permits from the flag state. The major compliance and enforcement tools are directed to prevent, deter and eliminate such illicit practices that are often popularly termed as IUU fishing. Flag states, port states and coastal states and, insofar as authorized by its Parties, even RFMOs, have different roles and obligations in securing compliance and enforcement on the high seas. There are, however, some measures that are common and may be considered as the constituent elements for compliance and enforcement regimes pertaining to the conservation of high seas living resources. The ratification of the FSA, the Compliance Agreement and regional and subregional fisheries agreements is identified under the FAO IPOA-IUU as one of the most essential commitments all states may take to deter and eliminate IUU. Once states adhere to these legal instruments, they may harmonize their different national positions to establish, as far as possible, a level playing field where states have identical legal compliance and enforcement obligations. The wider the number of ratifications of these treaties, the less likely it is to have non-parties acting as free riders thwarting conservation regimes agreed upon via cooperation. Other measures that can be taken by all states to facilitate compliance and enforcement over their fishing vessels include: the adoption of National Action Plans for Fisheries, legislation that obliges nationals to observe conservation rules agreed upon at RFMOs,[5] and the adoption of a national enforcement regime which provides for punishments that serve to deter nationals engaging in IUU fishing on the high seas or other offenders that enter the state as a port of call. The flag state obviously has the widest range of obligations stemming from its exclusive jurisdiction over the vessel. Consequently, it is legally responsible to take measures that ensure compliance and to exercise controls that enforce conservation measures. As we explained in the previous chapter, the role of both the port state and the coastal state since UNCLOS has been further developed and approximated to the rights and obligations these types of states have in cases of marine pollution from shipping and dumping at sea under the same Convention.[6] The development of these extended roles may be seen in itself as another tool to secure compliance and enforcement.

In order to adhere to their obligations to conserve living resources on the high seas, states adopt both compliance and enforcement measures. Compliance tools are usually in-built administrative obligations that are preventive rather than remedial in their approach. They help to secure adherence and to provide data on the fishing vessels and fishing operations on the high seas. The more effective compliance measures are, the less need there is to resort to enforcement. The FSA has been very specific in outlining what the compliance measures of flag states should be in order to secure the conservation of marine living resources.[7] Other regional and subregional agreements also spell out compliance measures and do not leave them at the discretion of flag states. However, other Agreements, notably the IWC, have so far failed to agree upon a compliance regime; discussions on the revised management scheme are still going on.

7.2 REGISTRATION OF FISHING VESSELS AND THE AUTHORIZATION TO FISH ON THE HIGH SEAS

As seen in the previous chapter, there are two major legal issues that affect compliance and enforcement of conservation measures on the high seas. The nationality of a vessel is most commonly asserted through vessel registration under the state's national merchant shipping or similar legislation, and the flag state has exclusive jurisdiction on the high seas to exercise enforcement with respect to vessels flying its flag. The nationality component for the registration of vessels is not an essential requirement under international maritime law, but the flag state must exercise control over vessels flying its flag. This is the prevalent interpretation of the term 'genuine link', the only condition that UNCLOS imposes upon states with respect to the registration of vessels.[8] Under international fisheries law, the issue of registration is often confused with the authorization to fish, in the sense that either of the two is used interchangeably with the other or granted instead of the other. This is probably so because, whilst UNCLOS is silent on the matter, international legal instruments relating to registration of vessels, including the 1974 Convention for the Safety of Life at Sea and the United Nations Convention on Conditions for Registration of Ships, exempt fishing vessels from registration. Nevertheless, many states require, through national fisheries legislation, that fishing vessels are entered on a register or record. This is essential to bestow flag state jurisdiction upon them in accordance with international law when they operate on the high seas. Most international fisheries agreements, whether global, regional or subregional, do not refer to registration of fishing vessels since this is a legal issue which essentially falls outside their scope; but they do require flag states to provide for the specific authorization to fish on the high seas in order to ensure effective control over fishing activities of vessels.[9] Registration of the vessel establishes flag state jurisdiction, which is a *sine qua non* for the flag states to exercise compliance and enforcement on the high seas. However, it is not considered to be, by itself, sufficient to ensure that flag states can control their fishing vessels to comply with conservation measures on the high seas. Consequently, post-UNCLOS legal instruments require that states should provide a specific licence or permit to fish, and that a fishing vessel may fish only under a specific authorization.[10] In sum, UNCLOS does not lay down any specific details on how states are to bestow their right of freedom of fishing on the high seas upon their nationals, but the prevalent trend in global, regional and subregional fisheries agreements is to require state parties to provide their fishing vessels with a specific authorization to fish. This serves to provide an important sense of direction because some flag states do not distinguish between the two systems of registration and authorization. Sometimes registration for the purposes of fishing is misconstrued as the kind of registration required for merchant shipping that is only administered by shipping authorities, thereby falling outside the jurisdictional scope of the fisheries agency of the flag state. Alternatively, the flag state may fail to register its fishing vessels with the negative consequence that this may have when it comes to a state's ability to enforce conservation measures on the high seas.[11] A vessel without nationality breaching conservation measures on the high seas may be subject to enforcement by a coastal or any other state, but this does not change the fact that such a vessel would not be accountable to a flag state which can impose specific conservation measures upon it. The system of authorization adopted by flag states needs to be pegged to, or else be included in, the registration of fishing vessels under their flag so that the authorization to fish satisfies also normal registration requirements such as information on the vessel itself, its operations, the owners and history of the ownership, and the nationality of the vessel. If the vessel is registered as a fishing vessel, registration must then be linked to a specific authorization to fish before undertaking any fishing activity. Both registration and authorization are essential compliance tools that implement the legal framework set by UNCLOS enabling states to exercise control over fishing vessels flying their flag in accordance with the qualifications to the freedom of fishing discussed above.

The obligation of flag states to exercise control over fishing vessels flying their flag has therefore mainly developed via the authorization system. Authorization to fish is granted by the state to fishing vessels registered under its flag, whether the crew is made up of nationals or not. Through this administrative and legal instrument, the flag state must ensure that vessels registered under its flag comply with conservation measures on the high seas. The authorization serves to ensure that the flag state secures compliance with the concomitant obligations it is legally bound to observe, whether these emerge from its national laws, rules of customary international law or from any treaty provisions to which it is party. The system of authorization leads to more effective compliance because in it, states may set specific parameters and conditions on how fishing on the high seas should be conducted. Surpassing these parameters would constitute a breach of the authorization conditions which flag states are then obligated to enforce. Under the FSA, state parties cannot allow their vessels to fish on the high seas if they are not duly licensed or authorized to fish, or are not fishing in accordance with the terms and conditions of a licence, authorization or permit.[12] The breach of such conditions by a vessel of a state that is party to the FSA constitutes a 'serious violation'[13] and is subject to mandatory sanctions under the Agreement. These are applicable in respect of masters and other officers of fishing vessels and shall include provisions which 'may permit, inter alia, refusal, withdrawal or suspension of authorizations to serve as masters or officers on such vessels'.[14] The FSA, for instance, obligates state parties to establish regulations to apply terms and conditions in these instruments that fulfil any obligations the flag state may have under subregional, regional or global fisheries agreements to which it is a party.[15] The FSA specifically lists fishing licences, authorization or permits as measures that flag states should adopt in order to control their vessels in taking conservation measures on the high seas.[16] The authorization system is also useful in order to facilitate monitoring and surveillance by port states and coastal states when a foreign fishing vessels enters port or else when such states are participants together with the flag state in a joint enforcement regime and involved in an observer programme, boarding and inspection scheme. The more details the authorization provides, the easier it is to corroborate information provided by the fishing vessels in order to avoid misreporting of catch and any other forms of abuse. The use of authorizations is essential in eliciting the necessary data which can then be circulated amongst state parties to an RFMO and the FAO. The FAO Compliance Agreement uses authorization as a compliance tool to provide leverage when obligating states to adopt sanctions.[17] The Agreement makes it mandatory upon the parties to adopt sanctions that shall be:

> of sufficient gravity as to be effective in securing compliance with the requirements of the Agreement and to deprive offenders of the benefits accruing from their illegal activities. Such sanctions shall, for serious offences, include refusal, suspension or withdrawal of the authorization to fish on the high seas.[18]

The Compliance Agreement obligates state parties to grant authorization only when the flag state is in a position to ensure that fishing vessels will comply with global, regional or subregional conservation and management measures, even if these are not the conservation measures adopted specifically by the flag state. Once the flag state is a party to the Compliance Agreement, it is bound to abide by them by virtue of its adherence to the same. This is identical to the situation under the FSA. Both the Compliance Agreement and the FSA endorse these global, regional and subregional agreements as basic standards of conservation reached via cooperation as advocated by UNCLOS and which, therefore, parties to them are bound to observe. This distinction between registration of fishing vessels and the authorization to fish may, however, lead to a particularly complex legal issue. Nationals may be in possession of an authorization to fish from their state of nationality that always has the right to impose its laws upon its nationals[19] but then operate a fishing vessel registered under the flag of another state. The legal dilemma arises either because the flag state may require that vessels registered under its flag fish on the high seas in accordance with its own authorization rules, or when the state of which the owners are nationals has, by virtue of its authorization, the right to exercise compliance and enforcement measures on the high seas. If neither of the two states agrees to waiver its authorization, the owner of the vessel is regulated by two authorization instruments. In this latter case, the flag state has exclusive jurisdiction with respect to the exercise of compliance and enforcement measures on the high seas, even if it does not require its vessels to operate therein in accordance with its own authorization to fish. Apart from this legal difficulty, the state of which the owners are nationals would meet with practical difficulties in exercising control over the vessel itself, namely because of its lack of presence, since the vessel may not re-enter the authorizing state's port.

The solution to such a situation lies in cooperation. Recent changes to international fisheries law, particularly under the FSA, allow duly authorized officers of an RFMO to carry out boarding and inspection of vessels of state parties to the FSA. This proves that enforcement action in respect of chartered vessels may be best undertaken through such organizations or arrangements. However, the success of authorizations as a compliance tool is not only dependent on the premise that vessels breaching the conditions of the authorization are struck off the register, or that the authorization is automatically cancelled when the fishing vessel ceases to be entitled to fly the flag of that state party. For this trigger mechanism to be effective, safeguards against reflagging must also be adopted. The harmonization of authorization procedures and conditions stipulated therein is indispensable to guarantee that states which take seriously the compliance with and the enforcement of conservation measures on the high seas are not prejudiced when their stricter conservation controls are simply avoided and vessels registered under their flag simply reflag to other states that do not exercise the same level of control over their fishing vessels. In other words, the more harmonized authorization procedures are the more difficult it would be for non-compliant vessels to resort to flag hopping and continue to fish in the area after being struck off the register of one or more states. The FSA, for instance, refers to the use of licences, permits and authorizations as a form of control by flag states if these adopt the same terms and conditions and are in accordance with the same procedures agreed at a global, regional and subregional level.[20] States are more eager to adhere to harmonized authorization measures as this would lessen the risks that any compliance and enforcement measures to fisheries conservation may prejudice the competitiveness of their ship register. It is not easy for states to harmonize authorizing procedures and measures. For instance, in order to discourage reflagging the FAO Compliance Agreement prohibits state parties to register and authorize fishing vessels to fish on the high seas if these have undermined conservation and management measures when they were previously registered under another flag state.[21] Nevertheless it is possible to waive such a prohibition on various grounds. It can be waived if the ownership of the fishing vessel has changed and the new owner proves that the previous owners have no further 'legal, beneficial or financial interest in the vessel'.[22] Another reason may be that the period of suspension for an authorization has expired and no other party has in the preceding three years withdrawn its authorization. There is also a blanket clause which allows flag state parties the discretion to grant an authorization even if the reasons for prohibiting it may subsist. The same party must take into consideration all relevant facts, including the circumstances when another party has previously withdrawn the fishing authorization.[23] This blanket clause leaves too much discretion in the hands of the flag state and waters down the obligations that were originally intended to deter reflagging. Once too much discretion is left in the hands of the flag states to register fishing vessels, free riders are likely to take advantage of this loophole, undermining the Agreement's enforcement regime and prejudicing states that seek stricter controls. The Compliance Agreement thus provides a way out from the same registration/authorization constraints it establishes that aim to curb reflagging. The discretion is absolute[24] because the state party is not obliged to justify or verify its decision when granting the authorization before any other independent body, although it is obliged to inform the FAO.[25] This blanket provision apparently still did not serve as an enticement to states renowned to be flags of convenience to adhere to the Agreement. Certain coastal states and states parties to fisheries agreements have successfully adopted a system of joint authorization for fishing on the high seas[26] which serves to deter reflagging and to ensure that vessels fishing on the high seas in areas subject to the RFMO abide by the same conservation standards and are in a position to control their vessels to comply with such standards. Other states have used fishing vessels' positive track records in abiding by compliance and enforcement measures as established under the RFMO to which they are parties to determine whether a fishing vessel is authorized to fish or not to fish on the high seas areas, subject to the RFMO agreement. By negative listing non-compliant vessels, such states would, in accordance with the provisions of the RFMO, declare that negatively listed fishing vessels are deemed 'not authorized to fish' and the vessels and their catch are classified as IUU by the state parties. This aspect will be dealt with in more detail below under 'listing of vessels'.

UNCLOS may not specifically require states to establish an authorization system such that their nationals can fish on the high seas, but doubtlessly such a system is the most efficient way for flag states to control their nationals in complying with the qualifications to the freedom of fishing. Authorizations render compliance and enforcement more effective, facilitate the exchange of data and information, and help making monitoring and surveillance as well as port controls much easier. Authorizations are also an efficient way of providing leverage when adopting sanctions. Above all, they constitute an example of best practice when it comes to the harmonization of terms and conditions of access for fishing vessels, which requires close coordination and cooperation amongst states whose EEZs border the high seas and/or amongst distant water fishing states exploiting the same species or operating in the same region. Through authorizations, fishing vessels belonging to all these stakeholders can operate under harmonized regulations.[27] Therefore, the requirement to use authorizations under post-UNCLOS multilateral agreements and the vast majority of RFMOs should be seen as a confirmation that general state practice adopts this compliance tool to ensure that the UNCLOS obligations concerning the conservation of high seas living resources are fulfilled and that the balance of interests between flag states, coastal states and the international community is maintained.

7.3 CONTROL, MONITORING AND SURVEILLANCE (CMS)

Even before the negotiation of the 1982 UNCLOS, states had already used various tools to exercise CMS in order to ensure that vessels on the high seas comply with and enforce their conservation obligations. Compliance and enforcement tools are necessarily interrelated, and some measures can be perceived as both one and the other. Some authors distinguish between non-compliance and non-implementation. They argue that whilst a state may be compliant because it has taken measures such as the promulgation of legislation and the setting up of an administrative framework to fulfil the obligations of a treaty to which it is party, it may still not implement it by failing to take effective action and develop further the regulatory regime.[28] Control by the flag state is mainly achieved if it rigorously follows compliance measures. In turn, monitoring and surveillance on the high seas ensure that flag states implement conservation measures and prevent IUU fishing. CMS tools are considered to be the cornerstones of most management and enforcement regimes, without which the deterrent quality of the latter is grossly diminished. In order to be both comprehensive and effective, CMS measures must address fishing operations from their commencement and right through the point of landing until the product is eventually placed on the market. This would also include the regulation of transshipment and sale of catches.

The FAO IPOA-IUU mentions also other measures that involve capacity and awareness building amongst fishing operators and the funding of CMS programmers to maximize their effectiveness. According to the same IPOA, promoting knowledge and understanding of CMS tools on a national level is also an important way to achieve better CMS.[29] In line with UNCLOS, the FAO IPOA-IUU singles out cooperation amongst states as essential in guaranteeing successful CMS of high seas fisheries to prevent, deter and eliminate IUU fishing. Cooperation is presently on the increase as a means to secure compliance with international law. It is actually preferred to confrontation and the establishment of adjudicatory bodies to settle disputes. In practice states have, over the years, adopted various methods to control, monitor and survey fisheries in a comprehensive manner. The setting up of authorization systems and the maintaining of records on vessels and gear have already been referred to and, as has been emphasized, these measures guarantee that states have better control over fishing operations which their vessels may conduct on the high seas. The FSA, for instance, specifies that compliance and enforcement measures undertaken by the flag state:

> shall include (a) control of such vessels on the high seas by means of fishing licenses, authorizations or permits in accordance with any applicable measures and procedures agreed at subregional, regional or global level, (b) establishment of regulations[30]. . . (d) requirements for marking of fishing vessels and fishing gear for identification in accordance with uniform and internationally recognizable vessel and gear marking systems, such as the Food and Agriculture Organization of the United Nations Standard Specifications for the Marking and Identification of Fishing Vessels[31], (e) requirements for recording and timely reporting of vessel position, catch of target and non-target species, fishing effort and other relevant fisheries data in accordance with subregional, regional and global standards for collection of such data.[32]

States may consequently use such measures to have the requisite information and data on catches and on the fishing effort of their fishing fleet. This leads to the compilation of useful data essential for the formulation of effective conservation measures. The most common and widely used CMS measures are: the compilation of data, access to it, exchange of related information with RFMOs and other parties, reporting, observer programmes, vessel monitoring systems, internationally agreed boarding and inspection regimes,[33] as well as listing of vessels. These CMS measures will now be examined in more detail to determine whether they impinge upon the traditional interpretation of the freedom of fishing as qualified under UNCLOS.

7.3.1 Submission of Data, Reporting and Access to Information

Compliance with and effective implementation of treaties depends upon the compilation of information and data.[34] The compilation and submission, as well as reporting, of information is a ubiquitous obligation in treaties addressing the conservation of living resources, including those regulating marine living resources outside national jurisdiction. UNCLOS obligates states 'to contribute and exchange of data on a regular basis through competent international organizations whether subregional, regional or global, where appropriate, and with participation by all States concerned'.[35] The term, 'all States concerned' seems to imply that this obligation involves not only the parties to an international fisheries organization but all states participating in the fishery or which in some way have 'an interest' in the resource.[36]

The duty to inform, to provide access to information and to report accordingly, fulfills also another obligation which states have under UNCLOS, namely to cooperate when they fish for the same species or in the same areas on the high seas.[37] UNCLOS left the details for both these obligations to be worked out in cooperation agreements at regional and subregional level. States have done so, and both reporting as well as the submission of information and data is required in most, if not all, fisheries agreements. Access to information is a means to secure compliance and guarantee transparency.[38] It is an obligation that has prevailed and been adopted in most conservation treaties following the UNCED process. The FAO Compliance Agreement provides that:

> Parties shall cooperate as appropriate in the implementation of this Agreement, and shall, in particular, exchange information, including evidentiary material, relating to activities of fishing vessels in order to assist the flag State in identifying those fishing vessels flying its flag reported to have engaged in activities undermining international conservation and management measures, so as to fulfil its obligations under Article III.

The Compliance Agreement requires parties to ensure that all fishing vessels flying their flag are to provide the national authorities with the information on their operations 'as may be necessary to enable the Party to fulfil its obligations under this Agreement'. The Agreement then gives an inclusive list of these measures, namely information on the area where the vessel operates, its catches and landings.[39] The Compliance Agreement imposes an obligation upon parties to maintain exhaustive records of fishing vessels flying their flag and authorized to fish on the high seas.[40] These vessels so recorded have to be marked in a way that they can be identified in accordance with generally accepted standards.[41] The parties are obliged to exchange information amongst themselves and report any fishing vessels undermining international conservation and management measures. This mutual monitoring role helps flag state parties to 'fulfil their obligations listed in Article II'. It is also an obligation upon parties to report information on fishing vessels that fly the flag of non-parties if these undermine the effectiveness of international conservation and management measures.[42]

The parties have an obligation to exchange information with the FAO by making information on fishing vessels entitled to fly their flag readily available. For each vessel recorded by it, the flag state is to submit a list of information specified in article VI of the Agreement. Some of this information is compulsory,[43] but some information is additional and shall be provided to the FAO by the Parties 'to the extent practicable'. Any modifications must be reported, and the FAO is to circulate this information to other parties and to other fisheries organizations, subject to any restrictions imposed by the party.[44] The flag state parties must 'promptly inform' FAO about any additions or deletions to the record of fishing vessels, particularly when this involves the non-renewal or withdrawal of authorizations for reasons of non-compliance, the decommissioning, scrapping and loss of fishing vessels recorded, and when the fishing vessel is no longer entitled to fly its flag.[45] Flag state parties are obligated to report promptly to FAO all the relevant information relating to activities by fishing vessels entitled to fly their flag that undermines the effectiveness of international conservation and management measures. This would include not just information to identify the fishing vessel involved but also information on what type of measures the flag state has imposed with respect to such activities by the fishing vessel involved.

Parties that have 'reasonable ground' to believe that a fishing vessel not entitled to fly its flag has engaged in any activity that undermines the effectiveness of international conservation and management measures 'shall draw this to the attention of the Flag State' and may, as appropriate, bring it to the attention of the FAO. It shall provide the flag state with full supporting evidence and may provide the FAO with a summary of such evidence. FAO shall not circulate such information until such time as the flag state has had an opportunity to comment on the allegation and evidence submitted, or to object as the case may be. The FSA list of enforcement measures includes the:

> establishment of a national record of fishing vessels authorized to fish on the high seas and provision of access to the information contained in that record on request by directly interested States, taking into account any national laws of the flag State regarding release of such information.[46]

It also imposes on state parties an obligation to require that, through reporting via inspection schemes, unloading reports, the monitoring of landed catches and market statistics, they will exercise control over their vessels' fishing operations. Multilateral, regional and subregional agreements usually obligate state parties to adopt a standard format when compiling or submitting information in order to enable a comparative assessment of the data provided. For instance, the FSA establishes that state parties are to provide for the marking of fishing vessels and fishing gear for identification in accordance with uniform and internationally recognizable vessel and gear marking systems, such as the FAO Standard Specifications for the Marking and Identification of Fishing Vessels.[47] Under ICCAT, for example, contracting and cooperating non-contracting parties, entities and fishing entities (CPCs)[48] are to submit data both to the Standing Committee on Research and Statistics (SCRS)[49] and to the Conservation and Management Measures Compliance Committee by means of standardized national reports and ICCAT reporting tables. This collection of data and reporting is to be submitted prior to the Annual Meeting by 31 July of each year.

There are various ways in which data and information may be collected. Apart from the specific obligation to provide information, most compliance and enforcement measures such as authorizations, licences and vessel markings, as well as the observer programmes, are all oriented towards the compilation of data and information. Under the FSA, state parties must require their fishing vessels to record and timely report vessel position, catch of target and non-target species, fishing effort, and other relevant fisheries data in accordance with sub regional, regional and global standards for collection of such data.[50] Furthermore, the FSA obligates parties to establish national records of fishing vessels authorized to fish on the high seas and to provide access to the information contained in these records on request by 'directly interested States', taking into account the national laws of the flag states with respect to release of such information.[51] Under the FSA the flag state is obliged to provide information on the outcome of the investigations to all states having an interest in or affected by the alleged violation.[52]

The obligation to submit information is, however, not always enforceable or, rather, enforced, even when included in treaties. Under ICCAT, for example, CPCs sometimes submit only partial, late or no data at all without incurring penalties. So, at times, these compliance tools are merely administrative measures rather than legally binding obligations, although there is a trend to have this changed. For instance, since 2005 ICCAT recommendations require CPCs to provide explanations for failed reporting and to submit plans to correct such deficiencies. It is the role of an institution under ICCAT, namely the Permanent Working Group for the Improvement of the ICCAT Statistics and Conservation Measures (PWG), to identify these shortcomings since these greatly affect stock assessments. ICCAT CPCs are also obliged to report any violations to the flag state and follow-up action is sought.

Under the IOTC, data collection and reporting are mandatory. The Species Working Parties peer review stock assessment with the secretariat, maintaining a role in stock assessment to ensure that parties which do not have the required scientific capacities would still have access to relevant information. NAFO obligates contracting parties to collect data on catch and effort as well as to submit reports about port and at-sea inspections and on the observer programme. Data is also collected from vessel monitoring systems messages and aerial surveillance. In 1998 the NEAFC adopted a Scheme of Control and Enforcement which, amongst other things, renders obligatory upon contracting parties the duty to report to the Secretary the monthly catches of regulated species that were landed or transshipped. Contracting parties are also obligated to collect data on infringement, port and at-sea inspections and boarding, as well as data from Vessel Monitoring Systems. Under both the NAFO and the NEAFC, all vessels must transmit to national Fisheries Monitoring Centres automatic positional and other reports every two hours. These national Fisheries Monitoring Centers then forward the data and reports to the NAFO and NEAFC Secretariats. To ensure uniform messaging, both NAFO and the NEAFC have developed the North Atlantic Format for harmonized, comprehensive electronic messaging transmitted from vessels' monitoring systems.

The GFCM data on catch, effort, scientific trawl and acoustic survey is collected through the GFCM and FAO regional projects, and from the contracting parties. In this respect the Mediterranean Fishery Statistics Information System (MEDFISIS) services the Commission by reformatting and aggregating the data submitted. Data collection under the CCAMLR is rather vast, and all vessels participating in exploratory fisheries have mandatory obligations to abide by research requirements and tagging procedures. Examples of data collection under the CCAMLR, besides fishery catch and effort, include data collected by scientific observers on by catch and incidental mortality of sea birds and marine mammals. Scientific survey programmes that are fishery-independent carry out biomass estimates and collect biological information. The data from the CCAMLR observer programme is also collected in a standardized format and is submitted to the CCAMLR. Such data is utilized both by the Commission's scientific committee and by its various working groups. Besides, under CCAMLR the flag state parties must provide information to the Commission on the owner or charterer and notify it that the master of the fishing vessel has been informed of the regulatory measures in force when fishing in the convention area. CCAMLR has been particularly active and has adopted a comprehensive approach to address IUU fishing. All members of the CCAMLR are compelled to submit a catch documentation scheme.

Under the Donut Hole Convention the parties annually submit catch and effort statistics to the Scientific and Technical Committee established under the Convention as well as information regarding the location and the time when fishery operations were conducted. Parties must also report any incidental taking of other marine living resources, including anadromous species. Any vessel of the contracting parties that wishes to fish in the Donut Hole Area must notify all the other parties 48 hours in advance, whilst information regarding the location of any transshipment of fish must be made 24 hours in advance. Parties must regularly inform the other parties about catch data. Under the WCPFC, all members and cooperating non-members are obligated to provide data on catch, effort, biological and other data on an annual basis or as otherwise directed by the Commission. Data must be provided in accordance with Annex I of the FSA.

State practice clearly shows a trend to apply the UNCLOS obligation for states to report and provide information via international, regional and subregional fishery organizations to other states for the conservation of high seas living resources. Unreported fishing is considered to be one of the three main anthropogenic activities which in a direct manner threaten the conservation of living resources on the high seas. Submitting and providing information and reporting is directly linked to the obligation to achieve sustainable fisheries. This explains the widespread adherence by states to these compliance tools, whether they are parties or not to a fisheries agreement; a factor which highlights the likelihood that submission and access to information as well as reporting has achieved the status of customary international law.

The major counter argument against the claim of universal adherence to this obligation is whether exchange of information and reporting, even as it is worded under UNCLOS, is applicable and enforceable against non-parties to fisheries agreements. Indeed, the difficulty in such cases is also a practical one. For instance, non-parties may lack the infrastructure to adopt information provision measures as they are not members of the organization establishing them. The evolution of the status of a cooperating non-member under international fisheries law has addressed this difficulty to some extent. However, not all fisheries organizations allow distant water fishing[53] as members or cooperating non-members. Furthermore, in those high seas areas which are not covered by a fisheries agreement there would not be any system to regulate the collection and dissemination of information. Although in the latter case it is hardly likely that a state may challenge another for breaching international law by failing to provide information, the matter is entirely different in the case of those high seas areas covered by a fisheries agreement that requests even non-parties to submit information. For example, NAFO classifies as IUU those vessels of non-parties that fail to provide information regarding the location where they caught the species on board. This brings to the fore a legal dilemma that has not yet been addressed by an international tribunal and which leaves much ground for legal speculation. In such cases, would the provisions of the fisheries agreement, as a specific and more recent legal development, supersede UNCLOS, or would enforcing such provisions vis-à-vis non-parties constitute a breach of international law? There are arguments for and against these two polarized positions. On the one hand, as stated above, UNCLOS itself establishes an obligation upon states to cooperate with each other in the conservation and management of living resources on the high seas, particularly those states whose nationals exploit the same species or different species in the same areas.[54] UNCLOS obligates these states to establish 'as appropriate' regional and subregional fisheries organizations to this end. This implies that states are obligated to set up and to cooperate with these fisheries organizations if they exploit living resources on high seas areas which fall within the organization's geographical ambit. Conservation of these species is optimized if subjected to a compliance and enforcement regime formulated via a cooperation agreement in this manner. Any state whose nationals exploit species in such areas may be deemed to be *prima facie* jeopardizing the conservation of species if it fails to observe the conservation measures the organization seeks to implement and enforce. UNCLOS itself obligates states to cooperate in this respect when their nationals fish for the same species and in the same areas on the high seas.[55] The conservation measures adopted at the regional or subregional level, or in certain cases like the FSA applied with respect to specific species on a global level, may thus be deemed to constitute the basic conservation measures required to achieve sustainable fisheries.[56] Their disregard or infringement by non-parties prejudices those states that have painstakingly followed the UNCLOS obligation to cooperate in this manner.

It is however also important to note that the regional and subregional agreements as well as the FSA are not automatically binding on UNCLOS parties; hence their legal status as a continuation of section 2 of Part VII of UNCLOS is uncertain. The conditions established under this section of UNCLOS constitute the qualification to the freedom of fishing[57] and, although it is true that the FSA and these regional and subregional agreements were negotiated to implement the applicable provisions of section 2, there was no agreement that parties to UNCLOS are obligated to adhere to these legal instruments. Therefore their enforcement cannot be automatically considered to emerge from customary international law, as is the case with the norm-creating character of the UNCLOS provisions.

The position of these legal instruments stands to be challenged by non-parties particularly because one of the conditions[58] under section 2 of Part VII of UNCLOS permits states to take unilateral conservation measures. Therefore, if unilateral conservation measures do not oblige states to submit or provide access to information relating to their fisheries operations, they cannot suffer any negative consequences as a result. This situation queries the legality of those provisions under fisheries agreements that subject non-parties to sanctions or some other form of negative treatment if they do not submit information or refuse access to it by other states, where it is so required by international, regional and sub-regional agreements.[59] This may be deemed to be discriminatory[60] against non-parties and tantamount to restricting their freedom of fishing. On the other hand, as explained above, widespread adherence to the obligation to submit relevant information and to allow its access to others may have come to form part of a set of minimum conservation standards[61] that may have crystallized into customary international law and which are therefore enforceable against all states exploiting living resources on the high seas. The same applies to other compliance and enforcement measures, although perhaps no other measure is as widely adopted as the obligation to report and provide information and data. The consistency with which states have adhered to this obligation constitutes strong evidence that they have acquiesced to it as a minimum requirement essential to safeguard the conservation of species that various states exploit on the high seas.

Evidence of state practice to support the latter argument may also be drawn from soft law instruments that have influenced the negotiation of compliance regimes under conservation treaties. The widespread adherence to the obligation of reporting is perhaps best highlighted by the fact that unreported fishing is perceived as one of the major causes of unsustainable exploitation of fisheries. 'Unreported fishing' on the high seas is defined in the FAO IPOA-IUU as:

> either fishing activities which have not been reported or misreported to the relevant national authority in contravention of national laws or regulations or undertaken in the area of competence of a relevant regional fisheries organization, which have not been reported or have been misreported in contravention of the reporting procedure of the organization.[62]

This definition does not distinguish between state parties and non-parties. Although the FAO IPOA-IUU is not a legally binding document, it was concluded after intensive negotiations in international fora reflecting predominant state practice. *Prima facie* this definition establishes the prevalent opinion amongst states with respect to the meaning of unreported fishing. Similarly, the UNEP guidelines on shared resources require states to cooperate, *inter alia*, to exchange information and to exercise notification and consultation on the basis of good faith and good neighbourliness.[63] Although these guidelines were agreed upon as a non-legally binding instrument, many of their provisions have been adopted in the major wildlife treaties. The duty to exchange information is a classic example.

The CBD provides no system of international inspection or observer system but establishes numerous incentives to induce compliance by the state[64] which has jurisdiction over resources. It identifies exchange of information as a method to promote compliance. It invites parties to share their experiences with the secretariat of the CBD. It does not have a reporting procedure with overview and comments from treaty bodies, but it requires each party to present to the Conference of the parties reports on measures taken by it to implement the Convention and to assess their effectiveness in meeting objectives of the convention.[65] Responsibility for compliance under the CBD in areas beyond national jurisdiction will generally fall within the competence, if any, of appropriate international and regional bodies. Parties are to cooperate as far as possible with other parties directly or through competent international organizations in areas of mutual interest.[66] The CBD asserts that its provisions do not affect parties' rights and obligations deriving from other international agreements to which they have adhered, unless their exercise would damage or threaten biodiversity.[67] It also requires that parties implement their rights and obligations under UNCLOS implying that the UNCLOS provisions on enforcement, compliance and dispute settlement can be applied to issues regulated by the CBD.[68]

Despite the uncertainties, the arguments and the counter arguments as to whether this obligation has indeed crystallized into customary international law, it is evident that currently multilateral implementation procedures are taking the form of reporting and data compilation systems. Implementation review is based on national reporting and other information submitted by the parties. State practice shows that the trend under current international law is to prefer compliance measures as opposed to elaborate, time-consuming and costly enforcement and litigation mechanisms. The FSA and other regional and subregional treaties establish that states are obligated to provide access to the information on request by directly interested states,[69] but whether these treaty provisions are binding on non-parties can only be resolved if the state alleging a breach of international law because another state failed to provide it with information proves that a rule of customary international law to this effect exists. If this is found to be the case, then this compliance tool has served to further fine-tune the interpretation of freedom of fishing rendering any distant water-fishing state accountable towards other states by providing information about fisheries operations carried out by vessels flying its flag, their compliance records and by reporting enforcement measures taken in their regard irrespective of whether or not it is party to a fisheries agreement.

7.3.2 The Vessel Monitoring System

The FSA has an enforcement regime[70] that requires parties to implement and enforce conservation and management measures through effective monitoring, surveillance and control (CMS).[71] It obligates parties to impose requirements for monitoring, control and surveillance of such vessels, their fishing operations and related activities.[72] As mentioned above, one of the most common ways of affecting CMS on the high seas is through the establishment of a vessel monitoring system (VMS). Many regional and subregional fisheries agreements have a VMS. ICCAT, for instance, obligates CPCs to collect data via a VMS which is forwarded to the flag state and to the ICCAT secretariat. Under NAFO, all contracting parties must ensure that the vessels flying their flag which fish in the NAFO Convention Area must be equipped with a vessel monitoring system. Contracting parties forward data collected from the scientific survey to the Scientific Council which uses it to develop stock assessments and other scientific advice on the species falling within the scope of the Convention. Under NEAFC, all vessels fishing outside the EEZs must be equipped with a VMS. The system operates successfully, and the secretariat provides a fully automated system with the latest information on fishing activities to those contracting parties having an inspection presence. Joint work with NAFO is leading to the development of a comprehensive table of message types that can be transmitted through a VMS. The VMS under the CCAMLR covers finfish and excludes krill fisheries. Data is transmitted to flag state Fisheries Monitoring Centres and communicated to the Secretariat. All vessels licensed under flag state parties to the Commission must be equipped with a satellite VMS with continuous reporting. This data is mainly used to corroborate evidence on landings, with an exception regarding exploratory fisheries. In the latter case it is the flag state which reports to the CCAMLR after the vessel has left the area. The VMS is compulsory on all vessels, and the data generated regarding the location is to be shared with all parties on a real-time basis. The WCPFC Vessel Monitoring System is compulsory for all vessels fishing in the Convention Area.[73] Cooperating non-members are to ensure compatibility between national and high seas vessel monitoring systems. The VMS has become widespread and is being utilized in most areas where there are agreements regulating high seas fisheries. It permits effective and precise monitoring and surveillance, and those agreements which do not as yet operate a VMS are largely working on it.[74]

7.3.3 Observer Programmes

Shared inspection in some international fisheries agreements goes back to the first half of the twentieth century. It was not followed by all agreements; the 1937 International Agreement for the Regulation of Whaling, for instance, mandated only national observers. International scrutiny was limited to the reviewing of reports, and it was already apparent that this was insufficient and that an international observer programme was essential to secure compliance.[75] When the 1937 agreement was revised and the IWC established, it took till the early 1970s for the International Observer Programme to become 'fully operative in all areas where whaling is undertaken by member countries'.[76] The International Observer Programme under the IWC was eventually extended to aboriginal subsistence whaling, but it lapsed with the advent of the moratorium. The last observers were appointed by the IWC in 1986, and since the resumption of whaling by Norway it has not been reinstated. As a result, data collection on whaling through the IWC observer programme is stalled. The observer programme has fared better under other agreements. The FSA obligates parties to verify the catch of target and non-target species through such means as observer programmes.[77] Under ICCAT, an important compliance measure was undertaken in 2005 with the establishment of the Regional Observer Programme. Under this programme all CPC fishing vessels[78] must have an ICCAT observer on board during all transshipments in the area covered by the Convention. The Observer Programme, which is coordinated by the Secretariat, is funded by the CPCs themselves, but when fees are not paid no observer is assigned to the vessel thereby compromising this important compliance scheme. The National Observer Programme of the IOTC is much more limited than that under ICCAT. Originally it was not mandatory, and CPCs were only encouraged to implement it, but a binding resolution concluded in 2002 obligates contracting parties to implement this system on 10 per cent of their vessels and non-contracting parties only with respect to vessels that are 24m or larger. The project was reviewed in 2006. Compared to other regional fishery organizations, NAFO has had, since 1998, a very strong and well organized observer programme, which is mandatory upon all vessels of contracting parties fishing in the NAFO Regulatory Area. As stated above, all reports are forwarded to the flag state and copied to the Secretariat to secure monitoring and compliance. More recently, NAFO has launched a Pilot Project on Observer, Satellite Tracking and Electronic Reporting to test a real time electronic reporting system by observers and vessel masters.

The observer programme referred to as the CCAMLR Scheme of International Scientific Observation has 100 per cent coverage. The observers are independent scientific observers and the programme covers all finfish. An observer programme for Krill coverage is on a voluntary basis. Under the CCAMLR, the observer and inspection scheme is different from the usual surveillance carried out under other similar agreements[79] because the Convention provides that observers are entitled to carry out observation and inspection activities aboard vessels engaged in scientific research and harvesting. Such types of inspections may also relate to vessels that are not the ones boarded. Observers designated by parties to the CCAMLR may serve upon the vessels of other parties but remain subject to the sole jurisdiction of the state that has designated them. It is in fact the designating state that has the responsibility to certify that the observer is qualified, and parties can only designate their own nationals. The CCAMLR Commission has a list of all these observers registered by the designating states.[80] The listed observers may perform their duties even upon vessels of another state by agreement between states parties. Vessels carrying observers must be marked.[81]

The Observer Programme is also carried out rigorously under the Donut Hole Convention which specifies that each vessel must accept an observer from another party whilst fishing in the Convention area. If an observer from another party is not available, the flag state must appoint one of its own observers instead. Observers report both to the flag state and the observer state. The Donut Hole Convention enforcement regime allows for coverage by observers from non-flag states. Under the WCPFC, Guidelines for the implementation of the observer programme are specified in the Convention itself under Annex III. The ITATTCA agreement provides for an observer scheme that has 100 per cent coverage in order to verify that parties are in fact adhering to the quotas on incidental bycatch, particularly with respect to dolphins.

However, the observer programme is not adopted by all fisheries organizations or agreements. The NEAFC, for instance, does not have an observer programme. The GFCM has no regional observer programme and no vessel monitoring system, but both are envisaged under a control scheme adopted in 2005. Like the VMS, the observer programme is a CMS measure that states are not expected to comply with unless they are specifically bound to do so by a treaty obligation.

7.3.4 Boarding and Inspection

As explained above, UNCLOS does not go into details about specific enforcement measures that states are to adopt to ensure the conservation of living resources on the high seas. It leaves it up to states to conclude cooperation agreements between them 'with a view to taking the measures necessary for the conservation of living resources concerned'[82] when their nationals exploit the same species or different species in the same areas on the high seas. There are various RFMOs that allow for their parties to exercise boarding and inspection, but not all these agreements provide for their application on the high seas. The North Pacific Anadromous Stock Convention was the first fisheries agreement to introduce mutual boarding and inspection on the high seas.[83] Under this Convention any party is authorized to board a vessel of another member party on 'reasonable belief' that the other party is engaged in prohibited taking, whether directly or incidental. Authorized inspectors under NAFO are allowed to inspect catch, nets and other gear, all fishing gear on and near working deck and readily available for use, and to examine relevant documents on board the vessel that these inspectors may deem necessary. Under the Donut Hole Convention,[84] enforcement measures require state parties to agree in advance that any authorized officials from other state parties may board and inspect the vessels flying their flag. When notified that a vessel flying their flag has infringed the provisions of the Convention, the parties must take appropriate measures in accordance with their laws and regulations and start investigating promptly. Furthermore, flag states must order fishing vessels to cease violations and leave the Convention Area at once.

Under CCAMLR, enforcement is based on a system of both observation and inspection obligations that have been carried out since 1998. The CCAMLR obligates state parties to allow observers/inspectors on board the vessel.[85] Once aboard, vessel observers or inspectors:

> shall have the authority to observe and inspect catch, nets and other fishing gear as well as harvesting and scientific research activities and shall have access to records and reports of catch and location data in so far as necessary to carry out their function.

The enforcement regime under the WCPFC[86] establishes a boarding and inspection procedure, and if this does not come into effect the FSA boarding and inspection procedure would apply in the interim period.

Although ICCAT obligates CPCs to establish an enforcement system on the high seas, there exists no provision under this Agreement to date for permitting mutual boarding or inspection.[87] The situation is the same under the GFCM. Some other fisheries agreements provide for inspection and boarding, but not on the high seas. NAFO, for instance, obligates contracting parties to carry out in-port inspections on vessels that are fishing in the NAFO Regulatory Area and, until such an inspection is carried out, port access and transshipment is denied for non-compliance. The vessel inspected must prove, even if its flag state is a non-party that it either caught the fish outside the NAFO Regulatory Area or else, if caught within the Area, that it did so in accordance with NAFO rules. Information on non-contracting party vessels is communicated to the flag state, the contracting parties and the NAFO secretariat. The latter informs other fishery organizations about the IUU activity. Under NAFO, all non-contracting parties' vessels can be inspected if the flag state or the vessel gives its prior consent, but if the flag state refuses consent and is not inspected the presumption of carrying out IUU fishing remains and no transshipment or landing of the catch can take place. Listing as IUU vessels of non-parties which refuse boarding and inspection when fishing in the high seas area within the geographical scope of the fisheries agreement is a very effective way of preventing vessels from carrying out IUU fishing on the high seas and breaching a conservation regime reached via cooperation by the other participants in the fishery.

The measure of deeming as IUU those vessels whose flag states refuse boarding and inspection by the parties to a fisheries agreement, when the flag state is not a party to that same agreement, may be interpreted in two diametrically opposed ways. On the one hand, such measures may be deemed to be an expression of the coastal states' rights to safeguard their interests with respect to the conservation of living resources on the high seas taken in accordance with UNCLOS within the context of a cooperation agreement. This argument is further strengthened by the fact that listing vessels as IUU does not involve exercising direct enforcement measures by the coastal states and other members of a fisheries agreement upon the vessel of the non-party. The state parties are not physically restricting the vessel's freedom to fish on the high seas area falling within the geographical scope of the agreement. By classifying such vessels and their catch as IUU they are taking preventive and remedial measures they are entitled to take as port states, namely to refuse to place on the market catches from vessels listed as IUU. In this respect port states cannot be challenged as going against the freedom of fishing or of imposing discriminatory measures.[88] They are allowed to implement whatever compliance and enforcement measures they deem necessary for the conservation of high seas fisheries, once a fishing vessel voluntarily enters their port.

Flag states not parties to the fisheries agreement may resist consenting to enforcement measures on the pretext that since they are not parties they are not bound to subject their vessels to comply with them.[89] They argue that refusal to abide by these measures should not lead to their suffering any negative repercussions as this would be tantamount to a violation of UNCLOS that prohibits the use of conservation measures and their implementation as a form of discrimination in form and/or in fact against other states.[90] Both the Compliance Agreement and the FSA consider conservation measures adopted via cooperation under fisheries agreements as the 'applicable conservation measures' for the exploitation of living resources in the area subject to the agreement. The FSA goes as far as to obligate its parties to subject themselves to the enforcement and compliance regimes of such cooperation agreements even if they are not parties to them. A state party to the FSA, if it is a member of or a participant[91] in a subregional or regional fisheries management organization or arrangement, may board and inspect fishing vessels of another party to the FSA in any high seas area falling within the jurisdictional scope of such an arrangement or organization, in order to ensure compliance with conservation and management measures for HMS and straddling fish stocks. This may happen even if that vessel's flag state is not a party to that particular regional organization or arrangement,[92] in the sense that once the flag state is a party to the FSA it is automatically bound to allow another state party through 'its duly authorized inspectors' to board and inspect its vessels without the flag state having to give its consent in those specific circumstances.

Boarding and inspecting procedures established under the FSA[93] may be considered to reflect common standards under maritime law. State parties to a subregional or regional fisheries organization or arrangement may opt to establish other procedures and schemes but, until such inspection and boarding procedures are adopted by the organization or the arrangement, the FSA procedures would apply for parties to that RFMO which are also parties to the FSA. Schemes adopted by RFMOs cannot be inconsistent with those established under the FSA, and neither can they be adopted unilaterally without the endorsement of the organization or arrangement. In sum, the states members of subregional and regional organizations must allow the right for mutual inspection, but they are permitted to make slight modifications to the inspection and boarding schemes listed in articles 21 and 22 of the FSA. States shall establish the procedures for boarding and inspection through the same regional or subregional organizations and arrangements.

The FSA specifies that these procedures must not discriminate against non-members and non-participants, and must be consistent with the FSA[94] and establish basic procedures for boarding and inspection. In fact, if states do not agree to such procedures under their respective regional and subregional fisheries organizations and arrangements, within two years of the adoption of the FSA the procedures stipulated under article 22 shall apply until such an agreement on the procedures is reached. Inspecting states are obligated to inform all states whose vessels fish in the region or subregion about the form of identification to be used by their inspectors. They can do so either directly or through the regional or subregional organization. If the master of a vessel refuses to accept boarding and inspection in accordance with the provisions of the FSA, the flag state party shall direct the master of the vessel to submit immediately to boarding and inspection, and if he remains non-compliant[95] it shall suspend the vessel's authorization to fish and order it to return immediately to port. The flag state shall advise the inspecting state of the action it has taken when the circumstances referred to in this paragraph arise.[96] Where there exist clear grounds for suspecting that a vessel flying the flag of a state party has violated regionally agreed conservation measures, the inspecting party, which must also be a member of the subregional or regional organization or arrangement, shall secure evidence[97] and notify the flag state immediately.[98] In the case of serious violations,[99] if the flag state 'failed to respond or take action as required',[100] the inspectors have the right to remain on board to secure evidence and may also require the vessel to proceed to the nearest port for a dockside inspection.[101] The flag state must respond to the notification within three working days from its receipt.[102] The flag state has two options, either to investigate and act accordingly,[103] or to authorize the inspecting state to do so itself.[104] The latter shall, 'without delay', communicate the results of the investigation to the flag state. If evidence so warrants that a violation has occurred, the flag state 'shall fulfil its obligation to take enforcement action with respect to the vessel', or authorize the inspecting state which specific enforcement measures it is to take in its stead. The inspecting state has no authority to enforce and prosecute without the flag state's consent, which retains the right to intervene throughout any stage of the enforcement process and particularly during the trial and penalty phase,[105] and may always exercise its jurisdiction.[106] Enforcement action taken by any state other than the flag state in respect of vessels that have engaged in activities contrary to subregional or regional conservation and management measures 'shall be proportional to the seriousness of the violation'. State parties which take any action in terms of article 21 that is unlawful or which exceeds what is reasonably required by law are subject to international liability for any damage or loss that ensues therefrom.[107]

Despite these developments under the FSA, one cannot say that boarding and inspection in areas subject to fisheries agreements can be enforced against vessels of non-parties without their approval, unless of course they are parties to the FSA or any other treaty which prescribes it.[108] Boarding and inspection are only applicable against state parties and, following the *Estai* case,[109] the flag state's prior consent is required even in such cases. The *Estai* case brought to the fore the difficulties that hamper inspection and enforcement regimes on the high seas, even if both Canada and Spain were parties to NAFO. When Canada's navy officers arrested the crew and seized the *Estai* on the high seas in a NAFO Regulatory Area, the Spanish fishing vessel was allegedly fishing for straddling fish stocks in contravention of internationally agreed conservation and management measures.[110] Spain argued that the Canadian Coastal Fisheries Protection Act, on the strength of which the Canadian navy officers acted, was in breach of international law because it extended Canada's jurisdiction to board and inspect vessels on the high seas. The EU, which on behalf of Spain and its other member states was involved in the exchange of letters throughout the dispute, reiterated that the implementation of these provisions of the Canadian Act against the *Estai*, a Spanish-flagged vessel, undermines the efforts of the international community, particularly with respect to the FSA framework, to achieve effective conservation through enhanced cooperation in the management of fisheries. Furthermore, Spain and the EU emphasized how Canada's actions on the high seas constituted a serious breach which goes far beyond the question of fisheries conservation. In other words, Spain and the EU did not even attempt to prove that the *Estai* was not actually infringing conservation measures within an area of the high seas subject to the NAFO, and based their legal argument on the inviolability of flag state jurisdiction in exercising enforcement measures on the high seas. Spain and the EU insisted that a coastal state cannot board, inspect a vessel and arrest the crew without the flag state's specific consent, as this constitutes a serious breach of international law. The coastal state's need to take immediate action to enforce conservation measures, even if these were agreed to via a cooperation agreement, can never justify the coastal state assuming enforcement powers which under international law are vested in the flag state. It is unfortunate that the Court had to decline going into the merits of the case and ruled that it lacked the necessary jurisdiction to take cognizance of it.[111] From a legal perspective, the only positive outcome of the *Estai* case was the eventual compromise agreement reached between Canada and the EU, including Spain, on the enforcement of conservation measures under the NAFO Agreement, which in a nutshell saw Canada amend its Coastal Fisheries Protection Act to renounce taking such enforcement measures against vessels flying the flags of EU member states without their consent. On the other hand, the EU member states had to take effective control to ensure that their vessels do not infringe such conservation measures. The two sides pledged that once either of them broke these two conditions such an agreement would be annulled.

The provisions of the FSA referred to above provide an exception but are applicable only vis-à-vis its parties, although one could possibly argue that the FSA has codified an expression of the right of coastal states to safeguard their interests in this manner as envisaged under UNCLOS. The latter argument would mean that the FSA has served to supplement the UNCLOS qualification to the freedom of fishing in the light of UNCLOS article 118 at least amongst its parties. Coastal states may, at best, take preventive measures as port states vis-à-vis those non-party flag states that refuse to comply with enforcement measures prescribed under a fisheries agreement. Intervention on the high seas upon non-party fishing vessels without the flag state's consent would constitute a breach of international law for violating the exclusive jurisdiction of the flag state, irrespective of whether the vessel was carrying out IUU or not.[112] The only exception to this situation is when a vessel on the high seas is without nationality, in which case the coastal state may intervene when such vessels violate international conservation and management measures on the high seas. A number of states have national legislation which includes vessels without nationality on the high seas as being subject to their jurisdiction.[113] Coastal states in such circumstances have assumed powers to seize and prosecute such vessels.[114] Apart from various types of CMS examined above, three other enforcement measures exercised by states to secure the implementation and enforcement of conservation measures on the high seas are: listing of vessels, internationally agreed market-related measures, and specific port state measures.

7.3.5 Listing of Vessels

Negative listing of fishing vessels is another method to eliminate IUU fishing employed by various fisheries organizations. The IWC lists vessels of non-parties and collates lists of vessels of parties which it registers and circulates.[115] Under the IWC, the purpose of registering whaling vessels belonging to parties was to track them whaling and to enable parties to identify and take action against vessels that bear flags of convenience. The register was compiled annually till 1990, but Japan, Norway and Iceland have since then refused to register their vessels anymore arguing that by giving such information the risk of sabotage to their whaling vessels had increased. Only Denmark, as a whaling state, presently registers its vessels. Under ICCAT, vessels that do not feature in the list are deemed not authorized to fish, to transship or to land species falling within the scope of the Convention and are therefore negative-listed. ICCAT obligates

CPCs to enforce these compliance measures through domestic legislation that would prohibit landing or transshipment from unauthorized vessels. Under ICCAT, non-compliance may lead to trade restrictions or removal from the list of fishing vessels involved. Flag states which are negative listed are therefore deemed 'unauthorized' to fish in the high seas area falling within the jurisdictional scope of ICCAT.

Negative listing of vessels is an effective way of improving compliance with conservation measures because it would classify such vessels and their catch as IUU. As explained earlier, by negatively listing a vessel state parties to a fisheries agreement would not be directly and physically preventing these vessels of non-parties from fishing on the high seas in the RFMO area. This approach would therefore still be acceptable under UNCLOS because the coastal states or other members of the RFMO would be relying on their domestic legislation addressing port state controls on fisheries. This is, in fact, an approach adopted by ICCAT. Once it is listed as IUU, the fishing vessel would not be allowed to tranship or land any species protected under the Convention in any of the ports of ICCAT's CPCs. Under the GFCM, an IUU vessel list has to be published[116] based on information which both contracting parties and cooperating non-contracting parties transmit annually to the Secretariat. Enforcement is mainly left up to the contracting parties, although GFCM is cooperating with ICCAT on transshipment measures for large-scale long line fishing vessels. It has no enforcement measures that are potentially in conflict with UNCLOS. Vessels licensed to fish in the Area under the competence of the CCAMLR are listed as 'regulated vessels'.[117] Parties are obligated to furnish the Commission with a list of their flag vessels intending to harvest in the Convention area, and to provide details on each vessel such as its call sign, home port and nationality.

7.4 INTERNATIONALLY AGREED MARKET-RELATED MEASURES

IUU fishing thrives upon market demands. The higher the market value of the species, the more likely it is that fishermen will disregard conservation measures and engage in IUU fishing. The value of a catch may be so lucrative that flag states would be reluctant to curb unsustainable exploitation of living resources on the high seas by vessels flying their flag. Furthermore, as pointed out above, the adoption and enforcement of conservation measures may impinge upon the competitiveness of a state once its nationals are free to register their vessels under another state that refuses to do the same. In order to prevent illegally caught fish from being placed on the market, fisheries organizations have utilized trade sanctions and other market related measures against other states whose vessels fail to observe, adopt or enforce conservation measures on the high seas. This has served to entice flag states to exercise more control over their vessels and to discourage IUU fishing in general. The regulation of trade in endangered marine species is also subject to a multilateral treaty, the Convention on International Trade of Endangered Species of Wild Flora and Fauna (CITES), which is ratified by 172 Parties.[118] The coming into force of CITES on 1 July 1975 predates the coming into force of UNCLOS and various other conservation agreements which also regulate the conservation of marine living resources. 'Introduction from the sea' is one of the four elements constituting the definition of trade under CITES.[119] CITES parties, conservation organizations and NGOs have sought to include in the CITES appendices commercially exploited aquatic species[120] that faced the risk of unsustainable exploitation. This has had various repercussions amongst parties to fisheries organizations, some members of which severely oppose the listing of commercially exploitable species in the CITES appendices. Therefore, when it comes to the enforcement of market-related measures, CITES provisions may overlap and conflict with those of the WTO, UNCLOS, CBD and regional and subregional fisheries agreements. Although this situation is a further example of fragmentation amongst applicable regimes for the conservation of high seas living resources, it has spurred fisheries organizations, led by the FAO, to work together with the CITES secretariat. This has served to trigger an in-house upgrading exercise within various fisheries organizations to improve upon compliance and enforcement measures, utilizing also market-related measures to curb illegal trade and to improve the sustainability of these species. ICCAT, for example, has managed to use trade sanctions rather effectively to improve the sustainable exploitation of bluefin tuna. Many conservation organizations made various attempts to list bluefin tuna in Appendix II of CITES.[121] ICCAT state parties have, in their vast majority, opposed such an approach,[122] but political pressure produced the required counter effect and led ICCAT parties to develop a more effective enforcement regime. At the 1992 CITES meeting in Kyoto, the US, Japan and Canada supported ICCAT's recommendation to require a trade monitoring programme for bluefin tuna.[123] This trade monitoring programme requires contracting parties to provide statistical data to enhance the monitoring of trade in the species in the Atlantic and to ensure that all imported bluefin tuna would be accompanied by an ICCAT Bluefin Statistical Document. There were also instances where listing of marine species under CITES facilitated the enforcement of conservation measures under other fisheries conventions. The listing of the Patagonian toothfish in Appendix II of CITES has served to improve the enforcement of the catch limits for this species under the CCAMLR, which had been unable to do so effectively since only 24 out of the 56 nations that trade in the fish are parties to it. The limited membership of CCAMLR was the main culprit behind its enforcement problems because almost 50 per cent of the toothfish sold in international trade were caught by vessels, either operated illegally or did not report their catch, which were registered in flag states not parties to it or else landed their catch in non-party port states, thus avoiding its enforcement obligations. CITES' vast definition of the term *trade* and wide membership served to overcome CCAMLR's vulnerable position by extending trade controls to all states involved in the toothfish trade.

With respect to conflicts that may arise between CITES and fisheries conventions, it must be pointed out that parties to CITES[124] who are also parties to another international agreement affording protection to marine species listed in its Appendix II, are relieved from the obligations related to trade in these specimens that are taken by ships registered in those parties and in accordance with such other international agreements.[125] However, the exemption is specific to agreements in force at the time of the coming into force of CITES.[126] In this context, the export of a specimen taken in accordance with the CITES Article XIV paragraph 4 would only require a certificate from a management authority of the state of introduction to the effect that the specimen was taken in accordance with the provisions of an other relevant international agreement rather than of an export permit.[127] Therefore, if a species managed under ICCAT's provisions was listed in Appendix II as, for example, the Atlantic Bluefin tuna *Thunnus thynnus*, the obligations of CITES parties that are also members of ICCAT would be modified through the application of Article XIV(4) and (5). This exemption does not apply to a convention that came into force after CITES' coming into force in 1975. Clearly this excludes UNCLOS and its provision prohibiting discrimination in form and in fact in the taking and implementation of conservation measures on the high seas.

This situation has led to a further development with the conclusion of a Memorandum of Understanding between FAO and CITES. The memorandum binds these two organizations to review the scientific, legal and technical evaluation of commercially exploited aquatic species listed or proposed for listing in the CITES Appendices, and to consult one another on the matter. In the case of species that are already listed or set to become so, FAO will work with CITES and exporting countries to improve the monitoring and management of fisheries resources and help them ensure that exports come only from responsibly managed operations. FAO commits itself to help national authorities strengthen fishery management across the board.

The implementation of trade sanctions has generated notorious political disputes at the WTO level. The tuna–dolphin[128]and shrimp–turtle[129] 'wars' have become synonymous with the inability of the international community to find a solution where the application of environmental trade measures would not be used or readily classified as non-tariff trade barriers. In the WTO Fisheries–Trade issues, the need to safeguard fisheries from over-exploitation is acknowledged, but little has been done to address the situation in an objective manner, and the use of trade sanctions in fisheries agreements (as in any conservation agreement) is still disputed. A possible solution may lie in developing the eco-labelling of fishery products. The WTO Doha Agenda addresses eco-labelling, acknowledging that it plays an important role in developing market-based incentives that ensure for consumers seafood products from well-managed stocks and sustainable fisheries. There are still, however, various obstacles to achieving this goal, notably the absence of internationally agreed guidelines for labelling and certification of products that inevitably leads to lack of transparency and misinformation with respect to the choice of products. Furthermore, developing countries must be given sufficient time to adjust and to receive assistance for their capacity building. Given their economic reliance on fisheries, they require time to absorb negative socio-economic impacts when adopting eco-labelling of fishery products. The Doha Agenda also launches negotiations on the relationship between existing WTO rules and specific trade obligations set out in multilateral environmental agreements, fishery management organizations and WTO rules. The objective is to clarify overlap and conflicting rules that in the end prevent the harmonization of an international regime for the conservation of marine living resources on the high seas.

Despite their being particularly effective, market-based sanctions will remain controversial for the years to come, and it is unlikely that guidelines on eco-labelling of fish products would be adopted soon. Internationally agreed market-based measures adopted by a group of states with a diverse economic status and which are not tailor-made to accommodate geopolitical market conditions stand a better chance of acquiescence. Contrary to unilateral or regionally exclusive measures, the adoption of internationally agreed trade sanctions achieved via cooperation, which are applied evenly and indiscriminately, should not constitute discrimination in form or fact against fishermen of other states. This, however, requires such trade compliance and enforcement measures to be applied equitably, allowing all states the opportunity to adhere to them or at least acquire the status of a cooperating non-member. The UNCLOS provision prohibiting discrimination stresses that the above-mentioned underlying conditions cannot be dispensed with, in order to rebut the claim that trade sanctions adopted are a violation of article 119(3) of UNCLOS.

7.5 PORT STATE CONTROL

The role of the port state in securing compliance and enforcement measures is actually based on the sovereign jurisdiction that a state has over vessels which voluntarily enter its ports. Although there are certain IMO international standards and rules the port state must abide by,[130] the port state's actions are an exercise of national jurisdiction and the implementation of its own laws. The port state is free to enforce its own rules and laws in its own ports. The FAO IPOA-IUU identifies port state measures as one of the major tools available to secure compliance with and the enforcement of international conservation regimes. Port states are in an ideal position to curb IUU fishing because they can enact national laws that require certain procedures like the catch documentation scheme to corroborate information submitted by flag states or otherwise verify whether conservation rules like catch quotas or the use of permitted fishing gear were abided by. They can also, to a certain extent, lessen the negative impact caused by the two main obstacles to an effective enforcement regime, namely the abuse of flag state jurisdiction and reflagging since it is the port state's rules that apply with respect to the catch once it is landed or transshipped in its port.

Port states can exercise control when flag states are unable or unwilling to act, whether they are obligated to do so under a fisheries agreement or not. Nevertheless, various fisheries agreements include provisions to obligate state parties to take port control measures. Fisheries agreements may bind parties to act in a certain manner when exercising port state jurisdiction. For instance, the FAO Compliance Agreement establishes that when a fishing vessel is voluntarily in the port of a party other than its flag state, that party, where it has reasonable grounds for believing that the fishing vessel has been used for an activity that undermines the effectiveness of international conservation and management measures, shall promptly notify the flag state accordingly. Parties may make arrangements regarding the undertaking by port states of such investigatory measures as may be considered necessary to establish whether the fishing vessel had indeed been used contrary to the provisions of this Agreement.[131] Under the FSA, the port state may provide for the regulation of transshipment on the high seas to ensure that the effectiveness of conservation and management measures is not undermined.[132] It may also address fishing activities to ensure compliance with subregional, regional or global measures, including those aimed at minimizing catches of non-target species.[133] The port state has the right and duty to take measures 'in accordance with international law' to promote the effectiveness of internationally agreed conservation and management measures.[134] In so doing the port state cannot discriminate against the vessel of any state. The port state 'may' inspect vessels that voluntarily entered port or an offshore terminal, and it may also adopt national regulations empowering its authorities to prohibit landings and transshipments where catch has been taken in a manner which undermines the effectiveness of internationally agreed measures on the high seas. These measures may be applied, in accordance with international maritime law, to both parties and non-parties to the FSA as well as to parties' and non-parties' regional or subregional organizations or arrangements. This aspect of the FSA enforcement regime is akin to article 218 of UNCLOS that regulates enforcement by port states with respect to marine pollution. Contrary to these UNCLOS provisions, the FSA does not provide anything for the port state to institute proceedings against the vessel but only to carry out the inspection of the documents, fishing gear or catch on board the fishing vessel. Nor does the FSA specifically provide that the port state may carry out an inspection if another state requests it, as in the case of port state enforcement powers under UNCLOS.[135] The provisions of the FSA do not actually stop it from doing so if it decides to take these measures because, in accordance with international law, nothing affects the port state's exercise of sovereignty over ports in its territory. In fact, nothing in this provision constrains the port state to take action only if there is an alleged violation. Once the vessel voluntarily entered port and it has national regulations permitting it to do so, the port state can proceed to inspect it. It has no obligation either to inform or request the flag state's permission to do so. The FSA provides that, if it is established that the vessel has undermined the effectiveness of subregional, regional or global conservation and management measures on the high seas, 'relevant national authorities' may prohibit landings and transshipments.

The Port Inspection Scheme[136] was established under ICCAT in 1997, but not all CPCs implement it. The NEAFC has also adopted a system of port state control by listing non-contracting parties vessels that are deemed to be IUU fishing in order to deter landings in the contracting parties' ports. Acceding states parties to CCAMLR[137] are also required to produce catch documentation scheme documents before they can import toothfish. Consequently there has been, since 2003, a mandatory port inspection upon all toothfish vessels. Unless this is carried out, all vessels carrying toothfish are denied port access, landing or transshipment. In turn, the secretariat is duty bound to inform all contracting parties and catch documentation scheme parties. The WCPFC also provides[138] an inspection procedure for the port state which allows it to prohibit landings and transshipment if the catch was taken as a result of non-compliance. The Convention lays down the procedure for transshipment both at sea and in port.[139]

The need for standardizing port control procedures is also acquiring international attention, as this would enhance the process of verifying the validity of data and render more effective and efficient other enforcement measures. UNCLOS did not elaborate on the role of the port state in implementing conservation measures. Developments in post UNCLOS agreements, as we have seen, have bridged this lacuna by supplementing it with norms that follow the UNCLOS provisions on the role of port states in combating marine pollution. The IMO Rules for Port State Controls are the only parameters port states must observe, since they are free to include any port control measures they deem fit. In this respect international legal instruments can only act as catalysts because the port state is free to act as it deems fit without having to wait for international law to develop. Since port state controls may lead to the enforcement of conservation measures of multilateral, regional or subregional agreements even vis-à-vis non-parties, this may serve to encourage states to adhere to these fishery agreements. Non-party states cannot claim that they are not bound by these conservation measures because the port state has the jurisdiction to enforce its own laws even upon foreign fishing vessels in its own ports.

7.6 SETTLEMENT OF DISPUTES

The settlement of disputes has been referred to in all the chapters of this book. The various examples of case law quoted have also shown the particular role international adjudicating bodies play in the harmonization of applicable rules. This part will focus briefly on this aspect and on the settlement of disputes as an important tool to ensure compliance. Each flag state is the judge of its own performance on the high seas, and in the taking of conservation measures, their implementation and their enforcement. In order to control abuse, parties to an agreement normally attempt to curb the discretion of flag state jurisdiction by bestowing powers upon a centralized independent and regulatory authority to ensure compliance and enforcement whenever obligations on the high seas are not observed. The establishment of ITLOS under UNCLOS has widened the choice of forum for any dispute concerning the law of the sea, including the conservation of marine living resources. Under article 286, UNCLOS provides for compulsory dispute settlement regarding its interpretation and application where no settlement has been reached by peaceful means in accordance with the Charter of the United Nations.[140] It provides states, even third parties, with the right to seek settlement regarding the application and interpretation of UNCLOS or any treaty to which they are parties.[141] The establishment of dispute settlement mechanisms is therefore an important step in resolving ambiguous treaty provisions or when it is unclear that rules of customary international law are in harmony with treaty law. Consensus for the need to establish dispute settlement mechanisms that are more specialized than the ICJ and even ITLOS itself is reflected in the FSA. This Agreement obligates state parties to settle disputes by peaceful means[142] and, in accordance with UNCLOS, it provides a mechanism for compulsory settlement of disputes by laying down that the provisions of Part XV of UNCLOS are to apply to FSA parties whether they are parties to UNCLOS or not.[143] No dispute therefore can remain unresolved.

The FSA, however, goes beyond UNCLOS Part XV in three ways. First, it stresses the obligation to cooperate in order to prevent disputes, and it does so by agreeing on efficient and expeditious decision-making procedures with regional fisheries organizations as well as by strengthening decision-making procedures as necessary.[144] Secondly, it broadens the scope of the law to be applied by the court or the tribunal. Here it differs from UNCLOS because, whilst the court or tribunal is required to apply the provisions of UNCLOS itself and other non-incompatible rules of international law, the FSA, besides these two sources, allows national courts to apply any relevant subregional, regional and global fisheries agreement addressing conservation and management of HMS and SFS.[145] Such conservation measures are defined in the FSA as 'measures to conserve or manage one or more species of living marine resources that are adopted and applied consistent with the relevant rules of international law as reflected in the Convention (UNCLOS) and this agreement'.[146] Thirdly, it seeks to overcome any unresolved dispute that may result when regional and subregional fisheries organizations do not have compulsory dispute settlement mechanisms at their disposal. It does so by obligating state parties to apply the compulsory dispute settlement procedure under article 287 of UNCLOS in matters concerning the interpretation and application of subregional, regional and of global fisheries agreements addressing the conservation and management of HMS and straddling stocks.[147] In more ways than one, therefore, it extends the scope of UNCLOS with respect to dispute settlement, addressing situations that even UNCLOS may leave unresolved. This ensures that in case of any disputes between parties leading to a deadlock, the absence of compliance monitoring, as well as effective enforcement, are still addressed.

Regional and subregional fisheries agreements have been more cautious. Under ICCAT there is no dispute settlement mechanism at present. Under the IOTC disputes are to be settled by the Commission, and where the Commission is unsuccessful they will be referred for settlement to a conciliation procedure. If still unsettled, the dispute will be referred to the ICJ unless the parties agree to another method of settlement. Under the NEAFC there is a fast track mechanism for dispute settlement; currently this operates on a voluntary basis which will eventually be legally binding following an amendment to the Convention that was unanimously adopted at the 2004 Annual Meeting. The GFCM Agreement has an article[148] that provides for the establishment of a committee to which disputes amongst contracting parties may be referred.[149] The Donut Hole Convention does not specifically provide for dispute settlement procedures, but when parties fail to reach consensus on annual harvests they are to determine annual harvests by the fallback formula found in Part 1 of the Annex to the Convention.[150] The Commission for Conservation of Southern Bluefin Tuna has been put to the test with respect to the applicable mechanism for dispute settlement. Article XIV of the Convention provides directory provisions on dispute settlement, and in case these dispute settlement measures fail Annex I includes instructions for the creation of an arbitral tribunal; but when a dispute arose between Australia and New Zealand against Japan, all of which are parties to the Convention, they referred the matter under dispute to ITLOS and did not adopt the procedure set up under the CCSBT. Article XXV of the CCAMLR addresses dispute settlement between the parties in the case of interpretation or application of the Convention. The parties shall attempt to resolve the issue via negotiation, inquiry, mediation, conciliation, arbitration, judicial settlement or other peaceful means of their own choice. If the parties still do not manage to settle their dispute, then they are to resort to the ICJ or arbitration, and where the parties fail to agree whether to take the dispute to the ICJ they must seek to resolve it by one of the peaceful means mentioned above. Dispute settlement under the WCPFC is provided for under article 31 Part VIII of the Convention which applies to any dispute between the members of the Commission, whether they are parties to the agreement or not.

7.7 CONCLUSION

Compliance and enforcement have been termed as international law's greatest weakness and, true to this statement, there are innumerable practical and even legal difficulties to ensure compliance and enforcement when it comes to regulating the conservation of living resources on the high seas.

The vast areas subject to monitoring and compliance render enforcement very costly and not available to all states, because not all have the adequate financial backing. Space technology, for instance, is the most effective but also the most expensive. From a legal perspective we have seen how, unless the flag state acquiesces to conservation measures, no enforcement can be exercised against it on the high seas for breaching conservation measures adopted via cooperation.[151] The two most common legal obstacles that seriously hamper effective compliance and enforcement result from flag state abuse of their exclusive jurisdiction or their lack of control over their vessels. One can, however, trace a number of measures which aim at detecting and penalizing irregularities that may be considered as the constituent elements for compliance and enforcement in conservation regimes on the high seas. Compliance measures under the FSA and other agreements include authorizations, licensing, reporting and exchange of information between the flag state and the vessel owners and between the flag state and the secretariat of the fisheries agreements and other parties. Another important compliance tool is the observer programme adopted by some regional and subregional agreements.[152] The presence of an independent observer on a fishing vessel is instrumental in securing compliance and reporting any breaches of international conservation rules committed on the high seas. Reporting and data are also collected from observers and can be used to formulate lists of fishing vessels which are either presumed to be IUU fishing or certified to have satisfied compliance measures. Reporting and exchange of information are mainly applicable and most effective under a cooperation agreement, whilst licensing and authorizations can even be adopted unilaterally. It is needless to say that cooperation in itself is instrumental in securing better compliance, and UNCLOS itself obliges states to cooperate in the conservation and management of living resources on the high seas especially when states fish for the same species or in the same area.[153] As stated above, however, it is still permissible for states under UNCLOS to restrict themselves to take only unilateral conservation measures.[154] Apart from providing for enforcement measures, treaties sometimes also establish dispute settlement mechanisms to compel state parties to ensure compliance. They do so both indirectly when compulsory settlement of disputes acts as a deterrent, and also directly since this serves to resolve conflicts amongst parties and ensures that they comply with their conservation obligations.

The main acts of enforcement practised by states on the high seas are: surveillance, control, monitoring, search and inspection, stopping and boarding vessels, negative listing as well as reporting.[155] Arrest, seizure, and detention can also happen if a vessel voluntarily enters the port of a state party[156] or if the vessel belongs to a flag state that is also a party to a fisheries agreement which permits its vessels to be escorted from the high seas to the port state party. In such cases the flag state's consent is always required, even amongst parties to the agreement.[157] The application of sanctions, including internationally agreed market-related measures are also sometimes resorted to, particularly under regional and subregional fisheries agreements. A minimum level of enforcement is required to induce compliance. Fisheries agreements may themselves include compliance measures such as standard reporting, but enforcement in the sense of apprehension for wrongdoing remains essential. Otherwise competitiveness suffers because of loss of revenue, unemployment and unfair competition. Cooperative efforts via adherence to fishery agreements may be spurred by the high costs involved in taking enforcement and compliance measures, particularly when acting unilaterally. Expenses for surveillance costs, search and other enforcement efforts may exceed the benefits obtainable from the fishery. The best option for states is therefore to standardize and harmonize enforcement procedures that contribute to increasing net benefits. Greatly effective, for instance, has been the employment of a regional register of fishing vessels, adopted by the South Pacific Island States,[158] to promote compliance.

The setting up of ITLOS and the other dispute settlement mechanisms in treaties and RFMOs are a reaction to the ever-increasing developments under the law of the sea that have transformed it into a specialized branch of international law. These achievements may thus provide stronger and more responsive jurisprudence, but in itself this also risks causing the fragmentation of the international adjudicating system, thus diminishing the ICJ's central role as the principal judicial organ of the UN.[159] On the other hand, examples of dispute settlement have been referred to in the discussion because such procedures play a fundamental role in the harmonization process of conflicting rules which emerge from different sources or which originate from different fora. When negotiating treaties, states seek harmonization by streamlining and coordinating legal norms, whilst adjudicating bodies are bound to identify the most adequate legal techniques to avoid, minimize or mitigate conflict of applicable norms. Achieving harmonization becomes a question of interpretation rather than conflict resolution. The ILC[160] quotes the relationship between fisheries agreements and UNCLOS as an example of this kind.[161] It refers to the *Southern Bluefin Tuna* Case where the tribunal delved into the relationship between UNCLOS and the CCSBT and determined the applicable provisions that were to settle the dispute. In a landmark decision, it concluded that the CCSBT applied as both *lex specialis* and *lex posterior*.[162] This demonstrates to what extent legal techniques can resolve fragmentation and conflicts between laws, particularly between framework and implementation treaties. The tribunal held that international legal obligations benefit from a process of accretion and accumulation.[163] The adjudicating tribunal opted to coordinate the interpretation of applicable legal instruments and to consider them as mutually supportive.

NOTES

1. See Birnie, P., Boyle, A. and Redgwell, C. (2009), *International Law and the Environment*, 3rd edn, Oxford: Oxford University Press, pp 44–5, 47 and 84–6.
2. See the *Gabčikovo–Nagymaros Dam* case, ICJ Reports (1997), 7 at para 140.
3. See the preamble of the FSA and the FAO Compliance Agreement as well as the FAO IPOA–IUU and FAO Code of Conduct, all of which emphasize sustainable fisheries.
4. See above Chapters 3, 4 and 5.
5. See *Fisheries Jurisdiction Case (Spain v Canada)*, ICJ Rep., 1998. This dispute demonstrated the dire need for the promotion of an effective implementation agreement of those provisions under UNCLOS that address straddling fish stocks and HMS. See Freestone, D. (1995), 'The 1995 Agreement between Canada and the EU over Fishery Control and Enforcement in the NAFO Regulatory Area', *European Environmental Law Review*, **4** (10), 270–72; Sullivan, M.S. (1997), 'The Case in International Law for Canada's Extension of Fisheries Jurisdiction beyond 200 miles', ODIL, **28** (3), 203–68.
6. Under Part XII of UNCLOS, section 6.
7. See FSA article 18(3).
8. See UNCLOS article 90 on the right of navigation and article 91 on the nationality of ships.
9. See discussion in chapter 6. UNCLOS provides that 'all States have the right for their nationals to engage in fishing on the high seas' subject to their treaty obligations; the rights, duties and interests of coastal states with respect to straddling stocks, highly migratory species, marine mammals, anadromous and catadromous species, and the provisions of section 2 of Part VII of the Convention. UNCLOS also provides that 'States have the duty to take or to cooperate with other States in taking such measures for their respective nationals as may be necessary for the conservation of living resources of the High Seas'. These two provisions, found in section Two of Part VII, establish that right to freedom of fishing and duty to conserve marine living resources on the high seas vest in the state, which in turn exercises this right by authorizing its nationals to fish subject to these same obligations. The term 'nationals' refers both to natural persons as well as to the fishing vessels registered under its flag.
10. See paper by Kuemlangan, B., (2000), 'National Legislative Options to combat IUU Fishing' prepared for the Expert Consultation on Illegal, Unreported and Unregulated Fishing Organized by the Government of Australia in Cooperation with FAO, Sydney, Australia, 15–19 May. The paper is available at: http://www.daff.gov.au.
11. In Thailand, for example, there is a system of registration for fishing vessels but this requirement is not abided by as it is seen to overlap with or lead to a duplication of powers of the authority responsible for shipping. Consequently, the Thai authority responsible for fisheries does not implement a fishing vessel register, and Thai fishing vessels on the high seas are not subject to its jurisdiction. In Tonga, although registration of local fishing vessels is required to ensure compliance with national standards for safety-at-sea and to serve as a record of the level of fishing capacity, there is no national legal obligation to link fishing vessel registration with the authorization to fish, with the result that a licence to fish may still be issued to a vessel which is not registered and renders futile the purpose for which registration is required.

12. See FSA article 18(3)(b)(ii) and (iii) where state parties shall require their vessels fishing on the high seas to carry the licence, authorization or permit on board at all times and to produce it on demand for inspection by a duly authorized person.
13. See FSA article 21(11)(a): 'a serious violation means: (a) fishing without a valid licence, authorization or permit issued by the flag State in accordance with article 18, paragraph 3(a)'.
14. Ibid, article 19(2).
15. See ibid, article 18(3)(b)(i).
16. See ibid.
17. It is obligatory upon the parties to the Compliance Agreement to take enforcement measures if fishing vessels flying its flag contravene the provisions of the Agreement. The Compliance Agreement, however, leaves it up to the parties whether to include such contraventions as offences under national legislation.
18. Article III(8).
19. The FAO checklist for recommended actions under its IPOA-IUU urges all states to make it a violation of their law for their nationals to breach the fishery conservation and management laws of any other state or to undermine the effectiveness of conservation and management measures adopted by a fisheries organization. States are also to discourage their nationals from reflagging fishing vessels, or from initially registering new vessels, in states that are identified by a fisheries organization as undermining the effectiveness conservation and management measures adopted by it. All states should also ensure that their nationals are aware of the effects of IUU fishing, and should discourage them from doing business with those engaged in IUU fishing.
20. See Molenaar, E.J. (2003), 'Participation, Allocation and Unregulated Fishing; the Practice of Regional Fisheries Management Organizations', IJMC, **18** (4), 457–80, (2003); Sydnes, A.K. (2001), 'Regional Fishery Organizations: How and Why Organizational Diversity Matters', ODIL, **32** (4), 349–72.
21. See Compliance Agreement article III(5)(a)(b).
22. Ibid, article (5)(c).
23. It should determine that it is so by ensuring that granting such vessel an authorization to fish on the high seas would not undermine the object and purpose of this agreement.
24. Even if the agreement lays down that, to do so, the state party must take into account the relevant facts and the circumstances as to why the authorization was withdrawn by another state.
25. See article VI(9). This information shall include pertinent data permitting the identification of the fishing vessel and the owner or operator and, as appropriate, any other information relevant to the party's decision. It leaves it entirely upon the state party to decide.
26. See below at note 27.
27. So far the best example of such type of cooperation has been the Regional Registry of the Forum Fisheries Agency, an information database of fishing vessels operating in the region. Each vessel is given a unique regional registration number which guarantees that it can be licensed. Without a regional registration number, no fishing vessel may be licensed to fish in the region. The registration may be withdrawn or suspended if the vessel has been involved in a serious violation of the fisheries laws of any of the member countries of the Forum Fisheries Agency. The Forum Fisheries Agency (FFA) is established by the South Pacific Forum Fisheries Agency Convention, 10 July 1978. Its 16 members are Australia, Cook Islands, Federated States of Micronesia, Fiji, Kiribati, Marshall Islands, Nauru, New Zealand, Niue, Palau, Papua New Guinea, Samoa, Solomon Islands, Tonga, Tuvalu and Vanuatu.
28. See Birnie, Boyle and Redgwell (2009), p 207 and footnote 205.
29. See FAO IPOA-IUU para 24.8.
30. FSA article 18(3)(b) lays down '(i) to apply terms and conditions to the licence authorization or permit sufficient to fulfil any subregional, regional, global obligations of the flag state; (ii) prohibit fishing on the high seas by vessels which are not duly licensed or

authorized to fish, or fishing on the high seas by vessels otherwise than in accordance with the terms and conditions of a licence, authorization or permit; (iii) require vessels fishing on the high seas to carry the licence, authorization or permit on board at all times and to produce it on demand for inspection by a duly authorized person; and (iv) ensure that vessels flying its flag do not conduct unauthorized fishing within areas under the national jurisdiction of other States.'

31. See ibid, article 18(3).
32. See ibid.
33. See Riddle K. (2003), 'Illegal, Unreported And Unregulated Fishing: Is International Cooperation Contagious?', ODIL **37**, (3–4), 275.
34. See Birnie, Boyle and Redgwell (2009); see also Honneland, G. (1998), 'Compliance in the Fishery Protection Zone Around Svalbard,' ODIL, **29** (4), 339–60 (1998) and (2000), 'Enforcement Cooperation between Norway and Russia in the Barents Sea Fisheries', ODIL, **31** (3), 249–68.
35. See UNCLOS article 119(2).
36. The term 'concern' is linked to 'legal interest'; see above Chapter 2, pp 38–40, on the status of marine living resources and the meaning of biological diversity as a common concern of humankind. The phrase 'common concern of humankind' was used in the preamble of both the UNFCCC and the CBD, and referred precisely to this link. In this respect one may interpret the inclusion of this phrase in the CBD as expressing the interest which humanity has in the conservation of biological diversity.
37. See UNCLOS article 118.
38. See FSA article 18(3)(c), but it is to be noted that under the whaling convention some whaling states have refused to provide access to information about their vessels on the pretext that this leads to sabotage by terrorist anti-whaling groups; see also Gillespie, A. (2003), 'The Search for a New Compliance Mechanism within the International Whaling Commission', ODIL **34** (3–4),349–68.
39. See FAO Compliance Agreement Article III(7).
40. Ibid, Article IV.
41. Article III (6). Examples of such standards would include the FAO Standard Specifications for Marking and Identification of Fishing Vessels.
42. Article VIII(3) lists provisions relating to non-parties; sub para (2) specifically obligates parties to cooperate 'in a manner consistent with the Agreement and with international law to the end that fishing vessels entitled to fly the flags of non-Parties do not engage in activities which undermine the effectiveness of international conservation and management measures.'
43. The information is requested under article VI(1).
44. Ibid, sub para (4).
45. Ibid, article VI(5).
46. See FSA article 18(3)(c).
47. See ibid, article 18(3)(d).
48. ICCAT has as members or contracting parties 42 members from five continents, but in 1994 it created also a special status known as 'cooperating non-contracting parties', which was revised in 1997 to include also a non-contracting entity or fishing entity. Contracting parties, fishing entities and cooperating non-contracting parties are collectively referred to as CPCs.
49. This is held under two separate tasks. In Task I they must report annual catch by species, gear region and flag. Task II requires reporting on monthly catches and fishing effort statistics for each species by small area.
50. FSA article 18(3)(e).
51. Ibid, article 18(3)(c).
52. Ibid, article 20(3).
53. Or other states not part of the geographical area within the scope of the organization/agreement. See Freestone, D. (1995).
54. UNCLOS article 118.

55. Ibid.
56. Post UNCLOS multilateral agreements, such as the FSA and the FAO Compliance Agreement, interpret conservation measures to be those applied by regional and subregional fisheries organizations where these exist.
57. See UNCLOS article 87(1)(e).
58. See ibid, article 117.
59. With respect to the species they exploit or the areas where they fish on the high seas.
60. Article 119(3) under section two of UNCLOS specifically obligates states to ensure that conservation measures and their implementation (hence including their enforcement) does not discriminate 'in form or in fact' against fishermen of any state.
61. This is the case, for instance, of prohibition of drift net fishing.
62. See FAO IPOA-IUU para 3.2.
63. See Birnie, Boyle and Redgwell (2009); see also Orrego Vicuna, F. (1993), 'Towards an Effective Management of High Seas Fisheries and the Settlement of Pending Issues of the Law of the Sea', ODIL, **24** (1), 81–92.
64. See CBD article 17.
65. Ibid, article 26.
66. Ibid, article 5.
67. Ibid, article 22.
68. See Birnie, Boyle and Redgwell (2009), p 588.
69. See FSA article 18(3)(c). They have to do so taking into account any national laws of the flag state regarding release of such information.
70. FSA bases enforcement measures on cooperation; see its article 5.
71. FSA article 5(l).
72. See ibid, 18(3)(i). These include '(i) the implementation of national inspection schemes and subregional and regional schemes for cooperation in enforcement pursuant to articles 21 and 22, including requirements for such vessels to permit access by duly authorized inspectors from other States; (ii) the implementation of national observer programmes and subregional and regional observer programmes in which the flag State is a participant, including requirements for such vessels to permit access by observers from other States to carry out the functions agreed under the programme; and (iii) the development and implementation of vessel monitoring systems, including, as appropriate, satellite transmitter systems, in accordance with any national programmes and those which have been subregionally, regionally or globally agreed among the States concerned.'
73. Ibid, article 24(8).
74. For example, the GFCM has no vessel monitoring system but envisages to introduce it under a control scheme adopted in 2005. See the Report of the FAO concerning UNGA resolutions A/RES/57/141 on Oceans and the Law of the Sea, p 3 para 2.2; see also Sydnes, A.K. (2001); Molenaar, E.J., (2000), 'Satellite-based VMS for Fisheries Management: International Legal Aspects', IJMC, **15** (1), 65–109.
75. See Gillespie, A. (2003) 349.
76. IWC 24th report (1974), p 20. In the mid-1950s Norway had proposed international observers on all factory ships, but there were various political and practical difficulties to the adoption of the proposal.
77. See FSA article 18(3)(g)(ii).
78. Established only for large scale tuna long line fishing vessels authorized for transshipment.
79. CCAMLR article XXIV. The Convention does not provide as to how this will be addressed but calls for the establishment of a set of principles.
80. This was established by the CCAMLR by a decision of the Commission at its 6th session on 6 November 1988.
81. This is done by means of a pennant or flag approved by the Commission.
82. UNCLOS article 118.
83. It was actually introduced by its predecessor. With respect to the Anadromous Stocks

Convention: inspection is directed at an examination of logs, docs, catch and other articles on board. See article V(2).

84. The Conservation and Management of Pollock Resources in the Central Bering Sea, commonly referred to as the Donut Hole Convention, was signed in Washington on June 16, 1994 by China, South Korea, Russia and the United States. Japan and Poland also signed the Convention in Washington on 4 August 1994 and 25 August 1994 respectively. See Canfield, J. (1993), 'Recent Developments in Bering Sea Fisheries Conservation and Management', ODIL, **24** (3), 257–89.
85. See CCAMLR article V.
86. See WCPFC article 26.
87. It has, however, an observer programme. The PWG is responsible for monitoring and addresses non-compliance, but it must rely on the approval of the ICCAT Commission to remedy any wrongdoing. Under NAFO, enforcement depends on the NAFO Scheme of Joint International Inspection and Surveillance which encompasses all vessels fishing in the NAFO Regulatory Area.
88. They list as IUU vessels that refuse to comply with boarding and inspection measures which would verify whether the vessel was IUU fishing or not. They apply such measures even with respect to vessels whose flag states are parties to the agreement prescribing boarding and inspection.
89. The basis for this argument and counter argument is based on UNCLOS which affirms that flag states have exclusive jurisdiction with respect to compliance and enforcement on the high seas but also subjects the freedom of fishing to coastal states' rights, duties and interests. The Convention leaves it up to the states concerned to sort out how to reach this delicate legal balance by concluding fisheries agreements. Nothing in UNCLOS, however, constrains states to refrain from exercising their freedom of fishing on the high seas if they are not party to an agreement applicable to the area where they fish.
90. See UNCLOS article 119(3).
91. This may include collaborating non-members if the latter agree.
92. See however FSA article 21(15) which allows the state parties members of a regional or subregional fisheries management organization or arrangement to limit the application of this provision only between themselves if the organization or arrangement has established 'an alternative mechanism which effectively discharges the obligation under this Agreement'. This would therefore not allow state parties to the FSA, which are also members of such an organization or agreement, to board and inspect fishing vessels of state parties that are not members of the same organization or arrangement as the FSA provides for under article 21(1).
93. FSA articles 21 and 22.
94. Ibid.
95. Unless by way of exception, it is necessary to delay the boarding and inspection in accordance with generally accepted international regulations, procedures and practices relating to safety at sea.
96. FSA article 22(4).
97. In the case of a serious suspicion, the inspecting state has the right to remain on board to secure evidence and may also require the vessel to proceed to the nearest port for dockside inspection. See FSA article 21(8).
98. Ibid, article 21.
99. An exclusive list of which is provided under the FSA; see article 21(11).
100. Ibid, article 21(8).
101. Ibid.
102. Unless another time period is established by the sub regional or regional enforcement procedures.
103. It must act in accordance with its obligations under FSA article 19.
104. Ibid, FSA article 21(5) (6).
105. Ibid, article 21(2).

106. This is in accordance with ibid, article 19.
107. Ibid, article 21(18).
108. The FAO IPOA-IUU makes it clear that this measure is binding only upon state parties to those agreements which prescribe it, like the FSA. UNCLOS itself subjects the freedom of fishing of states to their treaty obligations. See UNCLOS article 116(a).
109. The *Estai Case, Fisheries Jurisdiction case (Spain v Canada)*, ICJ General List No. 96 (1998).
110. The Canadian Coastal Fisheries Protection Act, on the basis that the straddling stocks of the Grand Banks of Newfoundland 'are a major renewable world food resource' and that these stocks 'are threatened with extinction', sought to enforce compliance with conservation and management measures taken under the Convention for Future Multilateral Cooperation in the Northwest Atlantic Fisheries (done at Ottawa 24 October 1978, Canada Treaty Series 1979 No. 11) even against foreign vessels 'which fish in contravention of such conservation and management measures'. The Act provided 'Protection officers' to board and inspect such fishing vessels found within the NAFO Regulatory Area in order to ensure compliance with this Act.
111. Canada and Spain had both adhered to the compulsory jurisdiction clause of the ICJ Statute article 36(2), but on 10 May 1994, Canada deposited with the Secretary General of the UN a statement which held that Canada's acceptance of the compulsory clause was terminated with respect to, *inter alia*, disputes arising out of or concerning management measures taken by Canada with respect to vessels fishing in the NAFO Regulatory Area and the enforcement of such measures.
112. A vessel may be deemed as conducting IUU, but it is still up to its flag state to take enforcement measures. The breach of conservation measures does not justify an intervention by the coastal state.
113. See, for example, the *US Magnuson-Stevens Fishery Conservation and Management Act* 16 U.S.C. 1801 and 16 U.S.C. 1903 (c); see also Riddle (2003), 273.
114. UNCLOS article 104 lays down that retention or loss of nationality is determined by the law of the state from which nationality is derived; see also article 92 on the status of ships.
115. In operation since 1979; see IWC 30th Report (1980), 32.
116. In 2006.
117. Vessels not listed are presumed to be IUU unless the contrary is proved.
118. As per information obtained in October 2007 from CITES website, www.cites.org.
119. See article I of CITES where trade is defined as having four elements: import, export, re-export and introduction from the sea.
120. No marine species taken in a large-scale, industrial commercial fishery have yet been listed on CITES, although all sturgeon and paddlefish *Acipenseriformes spp.* are listed in either Appendix I or in Appendix II and traded in significant quantities according to certain quotas. A growing number of commercially exploited fish have come under CITES controls in recent years; the Patagonian toothfish, the basking and whale sharks were included in Appendix II in 2002, and the great white shark and the humphead wrasse in 2004. The CITES Conference of the Parties at The Hague in May 2007 expanded CITES coverage to include the European eel and sawfish in Appendix I (except for one species of sawfish in Appendix II). Cetaceans are also all listed. Nevertheless, the moratorium under the IWC supersedes the CITES provisions by virtue of its article XIV paras 4 and 5.
121. To list species in the CITES Appendix II, a state party must make the proposal that would need to be supported by two-thirds of the other state parties.
122. See also Rubin Alana, R. (2007), 'Rock the Boat: The Plight of the Southern Bluefin Tuna', Michigan State University College of Law, 2007 http://www.animallaw.info/articles/ddusbluefintuna.htm.
123. See ICCAT recommendation 92-01 concerning the ICCAT Bluefin Tuna Statistical Document Programme, Madrid, ICCAT (1992).
124. See CITES article XIV, para 4.

125. Winjstekers, W. (2001), *The Evolution of CITES: Reference to the Convention on International Trade in Endangered Species of Wild Fauna and Flora,* 6th edn, CITES Secretariat, Geneva, Switzerland.
126. 1 July 1975. There are a number of fisheries conventions and agreements that were in force prior to that date. For example, the IATTC came into force on 3 March 1950 whilst ICCAT came into force on 21 March 1969.
127. CITES article XIV para 5.
128. GATT Case DS21 Dolphin–Tuna Case I, Mexico against the US, and later Dolphin–Tuna Case II GATT Case DS29 the European Community against the US.
129. WTO Case WT/DS 58 Complaint by India, Malaysia, Pakistan and Thailand against the US and WT/DS 61 Complaint by the Philippines against the US. Both complaints related to the prohibition of imports of shrimps and shrimp products from these states by the US because of the type of fishing gear used.
130. For example, the qualifications, the experience required and the training of port state control officers are set out in the IMO publication *Procedures for Port State Control.* It should follow that any officer associated with monitoring, control, surveillance and enforcement should be suitably qualified and trained in conformity with internationally agreed standards, but this is not always the case. See Rayfuse, R.G. (2004), *Non-Flag State Enforcement in High Seas Fisheries*, Leiden, Boston: Martinus Nijhoff Publishers.
131. See FAO Compliance Agreement article V para 2.
132. See FSA article 18(3)(h).
133. Ibid, article 18(3)(i).
134. See FSA article 23.
135. See UNCLOS article 218(3).
136. The scheme calls for port inspection both for flag and non-flag state vessels during off-loading or in-port transshipment.
137. Parties Members of its Commission are not included.
138. WCPFC article 27.
139. Ibid, article 29.
140. UNCLOS article 286 refers to the settlement reached by recourse to section 1 of Part XV.
141. ITLOS Statute article 31.
142. Ibid, article 27.
143. Ibid, article 30.
144. Ibid, article 28.
145. Ibid, article 30(5).
146. This is also referred to in the FAO Compliance Agreement which obligates state parties to take 'such measures that may be necessary to ensure that fishing vessels entitled to fly its flag do not engage in any activity that undermines the effectiveness of international conservation or management measures.'
147. ITLOS Statute, article 30(2); but state parties to the FSA may still opt for a different procedure when ratifying the FSA.
148. Article XVII of the Agreement establishes a committee composed of one member from each contracting party and an independent chairman chosen by the members of the committee. If the dispute is not settled by the committee it shall be referred to the ICJ.
149. Nevertheless, to date, the article establishing this committee has never been invoked.
150. This obligates them to prohibit directed fishing if the biomass is equal to or less than 1.67 million metric tons.
151. Articles 87 and 116 of UNCLOS establish the exclusivity of the flag state whereby the vessel is immune from interference by any other state.
152. It was also applied under the Whaling Convention, a multilateral treaty, but was suspended following the moratorium on whaling. See Gillespie, A. (2003), and (2002), 'Forum Shopping in International Environmental Law: The IWC, CITES and the Management of Cetaceans,' ODIL, **33** (1), 17–56; see also Burke, W.T. (1997), 'Legal

Aspects of the IWC Decision on the Southern Ocean Sanctuary', ODIL, **28** (3), 313–27 (1997).

153. See UNCLOS article 118.
154. Ibid, article 117.
155. Reporting as an enforcement tool is different from reporting as an administrative measure that is carried out to ensure compliance and provide data. As an enforcement tool it refers to reporting by third party states to inform the flag state or the fisheries organization or both that fishing vessels have infringed conservation measures.
156. In such circumstances the state concerned would be applying international law rules as a port state.
157. See above at note 7.
158. See above at note 27.
159. See, for example, the *MOX Plant Request for Provisional Measures Order Case (Ireland v United Kingdom)*, 3 December 2001, (ITLOS), ILR vol. 126 (2005) p 273, para 50. The negative effects on the environment caused by the operation of the MOX Plant, a nuclear facility at Sellafield in the UK, was raised at three different institutional procedures: under ITLOS, under the compulsory dispute settlement procedure set up under the OSPAR Convention, and under the regional rules of the EC/EURATOM treaty. All these three institutions had jurisdiction over the dispute which involved the multilateral and general rules of UNCLOS, the regional rules of OSPAR since the dispute related to pollution in the North Sea, and the application of EU law since both parties are members of the EU.
160. See Report of the Study Group of the International Law Commission entitled 'Fragmentation of International Law: Difficulties Arising from Diversification and Expansion of International Law'; document A/CN.4/L.682, 13 April 2006, 58th Session of the ILC, Geneva, para 9.
161. See ibid, p 21 para 29.
162. See ibid, p 23 para 38 and p 22 footnote 28; see also Churchill, R. (2007), 'The Jurisprudence of the International Tribunal for the Law of the Sea Relating to fisheries: Is There Much in the Net?', IJMC, **22** (3), 383–425.
163. *Southern Bluefin Tuna* case, ILM vol. 39 (2000), p 1388, para 52; see also Roach, J.A. (1995), 'Dispute Settlement in Specific Situations', 7 *Geo International and Environmental Law Review*, 775–84; see also Romano, C., (2001), 'The Southern Bluefin Tuna Dispute: Hints of a World to Come, Like it or Not', ODIL, **32** (4), 313–48; Stephens, T. (2004), 'The Limits of International Adjudication in International Law: Another Perspective on the Southern Bluefin Tuna Case', IJMC, **19** (2), 177–97.

8 Conclusion

8.1 THE NEED FOR HARMONIZATION AMONG APPLICABLE NORMS: AN OVERVIEW OF THE CURRENT STATE OF PLAY

The international community's attempt to conserve high seas living resources has generated a vast body of rules that span across different sectors of international law. Identifying applicable sources is not a plain sailing exercise as one needs to determine which legal sources apply and also how these must be interpreted in the light of contemporary state practice with respect to particular situations, given the constant development and specialized nature of this branch of law. The chances of conflict and ambiguity in the law increase as more rules are generated. The discussion in the previous chapters identifies various situations which prompt the need for harmonization among applicable rules of international law. The first and possibly the most common is the lack of coherence between prior and subsequent norms addressing the same circumstances. A number of treaties regulating living resources on the high seas already existed before UNCLOS was concluded. The 1982 Convention built upon their provisions and codified customary rules applicable at the time. It qualifies the freedom of fishing subjecting it to the rights, duties and interests of coastal states, other participants in the fishery and to the interests of the international community. The Convention requires states to accommodate their different interests via cooperation but does not elaborate upon what should be done if cooperation fails. It does not have any provisions on compliance and enforcement, even if it establishes compulsory dispute settlement.[1] The framework nature of the UNCLOS provisions in section two of its Part VII is understandable; they were negotiated when the extension of coastal state jurisdiction was rife and the conservation of high seas living resources was considered as part of a larger package deal. Section two of Part VII of UNCLOS secures an important balance of interests between coastal states and distant water fishing states but, as discussed earlier, some of its articles require states to further supplement it by other legal instruments.[2] There are various reasons why UNCLOS negotiators opted for this approach. A multilateral treaty may not be the best forum to negotiate specific conservation measures. For one thing, the conservation of marine species and the interests of participants in the fishery are often particular to the region and/or subregion; consequently regional agreements may achieve more effective substantive conservation measures. In the years that followed the conclusion of UNCLOS, states concluded various new agreements at the multilateral, regional and sub regional level, which apply to particular maritime zones[3] or to specific species.[4] A number of international norms that have developed via these post UNCLOS agreements aim to ensure that any measures taken outside or within areas subject to national jurisdiction must be compatible. They circumvent the ineptitude of previously existing rules or beef up obligations that are either too general or need to be updated to meet emerging needs. The process of spontaneous reviewing and fine-tuning of international law is essential to its nature as a thriving legal system but the absence of a centralized law-making body does not facilitate harmonization amongst this accretion of norms. The unity of the law suffers because there is no institutionalized coordination process. Even if the negotiating parties of a new treaty may specify its relationship vis à vis UNCLOS and other applicable norms, the parties of other treaties may refuse to adhere to it or to acquiesce to these more specialized and updated set of applicable norms.

The harmonization of norms may also become essential whenever specialized rules evolve from more general ones in a fragmented manner. Although as in the case of UNCLOS, the general law may be structured in a way which actually promotes more specialized legal instruments, there is the risk that some states would refuse to acquiesce to the more specialized norms, considering them as an encroachment upon their rights as laid down by the general law. For instance, the root cause of excessive fishing effort is directly linked to freedom of fishing, which allows all states to harvest living resources once they occur on the high seas, whilst taking the necessary conservation measures. The manner in which to fulfil this latter obligation is left to the discretion of the high seas fishing states. The post-UNCLOS era reflects the heightened level of concern over ecological matters and introduced a variety of new concepts, principles and approaches that aim at better and more integrated conservation of high seas living resources. Post-UNCLOS developments, particularly but not only in environmental fora, sought to strengthen the ecosystem approach, introduced the precautionary approach and expanded further the interpretation of the term 'conservation' to incorporate these two approaches and equating conservation with the 'sustainable use' of *all* marine living resources and their habitat. Fisheries agreements have been reviewed to reflect these developments. The precautionary approach is not referred to under UNCLOS but the other two concepts cannot be perceived as being in conflict with its provisions because they were already implied under section two of Part VII. In post UNCLOS treaties, sustainability is considered as an inclusive measure that takes into consideration even socio-economic concerns, besides environmental ones. This interpretation corroborates UNCLOS article 119, which refers to the taking of conservation measures to produce the maximum sustainable yield 'as qualified by relevant environmental and economic factors'. The ecosystem approach, which considers the conservation of high seas living resources as part of biological diversity, is also implied in UNCLOS article 119.[5] This provision establishes the obligation to take conservation measures for associated and dependent species. Furthermore, article 194[6] requires parties under Part XII[7] to take the necessary measures to 'protect and preserve rare or fragile ecosystems as well as the habitat of depleted, threatened or endangered species and other forms of marine life'. The ecosystem approach also manifests itself in the trend adopted by post-UNCLOS treaties to ensure consistency between conservation measures adopted by all participants in the fishery, whether they are high seas fishing states or coastal states. Despite these linkages between UNCLOS and the same Convention requiring states to cooperate and conclude agreements on the management and conservation of living high seas resources, parties to post UNCLOS treaties who claim that other participants' conservation measures must be compatible with theirs, may still meet with opposition from non-parties, who would insist that they have the discretion to choose which conservation measures to adopt on the high seas. These measures may fall short of the standards established by more specialized treaties. Even if the precautionary and ecosystem approach and sustainable use have become rules of customary international law, they would within this context generate various standards that may vary in degree, rendering the achievement of compatibility much more challenging than via the adoption of more certain and specific treaty rules.

The need for harmonization of applicable norms is usually also necessary when these emanate from different sources of international law, such as treaty and custom, since they may regulate the same issues differently. Gaps between these two sources are inevitable sometimes. Due to its very nature, custom is spontaneous, not easily decipherable and usually lags behind treaty regimes, which may be much more complex and under regular review by their parties in order to meet with emerging conservation requirements of living resources on the high seas. Nevertheless although custom may not adequately address the question of allocation of benefits as well as the restrictions on access and effort dictated by stock abundance, the general and broad obligations it imposes upon high seas fishing states form the very basis of the contemporary conservation regime. At the same time, customary norms may exceptionally even fine-tune earlier treaties and thereby generate ambiguity regarding the status of international law until the issue as to whether a new customary rule has superseded the provisions of an existing treaty is tested before an international tribunal. Until this happens, the lack of coherence between sources of treaty and customary law would encourage states to settle for more general and weaker measures, thereby undermining the more stringent conservation norms.

Harmonization of applicable conservation regimes is necessary whenever different fora apply and interpret the same rules in a diverse manner. This has happened for instance with the interpretation of the term 'conservation', which under contemporary law is assimilated with 'sustainable use' and therefore means taking without endangering a stock or species, allowing it enough time to recover in normal time and not threatening the reproduction of species through over-harvesting. At times, non-harvesting may prove to be a necessary conservation measure, so as to allow stocks to recover. Where science recommends non-use, this should be carried out on the basis of constituent management concepts like the precautionary and the ecosystem approach that appear to have become intrinsic to the obligation to take conservation measures. The vulnerability of particular species may require drastic conservation measures prohibiting use, or requiring the restriction of access to such species on the high seas because conservation is not possible in all or some areas beyond national jurisdiction.[8]

The last two decades have seen an increased impetus towards linkages between the formulation of conservation measures and scientific information as referred to in UNCLOS article 119.[9] Although there have been instances when the importance of this link has been ignored, this has been mainly due to political pressure, highly influenced by emotional and ethical principles rather than as an expression of the general trend in state practice since 1982. The ecosystem approach, which views the oceans as one large marine ecosystem, stresses the need to rely heavily upon scientific information and research in order to devise appropriate conservation measures for better governance. The precautionary approach, a fundamental component of modern conservation law and developed in environmental fora, urges action in the face of scientific uncertainty. Whilst it is essential when science is still unable to provide guidelines, the precautionary approach has discouraged governments from endorsing agreements that prohibit operations whose negative repercussions are uncertain for fear of burdening entire fishing communities without having tangible proof that their activities are detrimental to high seas living resources. Major international agreements, whether multilateral, regional or subregional, provide for in-house scientific bodies to review conservation measures in the light of regular scientific updates.[10] The more headway is made into integrating scientific information as a basis for adopting more stringent conservation measures, the more likely it is that states will adhere to further qualifications to the freedom of fishing. The imposition of conservation measures on the basis of claims dictated by dogmatic beliefs and emotional sentiments that are not shared by other states, due to cultural and historical reasons, is not tantamount to sound legal practice and is not suitable to resolve conservation problems. Such measures will only further intensify polarization at the expense of the continued unsustainable exploitation of marine living resources. This does not mean that behavioural and consumption patterns may not be required to change in order to implement the necessary conservation measures, but these must be based on scientific proof or, in the case of scientific uncertainty, upon evidence showing the risk that a good conservation status cannot be achieved unless such measures are taken.

International lawyers have been divided in their position as to how to deal with the accretion of international rules. Some have been critical of the specialization and subspecialization of general international law, seeing it as an erosion of its general principles and the emergence of conflicting rules of law and jurisprudence leading to forum shopping and loss of legal security. Others see it as a technical problem, a natural occurrence resulting from the increased international legal activity, which needs to be controlled by better streamlining and coordination.[11] This latter view is perhaps the best option to ensure better harmonization among international legal regimes addressing the conservation of high seas living resources, especially since UNCLOS, as a typical framework Convention, left it up to the states themselves to work out the details in separate agreements.[12] Despite these different views there appears however to be general consensus on the position established by the VCLT, namely that international law must be applied in its entirety and that the harmonization of applicable sources is an essential exercise.[13] In the words of Ed Miles,

> The management of the world ocean is characterized by a haphazard quilt of global, regional and national arrangements differentiated by activity and ocean but without effective mechanisms for achieving coordination across either oceans or activities. This fragmentation creates occasions for significant conflict and interferes with productive use of the oceans to a noticeable degree.[14]

8.2 A SUMMARY OF THE RECOMMENDATIONS FOR HARMONIZING APPLICABLE REGIMES

One of the legal techniques for harmonization which an adjudicating body has at its disposal emerges from article 30 of the VCLT. Generally speaking, state practice considers subsequent norms to supersede earlier norms.[15] The reason behind giving priority to more recent norms is pragmatic, in the sense that the successive norm would have probably evolved to provide for the needs of the subjects involved that may have emerged after the previous norms were established. The VCLT provides some guidance on what should prevail between an earlier and a later treaty but this is conditional to the subsequent law referring to the same subject matter. This qualification is not very helpful in determining whether the application of *lex posteriori* that supersedes the *lex priori* in accordance with the Vienna Convention would include the situation where the subject matter is dealt with by two different treaties whose objectives vary because they were negotiated in different fora. This is a typical situation that occurs when one comes to apply sources of international law regulating the conservation of marine living resources on the high seas. More recent treaties, whether they are environmental or fisheries treaties, may be regulating the same species or the same anthropogenic activities but their conservation objectives would include the ecosystem and the precautionary approach, which require a higher standard of conservation than that envisaged under the 1982 UNCLOS and the earlier fisheries treaties. The reasoning behind the VCLT's provisions to allow later norms to supersede older ones, only if they relate to the same subject matter, may be based on the presumption that commitments taken at a later stage may apply to different parties or have different beneficiaries. Nevertheless it is also absurd to retain norms that are proved to be outdated or insufficient due to changing circumstances or access to fresh information. As science provides the evidence on what kind of conservation measures are needed, it is futile to stick to previous norms that were not devised with the knowledge that is available today. This is particularly the case with conservation rules relating to marine living resources on the high seas, since the link with scientific information is an essential characteristic of this legal stream.

The general trend in state practice, in the case of treaties, is to accept the prevalent nature of the subsequent rule if the parties are identical. This is subject to the qualification that the new treaty must not depart from the previous one to such an extent that it interferes seriously either with the interests of other parties to that treaty, or impair the original purpose of that treaty or any multilateral treaties that are both general and norm creating affecting 'all members of the International community or which are deemed to have been concluded in the international interest.[16] The 1982 UNCLOS provides for the situation under two separate parts of the Convention, namely article 237 in Part XII and article 311 in Part XVII. In article 311 UNCLOS establishes that between state parties it shall prevail over the 1958 Conventions[17] and that it permits 'subsequent compatible treaties'.[18] More relevant to our discussion is article 237, which is found in Part XII of the 1982 Convention entitled Protection and Preservation of the Marine Environment. This provision establishes that:

> the provisions of this Part are without prejudice to specific obligations assumed by States under special conventions and agreement . . . which may be concluded in furtherance of the general principles set forth in this Convention. Specific obligations assumed by States under special conventions with respect to the protection and preservation of the marine environment should be carried out in a manner consistent with the general principles and objectives of this Convention.

This same article is referring both to subsequent and specialized treaties. Article 237 refers to general principles and objectives in 'this Convention', whilst articles 87(1) and 116(a)[19] refer to the subjection of the freedom of fishing to the Convention's provisions, not only to Part VII. In sum, UNCLOS permits subsequent and specialized treaties to take more stringent measures than those which it provides, as long as there is no inconsistency with its general principles and objectives. The legal practice that a subsequent norm takes priority over an earlier one applies not only when norms emerge from the same types of legal sources, but also between different ones. Although rare, norms of international law that have crystallized into custom may supersede the provisions of a treaty. This is in fact what the ICJ established in *Icelandic Fisheries Jurisdiction*[20] cases, with respect to the extension of coastal state jurisdiction for the exploitation of living resources vis à vis the 1958 Geneva Convention on Fisheries Conservation and Management.[21] In this particular dispute, the ICJ observed that practice showed how states had departed from the rigid position adopted by the 1958 Convention and thus acknowledged the crystallization of a new rule that superseded a previous norm codified in the 1958 treaty. The general nature of the UNCLOS provisions facilitate harmonization techniques for the purpose of interpreting the qualifications to the freedom within the context of subsequent and more specialized rules. The thrust of these provisions seems to probe for a mutually supporting role between UNCLOS and later treaties as well as rules of custom that are applicable for the conservation of high seas living marine resources.

Conflict ascertainment and resolution on the interpretation of applicable rules is an integral part of legal reasoning. Every primary rule that lays down individual rights and obligations presupposes the existence of secondary rules that provide for the powers of legislative agencies to generate, modify and apply these rules. A rule may be seen as a specific application of a principle and understood as *lex specialis* or *lex posterior* to it and becomes applicable not *instead* but as a *manifestation* of it, since the general nature of the original rule does not have much of a substantive character. As reiterated a number of times in the various chapters, achieving harmonization when determining the relationship between earlier and subsequent or general and specialized legal instruments becomes a question of interpretation rather than of conflict resolution, indicating that the secondary rule applies as an interpretation of the primary one, given that it is an elaboration of the latter. In sum, the general or earlier set of norms serve as the *rationale* for a more specific and subsequent rule. Mutual accommodation is easier between a framework agreement and a specific implementation agreement as in the case of UNCLOS and the FSA. Rather than the *lex posteriori* superseding the *lex priori* the application of the implementation agreement would prevail as the *lex specialis* while the framework instrument remains in the background as *lex generalis*. Through articles 237 and 311, UNCLOS allows modifying agreements that remain compatible with it. The open-ended nature of these two articles under the 1982 Convention transfers the competence to decide what should happen in case of a conflict to who applies the law. While this may work well between treaties of the same regime such as UNCLOS and the FSA, it is more difficult to implement with treaties concluded in environmental fora such as the 1979 Bonn Convention on Migratory Species or the more recent CBD. The most acute manifestation of incompatibility in international state practice concerns relations between instruments forming part of trade and environmental regimes.[22] In the case of incompatibility between environmental and fisheries treaties more recent state practice shows a trend to update fisheries agreements in accordance with environmental principles and concepts although the conflict remains as to what extent such environmental principles have encroached upon the freedom of fishing on the high seas. This explains the ambiguous compatibility clause in the CBD which provides:

> The provisions of the Convention shall not affect the rights and obligations of any contracting Parties derived from any existing international agreement, except where the exercise of those rights and obligations would cause serious damage or threat to biological diversity and . . . contracting Parties shall implement this Convention with the rights and obligations of States under the law of the Sea.[23]

This provision is unclear on what it is trying to achieve. It can be read as an exhortation to read applicable treaties as compatible with one another and that there is an overall obligation to cooperate to reach this aim, as is for instance more clearly expressed in article 237 of UNCLOS referred to above. Some authors contend however that article 311(3) of UNCLOS and article 22(1) of the CBD seem intent to cancel each other out.[24] This probably explains why the CBD provides for the UNCLOS provisions to prevail, although one can also interpret article 22(2) of the CBD as limiting the supremacy of the UNCLOS provisions insofar as there is a conflict with it, within the context of applying article 22(1).

The relationship of UNCLOS with other treaties addressing high seas fisheries was raised in the *Southern Bluefin Tuna* case[25] where UNCLOS was referred to as an umbrella Convention to an implementing agreement in relation to the dispute settlement system. In this case the international adjudicating body established that conflicts between successive treaties depend on the intent of the parties and the object and purpose of treaties so that there is no automatic preference. If treaties form part of a regime, the tendency has been to seek coordination[26] but emphasis should be put on guaranteeing those rights set up in the applicable Conventions. This is, however, precisely the bone of contention between environmental treaties, fisheries treaties and the freedom of fishing codified under UNCLOS, since it is the exercise of freedom of fishing *as qualified* by the need to take conservation measures that is at stake.

The ILC quotes the relationship between fisheries agreements and UNCLOS as an example of this sort.[27] The ILC refers to the *Southern Bluefin Tuna* Case where Japan had argued that the 1993 Convention on the Conservation of Southern Blue Fin Tuna (CCSBT) was the applicable treaty instead of UNCLOS. The tribunal held[28] that the *lex specialis* and the *lex posterior* do not set aside the general treaty but rather the general (primary) rule rests in the background, controlling as well as guiding the interpretation and application of the later and special norm. The CCSBT, according to the tribunal, applied as both *lex specialis* and *lex posterior*.[29] The fact remains, however, that any rule that fine-tunes the high seas freedoms is also a limitation on the freedom itself, to the extent that it lays down specific conditions and institutional modalities that must be met.

More recent treaties continue to require a higher standard of conservation backed by scientific information that was unavailable when UNCLOS was being negotiated. Such conservation standards require more intensive collective measures than those which UNCLOS prescribes or requires.[30] There are two main issues relating to conflicts between earlier and subsequent sources of international law. First, whether there should be state responsibility if a right in an earlier treaty is overruled because of incompatibility with another more recent treaty and, secondly, whether any further evolution of the law of conservation for high seas living resources is stuck in time due to the supremacy of the general nature of UNCLOS. In the end the role of current state practice prevails and the qualifications to the freedom of fishing will continue to develop albeit probably not in a universal manner and particularly not with respect to those states that persistently object to new rules that set more stringent parameters. For the settlement of conflicts across regimes or inside regimes, recourse to general dispute settlement would be best but even the applicable UNCLOS provisions bestow priority upon conservation measures reached via cooperation, so any conservation measures adopted via treaties, whether regional or subregional for particular zones on the high seas, are likely to be considered as providing, *prima facie,* the contemporary body of rules establishing the standard of conservation required as a qualification to the freedom of fishing.

Fisheries law and environmental law that adopt a species-based approach may be classified as 'specialized regimes'.[31] Some of the UNCLOS provisions[32] address the balance of rights and duties between coastal states and high seas fishing states with respect to straddling stocks, highly migratory species listed in Appendix I to the Convention, marine mammals as well as anadromous and catadromous species. Most of these UNCLOS provisions invite states to cooperate[33] and to enter into negotiations[34] or work through regional fisheries organizations or set up such organizations with a view to taking the necessary measures for the conservation of particular species. None of the applicable international legal instruments that succeeded UNCLOS, which were concluded on the strength of these provisions, can be seen as derogating from the general law embodied in the applicable UNCLOS articles. As specialized norms, post UNCLOS developments implement and support the provisions of the 1982 Convention and do not constitute a deviation from it. The various chapters of this book have examined these developments to see how they modify and update the UNCLOS provisions, translating the general legal principles embodied therein into substantive rules. These post UNCLOS developments do not operate in a vacuum; UNCLOS establishes the basic rights and duties, whilst they express to some extent how such rights and duties are to be implemented. This is for instance the case with the FSA. Rules addressing particular species, whether they originate from fisheries or environmental fora, are intended to take account of the particularities of the subject matter that were either not considered or only marginally addressed by the general legal framework. They develop to respond to the international community's need to regulate their inter relationships and operations. They are devised to regulate effectively general law but this would inevitably lead to the qualification of behavioural patterns and limit the discretion in the hands of the individual States. Consequently, specialized rules may be objected to for that reason. The application of specialized rules is therefore binding only upon states that consented to them but the more support they have, the more likely it is for an international adjudicating body to shift the burden of proof upon the state opposing them to prove that they have not acquiesced to them. To sum up, the general tendency that the specialized rule prevails, in the case of derogation from general law, arises only where it is considered to have acquired at least the same legal status.[35] Its validity cannot be seen in isolation from the general law. It is the general law which provides the rules as to how the specialized regime should operate and in which context it would do so. The specialized regime follows from the general regime and the two norms are to be interpreted in a mutually supportive manner. The nature of a rule as a specialized norm can also derive from the fact that it is regional in scope. This is particularly relevant in the case of the conservation of high seas living resources, as the implementation of conservation measures may need to be more specialized with respect to some species and in some regions due to vulnerable and geophysical characteristics or because of the commitments the participants in that fishery wish to adopt. It is accepted in fact that some conservation measures do not require universal state practice to be considered as binding. The development of specialized rules and of new 'branches of the law' is an inevitable consequence of the complexities involved and the requirements highlighted by scientific and technological developments.

The lack of a hierarchical relationship amongst applicable international law rules does not facilitate harmonization. There is no general order of precedence between international rules. Only norms that are classified as *jus cogens*[36] are distinguished by their non derogability. This means that a norm conflicting with them is null and void. Although there is no official exhaustive list of such norms, it is unlikely that the obligation to take conservation measures to ensure sustainability of high seas fish stocks as a common resource can be classified as *jus cogens*.[37] At best the obligation to ensure their sustainability for present and future generations may qualify as an *erga omnes* obligation, which if breached, provides any state with the legal standing to make an international claim.[38] Whilst all norms of *jus cogens* can be termed as an *erga omnes* obligation the converse is not necessarily true. Sources of international law which conflict with *erga omnes* obligations are not necessarily null and void.[39] Having no hierarchy under international law, however, does not mean that there is no superiority of one legal source over another. It is determined on a case-by-case basis. UNCLOS itself accepts treaty obligations between parties as opposed to custom. Similarly a more specialized treaty like the FSA may bear more weight upon parties than a framework treaty. In the *Southern Bluefin Tuna* case, the arbitral tribunal assessed the relationship between the 1982 UNCLOS and a fisheries treaty concluded as an implementation agreement to it, namely the 1993 CCSBT. The tribunal held that there is frequently a parallelism of treaties and that the universal range of international legal obligations benefits from a process of accretion and accumulation.[40] This argument made by the adjudicating tribunal stresses the need to coordinate the interpretation of applicable legal instruments and envisage them as mutually supportive. This is more likely to happen between framework treaties and implementation treaties but, as discussed above, it should also guide the application of norms as they emerge from the relationship between previous and subsequent or general and more specialized law sources.[41] The application of the whole body of law was in fact addressed by the Appellate Body of the WTO in the *Shrimp–Turtle*[42] case that made extensive references to international environmental law texts and considered the application of principles of customary and general international law in the interpretation of WTO covered agreements. The Appellate Body took into account article 56 of UNCLOS that natural resources could be both living and non living and also referred to Agenda 21 as well as to the resolution on assistance to developing countries adopted in conjunction with the 1979 Bonn Convention on the Conservation of Migratory Species of Wild Animals. Nevertheless the recourse to other sources of law helped the WTO Appellate body in interpretation but not for overriding the agreements of the WTO itself.

Fragmentation threatens the coherent nature of international law but the proliferation of subsequent and specialized rules remain necessary. The law cannot resolve in an abstract way any possible conflict that may arise between economic and environmental regimes or a universal law regime and a regional fisheries treaty. Different concerns are addressed via a variety of instruments and institutions, which prioritize conservation measures in a manner that appeases the interests of the parties. In the end, however, it is the conservation of the high seas living resources which is the underlying objective, irrespective of for which purpose the resources need to be conserved. This in itself has been the driving force behind any attempt for harmonization as an indispensable process for an effective conservation regime. The best methodology lies in ensuring cooperation that leads to compatible measures between all participants in a fishery. As was the case with the *Behring Fur Seals* dispute in 1898, however, all the stakeholders normally join in the concerted effort when it is the very survival of the stocks rather than their good conservation status which is at stake.

The legal techniques referred to above[43] may serve to interpret away discrepancies as well as apparent or potential conflicts between applicable laws. Other legal techniques that can be used may be 'in-built'. One of the direct negative consequences of fragmentation of norms is non-compliance. The harmonization of norms would greatly benefit from an effective compliance and enforcement regime that is binding amongst stakeholders.

This would avoid having each flag state acting as the judge of its own performance on the high seas regarding the taking of conservation measures, their implementation and enforcement. The FSA does proposes a compliance and enforcement regime that may serve as a fall back when states, participants in a fishery, do not manage to conclude one. To ensure widespread adherence a compliance and enforcement regime should not discriminate against any state but would subject the right of access by all, to the obligation to ensure a minimum standard of conservation that, if not met with, would then lead to the forfeiture of the same right. Enforcement measures reached via cooperation may also be considered by states as establishing the minimum standards required. It would be difficult for a state to prove that its unilateral enforcement measures, which are less stringent, are just as adequate. This would encourage states to adhere to the treaty and also establish clear compliance and enforcement measures which state parties may adopt against stateless ships that would otherwise act as free riders avoiding the obligations imposed by international, subregional and regional regulations.[44] Enforcement on the high seas remains the prerogative of the flag state in the vast majority of treaties, but the introduction of monitoring and compliance measures encouraged by the coming into force of the FSA[45] may require flag states to report to the RFMO of which it is a member, informing the parties upon the enforcement steps it took to verify the alleged breach of conservation measures.[46]

The FSA, for instance, addresses enforcement in a comprehensive manner based primarily but not exclusively on the concept of responsible flag state jurisdiction. It also provides for compulsory dispute settlement. It does so by listing a number of factors that states parties to fisheries organizations must take into account in order to establish cooperative measures in this respect. Apart from imposing obligations that serve as in-built compliance measures to prevent the breach of subregional and regional conservation and to establish management measures for straddling and highly migratory fish stocks, the FSA provides for other compliance and enforcement measures[47] for which the flag state is responsible when violations occur. The FSA obligates flag states to 'ensure compliance' by imposing mandatory measures to this end. This entails the obligation to enforce such measures 'irrespective of where' violations occur. This phrase seems to imply that flag states should take enforcement measures even when infringements are committed within areas subject to national jurisdiction, but the jurisdictional scope of the FSA only applies to areas beyond national jurisdiction.[48] A system devised to make flag state jurisdiction subject to a set of standards reached via cooperation and specifying flag state obligations on compliance would lead to a significant improvement[49] for harmonization purposes. An example of current state practice is the setting up of a regional registry system such as the one adopted among the Pacific island states. The latter system may be particularly useful if the unilateral adoption of conservation measures is required to meet certain basic standards. This would lead to the proper implementation of article 117. In reality, few areas on the high seas fall outside the geographical scope of some fishery agreement or other RFMOs. These RFMOs have sought to formulate, for the fishing regions they govern, conservation and management measures, which focus on the sustainable use of such living resources. Although the implementation of these conservation and management measures varies amongst states parties to the RFMOs and other collaborating states and fishing entities, it is the enforcement of such measures which remains the weakest link in the conservation regime devised.[50]

Harmonization may also be more easily achieved via compulsory dispute settlement mechanisms found in various applicable treaties. A number of RFMOs have bestowed dispute settlement powers upon a centralized independent and regulatory authority to ensure appropriate surveillance and monitoring of the parties' fishing vessels and to provide adequate enforcement in case of breach. The role of the port state is equally valuable to ascertain a coherent compliance and enforcement regime among participants in the same high seas fishery. Port state enforcement is by far the most effective way of curbing IUU fishing, especially since the rights of coastal states, of states participants to the same fishery and the international community as a whole, can only be enforced by the flag state. Other states may only intervene in their capacity as port states. The more intensive the network of port states adopting the same enforcement measures is, the less likely it is for non-parties to continue to jeopardize the conservation regime, and the higher the prospect of their adhering to the conservation regime reached via cooperation. When taken within the context of a fisheries agreement, state parties can also harmonize port state regulations that would penalize vessels whose flag states refuse to carry out their enforcement duties in an effective manner. Manifest inadequacies in high seas enforcement due to a wide range of illegal activities mentioned above have prompted post-UNCLOS agreements to strengthen flag and port state enforcement powers, to further develop regional enforcement arrangements and the use of an agreed sea boarding and inspection scheme as set out in the FSA and other agreements.

Other legal techniques that may be used for harmonization of applicable norms are more procedural and institutional. Cooperation for example is an indispensable technique, which may be exercised across the board amongst different fora having the same objectives. Cooperation between the parties to different treaties and the institutions related thereto, serves to facilitate compatibility amongst the different international regimes and in this manner help to avoid abuse of rights. The negotiation of new treaties is an exercise which often aims at establishing a harmonized approach in the face of ambiguity and conflicting interpretation that cannot otherwise be resolved. This is precisely the role of the post-UNCLOS MEAs and of those RFMOs which seek to clarify UNCLOS general rules.[51] It is essential however to ensure that any treaties aiming to supplement earlier ones do not lead to new forms of fragmentation. As highlighted above, linkages between previous and subsequent norms must be formally established to avoid creating another problem instead of resolving an existing one.

Cooperation is also the best means to support other legal techniques mentioned above that aim for harmonization. For instance, when a treaty or an RFMO limits access to high seas living resources only to those states that adopt specific conservation measures, this may be interpreted as a measure which is in conflict with the freedom of fishing as codified by UNCLOS, since the 1982 Convention permits unilateral measures. Such a conflict may, however, be resolved if this approach is perceived as an updated interpretation of the need to take the 'necessary' conservation measures established under UNCLOS article 117. In fact, neither the FSA nor the RFMOs interpret the duty to cooperate as excluding the right to take unilateral measures. Instead, they consider that the duty to cooperate also includes any unilateral measures, which are not in conflict but actually compatible with conservation measures reached via cooperation. Such an interpretation is supported by UNCLOS itself which obligates states to take conservation measures that are backed by scientific evidence, which safeguard the rights and interests of other participants and which aim at the sustainability of the resource.[52] Furthermore, whilst permitting the taking of unilateral conservation measures, UNCLOS qualifies this right by imposing the condition that any conservation measures adopted, whether unilaterally or otherwise, must be taken as 'necessary'. If an adjudicating body had to resolve such a conflict between the applicable sources of international law, it is highly likely that it would shift the burden of proof onto the state taking unilateral measures and request it to provide evidence that its measures still ensure sustainable exploitation. The widespread adherence to the FSA shows that seeking compatibility via cooperation is a dominant trend in current state practice. An aspect of conservation likely to cause conflict between prior and successive laws, as well as between treaty law and customary international law, relates to allocation issues. UNCLOS refers only indirectly to allocation when establishing the non-discrimination principle in article 119(3) and the provisions in Part V dealing with straddling stocks and HMS. There is a general acquiescence to the obligation that conservation implies also limiting effort, but article 119 attempts to curb the abuse when this principle is used to prevent different allocation quotas to new entrants in the fishery. UNCLOS does not support limitation of catch and fishing effort, and every state is treated alike even if the 1982 Convention refers to the establishment of the TAC or other conservation measures on the high seas by maintaining the MSY. Again, UNCLOS implies that limitations on allocation resulting from conservation measures can only be reached via cooperation in an agreement where states should give greater weight to scientific information when adopting their decision. This necessitates a need for the development of catch and effort information and data. Only in this way can reference points to set limits on catch and effort be adequate for conservation purposes. This should, in fact, be an overriding obligation amongst high seas fishing states, and whoever does not comply should not be given access to these resources. This approach is adopted by the FSA, but obviously it applies only to its parties with respect to straddling stocks and HMS. However, extending such a standard to the entire ecosystem or to all associated and dependent species may render fishing on the high seas impossible.[53] At any rate, general state practice does not appear to conform to this extended interpretation at this current point in time.

This link with scientific evidence may be seen as being intrinsic to the duty to cooperate in the taking of conservation measures. Successive laws duly emphasize the need for cooperation, which is also referred to in many of the UNCLOS provisions in Part VII and in articles 63 to 67 of Part V. Cooperation is thus the preferred option for ensuring effective conservation as opposed to claims for the further extension of coastal state jurisdiction and the taking of unilateral measures. Contrary to the times when UNCLOS was negotiated, further extensions and unilateral acts by coastal states are now perceived as the price paid for failure to agree. More recently, trends in state practice usually aim for stricter regulation via an RFMO as a cooperation measure rather than as a unilateral measure by a single State.[54] Examples of successful measures of this nature have been achieved, with general state practice conforming to the regulation of anadromous and catadromous species under UNCLOS. States acquiesce to the prohibition to access these species outside the jurisdiction of the coastal state of origin[55] because their life cycle makes it is impossible to implement effectively the duty to conserve such species on the high seas. Although it is true that the nature of such species permits the coastal state to exercise effective control, it also shows that states abide more readily by strict conservation measures, even on the high seas, when these are based on proven scientific information.

The harmonization of applicable regimes, and therefore the success of conservation measures in the coming years, will depend upon investment in research and independent scientific advice and cooperation between states to ensure the implementation of conservation measures formulated thereupon. These are the two management concepts which are best suited to address the major challenges that remain, namely the allocation of benefits from harvesting high seas resources and burden sharing for not doing so if this is required for conservation purposes. The adoption of sound and effective conservation measures requires the participation of all stakeholders. It cannot be dominated by one side without considering competing values and the need to accommodate socio-economic and environmental concerns. Non-parties and the reflagging of vessels remain a major cause of concern since free riders can jeopardize a conservation regime that has been painstakingly adopted by the other participants in the fishery. States, parties to RFMOs and multilateral treaties are adopting measures that lean more towards international management for shared resources, albeit limited to specific regions on the high seas falling within the geographical scope of a fisheries agreement.[56] Recent trends in state practice have steered away from associating high seas living resources with the common heritage regime, but both multilateral treaties like the FSA and regional treaties or RFMOs like NAFO have qualified even further the right of access to high seas living resources rendering it subject to the adoption of specific conservation measures[57] reached via cooperation. Allocation rights vis-à-vis new entrants are definitely the thorniest problem to resolve; new entrants cannot be excluded but in their turn they must accept existing arrangements. The UNCLOS provision, which requires sharing on the pretext of non-discrimination, does not refer to equality but, as in the *Icelandic Fisheries Cases*, implies equitable allocation of high seas fish stocks when in paragraph 1(a) it refers to catches to be qualified *inter alia* by 'relevant environmental and economic factors, including the requirements of developing States . . .'.

Despite the 'added-value' which regional agreements may bring about when regulating the conservation of species, the sustainable use of high seas living resources requires a harmonized legal framework on a global level. The species themselves and the maritime zones they occupy are diverse but also interdependent. Their regulation is such a complex exercise that it may also be perceived as an impossible task, which cannot be effectively addressed by international law. This kind of reasoning generates anarchic behaviour on the high seas. It seems that there are conflicting views on how international law should be applied to regulate the conservation of high seas living resources, especially when it comes to choosing the right methodology to achieve its objectives. Applicable regimes appear to promote two diametrically opposed management concepts. Whilst regulation and enforcement can be most effective if they are specialized and tailor made for the particular species and zones involved, the need of an ecosystem approach requires horizontal regulation that cuts across species, maritime zones, legal systems and political interests. The discussion in the previous chapters demonstrates that whilst an appropriate conservation regime should be based on the ecosystem approach, the more horizontal and multidisciplinary management concepts are, the harder it becomes to apply them in practice to ensure adequate regulation, effective enforcement and viable institutional governance.[58] Additionally, there are the usual legal and political difficulties that are intrinsic to an international legal system based on state sovereignty. These realities cannot be underestimated, particularly when regulating a common resource in the absence of a centralized law-making and compliance system. These inherent characteristics should serve to help us appreciate better the achievements made by international law to date. Rather than dismissing international law as being a low performer, the discussion in this book demonstrates that it has made some remarkable achievements despite the various handicaps it is riddled with. To some extent, it has managed to direct the international community towards a regulatory framework that addresses the exploitation of a common resource and instilled acquiescence amongst states to qualify the freedom of fishing by taking conservation measures. More recently, international law has evolved to adopt a more holistic approach promoting the vested interest which humanity as a whole has over the marine habitat and its biodiversity.[59] The various chapters have identified instances when treaties and RFMOs have resorted to legal measures, which adopt sanctions as port states against vessels of flag states that fish on the high seas and do not adopt certain standards of conservation reached via cooperation. This emerging trend proposes a harmonized system of international and regional regulation of such resources.

State practice at times may still be far away from translating this approach into substantive legal norms that are endorsed by the majority of states. Nevertheless successful conservation regimes demonstrate that incentives may be provided to fishing fleets to ensure appropriate management, which can stop the decline and help to replenish stocks that are threatened by excessive exploitation. Examples include: the introduction of community-based fishing rights, allocation to entire cooperatives and individual fishing quotas. Ensuring responsible access[60] to high seas living resources is a *sine qua non* rule for their good governance and the best way to achieve this is via the organization of stakeholder states in adopting compatible conservation measures. Such an approach would do away with any incentives that promote maximization of exploitation and ensures instead the sustainability of stocks through stability and profitability.

In the past, participants in a fishery normally started taking conservation measures only when fish stocks were on the brink of collapse. Modern society has the capacity to change this trend. Contemporary technology permits the surpassing of communication barriers, due to geophysical constraints. Scientific information is definitely more accurate and more diffused; globalization facilitates the adoption of compatible conservation measures even through the adoption of trade sanctions by both developed and developing states. Although enforcement on the high seas remains the prerogative of the flag state, trade sanctions would encourage states to comply with standards agreed via concerted efforts. Their wide adoption would also discourage flag hopping. The political environment remains hostile when it comes to the regulation of common resources and their sustainable use. Indeed, international law does not operate in a vacuum but within a *sui generis* legal system, which is dependent on arbitrary political interests that tend towards crisis-management. Nevertheless today's international community has more tools at its disposal from a technical perspective. It has also a wealth of political experience and a myriad of applicable regimes to ensure the sustainable use of high seas fisheries. Seeking the harmonization of applicable international law, instead of dwelling on its shortcomings and failures, is a good step forward whereby the international community can effectively promote the sustainability of marine living resources and their habitat.

NOTES

1. UNCLOS Part XV.
2. See UNCLOS articles 117, 118 and 119(2) as well as the cross references to article 116(b).
3. Examples include SEAFO in force on 13 April 2003, the Central Behring Sea Donut Hole treaty in force since 8 December 1995 and WCPFC which came into force on 19 June 2004.
4. Examples include the FSA itself, CCSBT in force on 20 May 1994 and IOTC in force since 27 March 1996.
5. See UNCLOS article 119(1)(b).
6. Ibid, article 194(5).
7. This Part relates to the Protection and Preservation of the Marine Environment, but there is no cross reference to it under Part VII. It mainly regulates anthropogenic activities leading to pollution. There is no reference to fishing at all.
8. Some anti-whaling states like the US have taken more stringent obligations than the ICRW with respect to whales, and have imposed sanctions upon states who failed to do the same.
9. See UNCLOS article 119(2); see also Von Zharen, M.W. (1999),'An Ecopolicy Perspective for Sustainable Living Marine Species', ODIL, **30**, (1), 1–42.
10. UNCLOS and the UNFSA do not have an in-house scientific body. The FAO Fisheries Section does not actually have a scientific body but it has two divisions that contribute to the collection and application of scientific information relating to fisheries. The Fisheries and Aquaculture Resources Use and Conservation Division (FIR) is responsible for all programmes and activities related to the management of responsible fisheries

and aquaculture. It provides advice, assistance and information to FAO Members on the effective identification and appraisal of the living marine resources and the development and implementation of management approaches and strategies. Furthermore the Statistics and Information Service (FIPS) is responsible for the collection, compilation, validation, analysis and dissemination of data on all aspects of world fisheries and aquaculture. It assists FAO Members on the development of international standards for statistics. It also serves to collect, verify and circulate statistics at the global and regional level. See http://www.fao.org/fishery/about/organigram/en. The CBD has its own scientific body. The Subsidiary Body on Scientific, Technical and Technological Advice (SBSTTA) reports directly to the Conference of the Parties (COP) and its other subsidiary bodies, and provides it with advice on how to implement the Convention. SBSTTA is made up of government representatives who are experts in the field. Its functions include: providing assessments of the status of biological diversity and the types of measures taken in accordance with the provisions of the Convention. The SBSTTA is set up under article 25 of the CBD and carries out its work according to a consolidated *modus operandi* found in annex III of Decision VIII/10. The Code of Conduct for Responsible Fisheries refers to the need for linkages with scientific bodies in its article 12. There are also scientific bodies set up in house by various RFMOs namely NAFO, SEAFO, CCAMLR, ICCAT, GFCM, CCSBT and IOTC. Most of these bodies are made up by scientists from the contracting parties although in the case of the CCSBT the chair of the scientific committee and the advisory panel are independent. NEAFC has ICES as its scientific advisory body, which is independent from the constituent treaty. See Meltzer, E. (2009), *The Quest for Sustainable Fisheries*, Ottawa: NRC Research Press, pp 270–90.

11. See Report of the Study Group of the International Law Commission, '*Fragmentation of International Law: Difficulties Arising from Diversification and Expansion of International Law*', document A/CN.4/L.682, 13 April 2006, 58th Session of the ILC, Geneva, para 9 and footnote 14; see also Gillespie, A. (2002), 'Forum shopping in international environmental law: The IWC, CITES and the management of cetaceans,' ODIL, **33** (1), 17–56; Joyner, C. C. (1995), 'The Antarctic Treaty System and the Law of the Sea–Competing Regimes in the Southern Ocean?', IJMC, **10** (2), 301–331.
12. The 1982 UNCLOS maintains that high seas fishing should be conducted according to articles 87 and 116 to 120 in Part VII and subject to articles 63 to 67 in Part V.
13. See Birnie, P., Boyle, A. and Redgwell, C.,(2009), *International Law and the Environment*, 3rd edn, Oxford: Oxford University Press, pp 4 and 42; Orrego Vicuna, F. (1999), *The Changing International Law of High Seas Fisheries*, Cambridge: Cambridge University Press, pp 1–2. Meltzer, E., (2009), pp 11 and 67 where the author quotes Ed Miles; see below at note 14.
14. Miles, E. (1979) 'The Management of Marine Regions: The North Pacific', 6 ODIL, vii–xxx at vii.
15. This is based on the Roman law maxim '*lex posteriori derogate lege priori*' and has often been listed as a principle of interpretation or conflict-resolution in international law. It has sometimes been regarded as a "*general principle of law recognized by civilized nations*" under article 38(1)(c) of the ICJ Statute and a customary rule of international law.
16. See VCLT articles 30 and 41. See also Brownlie, I. (2003), *Principles of Public International Law*, Oxford: Oxford University Press, p 600.
17. See UNCLOS article 311(1).
18. See ibid, article 311(3) which provides, 'Two or more States parties may conclude agreements modifying or suspending the operation of provisions of this Convention, applicable solely between them, provided that such agreements do not relate to a provision derogation from which is incompatible with the effective execution of the object and purpose of this Convention and provided further that such agreements do not affect the enjoyment by other states Parties of their right of performance of their obligations under this Convention.'

19. UNCLOS article 116(a) actually refers to the obligations of treaties to which the states are parties so this would also include UNCLOS.
20. See Birnie P., Boyle A. and Rodgwell, C. (2009), Oxford: p 651; see also the *Icelandic Fisheries Cases*, ICJ Reports, (1974), (*UK v Iceland*), at 31, para 72; (*FRG v Iceland*) at 200, para 64.
21. The 1958 Geneva Convention recognized in its article 6 only the special interest of the coastal state in the conservation of high seas fisheries adjacent to its territorial sea. See also Nelson, in Boyle and Freestone (eds), (1999), *International law and Sustainable Development*. Oxford: Oxford University Press, pp 113–118.
22. See Wolfrum R. and Nele, M. (2003), *Conflicts in International Environmental Law*, Berlin: Springer, pp 6–13, which article deals extensively with conflicts between environmental and other treaties.
23. CBD article 22(1), (2).
24. See Fitzmaurice M. and Elias O. (2005), *Contemporary Issues in the Law of Treaties*, Utrecht: Eleven International Publishing, p 341.
25. *Southern Bluefin Tuna (Jurisdiction and Admissibility) case, (Australia and New Zealand v Japan)*, Award of 4 August 2000, UNRIAA vol XXII (2004).
26. See above at note 16; the rights set up in the applicable conventions should be guaranteed and if a right is overruled because of incompatibility with another treaty then there should be state responsibility.
27. See ILC report, supra at note 11, p 21, para 29.
28. Ibid.
29. Ibid, p 23, para 38(c).
30. See UNCLOS articles 117 and 118 but also articles 63(2)–67.
31. See above at note 16.
32. Ibid, articles 63 to 67 in Part V are in themselves more specialized because they address the conservation of particular species.
33. Ibid, articles 64, 65, 116, and 118.
34. Ibid, articles 63, 64, 118.
35. International Law Commission, *Draft Articles on State Responsibility*, Commentary on Article 55, para 2 in Official Records of the General Assembly, 56th session, supplement No 10 (A/56/10) p 357.
36. Norms of *jus cogens* are also referred to as peremptory norms.
37. See *Gabčikovo–Nagymaros Dam Case*, ICJ Reports, (1997), 7, para 97, where the Court accepted Slovakia's argument that none of the norms that Hungary claimed to be *jus cogens* were in fact recognized as such but that sustainable development as an objective had acquired the status of customary environmental law; see ibid para 7.
38. See Chapter 2, p 38 et seq.
39. See commentary on *Draft Articles on Responsibility of States for Internationally Wrongful Acts*. ILC Yearbook 2001, vol. II, Part Two, pp 281–2. See also Byers, M. (1997), 'Conceptualizing the Relationship between *Jus Cogens* and *Erga Omnes* Rules', *Nordic Journal of International Law*, vol. 66 p 211.
40. *Southern Bluefin Tuna* case, ILM vol. 39 (2000) p 1388, para 52.
41. In the *Southern Bluefin Tuna* case the adjudicating body concluded that the relationship between UNCLOS and the CCSBT was such that interpreting the provisions independent of each other would not have been in line with the objective of the parties to both treaties. The tribunal observed that there were overlapping provisions to dispute settlement and the tribunal rightly acknowledged that the problem arose under both treaties.
42. WTO Case WT/DS 58 Complaint by India, Malaysia, Pakistan and Thailand against the US and WT/DS 61 Compliant by the Philippines against the US. Both complaints related to the prohibition by the US of imports from these States of shrimps and shrimp products.
43. See VCLT article 30. Other methods include: adopting procedural legal principles such as the hierarchy of laws or the application of the maxim that *lex specialis* supersedes the *lex generalis*.

44. Ships which do not sail under the flag of any state do not have right to the exclusivity of the flag state or to freedom of fishing, and any state on the high seas may take enforcement measures against them.
45. See FSA article 10.
46. See Stephens, T., (2004), 'The Limits of International Adjudication in International Law: Another Perspective on the Southern Bluefin Tuna Case,' IJMC, **19** (2) 177–97.
47. FSA Article 19(1).
48. See ibid, article 3 which explicitly specifies this with the exemption of articles 6 and 7. Therefore article 18(4) would apply to violations that occurred on the high seas even in areas outside the jurisdictional scope of the subregional or regional agreement.
49. See Burke, W.T. (1994), *The New International Law of Fisheries, UNCLOS 1982 and Beyond*, Clarendon Press, Oxford, p 345; see also Schurman, R.A. (1997), 'The Future of Regional Fisheries Cooperation in a Changing Economic Environment: The South Pacific Island Countries in the 1990s', ODIL, **28** (4), 369–404.
50. Riddle, K. (2006), 'Illegal Unreported and Unregulated Fishing: Is International Cooperation Contagious?', ODIL, **37** (3–4), 266.
51. As discussed in the previous chapters, the 1982 Convention's legal framework has left open to interpretation the duty to take conservation measures, the duty to cooperate with other participants in the fishery, and the implications of the qualifications to the freedom of fishing, particularly vis-à-vis the rights, duties and interests of coastal states.
52. See UNCLOS article 119. Moore, G., (1993), 'Enforcement without Force: New Techniques in Compliance Control for Foreign Fishing Operations based on Regional Cooperation', ODIL, **24**, (2), 197–204. See also Sydnes, A.K. (2001), 'Regional Fishery Organizations: How and why Organizational Diversity Matters', ODIL, **32** (4), 349–72.
53. See Burke, W.T. (1994).
54. See, for instance, ICCAT measures to regulate quotas on Tuna and NAFO in regulating fishing in the NAFO Regulatory Area as opposed to extension of coastal state jurisdiction pushed vigorously by Canada over straddling stocks on the Atlantic coast and Chile with its concept of '*mar presencial*'.
55. See UNCLOS articles 66 and 67; see also De Reynier, Y.L. (1998), 'Evolving Principles of International Fisheries Law and the North Pacific Anadromous Fish Commission', ODIL, **29** (2), 147–78.
56. A clear example is the NAFO Regulatory Area which, although part of the high seas, is subject to certain conservation measures which, whether the flag state is a NAFO party or not, if fishing vessels do not abide by are deemed to be IUU. See also Vidas, D. (2000), 'Emerging Law of the Sea Issues in the Antarctic Maritime Area: A Heritage for the New Century?', ODIL, **31** (1–2), 197–222.
57. This would even include allocation rights; see Molenaar, E.J., (2003), 'Participation, Allocation and Unregulated Fishing; The Practice of Regional Fisheries Management Organizations', IJMC, **18** (4), 457–480.
58. See difficulties with CCAMLR as described by Burke supra at 53.
59. See Orrego Vicuna (1999), pp 29–31.
60. Also referred to as '*dedicated access*'; see Hilborn, R., (2007), 'Moving to Sustainability by learning from Successful Fisheries', Ambio, **36** (4), Royal Swedish Academy of Sciences, p 297.

Bibliography

BOOKS

Attard, D.J. (1987), *The Exclusive Economic Zone in International Law*, Oxford: Clarendon Press

Birnie, P. (1985), *International Regulation of Whaling*, New York: Oceana Publications

Birnie, P., Boyle, A. and Redgwell, C. (2009), *International Law and the Environment*, 3rd edn, Oxford: Oxford University Press

Boyle, A. and Freestone D. (1999), *International Law and Sustainable Development: Past Achievements and Future Challenges*, Oxford: Oxford University Press

Brownlie, I. (2003), *Principles of Public International Law',* 6th edn, Oxford: Oxford University Press

Burke W.T. (1994), *The New International Law of Fisheries, the 1982 UNCLOS and Beyond*, Oxford: Clarendon Press

Burke, W.T. and McDougal, M.S. (1962), (1987) *The Public Order of the Oceans* New Haven, Connecticut: New Haven Press

Churchill, R.R. and Freestone, D. (eds) (1991), *International Law and Global Climate Change*, London: Graham & Trotman

Churchill, R.R. and Lowe, A.V. (1999), *The Law of the Sea*, 3rd edn, Manchester: Manchester University Press

De Ferion, O. (1958), *Le Droit de la Mer*, Paris: Droz

Dupuys, R.J. and Vignes, D. (1991), *A Handbook on the New Law of the Sea*, Volume I, The Hague: Hague Academy of International Law, Martinus Nijhoff Publishers

Fitzmaurice M. and Elias O. (2005), *Contemporary Issues in the Law of Treaties*, Utrecht: Eleven International Publishing

Gidel, G. (1932), *Le Droit International de la Mer en Temps de Paix*, Paris

Grotius (1609), *Mare Liberum*, J. Brown Scott (ed) (1916), Oxford: Oxford University Press

Harris, D.J. (2004), *Cases and Materials on International Law*, 6th edn, London: Sweet and Maxwell

Hey, E., *The Regime for the Exploitation of Transboundary Marine Fisheries Resources*, Dordrecht: Martinus Nijhoff

Johnson, D.M. (ed.) (1981), *The Environmental Law of the Sea*, Berlin: IUCN Environmental Policy Paper No. 18

Koers, A.W. (1973), *The International Regime of Marine Fisheries*, London: West Byfleet Fishing News

Meltzer, E. (2009), *The Quest for Sustainable Fisheries*, Ottawa: NRC Research Press

Meyers, H. (1967), *The Nationality of Ships*, The Hague: Martinus Nijhoff

O'Connell, D.P. (1984), *International Law of the Sea*, Vol. I, Oxford: Clarendon Press, chapter 14

Orrego Vicuna, F. (2003), *Le Droit de la Pêche en Haute Mer: Développement et Conservation des Resources, La Mer et Son Droit, Mélanges Offerts á Laurent Lucchini et Jean Pierre Quéneudec*, Paris: Pedone

Orrego Vicuna, F. (1999), *The Changing International Law of High Seas Fisheries*, Cambridge: Cambridge University Press

Oxman, B. (1997), 'The International Commons, the International Public Interest and New Modes of International Law Making', in J. Delbrück (ed.) *New Trends in International Lawmaking: International 'Legislation' in the Public Interest*, Berlin: Ducker & Humblot

Pauwelyn, J. (2003), *Conflict of Norms in Public International: How WTO relates to other Rules of International Law*, Cambridge Studies in International and Comparative Law, Cambridge: Cambridge University Press

Rayfuse, R.G. (2004), *Non-Flag State Enforcement in High Seas Fisheries*, Leiden, Boston: Martinus Nijhoff

Schacter, O. (1998), 'Entangled Treaty and Custom' in Y. Dinstein and M. Tabory (eds) *International Law in a Time of Perplexity – Essays in Honour of Shabtai Rosenne*, Dordrecht: Martinus Nijhoff)

Shaw, M.N. (2003), *International Law*, 5th edn, Cambridge: Cambridge University Press

Shelton, D. (ed.) (2000), *Commitment and Compliance: The Role of Non Binding Norms in the International Legal System*, Oxford: Oxford University Press

Shigeru Oda (1989) *International Control of Sea Resources*, Dordrecht: Martinus Nijhoff

Van Heijnsbergen, P. (1997), *International Protection of Wild Flora and Fauna*, Amsterdam: Asd. IOS Press, Thesis Universiteit van Amsterdam

Winjstekers, W. (2001), *The Evolution of CITES: Reference to the Convention on International Trade in Endangered Species of Wild Fauna and Flora*, 6th edn, Geneva: CITES Secretariat

Wolfrum, R. and Nele M. (2003), *Conflicts in International Environmental Law*, Berlin, London: Springer

Zoi Varfis, C. (1994), 'La Conservation et l'Exploitation des resources biologiques marins' in Dommen, C. and Cullet, P. (eds), *General Convention des nations Uniés sur le Droit de la Mer et la Conservation et l'Exploitation des Resources Biologiques Marines*, The Hague: Kluwer Law International

ARTICLES

Ball, W.S. (1999), 'The Old Grey Mare, National Enclosure of the Oceans', ODIL, **27** (1–2), 97–124

Balton, D.A. (1996), 'Strengthening the CLOS: The New Agreement on Straddling Fish Stocks and Highly Migratory Fish Stocks', ODIL, **27** (1–2), 125–52

Birnie, P. (1997), 'Are Twentieth–Century Marine Conservation Conventions Adaptable to Twenty First Century Goals and Principles?' Part II, IJMC, **12** (4), 488–532

Burke, W.T. (1997), 'Legal Aspects of the IWC Decision on the Southern Ocean Sanctuary', ODIL, **28** (3), 313–327

Burke, W.T. (1996), 'Introduction: Importance of the 1982 UN Convention on the Law of the Sea and Its Future Development', ODIL, **27** (1–2)

Burke, W.T. (1984), 'Highly Migratory Species and the New Law of the Sea', ODIL, **14**, 273, 283–293

Burke W.T., Freeberg, M. and Miles, E.L. (1994), 'United Nations Resolution on Driftnet Fishing: An Unsustainable Precedent for High Seas and Coastal Fisheries Management', ODIL **25** (2), 127–86

Byers, M. (1997), 'Conceptualising the Relationship between *Jus Cogens* and *Erga Omnes* Rules', *Nordic Journal of International Law*, **66**, 211

Caddy, J.F., and Mahon, R. (1995), 'Reference points for Fisheries Management', FAO Fisheries Technical Paper No. 347, Rome: FAO

Canfield, J. (1993), 'Recent Developments in Bering Sea Fisheries Conservation and Management', ODIL, **24** (3), 257–89

Churchill, R. (2007), 'The Jurisprudence of the International Tribunal for the Law of the Sea Relating to Fisheries: Is There Much in the Net?', IJMC, **22** (3), 383–425

Cicin-Sain, B. and Knecht, R.W. (1993), 'Implications of the Earth Summit for Ocean and Coastal Governance', ODIL, **24** (4), 323–54

Craig, A. (2001), 'Protecting the Oceanic Gardens of Eden: International Law Issues in Deep-Sea Vent Resource Conservation and Management', 13 Geo Int'l Envtl L Rev 563, 584

D'Amato, A. and Chopra, S. (1991), 'Whales: Their Emerging Right to Life', 85 Am. J. Int. L., 21–62

De Klemm C. (1989), 'Migratory Species in International Law', *Natural Resources Journal*, **29** (73), 935, 963, 964

De Reynier, Y.L. (1998), 'Evolving Principles of International Fisheries Law and the North Pacific Anadromous Fish Commission', ODIL, **29** (2), 147–78

Eichenberg, T. and Shapson, M. (2004) 'The promise of Johannesburg Fisheries and the WSSD', 34 Golden Gate UL Rev 587

Ellis, J. (2001), 'The Straddling Stocks Agreement and the Precautionary Principle an Interpretative Device and Rule of Law', ODIL, **32** (4), 289–312

Freestone, D. (1995), 'The 1995 Agreement between Canada and the EU over Fishery Control and Enforcement in the NAFO Regulatory Area', *European Environmental Law Review*, **4** (10), 270–72

Garcia, S. and Staples, D. (2000), 'Sustainability Reference Systems and Indicators for Responsible Marine Capture Fisheries: A Review of Concepts and Elements for a Set of Guidelines', *Marine and Freshwater Research*, 51, 385–426

Gillespie, A. (2003), 'The Search for a New Compliance Mechanism within the International Whaling Commission,' ODIL, **34** (3–4), 349–68

Gillespie, A. (2002), 'Forum Shopping in International Environmental Law: The IWC, CITES and the Management of Cetaceans', ODIL, **33** (1), 17–56

Goldie, L.F.E. (1969), 'Sedentary Species and Art 2(4) of the 1958 Convention on the Continental Shelf A Plea for a Separate Regime', 86 Am.J.Int.L.

Grzybowski, D. M. (et al) (1995), 'A Historical Perspective Leading Up to and Including the UN Conference on Straddling Fish Stocks and Highly Migratory Fish Stocks', *Pace Environmental Law Review*, **13** (1)

Hewison, G.J. (1996), 'The Precautionary Approach to Fisheries Management: An Environmental Perspective', IJMC, **11** (3), 301–32

Hilborn, R. (2007), 'Moving to Sustainability by Learning from Successful Fisheries', Ambio, **36** (4), Royal Swedish Academy of Sciences, 296–303

Honneland, G. (1998), 'Compliance in the Fishery Protection Zone Around Svalbard', ODIL, **29** (4), 339–60

Honneland, G. (2000), 'Enforcement Cooperation between Norway and Russia in the Barents Sea Fisheries', ODIL, **31** (3), 249–68

Jennings, R. (1981), 'What is International Law and How Do We Tell It When We See It?', 37 ASOI 59

Joyner, C. C. (1995), 'The Antarctic Treaty System and the Law of the Sea-Competing Regimes in the Southern Ocean', IJMC, **10** (2), 301–31

Joyner, C.C. and Taylor, Z. (2000), 'Marine Conservation versus

International Free Trade: Reconciling Dolphins with Tuna and Sea Turtles with Shrimp', ODIL, **31** (1–2), 127–50

Juda, L. (1999), 'Considerations in Developing a Functional Approach to the Governance of Large Marine Eco Systems', ODIL, **30** (2), 89–126

Juda, L. (2007), 'The European Union and Ocean Use Management; the Marine Strategy and the Marine Policy', ODIL, **38** (3), 259–82

Koers (1973), 'The International Regime of Marine Fisheries', London: West Byfleet Fishing News

Kwiatkowska, B. (1993), 'The High Seas Fisheries Regime: at a Point of No Return?', IJMC, **8** (3), 327–58

Kwiatkowska, B. (1999), 'Inauguration of the ITLOS Jurisprudence: The Saint Vincent and the Grenadines v Guinea M/V Saiga Cases', ODIL, **30** (1), 43–78

Long and Grehan (2002), 'Marine Habitats', 17 *International Journal of Marine and Coastal Law* 237–8

McDorman T.L. (1998), 'Canada and Whaling an Analysis of Article 65 of the Law of the Sea Convention', ODIL, **29** (2), 179–94

Miles, E. (1979), 'The Management of Marine Regions: The North Pacific', 6 ODIL, vii–xxx

Meltzer, E. (2005), 'Global Overview of Straddling and Highly Migratory Fish Stocks: Maps and Charts Detailing RFMO Coverage and Implementation', IJMC, **20** (3–4), 571–604

Meltzer, E. (1994), 'Global Overview of Straddling and HMS : The Non Sustainable Nature of High Seas Fisheries', ODIL, **25** (3), 255–344

Miles, E.L. and Burke, W.T. (1989), 'Pressures on the United Nations Convention on the Law of the Sea of 1982 Arising from New Fisheries Conflicts: The Problem of Straddling Stocks', 20 ODIL 343, 344–57

Molenaar, E.J. (2007), 'Managing Biodiversity Beyond National Jurisdiction', IJMC, **22** (1), 89–124

Molenaar, E.J. (2003), 'Participation, Allocation and Unregulated Fishing: the Practice of Regional Fisheries Management Organizations', IJMC, **18** (4), 457–80

Molenaar, E.J. (2000), 'Satellite-Based VMS for Fisheries Management: International Legal Aspects', IJMC, **15** (1), 65–109

Moore, G. (1993), 'Enforcement without Force: New Techniques in Compliance Control for Foreign Fishing Operations based on Regional Cooperation', ODIL, **24** (2), 197–204

Morgera, E. (2004), 'Whale Sanctuaries: An Evolving Concept within the International Whaling Commission', ODIL, **35** (4), 319–38

Mossop, J. (2007), 'Protecting Marine Biodiversity on the Continental Shelf Beyond 200 Nautical Miles', ODIL, **38** (3)

Orrego Vicuna, F. (1993), 'Towards an Effective Management of High

Seas Fisheries and the Settlement of Pending Issues of the Law of the Sea', ODIL, **24** (1), 81–92

Oude Elferink, A. (1999), 'The Genuine Link Concept: Time for a Post Mortem?', Netherlands Institute for the Law of the Sea, Utrecht: Utrecht University

Oxman, B. (1995), 'Coastal States' Competences over High Seas Fisheries and the Changing Role of International Law Comment,' *Zeitxhrift Fur Auslandisches Offentliches Recht Und Volkerrecht* 55, 536

Riddle, K. (2003), 'Illegal, Unreported and Unregulated Fishing: Is International Cooperation Contagious?,' ODIL, **37** (3–4), 265–98

Roach, J.A. (1995), 'Dispute Settlement in Specific Situations', 7 Geo International and Environmental Law Review, 775–84

Romano, C. (2001), 'The Southern Bluefin Tuna Dispute: Hints of a World to Come, Like It or Not', ODIL, **32** (4), 313–48

Rubin A.R. (2007), 'Rock the Boat: The Plight of the Southern Blue Fin Tuna', Michigan State University College of Law, http://www.animal-law.info/articles/ddusbluefintuna.htm.

Schurman, R.A. (1997), 'The Future of Regional Fisheries Cooperation in a Changing Economic Environment: The South Pacific Island Countries in the 1990's', ODIL, **28** (4), 369–404

Shearer, I.A. (1986) 'Problems of Jurisdiction and Law Enforcement Against Delinquent Vessels', 35 *International and Comparative Law Quarterly*, 320–43

Sohn (1985), 'The Law of the Sea: Customary International Law Developments', 34 Am. UL Rev., 271, 278–9

Stephens, T. (2004), 'The Limits of International Adjudication in International Law: Another Perspective on the Southern Bluefin Tuna Case', IJMC, **19** (2), 177–97

Sydnes, A.K. (2001), 'Regional Fishery Organizations: How and Why Organizational Diversity Matters', ODIL, **32** (4), 349–72

Sullivan, M.S. (1997), 'The Case in International Law for Canada's Extension of Fisheries Jurisdiction Beyond 200 miles', ODIL, **28** (3), 203–68

Tanaka, Y. (2008), 'Reflections on the Conservation and Sustainable Use of Genetic Resources in the Deep Seabed Beyond the Limits of National Jurisdiction', ODIL, **39** (2) 129–49

Vidas, D. (2000), 'Emerging Law of the Sea Issues in the Antarctic Maritime Area: A Heritage for the New Century?', ODIL, **31** (1–2), 197–222

Vierdag, E.W. (1988), 'The Time of the "Conclusion" of a Multilateral Treaty: Article 30 of the Vienna Convention on the Law of Treaties and Related Provisions', 59 BYBIL 100

Von Zharen M.W. (1999), 'An Ecopolicy Perspective for Sustainable Living Marine Species', ODIL, **30** (1), 1–42

SELECTED MISCELLANEOUS DOCUMENTS AND FURTHER READING

Agenda 21, Chapter 17 adopted at the United Nations Conference on Environment and Development, Rio de Janeiro, 1992

Arico, S. and Sapin. C., 'Bioprospecting of Genetic Resources in the Deep Seabed Scientific, Legal and Policy Aspects', UNU-IAS Report (2005)

Baird, R. (2008), 'Australia's Response to Illegal Foreign Fishing: A Case of Winning the Battle but Losing the Law?', IJMC, **23** (1), 95–124

Balton, D.A. (2005), 'Managing Living Resources Multilaterally: Some Threshold Questions,' Deep Sea 2003: Conference on the Governance and Management of Deep Sea Fisheries, 1–5 December 2003, Queenstown, New Zealand, Part I Conference Reports, (ed) Ross Shotton (ed), Rome: FAO

Bialek, D. (2003), 'Sink or Swim: Measures Under International Law for the Conservation of the Patagonian Toothfish in the Southern Ocean', ODIL, **34** (2), 105–38

Burhenne, W.E., (ed) (1995), *International Environmental Law – Multilateral Treaties*, International Council of Environmental Law, Supplement 45, The Hague: Kluwer International

Burke, W.T. (1989), 'Fishing in the Behring Sea Donut: Straddling Stocks and the New International Law of the Sea', 16 Ecology LO, 285

Burke, W.T. (1996), 'Memorandum of Opinion on the Legality of the Designation of the Southern Ocean Sanctuary by the IWC', ODIL, **27** (3), 315–26

Campbell, H., Herrick, S.F. and Squires, D. (2000), 'The Role of Research in Fisheries Management: Conservation of Dolphins in the Eastern Tropical Pacific and the Exploitation of Southern Bluefin Tuna in the Southern Ocean', ODIL, **31** (4), 347–76

Cancun Declaration on Responsible Fishing, Cancun Conference on Responsible Fishing, Cancun, (1992).

Churchill, R.R. (1987), *EEC Fisheries Law*, Dordrecht: Martinus Nijhoff

Coastal Fisheries Protection Act, Canada (CR.S, 1985, c. C-33) (1985 as subsequently amended)

CBD Secretariat (November 2005), '*The International Legal Regime of the High Seas and the Seabed beyond the Limits of National Jurisdiction and Options for Cooperation for the Establishment of Marine Protected*

Areas in Marine Areas Beyond National Jurisdiction', CBD Technical Series, No. 19

CBD COP 2 Decision II/10 Study of the Relationship between the Convention on Biological Diversity and the United Nations Convention on the Law of the sea with regard to the Conservation and Sustainable Use of Genetic Resources on the Deep Seabed

CBD COP 2 Decision II/10 The Jakarta Mandate on the Conservation and Sustainable Use of Marine and Coastal Biodiversity (Basic Principles and Thematic Areas) (1995)

CBD COP 4 Decision IV/5 Jakarta Mandate Plan of Implementation Through a Multi-Year Programme of Work as amended by CBD SBSTTA Recommendation III/2. (1998)

CBD COP 6 Decision VI/3 Implementation of the Work of the SBSTTA Recommendation VI/2. (2002)

CBD COP 7 Decision VII/5 addressing Obstacles for the Implementation of Work relating to Marine Areas Beyond National Jurisdiction. (2004)

CBD COP 8 Decision VIII/21 Conservation and Sustainable Use of High Seas Biological Diversity Specifically Deep Sea Bed Genetic Resources Beyond National Jurisdiction. (2006)

CBD COP 8 Decision VIII/22 Integrated Marine and Coastal Area Management (2006)

CBD COP 8 Decision VIII/24 Marine Protected Areas Beyond National Jurisdiction (2006)

CBD SBSTTA 3, Recommendation III/2; amended Programme of Work stipulated by Jakarta Mandate, adopted at COP 4 by Decision IV/5 (1997)

CBD SBSTTA 8, Recommendation VIII/3 Extension of Time for the Programme of Implementation (March 2003).

De Hoogh, A. (1996), *Obligations Erga Omnes and International Crimes*, The Hague: Kluwer Law International

Djalal, H. (2006), 'The Emergence of the Concept of Fishing Entities: A Note', ODIL, **37** (2), 117–21

Dutton, P.H. and Squires, D. (2008), 'Reconciling Biodiversity with Fishing: A Holistic Strategy for Pacific Sea Turtle Recovery', ODIL, **39** (2), 200–222

European Union, Council Regulation (EEC) No 3094/86 of 7 October 1986 as a vessel with the nationality of a Member State on the ground that it has a genuine link with that Member State

European Union Maritime Strategy, *Towards a Future Maritime Policy for the Union: A European Vision for the Oceans and Seas*, (COM (2006) 275 Final Vol. II Annex SEC (2006) 689). Green Paper adopted by EU Commission on 7 June, 2006

FAO Code of Conduct for Responsible Fisheries, 1995
FAO IPOA for the Management of Fishing Capacity, 1999
FAO IPOA for Reducing Incidental Catch of Seabirds in Longline Fisheries, 1999
FAO IPOA for the Conservation and Management of Sharks, 1999.
FAO IPOA to Prevent, Deter and Eliminate Illegal, Unreported and Unregulated Fishing, 2001
FAO RFB/II/2001/7, '*Ecosystem-Based Management of Fisheries: Opportunities and Challenges For Co-Ordination between Marine Regional Fishery Bodies and Regional Seas Convention*', Rome, February, 2001
FAO Conference Resolution 15/93, which adopted the FAO Compliance Agreement, 1993
FAO Fisheries Department: Paper on the 'World Fisheries Situation', 1992
FAO Driftnet fisheries and their Impacts on non-target species: A World Wide Review, FAO Fisheries Technical Paper – T320, 1991
FAO Report of the Workshop on Data and Knowledge in Deep-Sea Fisheries in the High Seas, Rome, 5–7 November 2007, FAO Fisheries Report – R860, 2008
FAO The state of world highly migratory, straddling and other high seas fishery resources and associated species, FAO Fisheries Technical Paper – T495, 2006.
FAO Report of the Expert Consultation on International Guidelines for the Management of Deepsea Fisheries in the High Seas, Bangkok, 11–14 September 2007, FAO Fisheries Report – R855, 2008
FAO Summary information on the Role of International Fishery and other bodies with regard to the Conservation and Management of Living Resources of the High Seas, FAO Fisheries Circular – C908, 1996
FAO World review of Highly Migratory Species and Straddling Stocks FAO Fisheries Technical Paper – T337, 1994
FAO Managing Fishing Capacity: Selected Papers on Underlying Concepts and Issues, Fisheries Technical Paper – T386, 1999
FAO A Review of Measures Taken by Regional Marine Fishery Bodies to Address Contemporary Fishery Issues FAO Fisheries Circular – C940, 1999
FAO Report of the Workshop on Vulnerable Ecosystems and Destructive Fishing in Deep-sea Fisheries (Rome, 26-29 June 2007), FAO Fisheries Report – R829, 2008
FAO Implementation of the International Plan of Action to deter, prevent and eliminate, illegal, unreported and unregulated fishing. FAO Technical Guidelines for Responsible Fisheries – No. 9, 2002
FAO Living marine resources and their sustainable development – Some

environmental and institutional perspectives, FAO Fisheries Technical Paper – T353, 1995
FAO Some problems of the management of shared stocks, FAO Fisheries Technical Paper – T206, 1980
FAO Technical Assistance in Fisheries Monitoring Control and Surveillance: a Historical Perspective of FAO's Role, FAO Fisheries Circular – C882, 1994
FAO The conservation and management of shared fish stocks: legal and economic aspects, FAO Fisheries Technical Paper – T465, 2004
FAO Report of the Consultation on the Management of Fishing Capacity, Shark Fisheries and Incidental Catch of Seabirds in Longline Fisheries, Rome, Italy, 26–30 October 1998, FAO Fisheries Report – R593, 1999.
Farrier, D. and Tucker, L. (2000), 'Access to Marine Bioresources: Hitching the Conservation Cart to the Bioprospecting Horse', ODIL, **32** (3), 213–40
Friedheim, R. (2000), 'Designing the Ocean Policy Future: An Essay on How Am I Going to Do That?', ODIL, **31** (1–2), 183–96
Grafton, R.Q. (2005), 'Comment on What Restoration Schemes Can Do Or Getting It Right Without Fisheries Transferable Quotas', ODIL, **36** (4), 375–80
Hedley, C. (2001), 'The 1998 Agreement on the International Dolphin Conservation Program: Recent Developments in the Tuna Dolphin Controversy in the Eastern Pacific Ocean', ODIL, **32** (1), 71–92
Hey, E. (ed.) (1999), 'Developments in International Fisheries Law', The Hague: Kluwer Law International
Hu Nien-Tsu A., (Guest Editor) (2006), 'Introduction to the Special Issue on the Concept of Fishing Entities in International Law: A Decade of Practice', ODIL, **37** (2), 113–15
ICCAT Recommendation 92-01 on the ICCAT Bluefin Tuna Statistical Document Program, (1992).
IDDRI (Institut du Développement Durable et des Relations Internationales) No 04/2008 Conference Proceedings, *Governance of Marine Biodiversity beyond National Jurisdictions: Issues and Perspectives*, Rochette, J. and Billé, R. (eds), looseleaf publication (2008)
IMO Rules for Port State Controls, The Paris Memorandum of Port State Control, http://www.parismou.org/ParisMOU/Code+of+Good+Practice/xp/menu.4279/default.aspx (1982)
International Law Commission, 'Draft Articles on State Responsibility', Commentary supplement No 10 (A/56/10), ILC 53rd Session, (2001).
International Law Commission (2001), '*Draft Articles on Responsibility of States for Internationally Wrongful Acts*' ILC Yearbook Vol. II Part Two pp 281–282

International Law Commission (2006), Report of the Diversification and Expansion of International Law Study Group, 'Fragmentation of International Law: Difficulties Arising from Diversification and Expansion of International Law,' document A/CN.4/L.682, 13 April

IUCN Report on the High Seas Marine Protected Areas Workshop, organized by IUCN, WCPA and WWF, Spain, (2003)

IUCN Resolution No 8, 12th General Assembly of the IUCN, (1976)

IUCN Strategy entitled, '*Caring for the Earth a Strategy for Sustainable Living*', Gland, (1991)

IWC 24th report, 20, (1974)

IWC 30th Report, 32, (1980)

Johannesburg Plan of Implementation, adopted at the World Summit on Sustainable Development, Johannesburg, (2002)

Joseph, J. (1994), 'The Tuna–Dolphin Controversy in the Eastern Pacific Ocean: Biological Economic and Political Impacts', ODIL, **25** (1), 1–30

Joyner, C.C. and De Cola P.N. (1993), 'Chile's Presential Sea Proposal Implications for Straddling Stocks and the International law of Fisheries', ODIL, **24** (1), 99–121

Joyner, C.C. and Martell, E.A. (1996), 'Looking Back to See Ahead UNCLOS III and Lessons for Global Commons Law', ODIL, **27** (1–2) 73–96

Juda, L. (1997), 'The 1995 United Nations Agreement on Straddling Fish Stocks and Highly Migratory Fish Stocks: A Critique', ODIL, **28** (2), 147–66

Juda, L. (2003), 'Changing National Approaches to Ocean Governance: The United States Canada and Australia', ODIL, **34** (2), 161–88

Kirgis, F.L. Jr. (April 1990), 'Standing to Challenge Human Endeavours that Could Change the Climate', Editorial Comment, Am.J.Int.L., **84** (2)

Kuemlangan, B. (2000), 'National Legislative Options to combat IUU Fishing', paper prepared for the Expert Consultation on Illegal, Unreported and Unregulated Fishing Organized by the Government of Australia in Cooperation with FAO, Sydney, Australia, 15–19 May 2000, available at http://www.daff.gov.au

Kwiatkowska, B. (2003), 'Ireland v. United Kingdom (MOX Plant) Case: Applying the Doctrine of Treaty Parallelism', IJMC, **18** (1), 1–58

Lodge, M.W. (2006), 'The Practice of Fishing Entities in Regional Fisheries Management Organizations: The Case of the Commission for the Conservation and Management of Highly Migratory Fish Stocks in the Western and Central Pacific Ocean', ODIL, **37** (2), 113–15

Lyster, S. (1985), *International Wild Life Law*, Cambridge: Grotius Publications

Macdonald, J.M. (1995), 'Appreciating the Precautionary Principle as an Ethical Evolution in Ocean Management', ODIL, **26** (3), 255–86

McLaughlin, R. (2003), 'Foreign Access to Shared Marine Genetic Materials; Management Options for a Quasi-Fugacious Resource', ODIL, **34** (3–4), 297–348

Magnuson-Stevens Fishery Conservation and Management Act, 16 USC 1371, 1801 and 1903 (1976 as subsequently amended).

Miles, E.L. (1998), *Global Ocean Politics: the Decision Process at the Third United Nations Conference on the Law of the Sea, 1973–1982*, The Hague: Martinus Nijhoff

Miles, E.L. (ed.) (1989), *The Management of World Fisheries: Implications of Extended Coastal State Jurisdiction*, Seattle, Washington: University of Washington Press

Nordquist, M.H., & Moore, J.N. (eds.) (2001), *Current Marine Environmental Issues and the International Tribunal for the Law of the Sea*, The Hague, New York: Martinus Nijhoff

Munro and Lammers (1986), *Environmental Protection and Sustainable Development*, Dordrecht: Legal Experts Group Report (1986)

NAFO Measures on Port State Control, adopted at the 30th Annual Meeting in Vigo, Spain, September 2008 (looseleaf publication)

National Research Council Dolphins and the Tuna Industry Report (1992), USA

Orebech, P. (2005), 'What Restoration Schemes Can Do? Or, Getting It Right Without Fisheries Transferable Quotas', ODIL, **36** (2), 159–78

Orrego Vicuna, F. (1995), 'Trends and Issues in the Law of the Sea as Applied in Latin America', ODIL, **26** (2), 93–103

Prfirter, F. and Armas, M. (1995), 'Straddling Stocks and HMS in Latin American Practice and Legislation: New Perspectives in light of Current International Negotiations', ODIL, **26** (2), 127–150

Rigg, K., Parmentier, R., and Currie, D. (2003), 'Halting IUU Fishing: Enforcing International Fisheries Agreements', Varda Group Paper prepared for Oceana

Rio Declaration on Environment and Development (1992), A/CONF.151/26 (Vol. I), United Nations Conference on Environment and Development, Rio de Janeiro

Rome Declaration on Illegal, Unreported and Unregulated Fishing, FAO International Conference on Responsible Fishing, Rome (2005)

Scovazzi, T. (2004), 'Marine Protected Areas on the High Seas: Some Legal and Policy Considerations', IJMC, **19** (1), 1–17

Smith, B.D. (1988), *State Responsibility and the Marine Environment: The Rules of Decision*, Oxford: Clarendon Press

Stokke, O.S. (ed.) (2001), *Governing High Seas Fisheries: The Interplay of Global and Regional Regimes*, Oxford: Oxford University Press

Stokke, O.S. (2001), 'Managing Fisheries in the Barents Sea Loophole; Interplay with the UN Fish Stocks Agreement', ODIL, **32** (3), 241–62

St. John's Declaration on Specific Action to Improve Governance of High Seas Fisheries, Conference on Governance of High Seas Fisheries and the UN Fish Stocks Agreement: Moving from Words to Action, St John's, Canada, (2005)

Song, Y. (1997), 'The Canada–European Union Turbot Dispute in the North West Atlantic: An Application of the Incident Approach', ODIL, **28** (3), 269–312

Stockholm Declaration on the Human Environment, United Nations Conference on the Human Environment (1972)

Tahindro, A. (1997), 'Conservation and Management of Transboundary Fish Stocks: Comments in the Light of the Adoption of the 1995 Agreement for the Conservation of Straddling Stocks and Highly Migratory Fish Stocks', ODIL, **28** (1), 1–58

Truman Proclamation, No 2667, 10. Federal Registry. 12, 303 (1945)

UK Hydrographic Office Report, January 1, 2002 U.K. M.I.L., referred to in *British Year Book of International Law* (2001)

Ulfstein, Andersen and Churchill (1986), *The Regulation of Fisheries, Legal, Economic and Social Aspects*, Strasbourg: Council of Europe

UNGA Report of the Secretary General on Oceans and the Law of the Sea, UNGA 60th Session, Item 76 of the Provisional Agenda, A/60/63/ Add. 1, (2005)

UNGA Report of the Ad Hoc Open Ended Informal Working Group to Study Issues relating to the Conservation and Sustainable Use of Marine Biological Diversity Beyond the Areas of National Jurisdiction, presented to the UNGA 61st session, Agenda Item 69(a), Oceans and the Law of the Sea, A/61/65, (2006)

UNGA Resolution 2574, on Deep Sea Bed Mining (1969)

UNGA Resolution, 34/186, on Cooperation Between States that Share Natural Resources (1979)

UNGA Resolution, 43/53, on Protection of Global Climate for Present and Future Generations of Mankind (1988)

UNGA Resolution 44/225, on Large Scale Pelagic Driftnet Fishing and Its Impacts on the Living Marine Resources of the World's Oceans (1989)

UNGA Resolution 46/215, on Large Scale Pelagic Driftnet Fishing and Its Impacts on the Living Marine Resources of the World's Oceans (1991)

UNEP/IG/12/2 Draft Principles of Conduct in the Field of Environment for Guidance of States in the Conservation and Harmonious Utilization of Natural Resources Shared by Two or More States (1978)

UNEP/CBD/SBSTTA/8/INF/3/Rev.1 Marine and Coastal Biodiversity: Review, Further Elaboration and Refinement of the Programme of Work (2003)

World Commission on Environment and Development Report (1987), Gro Harlem Brundtland, et al, *Our Common Future*, Oxford: Oxford University Press

Index